On Grief and Reason

BY JOSEPH BRODSKY

Elegy for John Donne and Other Poems
Selected Poems
A Part of Speech
Less Than One
To Urania
Marbles
Watermark
On Grief and Reason
So Forth

JOSEPH BRODSKY

ON GRIEF AND REASON

ESSAYS

FARRAR, STRAUS AND GIROUX

NEW YORK

Farrar, Straus and Giroux

Copyright © 1995 by Joseph Brodsky
All rights reserved

Printed in the United States of America
First published in 1995 by Farrar, Straus and Giroux
5 7 9 10 8 6 4

The Library of Congress has catalogued the hardcover edition as follows:
Brodsky, Joseph.
    On grief and reason : essays / Joseph Brodsky — 1st ed.
    p.   cm.
    ISBN: 978-0-374-52509-5
    I. Title.
PG3479.4.R64P59   1994
814'.54—dc20   94-10872

The essays in this book have appeared, in slightly different
form, in The New Republic, Soho Square, The New York
Review of Books, Paris Vogue, Partisan Review, *the* Times
Literary Supplement, Dartmouth Alumni Magazine. The
New Yorker, *and* La Repubblica

"Homage to Marcus Aurelius," *originally published in* Campidoglio, *is reprinted with permission of Random House, Inc.*
Text copyright © *1994 by Joseph Brodsky.* "Wooing the Inanimate," *originally published as the introduction to* The Essential Thomas Hardy, *is reproduced by permission of The*
Ecco Press. *Introduction copyright © 1995 by*
Joseph Brodsky.

To Roger W. Straus, with gratitude

Contents

Blessed be all metrical rules that forbid automatic responses,
force us to have second thoughts, free from the fetters of Self.
—W . H . AUDEN

On Grief and Reason

Spoils of War

In the beginning, there was canned corned beef. More accurately, in the beginning, there was a war, World War II; the siege of my hometown, Leningrad; the Great Hunger, which claimed more lives than all the bombs, shells, and bullets together. And toward the end of the siege, there was canned corned beef from America. Swift, I think, was the brand name, although I may be wrong; I was only four when I tasted it for the first time.

It was perhaps the first meat we had had in a while. Still, its flavor was less memorable than the cans themselves. Tall, square-shaped, with an opening key attached to the side, they heralded different mechanical principles, a different sensibility altogether. That key skeining a tiny strip of metal to get the can open, was a revelation to a Russian child: we knew only knives. The country was still nails, hammers, nuts, and bolts: that's what held it together, and it was to stay that way for most of our lives. That's why, there and then, nobody could explain to me the sealing method used by these cans' makers. Even today, I don't grasp it fully. Then and there, I'd stare at my mother detaching the key, unbending the little tab and sticking it into the key's eye, and then turning the key time and again around its axis, in sheer bewilderment.

Long after their contents vanished into the cloaca, these tall, somewhat streamlined around the corners (like cinema screens!), dark red or brown cans with foreign lettering on their sides survived on many families' shelves and windowsills, partly as aesthetic objects, partly as good containers for pencils, screwdrivers, film rolls, nails, etc. Often, too, they would be used as flowerpots.

We were not to see them ever again—neither their jellied contents nor their shapes. With the passage of years, their value increased: at least they were becoming more and more coveted in schoolboys' trade. For a can like this, one could get a German bayonet, a navy belt buckle, a magnifying glass. Their sharp edges (where the can was opened) cost us many a cut finger. In the third grade, however, I was the proud owner of two of them.

II

If anybody profited from the war, it was us: its children. Apart from having survived it, we were richly provided with stuff to romanticize or to fantasize about. In addition to the usual childhood diet of Dumas and Jules Verne, we had military paraphernalia, which always goes well with boys. With us, it went exceptionally well, since it was our country that won the war.

Curiously enough, though, it was the military hardware of the other side that attracted us most, not that of our own victorious Red Army. Names of German airplanes—Junkers, Stukas, Messerschmidts, Focke-Wulfs—were constantly on our lips. So were Schmeisser automatic rifles, Tiger tanks, ersatz rations. Guns were made by Krupp, bombs were courtesy of I. G. Farben-Industrie. A child's ear is always sensitive to a strange, irregular sound. It was, I believe, this acoustic fascination rather than any actual sense of danger that attracted our tongues and minds to those words. In spite of all the good reasons that we had to hate the Germans—and in spite of the state propaganda's constant exhortations to that end—we habitually called them "Fritzes" rather than "Fascists" or "Hitlerites." Presumably because luckily we'd never known them in any other capacity than as POWs.

Similarly, we saw quite a lot of German military equipment in the war museums, which cropped up in the late forties everywhere. Those were our best outings—far better than the circus or the movies; and especially if our demobilized fathers were taking us there (those of us, that is, who had fathers). Oddly enough, they were quite reluctant to do so; but they'd answer in great detail our inquiries about the firepower of this or that German machine gun or the types of explosives used in this or that bomb. This reluctance was caused, not by their desire to spare gentle imaginations the horrors of war, or themselves the memories of dead friends and the guilty feeling of being alive. No, they simply saw through our idle curiosity and didn't approve of that.

III

Each one of them—our alive fathers, that is—kept, of course, some memento of that war. It could be a set of binoculars (Zeiss!), or a German U-boat officer's cap with appropriate insignia, or an accordion inlaid with mother-of-pearl, or a sterling-silver cigarette case, a gramophone, or a camera. When I was twelve, my father suddenly produced to my great delight a shortwave-radio set. Philips was the name, and it could pick up stations from all over the world, from Copenhagen to Surabaja. At least that was what the names on its yellow dial suggested.

This Philips radio was rather portable—by the standards of the time—a 10-by-14-inch brown Bakelite affair, with said yellow dial and a catlike, absolutely mesmerizing green eye indicating the quality of reception. It had, if I remember things correctly, only six tubes, and two feet of simple wire would do as its aerial. But here was the rub. To have an aerial sticking out of a window could mean only one thing to the police. To try to attach your radio to the building's main antenna required a professional's help, and that professional, in his turn, would pay unneeded attention to your set. One wasn't supposed to have a foreign radio, period. The solution was a web-like arrangement under the ceiling of your room, which is what I made. That way, of course, I couldn't get Radio Bratislava or, moreover, Delhi. But then I knew neither Czech nor Hindi. And as for the BBC, the Voice of America, or Radio Free Europe broadcasts in Russian, they were jammed anyway. Still, one could get programs in English, German, Polish, Hungarian, French, Swedish. I knew none of those languages; but then there was the VOA's *Time for Jazz*, with the richest-in-the-world bass-baritone of Willis Conover, its disc jockey!

To this brown, shining-like-an-old-shoe Philips set, I owe my first bits of English and my introduction to the Jazz Pantheon. When we were twelve, the German names on our lips gradually began to be replaced by those of Louis Armstrong, Duke Ellington, Ella Fitzgerald, Clifford Brown, Sidney Bechet, Django Reinhardt, and Charlie Parker. Something began to happen, I remember, even to our walk: the joints of our highly inhibited Russian frames harkened to "swing." Apparently I was not the only one in my generation who knew how to put two feet of plain wire to good use.

Through six symmetrical holes in its back, in the subdued glow and flicker of the radio tubes, in the maze of
contacts, resistors, and cathodes, as incomprehensible as the
languages they were generating, I thought I saw Europe.
Inside, it always looked like a city at night, with scattered
neon lights. And when at the age of thirty-two I indeed
landed in Vienna, I immediately felt that, to a certain extent,
I knew the place. To say the least, falling asleep my first
nights in Vienna felt distinctly like being switched off by
some invisible hand far away, in Russia.

It was a sturdy machine. When one day, in a paroxysm
of anger at my incessant fiddling with various frequencies,
my father threw it on the floor, its frame came apart, but it
kept receiving. Because I wouldn't dare take it to a professional radio mechanic, I tried to repair that Oder-Neisse-
like crack as best I could, using all sorts of glue and rubber
bands; but from then on, it existed in the form of two somewhat loosely connected bulky halves. Its end came when the
tubes gave out, although once or twice I managed to track
down their analogues through the grapevine of friends and
acquaintances. Yet even when it became just a mute box, it
still remained in our family—as long as the family itself
existed. In the late sixties, everyone bought a Latvian-made
Spidola, with its telescopic antenna and all sorts of transistors
inside. Admittedly, it had better reception and was more
portable. Still, I saw it once in a repair shop with its back
removed. The best I can say about the way it looked inside
was that it resembled some geographic map (roads, railroads,
rivers, tributaries). It didn't look like anything in particular;
it didn't even look like Riga.

IV

But the greatest spoils of war were, of course, films! There were lots of them, and they were mostly of Hollywood prewar production, with (as we were able to determine two decades later) Errol Flynn, Olivia de Havilland, Tyrone Power, Johnny Weissmuller, and others. They were mostly about pirates, Elizabeth I, Cardinal Richelieu, et cetera—nothing to do with reality. The closest they approached to our time was in *Waterloo Bridge* with Robert Taylor and Vivien Leigh. Since our government wasn't keen on paying for the rights, no credits were given and, as a rule, no names of characters or actors either. The show would start in the following fashion. The light dimmed, and on the screen, in white letters against a black background, this message would appear: THIS FILM WAS CAPTURED AS A MILITARY TROPHY IN THE COURSE OF THE GREAT WAR FOR OUR MOTHERLAND. It would flicker there for a minute or so; then the film started. A hand with a candle in it lit up a piece of parchment with THE ROYAL PIRATES, CAPTAIN BLOOD, or ROBIN HOOD in Cyrillic on it. That might be followed by an explanatory note indicating time and place of action, also in Cyrillic but often fashioned after Gothic script. Surely this was theft, but we in the audience couldn't care less. For that, we were too absorbed in reading subtitles and following the action.

Perhaps just as well. The absence of who was who on the screen imparted to these films the anonymity of folklore and the air of universality. They held us in greater sway and thrall than all the subsequent output of the neorealists or the *nouvelle vague*. The absence of credits made them openly archetypal at the time—the early fifties: the last years of Stalin's rule. The Tarzan series alone, I daresay, did more for de-Stalinization than all Khrushchev's speeches at the Twentieth Party Congress and after.

One should take into account our latitudes, our buttoned-up, rigid, inhibited, winter-minded standards of public and private conduct, in order to appreciate the impact of a long-haired naked loner pursuing a blonde through the thick of a tropical rain forest with his chimpanzee version of Sancho Panza and lianas as means of transportation. Add to that the view of New York (in the last bit of the series that was played in Russia), with Tarzan jumping off the Brooklyn Bridge—and almost an entire generation's opting out will become understandable.

The first thing that came in was, of course, the haircut. We all turned long-haired at once. That was immediately followed by stovepipe trousers. Ah, what pains, what subterfuge, what effort it cost to convince our mothers/sisters/aunts to convert our invariably black ballooning postwar pants into straight-leg precursors of yet unknown Levi's! But we were adamant—and so were our detractors: teachers, police, relatives, neighbors, who'd kick us out of school, arrest us on the street, ridicule us, call us names. That's why a man who grew up in the fifties and the sixties despairs today trying to buy a pair of pants; all this ridiculous, fabric-wasting, baggy stuff!

V

There was, of course, something more crucial to these trophy movies; it was their "one-against-all" spirit, totally alien to the communal, collective-oriented sensibility of the society we grew up in. Perhaps precisely because all these Sea Hawks and Zorros were so removed from our reality, they influenced us in a way contrary to that intended. Offered to us as entertaining fairy tales, they were received rather as parables of individualism. What would be regarded by a normal viewer as a costume drama with some Renaissance props was regarded by us as historical proof of individualism's precedence.

Showing humans against the backdrop of nature, a film always has documentary value. Connoting a printed page, a black-and-white film does all the more so. Given our closed, better yet our tightly shut, society, we were thus more informed than entertained. With what keenness did we scrutinize turrets and ramparts, vaults and moats, grilles and chambers that we'd seen on the screen! For we'd seen them for the first time in our lives! So we took all those papier-mâché, cardboard Hollywood props for real, and our sense of Europe, of the West, of history, if you will, always owed a great deal to those images. So much so that some among us who later would have landed in the barracks of our penal system frequently improved their diet by retelling plots and remembered details of that West to both guards and fellow inmates who'd never seen those trophy movies.

VI

Among those trophies one could occasionally bump into a real masterpiece. I remember, for instance, *That Hamilton Woman* with Vivien Leigh and Laurence Olivier. Also, I seem to recall *Gaslight* with the then very young Ingrid Bergman. The underground industry was very alert, and in no time one could buy, from a shady character in the public lavatory or in the park, a postcard-sized print of this or that actress or actor. Errol Flynn in his Sea Hawk outfit was my most sacred possession, and for years I tried to imitate the forward thrust of his chin and the autonomous motion of his left eyebrow. With the latter, I failed.

And before the twang of this sycophantic note dies away, let me mention here something else—something that I have in common with Adolf Hitler: the great love of my youth, whose name was Zarah Leander. I saw her only once, in what was called, then and there, *Road to the Scaffold* (*Das Herz einer Königin*), a story about Mary, Queen of Scots. I remember nothing about this picture save a scene where her young page rests his head on the stupendous lap of his condemned queen. In my view, she was the most beautiful woman who ever appeared on the screen, and my subsequent tastes and preferences, valid though they were in themselves, were but deviations from her standard. As attempts to account for a stunted or failed romantic career go, this one feels to me oddly satisfactory.

Leander died two or three years ago, I think, in Stockholm. Shortly before that, a record came out with several *Schlagers* of hers, among which was a tune called "Die Rose von Nowgorod." The composer's name was given as Rota, and it couldn't be anyone else but Nino Rota himself. The tune beats by far the Lara theme from *Doctor Zhivago*; the lyrics—well, they are blissfully in German, so I don't bother. The voice is that of Marlene Dietrich in timbre, but the singing technique is far better. Leander indeed sings; she doesn't declaim. And it occurred to me several times that had the Germans listened to that tune, they would not have been in the mood to march *nach Osten*. Come to think of it, no other century has produced as much schmaltz as ours; perhaps one should pay closer attention to it. Perhaps schmaltz should be regarded as a tool of cognition, especially given the vast imprecision of our century. For schmaltz is flesh of the flesh—a kid brother indeed—of *Schmerz*. We have, all of us, more reasons for staying than for marching. What's the point in marching if you are only going to catch up with a very sad tune?

VII

I suppose my generation was the most attentive audience for all that pre- and postwar dream factories' production. Some of us became, for a while, avid cineastes, but perhaps for a different set of reasons than our counterparts in the West. For us, films were the only opportunity to see the West. Quite oblivious of the action itself, in every frame we tried to discern the contents of the street or of an apartment, the dashboard of the hero's car, the types of clothes worn by heroines, the sense of space, the layout of the place they were operating in. Some of us became quite adept at determining the location in which a film was shot, and sometimes we could tell Genoa from Naples or, to say the least, Paris from Rome, on the basis of only two or three architectural ensembles. We would arm ourselves with city maps, and we would hotly argue about Jeanne Moreau's address in this film or Jean Marais's in another.

But that, as I said, was to happen much later, in the late sixties. And later still, our interest in films began to fade away, as we realized that film directors were increasingly of our own age and had less and less to tell us. By that time, we were already accomplished book readers, subscribers to *Foreign Literature* monthly, and we would stroll to the cinema less and less willingly, having realized that there is no point in knowing a place you are not going to inhabit. That, I repeat, was to happen much later, when we were in our thirties.

VIII

One day, when I was fifteen or sixteen, I sat in the courtyard of a huge apartment complex driving nails into the lid of a wooden box filled with all sorts of geological instruments which were to be shipped to the (Soviet) Far East—where I myself was about to follow, to join my team. It was early May, but the day was hot and I was bored out of my wits and perspiring. Suddenly, out of one of the top floor's open windows, came "A-tisket, a-tasket"—the voice was that of Ella Fitzgerald. Now this was 1955 or 1956, in some grimy industrial outskirt of Leningrad, Russia. Good Lord, I remember thinking, how many records must they have produced for one of them to end up here, in this brick-cum-concrete absolute nowhere, amid not so much drying-up as soot-absorbing bedsheets and lavender underpants! That's what capitalism is all about, I said to myself: winning through excess, through overkill. Not through central planning, but through grapeshot.

IX

I knew the tune, partly because of my radio, partly because in the fifties every city youth had his own collection of so-called bone music. "Bone music" was a sheet of X-ray film with a homemade copy of some jazz piece on it. The technology of the copying process was beyond my grasp, but I trust it was a relatively simple procedure, since the supply was steady and the price reasonable.

One could purchase this somewhat morbid-looking stuff (speak of the nuclear age!) in the same fashion as those sepia pictures of Western movie stars: in parks, in public toilets, at flea markets, in the then-famous "cocktail halls," where you could sit on a tall chair sipping a milkshake and think you were in the West.

And the more I think of it, the more I become convinced that this *was* the West. For on the scales of truth, intensity of imagination counterbalances and at times outweighs reality. On that score, as well as with the benefit of hindsight,

I may even insist that we were the real Westerners, perhaps the only ones. With our instinct for individualism fostered at every instance by our collectivist society, with our hatred toward any form of affiliation, be that with a party, a block association, or, at that time, a family, we were more American than the Americans themselves. And if America stands for the outer limit of the West, for where the West ends, we were, I must say, a couple of thousand miles off the West Coast. In the middle of the Pacific.

X

Somewhere in the early sixties, when the power of suggestion, headed by garter belts, began its slow exodus from the world, when we found ourselves increasingly reduced to the either/or of pantyhose, when foreigners had already started to arrive in planeloads in Russia, attracted by its cheap yet very sharp fragrance of slavery, and when a friend of mine, with a faintly contemptuous smile on his lips, remarked that perhaps it takes history to compromise geography, a girl I was courting gave me for my birthday an accordionlike set of postcards depicting Venice.

They belonged, she said, to her grandmother, who went to Italy for a honeymoon shortly before World War I. There were twelve postcards, in sepia, on poor quality yellowish paper. The reason she gave them to me was that, at about that time, I was full of two books by Henri de Regnier I'd just finished; both of them had for their setting Venice in winter: Venice thus was then on my lips.

Because the pictures were brownish and badly printed, and because of Venice's latitude and its very few trees, one couldn't tell for sure what season was depicted. People's clothes were of no help, since everyone wore long skirts, felt hats, top hats, bowlers, dark jackets: turn-of-the-century fashions. The absence of color and the general gloom of the texture suggested what I wanted them to suggest: winter, the true time of the year.

In other words, the texture and the melancholy it conveyed, because so familiar to me in my own hometown, made these pictures more comprehensible, more real. It was almost like reading relatives' letters. And I read them and reread them. And the more I read them, the more apparent it became that this was what the word "West" meant to me: a perfect city by the winter sea, columns, arcades, narrow passages, cold marble staircases, peeling stucco exposing the red-brick flesh, putti, cherubs with their dust-covered eyeballs: civilization that braced itself for the cold times.

And looking at these postcards, I made a vow that, should I ever get out of my native realm, I'd go in winter to Venice, rent a room on the ground—nay, the water—floor, sit down there, write two or three elegies, extinguishing my cigarettes on the damp floor, so that they'd hiss; and when the money was up, I'd purchase not a ticket back but a Saturday-Night Special and blow my brains out on the spot. A decadent fantasy, of course (but if you are not decadent at twenty, then when?). Still, I am grateful to the Parcae for allowing me to act out the better part of it. True, history is doing a rather brisk job at compromising geography. The only way to beat that is to become an outcast, a nomad; a shadow briefly caressing lace-like porcelain colonnades reflected in crystal water.

XI

And then there was the Renault 2CV that I saw one day parked on an empty street in my hometown, by the Hermitage's caryatided portico. It looked like a flimsy yet self-contained butterfly, with its folded wings of corrugated iron:

the way World War II airfield hangars were and French police vans still are.

I was observing it without any vested interest. I was then just twenty, and I neither drove nor aspired to drive. To have your own car in Russia in those days, one had to be real scum, or that scum's child: a *Parteigenosse*, an academician, a famous athlete. But even then your car would be only of local manufacture, for all its stolen blueprints and know-how.

It stood there, light and defenseless, totally lacking the menace normally associated with automobiles. It looked as if it could easily be hurt by one, rather than the other way around. I've never seen anything made of metal as unemphatic. It felt more human than some of the passersby, and somehow it resembled in its breathtaking simplicity those World War II beef cans that were still sitting on my windowsill. It had no secrets. I wanted to get into it and drive off—not because I wanted to emigrate, but because to get inside it must have felt like putting on a jacket—no, a raincoat—and going for a stroll. Its side-window flaps alone resembled a myopic, bespectacled man with a raised collar. If I remember things correctly, what I felt while staring at this car was happiness.

XII

I believe my first English utterance was indeed "His Master's Voice," because one started to learn languages in the third grade, when one was ten, and my father returned from his tour of duty in the Far East when I was eight. The war ended for him in China, yet his hoard was not so much Chinese as Japanese, because at that end of the story it was Japan that was the loser. Or so it seemed at the time. The bulk of the hoard was records. They sat in massive but quite elegant cardboard albums embossed with gilded Japanese characters; now and then the cover would depict a scantily attired maiden led to a dance by a tuxedoed gent. Each album would contain up to a dozen black shiny disks staring at you through their thick shirts, with their gold-and-red and gold-and-black labels. They were mostly "His Master's Voice" and "Columbia"; the latter, however, although easily pronounced, had only letters, and the pensive doggy was a winner. So much so that its presence would influence my choice of music. As a result, by the age of ten I was more familiar with Enrico Caruso and Tito Schipa than with fox-trot and tangos, which also were in abundance, and for which in fact I felt a predilection. There were also all sorts of overtures and classical hits conducted by Stokowski and Toscanini, "Ave Maria" sung by Marian Anderson, and the whole of *Carmen* and *Lohengrin*, with casts I no longer recall, though I remember how enthusiastic my mother was about those performances. In fact, the albums contained the whole prewar musical diet of the European middle class, which tasted perhaps doubly sweet in our parts because of the delay in its arrival. And it was brought to you by this pensive doggy, practically in its teeth. It took me at least a decade to realize that "His Master's Voice" means what it does: that a dog is listening here to the voice of its owner. I thought it was listening to the recording of its own barking, for I somehow took the phonograph's amplifier for a mouthpiece too, and since dogs normally run before their owners, this label all my childhood meant to me the voice of the dog announcing his master's approach. In any case, the doggy ran around the world, since my father found those records in Shanghai after the slaughter of the Kwangtong Army. Needless to say, they arrived in my reality from an unlikely direction, and I remember myself more than once dreaming about a long train with black shining records for wheels adorned with "His Master's Voice" and "Columbia," trundling along a rail laid out of words like "Kuomintang," "Chiang Kai-shek," "Taiwan," "Chu Teh"— or were those the railroad stations? The destination was presumably our brown leather gramophone with its chromium-steel handle powered by my measly self. On the chair's back hangs my father's dark blue Navy tunic with its golden epaulets, on the hat rack there is my mother's silver fox clasping its tail; in the air: "Una furtiva lagrima."

XIII

Or else it could be "La Comparsita"—the greatest piece of music in this century, as far as I am concerned. After this tango, no triumph is meaningful, either your nation's or your own. I've never learned to dance, being both self-conscious and truly awkward, but I could listen to these twangs for hours and, when there was no one around, move. Like many a folk tune, "La Comparsita" is a dirge, and at the end of that war a dirge rhythm felt more suitable than a boogie-woogie. One didn't want acceleration, one craved restraint. Because one vaguely sensed what one was heading for. Put it down, then, to our dormant erotic nature that we clung so much to things that as yet hadn't gone streamline, to the black-lacquered fenders of the surviving German BMWs and Opel-captains, to the equally shining American Packards and bearlike windshield-squinting Studebakers, with their double rear wheels—Detroit's answer to our all-absorbing mud. A child always tries to get beyond his age, and if one can't picture oneself defending the motherland, since the real defenders are all around, one's fancy may fly one into the incoherent foreign past and land one inside a large black Lincoln with its porcelain-knob-studded dashboard, next to some platinum blonde, sunk to her silk knees in the patent-leather cushions. In fact, one knee would be enough. Sometimes, just touching the smooth fender was enough. This comes to you via one of those whose birthplace went up in smoke, courtesy of a Luftwaffe air raid, from one of those who tasted white bread for the first time at the age of eight (or, if this idiom is too foreign for you, Coca-Cola at thirty-two). So put this down to that dormant eroticism and check in the yellow pages where they certify morons.

XIV

There was that wonderful khaki-green American thermos made of corrugated plastic, with a quicksilver, mirrorlike glass tube, which belonged to my uncle and which I broke in 1951. The tube's inside was an optical infinity-generating maelstrom, and I could stare at its reflections of itself in itself forever. That's presumably how I broke it, inadvertently dropping it on the floor. There was also my father's no less American flashlight, also brought from China, for which we pretty soon ran out of batteries, but its shining refractor's visionary clarity, vastly superior to the properties of my eye, kept me in thrall for most of my school years. Eventually, when rust started to fray its rim and its button, I took it apart and, with a couple of magnifying lenses, turned its smooth cylinder into a totally blind telescope. There was also an English field compass, which my father got from somebody with one of those doomed British PQs he'd meet off Murmansk. The compass had a phosphorescent dial and you could read its degrees under a blanket. Because the lettering was Latin, the indications had the air of numerals, and my sense was that my position's reading was not so much accurate as absolute. That's perhaps what was making that position unpalatable in the first place. And then there were my father's Army winter boots, whose provenance (American? Chinese? certainly not German) I can't recall now. They

were huge, pale yellow buckskin boots lined with what
looked to me like coils of lamb's wool. They stood more like
cannonballs than shoes on his side of the king-size bed, although their brown laces never were tied, since my father
wore them only at home, instead of slippers; outside, they'd
call too much attention to themselves and therefore their
owner. Like most of that era's attire, footwear was supposed
to be black, dark gray (boots), or, at best, brown. Up to the
1920s, I suppose, even up to the thirties, Russia enjoyed
some semblance of parity with the West as regards existential
gadgetry and know-how. But then it snapped. Even the war,
finding us in a state of arrested development, failed to fish
us out of this predicament. For all their comfort, the yellow
winter boots were anathema on our streets. On the other
hand, this made these shizi-like monsters last longer, and as
I grew up, they became a point of contention between my
father and me. Thirty-five years after the war they were good
enough for us to argue at length about whose right it was to
wear them. In the end he won, because he died with me
far away from where they stood.

XV

Among flags we preferred the Union Jack; among cigarette
brands, Camel; Beefeater among liquors. Clearly our choice
was dictated by sense of form, not substance. We can be
forgiven, though, because our familiarity with the contents
was marginal, because what circumstances and luck were
offering didn't constitute choice. Besides, we weren't so
much a mark vis-à-vis the Union Jack and, moreover, vis-à-
vis Camels. As for Beefeater gin bottles, a friend of mine
observed upon receiving one from a visiting foreigner that
perhaps in the same way we get kicks from their elaborate
labels, they get their kicks from the total vacancy on ours.

I nodded in agreement. He then slid his hand under a pile of magazines and fished out what I seem to remember as a *Life* magazine cover. It depicted the upper deck of an aircraft carrier, somewhere on the ocean. Sailors in their white tops stood on the deck looking upward—presumably at a plane or chopper from which they had been photographed. They stood in formation. From the air, the formation read: $E = mc^2$. "Nice, isn't it?" said my friend. "Uh-huh," I said. "Where was it taken?" "Somewhere in the Pacific," he said. "Who cares?"

XVI

Let's turn the light off, then, or let's shut our eyes tight. What do we see? A U.S. aircraft carrier in the middle of the Pacific. And it's me there on the deck, waving. Or by the 2CV's wheel, driving. Or in the "green and yellow basket" rhyme of Ella's singing, etc., etc. For a man is what he loves. That's why he loves it: because he is a part of it. And not a man only. Things are that way, too. I remember the roar produced by the then newly opened, imported from Lord-knows-where, American-made laundromat in Leningrad when I threw my first blue jeans into a machine. There was joy of recognition in that roar; the entire queue heard it. So with eyes shut let's admit it: we recognized something in the West, in the civilization, as our own; perhaps even more so there than at home. What's more, it turned out that we were prepared to pay for that sentiment, and quite dearly —with the rest of our lives. Which is a lot, of course. But anything less than that would be plain whoring. Not to mention that, in those days, the rest of our lives was all we had.

1986

The Condition We Call Exile, or Acorns Aweigh

~

As we gather here, in this attractive and well-lit room, on this cold December evening, to discuss the plight of the writer in exile, let us pause for a minute and think of some of those who, quite naturally, didn't make it to this room. Let us imagine, for instance, Turkish *Gastarbeiters* prowling the streets of West Germany, uncomprehending or envious of the surrounding reality. Or let us imagine Vietnamese boat people bobbing on high seas or already settled somewhere in the Australian outback. Let us imagine Mexican wetbacks crawling the ravines of Southern California, past the border patrols into the territory of the United States. Or let us imagine shiploads of Pakistanis disembarking somewhere in Kuwait or Saudi Arabia, hungry for menial jobs the oil-rich locals won't do. Let us imagine multitudes of Ethiopians trekking some desert on foot into Somalia (or is it the other way around?), escaping the famine. Well, we may stop here, because that minute of imagining has already passed, although a lot could be added to this list. Nobody has ever counted these people and nobody, including the UN relief organizations, ever will: coming in millions, they elude com-

Written for the Wheatland Conference, held in Vienna in November 1987.

putation and constitute what is called—for want of a better term or a higher degree of compassion—migration.

Whatever the proper name for this phenomenon is, whatever the motives, origins, and destinations of these people are, whatever their impact on the societies which they abandon and to which they come, one thing is absolutely clear: they make it very difficult to talk with a straight face about the plight of the writer in exile.

Yet talk we must; and not only because literature, like poverty, is known for taking care of its own kind, but mainly because of the ancient and perhaps as yet unfounded belief that, were the masters of this world better read, the mismanagement and grief that make millions hit the road could be somewhat reduced. Since there is not much on which to rest our hopes for a better world, and since everything else seems to fail one way or another, we must somehow maintain that literature is the only form of moral insurance that a society has; that it is the permanent antidote to the dog-eat-dog principle; that it provides the best argument against any sort of bulldozer-type mass solution—if only because human diversity is literature's lock and stock, as well as its *raison d'être*. We must talk because we must insist that literature is the greatest—surely greater than any creed—teacher of human subtlety, and that by interfering with literature's natural existence and with people's ability to learn literature's lessons, a society reduces its own potential, slows down the pace of its evolution, ultimately, perhaps, puts its own fabric in peril. If this means that we must talk to ourselves, so much the better: not for ourselves but perhaps for literature.

Whether he likes it or not, *Gastarbeiters* and refugees of any stripe effectively pluck the orchid out of an exiled writer's lapel. Displacement and misplacement are this century's commonplace. And what our exiled writer has in common with a *Gastarbeiter* or a political refugee is that in either case a man is running away from the worse toward the better. The truth of the matter is that from a tyranny one can be exiled only to a democracy. For good old exile ain't what it used to be. It isn't leaving civilized Rome for savage Sarmatia anymore, nor is it sending a man from, say, Bulgaria to China. No, as a rule what takes place is a transition from a political and economic backwater to an industrially advanced society with the latest word on individual liberty on its lips. And it must be added that perhaps taking this route is for an exiled writer, in many ways, like going home—because he gets closer to the seat of the ideals which inspired him all along.

If one were to assign the life of an exiled writer a genre, it would have to be tragicomedy. Because of his previous incarnation, he is capable of appreciating the social and material advantages of democracy far more intensely than its natives do. Yet for precisely the same reason (whose main by-product is the linguistic barrier), he finds himself totally unable to play any meaningful role in his new society. The democracy into which he has arrived provides him with physical safety but renders him socially insignificant. And the lack of significance is what no writer, exile or not, can take.

For it is the quest for significance that very often constitutes most of his career. To say the least, it is very often a literary career's consequence. In the case of the exiled writer, it is almost invariably the cause of his exile. And one is terribly tempted to add here that the existence of this desire in a writer is a conditioned response on his part to the vertical structure of his original society. (For a writer living in a free society, the presence of this desire bespeaks the atavistic memory every democracy has of its unconstitutional past.)

In this respect, the plight of an exiled writer is indeed much worse than that of a *Gastarbeiter* or the average refugee. His appetite for recognition makes him restless and oblivious to the superiority of his income as a college teacher, lecturer, small-magazine editor or just a contributor—for these are the most frequent occupations of exiled authors nowadays—over the wages of somebody doing menial work. That is, our man is a little bit corrupt, almost by definition. But then the sight of a writer rejoicing in insignificance, in being left alone, in anonymity is about as rare as that of a cockatoo in Greenland, even under the best possible circumstances. Among exiled writers, this attitude is almost totally absent. At least, it is absent in this room. Understandably so, of course, but saddening nonetheless.

It is saddening because if there is anything good about exile, it is that it teaches one humility. One can even take it a step further and suggest that the exile's is the ultimate lesson in that virtue. And that it is especially priceless for a writer because it gives him the longest possible perspective. "And thou art far in humanity," as Keats said. To be lost in mankind, in the crowd—crowd?—among billions; to become a needle in that proverbial haystack—but a needle someone is searching for—that's what exile is all about. Put down your vanity, it says, you are but a grain of sand in the desert. Measure yourself not against your pen pals but against human infinity: it is about as bad as the inhuman one. Out of that you should speak, not out of your envy or ambition.

Needless to say, this call goes unheeded. Somehow a commentator on life prefers his position to his subject and, when in exile, considers it grim enough not to aggravate it any further. As for such appeals, he considers them inappropriate. He may be right, although calls for humility are always timely. For the other truth of the matter is that exile is a metaphysical condition. At least, it has a very strong, very clear metaphysical dimension; to ignore or to dodge it is to cheat yourself out of the meaning of what has happened to you, to doom yourself into remaining forever at the receiving end of things, to ossify into an uncomprehending victim.

It is because of the absence of good examples that one cannot describe an alternative conduct (although Czeslaw Milosz and Robert Musil come to mind). Maybe just as well, because we are here evidently to talk about the reality of exile, not about its potential. And the reality of it consists of an exiled writer constantly fighting and conspiring to restore his significance, his leading role, his authority. His main consideration, of course, is the folks back home; but he also wants to rule the roost in the malicious village of his fellow émigrés. Playing ostrich to the metaphysics of his situation, he concentrates on the immediate and tangible. This means besmirching colleagues in a similar predicament, bilious polemics with rival publications, innumerable interviews for the BBC, Deutsche Welle, ORTF [French Radio-Television], and the Voice of America, open letters, statements for the press, going to conferences—you name it. The energy previously spent in food lines or petty officials' musty anterooms is now released and gone rampant. Unchecked by anyone, let alone his kin (for he is himself now a Caesar's wife, as it were, and beyond suspicion—how could his literate, perhaps, but aging spouse correct or contradict her certified martyr?), his ego grows rapidly in diameter and eventually, filled with CO_2, lifts him from reality—especially if he resides in Paris, where the Montgolfier brothers set the precedent.

Traveling by balloon is precipitous and, above all, unpredictable: too easily one becomes a plaything of the winds, in this case, political winds. Small wonder, then, that our navigator keenly listens to all the forecasts, and on occasion ventures to predict the weather himself. That is, not the weather of wherever he starts or finds himself en route, but the weather at his destination, for our balloonist is invariably homeward bound.

And perhaps the third truth of the matter is that a writer in exile is, by and large, a retrospective and retroactive being. In other words, retrospection plays an excessive (compared with other people's lives) role in his existence, overshadowing his reality and dimming the future into something thicker than its usual pea soup. Like the false prophets of Dante's *Inferno*, his head is forever turned backward and his tears, or saliva, are running down between his shoulder blades. Whether or not he is of elegiac disposition by nature is beside the point: doomed to a limited audience abroad, he cannot help pining for the multitudes, real or imagined, left behind. Just as the former fill him with venom, the latter fuel his fantasy. Even having gained the freedom to travel, even having actually done some traveling, he will stick in his writing to the familiar material of his past, producing, as it were, sequels to his previous works. Approached on this subject, an exiled writer will most likely evoke Ovid's Rome, Dante's Florence, and—after a small pause—Joyce's Dublin.

Indeed, we've got a pedigree, and a much longer one than that. If we want, we can trace it all the way back to Adam. And yet we should be careful about the place it tends to occupy in the public's and our own minds. We all know what happens to many a noble family over generations, or in the course of a revolution. Family trees never make or obscure the forest; and the forest is now advancing. I am mixing metaphors here, but perhaps I can justify this by remarking that to expect for ourselves the kind of future that we constitute for the above-mentioned few is imprudent rather than immodest. Of course a writer always takes himself posthumously: and an exiled writer especially so, inspired as he is not so much by the artificial oblivion to which he is subjected by his former state but by the way the critical profession in the free marketplace enthuses about his contemporaries. Yet one should go carefully about this type of self-estrangement, not for any other reason than a realization that, with the population explosion, literature, too, has taken on the dimensions of a demographic phenomenon. Per reader, there are simply too many writers around today. A couple of decades ago a grown man thinking about books or authors yet to be read would come up with thirty or forty names; nowadays these names would run in the thousands. Today one walks into a bookstore the way one enters a record shop. To listen to all these groups and soloists would overshoot a lifetime. And very few among those thousands are exiles, or even particularly good. But the public will read them, and not you, for all your halo, not because it is perverse or misguided, but because statistically it is on the side of normalcy and trash. In other words, it wants to read about itself. On any street of any city in the world at any time of night or day there are more people who haven't heard of you than those who have.

The current interest in the literature of exiles has to do, of course, with the rise of tyrannies. Herein perhaps lies our chance with the future reader, though that's the kind of insurance one would like to do without. Partly because of this noble caveat, but mainly because he can't think of the future in any other than the glowing terms of his triumphant return, an exiled writer sticks to his guns. But then why shouldn't he? Why should he try to use anything else, why should he bother probing the future in any other fashion, since it is unpredictable anyhow? The good old stuff served him well at least once: it earned him exile. And exile, after all, is a kind of success. Why not try another tack? Why not push the good old stuff around a bit more? Apart from anything else, it now constitutes ethnographic material, and that goes big with your Western, Northern, or (if you run afoul of a right-wing tyranny) even Eastern publisher. And there is always the chance of a masterpiece in covering the same turf twice, which possibility doesn't escape the eye of your publisher either, or at least it may provide future scholars with the notion of a "myth-making" element in your work.

But however practical-sounding, these factors are secondary or tertiary among those that keep an exiled writer's eyes firmly trained on his past. The main explanation lies in the aforementioned retrospective machinery that gets unwittingly triggered within an individual by the least evidence of his surroundings' strangeness. Sometimes the shape of a maple leaf is enough, and each tree has thousands of these. On an animal level, this retrospective machinery is constantly in motion in an exiled writer, nearly always unbeknownst to him. Whether pleasant or dismal, the past is always a safe territory, if only because it is already experienced; and the species' capacity to revert, to run backward—especially in its thoughts or dreams, since there we are safe as well—is extremely strong in all of us, quite irrespective of the reality we are facing. Yet this machinery has been built into us, not for cherishing or grasping the past (in the end, we don't do either), but more for delaying the arrival of the present—for, in other words, slowing down a bit the passage of time. See the fatal exclamation of Goethe's Faust.

And the whole point about our exiled writer is that he, too, like Goethe's Faust, clings to his "fair," or not so fair, "moment," not for beholding it, but for postponement of the next one. It's not that he wants to be young again; he simply doesn't want tomorrow to arrive, because he knows that it may edit what he beholds. And the more tomorrow presses him, the more obstinate he becomes. There is terrific value in this obstinacy: with luck, it may amount to intensity of concentration and then, indeed, we may get a great work of literature (the reading public and the publishers sense that, and this is why—as I've already said—they keep an eye on the literature of exiles).

More often, however, this obstinacy translates itself into the repetitiveness of nostalgia, which is, to put it bluntly, simply a failure to deal with the realities of the present or the uncertainties of the future.

One can, of course, help matters somewhat by changing one's narrative manner, by making it more avant-garde, by spicing the stuff with a good measure of eroticism, violence, foul language, etc., after the fashion of our free-market colleagues. But stylistic shifts and innovations greatly depend on the condition of the literary idiom "back there," at home, the links with which have not been severed. As for the spice, a writer, exiled or not, never wants to appear to be influenced by his contemporaries. Perhaps an additional truth about the matter is that exile slows down one's stylistic evolution, that it makes a writer more conservative. Style is not so much the man as the man's nerves, and, on the whole, exile provides one's nerves with fewer irritants than the motherland does. This condition, it must be added, worries an exiled writer somewhat, not only because he regards existence back home as more genuine than his own (by definition, and with all attendant or imagined consequences for normal literary process), but because in his mind there exists a suspicion of a pendulum-like dependency, or ratio, between those irritants and his mother tongue.

One ends up in exile for a variety of reasons and under a number of circumstances. Some of them sound better, some worse, but the difference has already ceased to matter by the time one reads an obituary. On the bookshelf your place will be occupied, not by you, but by your book. And as long as they insist on making a distinction between art and life, it is better if they find your book good and your life foul than the other way around. Chances are, of course, that they won't care for either.

Life in exile, abroad, in a foreign element, is essentially a premonition of your own book-form fate, of being lost on the shelf among those with whom all you have in common is the first letter of your surname. Here you are, in some gigantic library's reading room, still open . . . Your reader won't give a damn about how you got here. To keep yourself from getting closed and shelved you've got to tell your reader, who thinks he knows it all, about something qualitatively novel—about his world and himself. If this sounds a bit too suggestive, so be it, because suggestion is the name of the whole game anyhow, and because the distance exile puts between an author and his protagonists indeed sometimes begs for the use of astronomical or ecclesiastical figures.

This is what makes one think that "exile" is, perhaps, not the most apt term to describe the condition of a writer forced (by the state, by fear, by poverty, by boredom) to abandon his country. "Exile" covers, at best, the very moment of departure, of expulsion; what follows is both too comfortable and too autonomous to be called by this name, which so strongly suggests a comprehensible grief. The very fact of our gathering here indicates that, if we indeed have a common denominator, it lacks a name. Are we suffering the same degree of despair, ladies and gentlemen? Are we equally sundered from our public? Do we all reside in Paris? No, but what binds us is our book-like fate, the same literal and symbolic lying open on the table or the floor of the gigantic library, at various ends, to be trampled on or picked up by a mildly curious reader or—worse—by a dutiful librarian. The qualitatively novel stuff we may tell that reader about is the autonomous, spacecraft-like mentality that visits,

I am sure, every one of us, but whose visitations most of our pages choose not to acknowledge.

We do this for practical reasons, as it were, or genre considerations. Because this way lies either madness or the degree of coldness associated more with the pale-faced locals than with a hot-blooded exile. The other way, however, lies—and close, too—banality. All of this may sound to you like a typically Russian job of issuing guidelines for literature, while, in fact, it's simply one man's reactions to finding many an exiled author—Russian ones in the first place—on the banal side of virtue. That's a great waste, because one more truth about the condition we call exile is that it accelerates tremendously one's otherwise professional flight—or drift—into isolation, into an absolute perspective: into the condition at which all one is left with is oneself and one's language, with nobody or nothing in between. Exile brings you overnight where it would normally take a lifetime to go. If this sounds to you like a commercial, so be it, because it is about time to sell this idea. Because I indeed wish it got more takers. Perhaps a metaphor will help: to be an exiled writer is like being a dog or a man hurtled into outer space in a capsule (more like a dog, of course, than a man, because they will never retrieve you). And your capsule is your language. To finish the metaphor off, it must be added that before long the capsule's passenger discovers that it gravitates not earthward but outward.

For one in our profession the condition we call exile is, first of all, a linguistic event: he is thrust from, he retreats into his mother tongue. From being his, so to speak, sword, it turns into his shield, into his capsule. What started as a private, intimate affair with the language in exile becomes fate—even before it becomes an obsession or a duty. A living language, by definition, has a centrifugal propensity—and propulsion; it tries to cover as much ground as possible— and as much emptiness as possible. Hence the population explosion, and hence your autonomous passage outward, into the domain of a telescope or a prayer.

In a manner of speaking, we all work for a dictionary. Because literature *is* a dictionary, a compendium of meanings for this or that human lot, for this or that experience. It is a dictionary of the language in which life speaks to man. Its function is to save the next man, a new arrival, from falling into an old trap, or to help him realize, should he fall into that trap anyway, that he has been hit by a tautology. This way he will be less impressed—and, in a way, more free. For to know the meaning of life's terms, of what is happening to you, is liberating. It would seem to me that the condition we call exile is up for a fuller explication; that, famous for its pain, it should also be known for its pain-dulling infinity, for its forgetfulness, detachment, indifference, for its terrifying human and inhuman vistas for which we've got no yardstick except ourselves.

We must make it easier for the next man, if we can't make it safer. And the only way to make it easier for him, to make him less frightened of it, is to give him the whole measure of it—that is, as much as we ourselves can manage to cover. We may argue about our responsibilities and loyalties (toward our respective contemporaries, motherlands, otherlands, cultures, traditions, etc.) ad infinitum, but this responsibility or, rather, opportunity to set the next man— however theoretical he and his needs may be—a bit more free shouldn't become a subject for hesitation. If all this sounds a bit too lofty and humanistic, then I apologize. These distinctions are actually not so much humanistic as deterministic, although one shouldn't bother with such subtleties. All I am trying to say is that, given an opportunity, in the great causal chain of things, we may as well stop being just its rattling effects and try to play causes. The condition we call exile is exactly that kind of opportunity.

Yet if we don't use it, if we decide to remain effects and play exile in an old-fashioned way, that shouldn't be explained away as nostalgia. Of course, it has to do with the necessity of telling about oppression, and of course, our condition should serve as a warning to any thinking man toying with the idea of an ideal society. That's our value for the free world: that's our function.

But perhaps our greater value and greater function are to be unwitting embodiments of the disheartening idea that a freed man is not a free man, that liberation is just the means of attaining freedom and is not synonymous with it. This highlights the extent of the damage that can be done to the species, and we can feel proud of playing this role. However, if we want to play a bigger role, the role of a free man, then we should be capable of accepting—or at least imitating—the manner in which a free man fails. A free man, when he fails, blames nobody.

A Place as Good as Any

~

The more one travels, the more complex one's sense of nostalgia becomes. In a dream, depending on one's mania or supper or both, one is either pursued or pursues somebody through a crumpled maze of streets, lanes, and alleyways belonging to several places at once; one is in a city that does not exist on the map. A panicky flight originating as a rule in one's hometown is likely to land one helpless under the poorly lit archway in the town of one's last year's, or the year before's, sojourn. It is so much so that eventually your traveler finds himself unwittingly sizing up every locale he encounters for its potential value as a backdrop for his nightmare.

The best way to keep your subconscious from getting overburdened is to take pictures: your camera is, as it were, your lightning rod. Developed and printed, unfamiliar façades and perspectives lose their potent three-dimensionality and their air of being an alternative to one's life. Yet one can't click nonstop, one can't constantly put things in focus —what with clutching the luggage, the shopping bags, the spouse's elbow. And with a particular vengeance the unfamiliar three-dimensional invades the senses of unsuspecting innocents at railway stations, airports, bus stations, in a taxi, on a leisurely evening stroll to or from a restaurant.

Of these, railway stations are the most insidious. Edifices of arrival for you and those of departure for the locals, they insinuate travelers, tense with excitement and apprehension, straight into the thick of things, into the heart of an alien existence, pretending to be precisely the opposite by flashing their gigantic CINZANO, MARTINI, COCA-COLA signs—the fiery writing that evokes familiar walls. Ah, those squares in front of railway stations! With their fountains and statues of the Leader, with their feverish bustle of traffic and cinema billboards, with their whores, hypodermic youths, beggars, winos, migrant workers; with taxicabs and stocky cabdrivers soliciting in loud snatches of unfathomable tongues! The deep-seated anxiety of every traveler makes him register the location of the taxi stand in this square with greater precision than the order of appearance of the great Master's works in the local museum—because the latter won't constitute a way of retreat.

The more one travels, the richer one's memory gets with exact locations of taxi stands, ticket offices, shortcuts to platforms, phone booths, and urinals. If not often revisited, these stations and their immediate vicinities merge and superimpose on each other in one's mind, like everything that's stored for too long, resulting in a gigantic brick-cum-cast-iron, chlorine-smelling octopal ogre, submerged in one's memory, to which every new destination adds a tentacle.

There are apparent exceptions: the great mother, Victoria Station in London; Nerva's masterpiece in Rome or the garish monumental monstrosity in Milan; Amsterdam's Central with one of its fronton's dials showing the direction and speed of the wind; Paris's Gare du Nord or Gare de Lyon with the latter's mind-boggling restaurant, where, consuming superb *canard* under frescoes à la Denis, you watch through the huge glass wall trains departing down below with a faint sense of metabolic connection; the Hauptbahnhof near Frankfurt's red-light district; Moscow's Three-Railroad-Stations Square—the ideal place to ladle despair and indirection even for those whose native alphabet is Cyrillic. These exceptions, however, do not so much confirm the rule as form the core or kernel for subsequent accretions. Their Piranesean vaults and staircases echo, perhaps even enlarge, the seat of the subconscious; at any rate, they remain there—in the brain—for good, waiting for addition.

II

And the more legendary your destination, the more readily this gigantic octopus comes to the surface, feeding equally well on airports, bus terminals, harbors. Its real dainty, though, is the place itself. What constitutes the legend—artifice or edifice, a tower or a cathedral, a breathtaking ancient ruin or a unique library—goes first. Our monster salivates over these nuggets, and so do travel agencies' posters, jumbling Westminster Abbey, the Eiffel Tower, St Basil, the Taj Mahal, the Acropolis, and some pagodas in an eye-catching, mind-skipping collage. We know these vertical things before we've seen them. What's more, after having seen them, we retain not their three-dimensional image but their printed version.

Strictly speaking, we remember not a place but our postcard of it. Say "London" and your mind most likely will flash the view of the National Gallery or Tower Bridge with the Union Jack logo discreetly printed in a corner or on the opposite side. Say "Paris," and . . . There is perhaps nothing wrong with this sort of reduction or swapping, for had a human mind indeed been able to cohere and retain the reality of this world, the life of its owner would become a nonstop nightmare of logic and justice. At least its laws imply as much. Unable or unwilling to be held accountable, man decides to move first and loses either count or track of what he experiences, especially for the umpteenth time. The result is not so much a hodgepodge or a jumble as a composite vision: of a green tree if you are a painter, of a mistress if you are a Don Giovanni, of a victim if you are a tyrant, of a city if you are a traveler.

Whatever one travels for—to modify one's territorial imperative, to get an eyeful of creation, to escape reality (awful tautology though this is), the net result of course is feeding that octopus constantly hungry for new details for its nightly chow. The composite city of your subconscious sojourn—nay! return—will therefore permanently sport a golden cupola; several bell towers; an opera house à la Fenice in Venice; a park with gloom-laden chestnuts and poplars, incomprehensible in their post-Romantic swaying grandeur, as in Graz; a wide, melancholy river spanned by a minimum of six well-wrought bridges; a skyscraper or two. After all, a city as such has only so many options. And, as though semiconscious of that, your memory will throw in a granite embankment with its vast colonnades from Russia's former capital; Parisian pearl-gray façades with the black lace of their balconies' grillwork; a few boulevards petering out into the lilac sunset of one's adolescence; a gothic needle or that of an obelisk shooting its heroin into a cloudy muscle; and, in winter, a well-tanned Roman terra-cotta; a marble fountain; poorly lit, cave-like café life at street corners.

Your memory will accord this place a history whose particulars you probably won't recall but whose main fruit will most likely be a democracy. The same source will endow it with a temperate climate adhering to the four-seasons routine and segregating palm trees to railway stations' grillrooms. It will also give your city Reykjavík-on-Sunday-type traffic; people will be few if any; beggars and children, however, will speak the foreign tongue fluently. The currency will carry images of Renaissance scholars, the coins feminine profiles of the republic, but the numbers will still be recognizable, and your main problem—not of paying, but of tipping—can, in the end, be solved. In other words, regardless of what it says on your ticket, of whether you'll be staying at the Savoy or the Danieli, the moment you open your shutters, you'll see at once Notre-Dame, St. James's, San Giorgio, and Hagia Sophia.

For the aforesaid submerged monster digests legends as eagerly as reality. Add to that the latter's aspiration for the glory of the former (or the former's claim to enjoying, at least once upon a time, the status of the latter). Small wonder, then, that your city should, as though it's been painted by Claude or Corot, have some water: a harbor, a lake, a lagoon. Smaller wonder still that the medieval ramparts or molars of its Roman wall should look like an intended background for some steel-cum-glass-cum-concrete structures: a university, say, or more likely an insurance company headquarters. These are usually erected on the site of some monastery or ghetto bombed out of existence in the course of the last war. Small wonder, too, that a traveler reveres ancient ruins many times over the modern ones left in the center of your city by its fathers for didactic purposes: a traveler, by definition, is a product of hierarchic thinking.

In the final analysis, however, there is no hierarchy between the legendary and the real, in the context of your city at least, since the present engenders the past far more energetically than the other way around. Every car passing through an intersection makes its equestrian monument more obsolete, more ancient, telescoping its great local eighteenth-century military or civic genius into some skin-

clad William Tell or other. With all four hooves firmly on
the plinth (which, in the parlance of sculpture, means that
the rider has died not on the battlefield but in his own,
presumably four-poster bed), this monument's horse would
stand in your city more as an homage to an extinct means
of transportation than to anyone's particular valor. The birds'
ca-ca on the bronze tricorn is all the more deserved, for
history long since exited your city, yielding the stage to the
more elementary forces of geography and commerce. Therefore, your city will have not only a cross between a bazaar
in Istanbul and Macy's; no, a traveler in this city, should he
turn right, is bound to hit the silks, furs, and leather of via
Condotti and, if he turns left, to find himself buying either
fresh or canned pheasant at Fauchon (and the canned one
is preferable).

For buy you must. As the philosopher would have put
it, I purchase, therefore I am. And who knows that better
than a man in passage? In fact, every well-mapped trip is in
the end a shopping expedition: indeed, one's whole passage
through the world is. In fact, next to taking pictures, shopping comes in second at sparing one's subconscious an alien
reality. In fact, that's what we call a bargain, and with a
credit card you can go on infinitely. In fact, why don't you
simply call your whole city—it surely ought to have a
name—American Express? This will make it as legal as being
included in the atlas: no one will dare to challenge your
description. On the contrary, many would claim they've
been there, too, a year or so ago. To prove this, they'll
produce a bunch of snapshots or, if you are staying for a
meal, even a slide show. Some of them have known Karl
Malden, that city's dapper old mayor, personally for years
and years.

III

It is an early evening in the town of your memory; you are sitting in a sidewalk café under drooping chestnuts. A traffic light idly flashes its red-amber-green eye above the empty intersection; higher up, swallows crisscross a platinum, cloudless sky. The way your coffee or your white wine tastes tells you that you are neither in Italy nor in Germany; the bill tells you that you are not in Switzerland, either. All the same, you are in Common Market territory.

On the left, there is the Concert Hall, and on the right there is the Parliament. Or it is the other way around: with architecture like this, it's hard to tell the difference. Chopin came through this town, so did Liszt, and so did Paganini. As for Wagner, the book says he went through this place three times. So did, it seems, the Pied Piper. Or maybe it's just Sunday, vacation time, midsummer. "In summer," the poet said, "capitals grow empty." An ideal season for a coup d'état, then, for introducing tanks into these narrow cobblestone streets—almost no traffic whatsoever. Of course, if this place is indeed a capital . . .

You have a couple of phone numbers here, but you've tried them already twice. As for the goal of your pilgrimage, the National Museum, justly famous for its Italian Masters, you went there straight from the train, and it closes at five. And anyhow, what's wrong with great art—with Italian Masters in particular—is that it makes you resent reality. If, of course, this is a reality . . .

So you open the local *Time Out* and consider theater. It's Ibsen and Chekhov all over the place, the usual Continental fare. Luckily, you don't know the language. The National Ballet appears to be touring Japan, and you won't sit through *Madama Butterfly* for the sixth time even if the set was designed by Hockney. That leaves movies and pop groups, yet the small print of these pages, not to mention the bands' names, makes you briefly nauseous. On the horizon looms further expansion of your waistline in some Lutèce or Golden Horseshoe. It is actually your widening diameter that narrows your options.

The more one travels, though, the better one knows that curling up in a hotel room with Flaubert won't do either. The sounder solution is a stroll in an amusement park, half an hour in a shooting gallery, or a video game—something that boosts the ego and doesn't require knowledge of the local tongue. Or else take a taxi to the top of the hill that dominates the view and offers a terrific panorama of your composite city and its environs: the Taj Mahal, the Eiffel Tower, Westminster Abbey, St. Basil—the whole thing. This is yet another nonverbal experience; a "wow" will suffice. That's, of course, if there is a hill, or if there is a taxi . . .

Return to your hotel on foot: it's downhill all the way. Admire shrubs and hedges shielding the stylish mansions; admire the rustling acacias and somber monoliths of the business center. Linger by well-lit shop windows, especially those selling watches. Such a variety, almost like in Switzerland! It's not that you need a new watch; it's just a nice way of killing time—looking at the watches. Admire toys and admire lingerie: these appeal to the family man in you. Admire the clean-swept pavement and perfect infinity of avenues: you always had a soft spot for geometry, which, as you know, means "no people."

So if you find somebody in the hotel bar, it's most likely a man like yourself, a fellow traveler. "Hey," he'll say, turning his face toward you. "Why is this place so empty? Neutron bomb or something?"

"Sunday," you'll reply. "It's just Sunday, midsummer, vacation time. Everyone's gone to the beaches." Yet you know you'll be lying. Because it is neither Sunday nor the Pied Piper, nor the neutron bomb nor beaches that make your composite city empty. It is empty because for an imagination it is easier to conjure architecture than human beings.

1986

Uncommon Visage

The Nobel Lecture

I

For someone rather private, for someone who all his life has preferred his private condition to any role of social significance, and who went in this preference rather far—far from his homeland, to say the least, for it is better to be a total failure in a democracy than a martyr, or *la crème de la crème*, in a tyranny—for such a person to find himself all of a sudden on this rostrum is a somewhat uncomfortable and trying experience.

This sensation is aggravated not so much by the thought of those who stood here before me as by the memory of those who have been bypassed by this honor, who were not given this chance to address *urbi et orbi*, as they say, from this rostrum, and whose cumulative silence is sort of searching, to no avail, for release through this speaker here.

The only thing that can reconcile one to this sort of situation is the simple realization that—for stylistic reasons, in the first place—one writer cannot speak for another writer, one poet for another poet especially; that had Osip Mandelstam or Marina Tsvetaeva or Robert Frost or Anna Akhmatova or Wystan Auden stood here, they couldn't have helped but speak precisely for themselves; and they, too, might have felt somewhat uncomfortable.

These shades disturb me constantly; they are disturbing me today as well. In any case, they do not spur one to eloquence. In my better moments, I deem myself their sum total, though invariably inferior to any one of them individually. For it is not possible to better them on the page; nor is it possible to better them in actual life. And it is precisely their lives, no matter how tragic or bitter they were, that often move me—more often, perhaps, than the case should be—to regret the passage of time. If the next life exists—and I can no more deny them the possibility of eternal life than I can forget their existence in this one—if the next world does exist, they will, I hope, forgive me, and the quality of what I am about to utter: after all, it is not one's conduct on a podium that dignity in our profession is measured by.

I have mentioned only five of them, those whose deeds and whose lot matter so much to me, if only because if it were not for them, I, as both a man and a writer, would amount to much less; in any case, I wouldn't be standing here today. There were more of them, those shades—better still, sources of light: lamps? stars?—more, of course, than just five. And each one of them is capable of rendering me absolutely mute. The number of those is substantial in the life of any conscious man of letters; in my case, it doubles, thanks to the two cultures to which fate has willed me to belong. Matters are not made easier by thoughts about contemporaries and fellow writers in both these cultures, poets and fiction writers whose gifts I rank above my own, and who, had they found themselves on this rostrum, would have come to the point long ago, for surely they have more to tell the world than I do.

I will allow myself, therefore, to make a number of

remarks here—disjointed, perhaps stumbling, perhaps even perplexing in their randomness. However, the amount of time allotted to me to collect my thoughts, as well as my very occupation, will, or may, I hope, shield me, at least partially, against charges of being chaotic. A man of my occupation seldom claims a systematic mode of thinking; at worst, he claims to have a system—but even that, in his case, is a borrowing from a milieu, from a social order, or from the pursuit of philosophy at a tender age. Nothing convinces an artist more of the arbitrariness of the means to which he resorts to attain a goal—however permanent it may be—than the creative process itself, the process of composition. Verse really does, in Akhmatova's words, grow from rubbish; the roots of prose are no more honorable.

II

If art teaches anything—to the artist, in the first place—it is the privateness of the human condition. Being the most ancient as well as the most literal form of private enterprise, it fosters in a man, knowingly or unwittingly, a sense of his uniqueness, of individuality, of separateness—thus turning him from a social animal into an autonomous "I." Lots of things can be shared: a bed, a piece of bread, convictions, a mistress, but not a poem by, say, Rainer Maria Rilke. A work of art, of literature especially, and a poem in particular, addresses a man tête-à-tête, entering with him into direct —free of any go-betweens—relations.

It is for this reason that art in general, literature especially, and poetry in particular, is not exactly favored by champions of the common good, masters of the masses, heralds of historical necessity. For there, where art has stepped, where a poem has been read, they discover, in place of the anticipated consent and unanimity, indifference and polyphony; in place of the resolve to act, inattention and fastidiousness. In other words, into the little zeros with which the champions of the common good and the rulers of the masses tend to operate, art introduces a "period, period, comma, and a minus," transforming each zero into a tiny human, albeit not always a pretty, face.

The great Baratynsky, speaking of his Muse, characterized her as possessing an "uncommon visage." It's in acquiring this "uncommon visage" that the meaning of human existence seems to lie, since for this uncommonness we are, as it were, prepared genetically. Regardless of whether one is a writer or a reader, one's task consists first of all in mastering a life that is one's own, not imposed or prescribed from without, no matter how noble its appearance may be. For each of us is issued but one life, and we know full well how it all ends. It would be regrettable to squander a single chance by assuming someone else's appearance, someone else's experience, whether by reducing or by expanding this single chance in a tautology—regrettable all the more because the heralds of historical necessity, at whose urging a man may be prepared to agree to this tautology, will not go to the grave with him, or give him so much as a thank-you.

Language and, presumably, literature are things that are more ancient and inevitable, more durable than any form of social organization. The revulsion, irony, or indifference often expressed by literature toward the state is essentially the reaction of the permanent—better yet, the infinite—against the temporary, against the finite. To say the least, as long as the state permits itself to interfere with the affairs of literature, literature has the right to interfere with the affairs of the state. A political system, a form of social organization, like any system in general, is by definition a form of the past tense that aspires to impose itself upon the present (and often on the future as well); and a man who works in grammar is the last one who can afford to forget this. The real danger for a writer is not so much the possibility (and often the certainty) of persecution on the part of the state as it is the possibility of finding oneself mesmerized by the state's features, which, whether monstrous or undergoing changes for the better, are always temporary.

The philosophy of the state, its ethics—not to mention its aesthetics—are always "yesterday." Language and literature are always "today," and often—particularly in the case where a political system is orthodox—they may even constitute "tomorrow." One of literature's merits is precisely that it helps a person to make the time of his existence more specific, to distinguish himself from the crowd of his predecessors as well as his like numbers, to avoid tautology—that is, the fate otherwise known by the honorific term "victim of history." What makes art in general, and literature in particular, remarkable, what distinguishes them from life, is precisely that they abhor repetition. In everyday life you can tell the same joke thrice and, thrice getting a laugh, become the life of the party. In art this sort of conduct is called "cliché."

Art is a recoilless weapon, and its development is determined not by the individuality of the artist but by the dynamics and the logic of the material itself, by the previous fate of the means that each time demand (or suggest) a qualitatively new aesthetic solution. Possessing its own genealogy, dynamics, logic, and future, art is not synonymous with, but at best parallel to, history; and the manner by which it exists is by continually generating a new aesthetic reality. That is why it is often found "ahead of progress," ahead of history, whose main instrument is—should we not, once more, improve upon Marx—precisely the cliché.

Nowadays, for example, there exists a rather widely held

view, postulating that in his work a writer, in particular a poet, should make use of the language of the street, the language of the crowd. For all its democratic appearance, and its palpable advantages for a writer, this assertion is quite absurd, and represents an attempt to subordinate art, in this case literature, to history. It is only if we have resolved that it is time for *Homo sapiens* to come to a halt in his development that literature should speak the language of the people. Otherwise it is the people who should speak the language of literature.

On the whole, every new aesthetic reality makes man's ethical reality more precise. For aesthetics is the mother of ethics. The categories of "good" and "bad" are, first and foremost, aesthetic ones, at least etymologically preceding the categories of "good" and "evil." If in ethics not "all is permitted," it is precisely because not "all is permitted" in aesthetics, because the number of colors in the spectrum is limited. The tender babe who cries and rejects the stranger who, on the contrary, reaches out to him, does so instinctively, makes an aesthetic choice, not a moral one.

Aesthetic choice is a highly individual matter, and aesthetic experience is always a private one. Every new aesthetic reality makes one's experience even more private; and this kind of privacy, assuming at times the guise of literary (or some other) taste, can in itself turn out to be, if not a guarantee, then a form of defense, against enslavement. For a man with taste, particularly with literary taste, is less susceptible to the refrains and the rhythmical incantations peculiar to any version of political demagogy. The point is not so much that virtue does not constitute a guarantee for producing a masterpiece as that evil, especially political evil, is always a bad stylist. The more substantial an individual's aesthetic experience is, the sounder his taste, the sharper his moral focus, the freer—though not necessarily the happier—he is.

It is precisely in this applied, rather than Platonic, sense that we should understand Dostoevsky's remark that beauty will save the world, or Matthew Arnold's belief that we shall be saved by poetry. It is probably too late for the world, but for the individual man there always remains a chance. An aesthetic instinct develops in man rather rapidly, for even without fully realizing who he is and what he actually requires, a person instinctively knows what he doesn't like and what doesn't suit him. In an anthropological respect, let me reiterate, a human being is an aesthetic creature before he is an ethical one. Therefore, it is not that art, particularly literature, is a by-product of our species' development, but just the reverse. If what distinguishes us from other members of the animal kingdom is speech, then literature—and poetry in particular, being the highest form of locution—is, to put it bluntly, the goal of our species.

I am far from suggesting the idea of compulsory training in verse composition; nevertheless the subdivision of society into intelligentsia and "all the rest" seems to me unacceptable. In moral terms, this situation is comparable to the subdivision of society into the poor and the rich; but if it is still possible to find some purely physical or material grounds for the existence of social inequality, for intellectual inequality these are inconceivable. Equality in this respect, unlike in anything else, has been guaranteed to us by nature. I speak not of education but of the education in speech, the slightest imprecision in which may trigger the intrusion of false choice into one's life. The existence of literature prefigures existence on literature's plane of regard—and not only in the moral sense, but lexically as well. If a piece of music still allows a person the possibility of choosing between the passive role of listener and the active one of performer, a work of literature—of the art which is, to use Montale's phrase, incurably semantic—dooms him to the role of performer only.

In this role, it would seem to me, a person should appear more often than in any other. Moreover, it seems to me that, as a result of the population explosion and the attendant, ever-increasing atomization of society (i.e., the ever-increasing isolation of the individual), this role becomes more and more inevitable for a person. I don't suppose that I know more about life than anyone of my age, but it seems to me that, in the capacity of an interlocutor, a book is more reliable than a friend or a beloved. A novel or a poem is not a monologue but a conversation of a writer with a reader, a conversation, I repeat, that is very private, excluding all others—if you will, mutually misanthropic. And in the moment of this conversation a writer is equal to a reader, as well as the other way around, regardless of whether the writer is a great one or not. This equality is the equality of consciousness. It remains with a person for the rest of his life in the form of memory, foggy or distinct; and sooner or later, appropriately or not, it conditions a person's conduct. It's precisely this that I have in mind in speaking of the role of the performer, all the more natural for one because a novel or a poem is the product of mutual loneliness—of a writer, or a reader.

In the history of our species, in the history of *Homo sapiens*, the book is an anthropological development, similar essentially to the invention of the wheel. Having emerged in order to give us some idea not so much of our origins as of what that *sapiens* is capable of, a book constitutes a means of transportation through the space of experience, at the speed of a turning page. This movement, like every movement, becomes a flight from the common denominator, from an attempt to elevate this denominator's line, previously never reaching higher than the groin, to our heart, to our consciousness, to our imagination. This flight is the flight in the direction of "uncommon visage," in the direction of the numerator, in the direction of autonomy, in the direction of privacy. Regardless of whose image we are created in, there are already five billion of us, and for a human being there is no other future save that outlined by art. Otherwise, what lies ahead is the past—the political one, first of all, with all its mass police entertainment.

In any event, the condition of society in which art in general, and literature in particular, are the property or prerogative of a minority appears to me unhealthy and dangerous. I am not appealing for the replacement of the state with a library, although this thought has visited me frequently; but there is no doubt in my mind that, had we been choosing our leaders on the basis of their reading experience and not their political programs, there would be much less grief on earth. It seems to me that a potential master of our fates should be asked, first of all, not about how he imagines the course of his foreign policy, but about his attitude toward Stendhal, Dickens, Dostoevsky. If only because the lock and stock of literature is indeed human diversity and perversity, it turns out to be a reliable antidote for any attempt—whether familiar or yet to be invented—toward summary solutions to the problems of human existence. As a form of moral insurance, at least, literature is much more dependable than a system of beliefs or a philosophical doctrine.

Since there are no laws that can protect us from ourselves, no criminal code is capable of preventing a true crime against literature; though we can condemn the material suppression of literature—the persecution of writers, acts of censorship, the burning of books—we are powerless when it comes to its worst violation: the neglect of books, the nonreading of them. For that crime, a person pays with his whole life; if the offender is a nation, it pays with its history. Living in the country I live in, I would be the first one prepared to believe that there is a set dependency between a person's material well-being and his literary ignorance. What keeps me from doing so is the history of the country in which I was born and grew up. For, reduced to a cause-and-effect minimum, to a crude formula, the Russian tragedy is precisely the tragedy of a society in which literature turned out to be the prerogative of the minority: the celebrated Russian intelligentsia.

I have no wish to enlarge upon the subject, no wish to darken this evening with thoughts of the tens of millions of human lives destroyed by other millions, since what occurred in Russia in the first half of the twentieth century occurred before the introduction of automatic weapons—in the name of the triumph of a political doctrine whose unsoundness is already manifested in the fact that it requires human sacrifice for its realization. I'll just say that I believe—not empirically, alas, but only theoretically—that for someone who has read a lot of Dickens, to shoot his like in the name of some idea is somewhat more problematic than for someone who has read no Dickens. And I am speaking precisely about reading Dickens, Sterne, Stendhal, Dostoevsky, Flaubert, Balzac, Melville, Proust, Musil, and so forth; that is, about literature, not about literacy or education. A literate, educated person, to be sure, is fully capable, after reading some political treatise or tract, of killing his like, and even of experiencing, in so doing, a rapture of conviction. Lenin was literate, Stalin was literate, so was

Hitler; as for Mao Zedong, he even wrote verse. What all these men had in common, though, was that their hit list was longer than their reading list.

However, before I move on to poetry, I would like to add that it would make sense to regard the Russian experience as a warning, if for no other reason than that the social structure of the West up to now is, on the whole, analogous to what existed in Russia prior to 1917. (This, by the way, is what explains the popularity in the West of the nineteenth-century Russian psychological novel and the relative lack of success of contemporary Russian prose. The social relations that emerged in Russia in the twentieth century presumably seem no less exotic to the reader than do the names of the characters, which prevent him from identifying with them.) For example, the number of political parties, on the eve of the October coup in 1917, was no fewer than what we find today in the United States or Britain. In other words, a dispassionate observer might remark that in a certain sense the nineteenth century is still going on in the West, while in Russia it came to an end; and if I say it ended in tragedy, this is, in the first place, because of the size of the human toll taken in the course of that social—or chronological—change. For in a real tragedy, it is not the hero who perishes; it is the chorus.

III

Although for a man whose mother tongue is Russian to speak about political evil is as natural as digestion, I would like here to change the subject. What's wrong with discourses about the obvious is that they corrupt consciousness with their easiness, with the speed with which they provide one with moral comfort, with the sensation of being right. Herein lies their temptation, similar in its nature to the temptation of a social reformer who begets this evil. The realization, or rather the comprehension, of this temptation, and the rejection of it, are perhaps responsible to a certain extent for the destinies of many of my contemporaries, responsible for the literature that emerged from under their pens. It, that literature, was neither a flight from history nor a muffling of memory, as it may seem from the outside. "How can one write poetry after Auschwitz?" inquired Adorno; and one familiar with Russian history can repeat the same question by merely changing the name of the camp—and repeat it perhaps with even greater justification, since the number of people who perished in Stalin's camps far surpasses the number of German prison-camp victims. "And how can one eat lunch?" the American poet Mark Strand once retorted. In any case, the generation to which I belong has proven capable of writing that poetry.

That generation—the generation born precisely at the time when the Auschwitz crematoria were working full blast, when Stalin was at the zenith of his godlike, absolute power, which seemed sponsored by Mother Nature herself—that generation came into the world, it appears, in order to continue what, theoretically, was supposed to be interrupted in those crematoria and in the anonymous common graves of Stalin's archipelago. The fact that not everything got interrupted, at least not in Russia, can be credited in no small degree to my generation, and I am no less proud of belonging to it than I am of standing here today. And the fact that I am standing here today is a recognition of the services that generation has rendered to culture; recalling a phrase from Mandelstam, I would add, to world culture. Looking back, I can say now that we were beginning in an empty—indeed, a terrifyingly wasted—place, and that, intuitively rather than consciously, we aspired precisely to the re-creation of the effect of culture's continuity, to the reconstruction of its forms and tropes, toward filling its few surviving, and often totally compromised, forms with our own new, or appearing to us as new, contemporary content.

There existed, presumably, another path: the path of further deformation, the poetics of ruins and debris, of minimalism, of choked breath. If we rejected it, it was not at all because we thought that it was the path of self-dramatization, or because we were extremely animated by the idea of preserving the hereditary nobility of the forms of culture we knew, the forms that were equivalent, in our consciousness, to forms of human dignity. We rejected it because in reality the choice wasn't ours but, in fact, culture's own—and this choice, again, was aesthetic rather than moral.

To be sure, it is natural for a person to perceive himself not as an instrument of culture but, on the contrary, as its creator and custodian. But if today I assert the opposite, it's not because toward the close of the twentieth century there is a certain charm in paraphrasing Plotinus, Lord Shaftesbury, Schelling, or Novalis, but because, unlike anyone else, a poet always knows that what in the vernacular is called the voice of the Muse is, in reality, the dictate of the language; that it's not the language that happens to be his instrument, but that he is language's means toward the continuation of its existence. Language, however, even if one imagines it as a certain animate creature (which would only be just), is not capable of ethical choice.

A person sets out to write a poem for a variety of reasons: to win the heart of his beloved; to express his attitude toward the reality surrounding him, be it a landscape or a state; to capture his state of mind at a given instant; to leave—as he thinks at that moment—a trace on the earth. He resorts to this form—the poem—most likely for unconsciously mimetic reasons: the black vertical clot of words on the white sheet of paper presumably reminds him of his own situation in the world, of the balance between space and his body. But regardless of the reasons for which he takes up the pen, and regardless of the effect produced by what emerges from under that pen on his audience—however great or small it may be—the immediate consequence of this enterprise is the sensation of coming into direct contact with language, or more precisely, the sensation of immediately falling into dependence on it, on everything that has already been uttered, written, and accomplished in it.

This dependence is absolute, despotic; but it unshackles as well. For, while always older than the writer, language still possesses the colossal centrifugal energy imparted to it by its temporal potential—that is, by all the time lying ahead. And this potential is determined not so much by the quantitative body of the nation that speaks it (though it is determined by that, too) as by the quality of the poem written in it. It will suffice to recall the authors of Greek or Roman antiquity; it will suffice to recall Dante. And that which is being created today in Russian or English, for example, guarantees the existence of these languages over the course of the next millennium also. The poet, I wish to repeat, is language's means for existence—or, as my beloved Auden said, he is the one by whom it lives. I who write these lines will cease to be; so will you who read them. But the language in which they are written and in which you read them will remain, not merely because language is a more lasting thing than man, but because it is more capable of mutation.

One who writes a poem, however, writes it not because he courts fame with posterity, although often he hopes that a poem will outlive him, at least briefly. One who writes a poem writes it because the language prompts, or simply dictates, the next line. Beginning a poem, the poet as a rule doesn't know the way it is going to come out; and at times he is very surprised by the way it turns out, since often it turns out better than he expected, often his thought carries him further than he reckoned. And that is the moment when the future of language invades its present.

There are, as we know, three modes of cognition: analytical, intuitive, and the mode that was known to the biblical prophets: revelation. What distinguishes poetry from other forms of literature is that it uses all three of them at once (gravitating primarily toward the second and the third). For all three of them are given in the language; and there are times when, by means of a single word, a single rhyme, the writer of a poem manages to find himself where no one has ever been before him, further, perhaps, than he himself would have wished to go. The one who writes a poem writes it above all because verse writing is an extraordinary accelerator of consciousness, of thinking, of comprehending the universe. Having experienced this acceleration once, one is no longer capable of abandoning the chance to repeat this experience; one falls into dependency on this process, the way others fall into dependency on drugs or alcohol. One who finds himself in this sort of dependency on language is, I suppose, what they call a poet.

1987

(Translated by Barry Rubin)

Acceptance Speech

~

Members of the Swedish Academy, Your Majesties, ladies and gentlemen, I was born and grew up on the other shore of the Baltic, practically on its opposite gray, rustling page. Sometimes on clear days, especially in autumn, standing on a beach somewhere in Kellomäki, a friend would point his finger northwest across the sheet of water and say: See that blue strip of land? It's Sweden.

He would be joking, of course: because the angle was wrong, because according to the law of optics, a human eye can travel only for something like twenty miles in open space. The space, however, wasn't open.

Nonetheless, it pleases me to think, ladies and gentlemen, that we used to inhale the same air, eat the same fish, get soaked by the same—at times—radioactive rain, swim in the same sea, get bored by the same kind of conifers. Depending on the wind, the clouds I saw in my window were already seen by you, or vice versa. It pleases me to think that we have had something in common before we ended up in this room.

And as far as this room is concerned, I think it was empty just a couple of hours ago, and it will be empty again a couple of hours hence. Our presence in it, mine especially, is quite incidental from its walls' point of view. On the whole, from space's point of view, anyone's presence is incidental in it, unless one possesses a permanent—and usually inanimate—characteristic of landscape: a moraine, say, a hilltop, a river bend. And it is the appearance of something or somebody unpredictable within a space well used to its contents that creates the sense of occasion.

So being grateful to you for your decision to award me the Nobel Prize for literature, I am essentially grateful for your imparting to my work an aspect of permanence, like that of a glacier's debris, let's say, in the vast landscape of literature.

I am fully aware of the danger hidden in this simile: of coldness, uselessness, eventual or fast erosion. Yet if that debris contains a single vein of animated ore—as I, in my vanity, believe it does—then this simile is perhaps prudent.

And as long as I am on the subject of prudence, I should like to add that through recorded history the audience for poetry seldom amounted to more than 1 percent of the entire population. That's why poets of antiquity or of the Renaissance gravitated to courts, the seats of power; that's why nowadays they flock to universities, the seats of knowledge. Your academy seems to be a cross between the two; and if in the future—in that time free of ourselves—that 1 percent ratio is sustained, it will be, not to a small degree, due to your efforts. In case this strikes you as a dim vision of the future, I hope that the thought of the population explosion may lift your spirits somewhat. Even a quarter of that 1 percent would make a lot of readers, even today.

So my gratitude to you, ladies and gentlemen, is not entirely egotistical. I am grateful to you for those whom your decisions make and will make read poetry, today and tomorrow. I am not so sure that man will prevail, as the great man and my fellow American once said, standing, I believe, in this very room; but I am quite positive that a man who reads poetry is harder to prevail upon than one who doesn't.

Of course, it's one hell of a way to get from St. Petersburg to Stockholm; but then, for a man of my occupation, the notion of a straight line being the shortest distance between two points lost its attraction a long time ago. So it pleases me to find out that geography in its own turn is also capable of poetic justice.

Thank you.

1987

After a Journey, or
Homage to Vertebrae

No matter how horrid, or else vapid, a day has turned out to be, in the end you stretch out on your bed—and you are no longer an ape, a man, a bird, or even a fish. Horizontality in nature is rather of a geological denomination and has to do with deposits: it is an homage to vertebrae and designed for the future. The same, on the whole, goes for all sorts of travel notes and memoirs: the mind there seems to get flat on its back and give up resistance, preparing for a rest rather than for settling scores with reality.

Sketching from memory: 1978, a journey to Brazil. Hardly a journey to speak of: a junket, really, in the name of international cultural exchange; just took a plane at 9 p.m. (total mess at the airport: Varig overbooked the flight two to one; the result the usual railway-station panic; the staff lackadaisical and indifferent—you sense you are dealing with a state—the company is nationalized, and everyone is a state employee). The plane was crammed, babies screaming, the back of my seat would not budge; all night I stayed vertical, with sleeping pills piling up in the abdomen. Bearing in mind that I had flown in from England just forty-eight hours before. Stifling, musty, etc. On top of everything else, instead of nine hours, the flight took twelve, since we touched

down first in São Paulo—pleading fog in Rio, but in fact half
the passengers had tickets precisely for São Paulo.

From the airport to downtown the taxi is rushing along
the right (?) bank of that famous January River, overgrown
with cranes and ocean ships—freighters, tankers, etc. Here
and there looms a gray bulk of the Brazilian Navy. (One
morning I walk out of the hotel and see Alexander Vertinsky's
couplet sailing into the harbor: "When we see the tall Brazilian cruiser, sailors'll tell us tales about a geyser.") So, on
the left, there are ships and the harbor; on the right, every
hundred or so meters, cocoa-shaded kids playing soccer.

Speaking of the latter, I must note that Brazil's triumphs
in this particular sport are no longer surprising when you've
seen the way people drive here. What is really puzzling,
with this kind of dribbling traffic, is the growth of the country's population. A local driver is a cross between Pelé and
a kamikaze. Apart from that, the very first thing you spot is
the prevalence of VW Bugs. It is virtually the only make
available here. Now and then, of course, you may notice a
Renault, a Peugeot, or a Ford, but they are clearly in the
minority. The same goes for telephones—all of them are
Siemens (and Schuckert). In a word, the Germans are in the
saddle here, one way or another. (Was it Franz Beckenbauer
who said, "Soccer is the most essential of all inessential
things"?)

They lodge us at the Gloria Hotel, an old-fashioned, fourteen-
floor affair with an extremely weird system of elevators requiring constant hopping from one to another. In the week
I stayed at this place I got used to it as to some kind of
womb—or the entrails of an octopus. In a certain sense, the
hotel was much more absorbing than the world outside.
Rio—at least the part I managed to see—is a very monotonous city, with all its riches and its poverty, both by accident

and by design. The two- or three-kilometer strip between the ocean and the looming cliffs is entirely overgrown with utterly moronic—à la that idiot Le Corbusier—beehive "structures." As though the vista denies man imagination. Perhaps it does. The eighteenth and the nineteenth centuries are completely wiped out. Occasionally you can bump into the debris of the mercantile style of the turn of the century, with its surreal medley of arcades, balconies, winding stairs, turrets, gates, and whatnot. But this is rare, and of no relief. And equally rare and relief-free are the small three- or four-floor hotels in the back streets behind the concrete-cum-stucco giants, or in the narrow lanes climbing up the hills at a minimum seventy-five-degree angle, winding up into an evergreen forest, the real jungle. There, in these narrow streets, in little villas and cobbled-up tenements, dwells the local population, employed mainly by the tourist outfits: extremely poor, somewhat desperate, but on the whole not overly protesting. At night, at every ten meters or so, you are offered a fuck, and later the West German consul treated us to the observation that prostitutes in Rio do not take money—or at least do not expect to get any, and are surprised if a client offers to pay.

It felt as if his excellency was right. Still, no opportunity to prove this personally ever arose, since I was kept occupied, as they say, from morn till night by a leggy Nordic delegate—or was she just an observer?—whose hairdo as well as a rather humdrum style of surrender brought memories of the same latitude and of N.N., with the difference that the latter was neither rude nor vain (and that I was younger and better then, and had N. not introduced me to her breadwinner and their bilious offspring, I could, who knows, have overcome this shortcoming and arrived at a less bitter end). On the third day of my stay in Rio—and the second day of the Nordic Games—we went to the beach at Copacabana, where, while I was getting sun, I was eased out of four hundred bucks as well as my favorite watch, which had been given to me by Liz Frank in Massachusetts six years before. The theft was staged splendidly, and as with everything here, nature was involved as well—this time in the guise of a light brown German shepherd loitering on the beach who, now and then, at his master's instigation, pulled at a traveler's pants. The traveler would not, of course, suspect a quadruped: a nice doggy jumping around, so what! The biped, in the meantime, voids your pockets, leaving you—very considerately—with a couple of cruzeiros for the bus trip back to the hotel. So potentially costly experiments were out of the question, whatever the German consul claimed while treating us to an impressive homebrew that glittered with all the colors of the rainbow. To be fair to him, though, he did usefully warn us against splashing in the ocean, citing both the extraordinary undertow and two members of the Hungarian mission only last week gobbled up by sharks in plain view of the city.

The beaches in Rio are indeed tremendous. When the plane starts to descend onto this continent, you have the impression that almost all the Brazilian coast is one uninterrupted beach, from the equator to Patagonia. From the top of Corcovado—the rock dominating the town and crowned with a twenty-meter-high statue of Christ (given to the city by none other than Mussolini)—one can see all three of them: Copacabana, Ipanema, and Leblon, and many others to the north and south of Rio, as well as the endless mountain chains at whose foothills are scattered the white concrete stalagmites of the city. On a clear day you feel that all your eye ever beheld before is but the measly, lackluster pickings of an arrested imagination. The local vistas can teach human as well as divine fantasy a lesson or two; it's places like this that give geography its good name.

As I stayed here for a week only, what I am saying amounts, by definition, to no more than first impressions. This said, I can only add that Rio is a most abstract place. This is a city which, no matter how many years you spend there, won't generate many memories. For a native of Europe, Rio is biological neutrality incarnate. Not a single façade, not one little lane or gateway, evokes any associations. It is a city of this century: nothing colonial, or even Victorian, with the exception perhaps of the edifice hulking over the passenger pier, resembling simultaneously St. Isaac's Cathedral and Washington's Capitol. Thanks to this indistinct (octagons, cubes, boxes), impersonal character, thanks to the beaches, which in their scale and generosity almost offset the ocean itself, thanks to the intensity, density, diversity, and total unfamiliarity of the local vegetation, which neither corresponds to nor echoes any species a European is used to, Rio gives one a sense of a total flight from the known reality. Into pure geometry, or into pure elements. All that week I felt like a former Nazi or Arthur Rimbaud: everything is behind, and just a blinking green light ahead.

"It could even be," I would say to myself, "that all of European culture, with its cathedrals, its Gothic, its Baroque, its rococo, its volutes, scrolls, pilasters, acanthi, etc., is nothing but the ape's longing for its forever-lost forest." Isn't it indeed telling that culture as we know it flourished precisely around the Mediterranean, where vegetation begins to change and, as it were, stops abruptly at the sea as if poised to leap over to its true homeland? That, in other words, architecture begins precisely where nature gives up, and that this may be true of all art? That literature is a continuation of the jungle by other means?

As far as our glorious congress was concerned, it was an event excruciating in its boredom, vacuity, and total dearth of any connection with either jungle or literature. For this reason alone, as well as for the utter sordidness of what followed, I'd better change the names of those I came to know there. I wish I could change mine, too, and for the same reasons. Julio Llianos, Tor Ostberg, and, possibly, I myself—plus of course the Great Translator—were the only writers in attendance. Initially I resolved just to ignore this delirium, but when every morning you bump into delegates (male and female deli-gators) at breakfast, in the hall, in the corridors, the whole thing little by little starts to acquire aspects of reality. Toward the end I was fighting like a lion for the creation of a PEN Club section for Vietnamese writers-in-exile. I got all worked up and tears were interfering with my speech.

Eventually a polygon began to take shape: Ulrich von Tirn with his wife and Samantha (a subtriangle), Fernando B. (Portuguese) with his wife, Thomas (a Swede) with a lady from Denmark, and me with my Nordic charge. Anonymity is adultery's oxygen, and nothing fills up one's lungs with it like being abroad. In this (plus or minus two furtive, stocky West Germans, half drunk and half insane) company we wandered from one watering hole to another, munched and sipped. Every day, bumping into one another at breakfast in the hotel's cafeteria or in the hall, we would pose one and the same question: "What's on for tonight?" The answer usually contained the name of a restaurant espied by one of us during the daytime or an establishment where the city fathers intended to entertain us, with the pomp, orations, libations, etc., the fathers are so good at. The opening of the congress was attended by the President of the country, General Figueiredo, who uttered three phrases, sat in the presidium for a while, patted Julio Llianos on the equally Latin

American shoulder, and left accompanied by a huge caval-
cade of bodyguards, cops, generals, admirals, and photog-
raphers from all the local papers, who were snapping his
picture with the fervor of people convinced that a lens was
capable not only of capturing the great man's epidermis but
of penetrating his lobes as well. It was amusing to watch all
these flunkies, athletic, youngish, ready any minute to
change their master or banner, clad in their blazers, ties,
and starched shirts offsetting their highly tensed, sun-baked
snouts. The state-bred genus, a cross between a parrot and
a monkey. Plus the pining for France and the nonstop quoting, now Victor Hugo, now André Malraux, with rather practiced accents. The Third World has inherited everything,
including the inferiority complex, of the First and Second.

"When are you flying back?" Ulrich asked me. "Tomorrow," I replied. "Lucky you," he said, for he was staying
on in Rio, where he had come with his wife, presumably to
salvage their marriage, at which he had already—apparently
in no time—succeeded. So for a while he would be stuck in
Rio, going to the beach with the local teachers of German
lit. and, at night, in the hotel, slipping out of his bed, in his
PJ top or bottom, sliding downstairs, and scratching at Samantha's door. Her room was right under his: 1161 and 1061.
You can change dollars into cruzeiros but not cruzeiros into
dollars.

I had planned to stay in Brazil for about ten days after the
congress—either to rent a cheap room somewhere around
the Copacabana, go to the beach, bathe, and get a suntan,
or else to take a trip to Bahia and try to sail up the Amazon
River, and then on to Cuzco, and from Cuzco—to Lima,
and then back to New York. But the money was stolen, and
although I could have gotten five hundred from American
Express, I did not do it. That continent, and that country in

particular, do interest me, but I am afraid that, as it is, I've seen more of this world than I've digested. The state of my health wasn't a consideration; at worst, it was a hindrance. After all, it would have been quite amusing for a Russian author to kick the bucket in the jungle: this hadn't happened in a while. But my ignorance as regards South American matters is so immense that even the most disastrous experience probably could not have enlightened me by one iota. There is something revolting in all this drifting along the surface, a camera in your hands, with no particular goal in mind. In the nineteenth century one could still do a Jules Verne or a Humboldt: in the twentieth, flora and fauna should be left to their own devices. In any case, I have seen the Southern Cross, and the young moon flat on its back. As to the destitution of the *favelas*—may the ones capable of forgiving forgive me for remarking that it, the destitution, is in tune with the uniqueness of the local landscape. Against such a backdrop, the ocean and the mountains, the social drama is looked at askance, and not by the spectators only but by the victims as well. Beauty always renders reality somewhat senseless; here beauty constitutes reality's major part.

A nervous person should not, and in fact cannot, keep a diary. Of course, I would prefer to arrest, or retain, something of these seven days—if only those kebabs, so monstrous in their volume (*churrasco rodízio*)—but by the second day I already felt like packing, like going back to New York. Of course, Rio is more chic than Sochi, the Côte d'Azur, Palm Beach, or Miami, regardless of the thick shroud of exhaust fumes, all the more unbearable in the local heat. But—and this may be the most important point—the essence of all my travels (their side effect, rather, turning into their essence) is in returning here, to Morton Street—in a more and more minute elaboration of the new meaning invested in my notion of "home." The more often you return to it, the more real this doghouse becomes. And the more abstract are the lands and waters I sashay through. I will probably never return to Liteynyi 27, and 44 Morton is but a last-ditch attempt to get away from perceiving the world as a one-way street.

After victory in the battle for the Annamites-in-exile, it emerged that it was Samantha's birthday—she was either thirty-five or forty-five; and Ulrich with his wife, ditto Fernando B., Samantha with the Great Translator (he may after all have indeed been the main writer among us, for the reputation of this whole continent rested precisely on him) went to the restaurant to celebrate. Stupefied by alcohol, I began to pester the Great Translator regarding his living merchandise—to the effect that they all, like the nineteenth-century gringos, for instance, plundered from our European brethren, plus, of course, the gringos themselves, with a touch of local color. That *One Hundred Years of Solitude* is just another Thomas Wolfe, whom (wasn't it unfortunate!) I'd happened to read right before the *Hundred Years*; the sense of "overcongestedness" was instantly recognizable. The Great Translator cozily and lazily was fending me off, saying yes, sure, there is an inevitable longing for the world culture, our European fellows themselves are not without this sin, and as for my own Eurasians, they are more guilty than most. That psychoanalysis had not yet taken root under the equator, and therefore his charges are still permitted to fantasize about themselves there, unlike, say, the gringos these days. Squeezed between Samantha and his uncomprehending spouse, Ulrich declared that modernism was the true culprit, and that after its rarefactions the reader gets a craving for real chow and all these Hispanic spices, etc., and that, generally, Borges was one thing and all this cheerful psychedelic blather was something else. "And Cortázar," I added. "*Ja*, Borges and Cortázar," said Ulrich, rolling his eyes toward Samantha, because he was wearing shorts and Samantha's hand was moving into them under the table from the left, unaware that the spouse was after the same goods from the right. "Borges and Cortázar," Ulrich repeated. Then, out of the blue, the other German duo pops up, quite high, and entices the salvaged wife, the Great Translator, and the Portuguese couple away to some party, while Samantha, Ulrich, and I shuffle back toward the Gloria along the Copacabana. In the process they both take off all their clothes and wade into the ocean, where they disappear sharks only know for how long, while I sit on the empty beach guarding their stuff and hiccuping; and I have the sensation that all this has already happened to me at some point in the past.

A drunk, especially a foreigner, especially a Russian, especially at night, is always a little concerned whether he will be able to find his way back to his hotel, and this concern gradually makes him sober.

In my room at the Gloria—rather chic by any standard (I was, after all, an honorary member of the American delegation)—there was a huge, lake-like mirror, dark and made almost velvet by thick reddish duckweed. It did not so much reflect as absorb what was happening in the room, and often, particularly in the dark, I seemed to myself like a naked perch slowly meandering in it, among the weeds, now submerging, now approaching the surface, now submerging again. This sensation was much stronger than the reality of the sessions, chatting with the delegates, attending press conferences, as though all these events were occurring somewhere in the background, at the bottom, knee-deep in silt. Perhaps this had to do with the naggingly hot weather, against which this lake was a subconscious refuge, since air conditioning at the Gloria was nonexistent. Anyhow, descending to the conference hall, or going out to the city, I had to make an effort, as though putting my eyesight manually into focus—as well as my mind, and ear, in order to tear my mind off that glass. Something like that happens with verses, pursuing you relentlessly although totally unrelated to the present moment—with your own or with someone else's, more often with someone else's; and with English even more frequently than Russian, especially with Auden's. The lines are just another kind of seaweed, and your memory is like a perch meandering among them. On the other hand, perhaps this impression could be explained by an unwitting narcissism, one's image acquiring in the mirror, thanks to the decaying amalgam, a shade of detachment, a certain extemporal savor; for the essence of any reflection is interest not so much in one's own person as in the very fact of viewing oneself from without. As for my Nordic distraction, all this was somewhat alien to her, and her interest in the mirror was briskly female and a touch pornographic: twisting her neck, she scrutinized the process or, rather, her enterprising self at it—in any case, not the weeds, or, moreover, the perch. To the left and to the right of the lake hung two color lithographs showing mango harvesting by half-dressed Negresses and a panoramic view of Cairo. Below mooned the gray of a broken TV set.

Among the delegates there were two remarkably scummy specimens: an old female stoolie from Bulgaria and a degenerate elderly literary critic from the DDR. She spoke English, he German and French, and as a result, on hearing them speechify, one (or at least I) had a most extraordinary sense of the soiling of civilization. It was particularly painful to listen to all this homeland-made drivel in English, since

English is somehow entirely unfit for this stuff—although, who knows, some hundred years ago one might have had the same reaction in Russian. I did not retain their names: she was sort of Rosa Khlebb–like, a major in the reserves, I guess: gray dress, poring over the files, thick spectacles, always on duty. He was even better, though: a critic with a clearance, more a windbag than a scribbler—with output at best something like "The Style of the Early Johannes Becher" (who penned that sonnet upon Stalin's seventieth birthday beginning with the words "I was awakened today by the sound of a thousand nightingales singing simultaneously . . ." *Eine tausend Nachtigallen . . .*). When I got up to mumble something on behalf of the Annamites, those two started booing, and the Deutsche Demokratische even inquired of the Presidium what country I represented. Then, *après* voting on the Vietnamese matter, this shitface ambles toward me and starts something like "But we do not know their literature, and can you really read that language of theirs anyhow, and we are *Europeans*, after all, aren't we," and so on. To this I reply that Indochina's population is *n* times larger than that of the Demokratische and the non-Demokratische put together, so chances are it harbors some equivalents of Anna Seghers *und* Stefan Zweig. On the whole, though, this kind of act reminds one mostly of the Gypsies at a country fair, who corner you and, screwing your territorial imperative, dive straight into your muzzle, which is something you allow only to your ex, and not too often at that! Cause who spares anything from a distance? Those guys, too, grab you by the button, roll their *r*'s as if this were Trocadero, and flash their Italian-framed glasses. The Continental crowd melts down on the spot, because it's polemics, mumbo-jumbo, a quote from either Feuerbach or Hegel, or some other bearded windbag, a shock of gray hair, and a total high from their own cadences and logic.

Afrostan goes in for that, too, even more so than the Europeans. There was a lot of it here—from Senegal, Côte d'Ivoire, and I don't recall anymore where else. The polished ebony pates, portly frames, in super fabrics, loafers from Balenciaga, etc., with Parisian experience under their belts, because it's no life for the Left Bank *gauchiste* if she never had a revolutionary Negro from the Third World—and that's where their action was, since the local fellahs and Bedouins cut no ice with them, not to mention the Annamites. "Your colored brothers are suffering," I wail. "No," they answer, "we have already cut a deal with the Deutsche Demokratische, and Léopold Sédar Senghor himself told us not to." On the other hand, had this congress been held not in Rio but among pine trees and squirrels—who knows—maybe they would have cackled differently. Here, of course, everything was too familiar—palms and lianas, vociferous parrots. Perhaps the pale-face latitudes are a more suitable venue for such displays of guilt and compassion, late as these usually are. Or perhaps an underdog, once well fed, barks no differently from the top dog. Or, at any rate, craves a leash.

The lousiest were the moments when all this caused aches here and there, left of the sternum; in general, when something goes bust in an Englishless place, I feel most uncomfortable. As Auden used to say, Most of all I dread croaking at some big hotel to the consternation of the personnel. That's how, I suppose, it's going to happen nevertheless, and the papers will be left in awful disarray, but one does not think about this although one should. And one does not think about it not because one does not feel like thinking this way but because that thing—let's call it nonexistence, though a shorter noun could easily be found—does not want one to divulge its secrets, and scares one out of pondering them with its proximity. So even later, when, after getting scared and after getting over it, you think about this, you write nothing down anyway. Generally it is odd that the mind turns itself from an ally, which it should be at the moment of going bust, into a fifth column, reducing one's resistance, not that high to begin with. And one ponders not how to get out of this bind but contemplates, rather, one's own mind-painted scenes of the final macabre. I was lying on my back at the Gloria, staring at the ceiling, waiting for the nitro to take effect and for the appearance of my Nordic escort, who had only the beach on her mind. But at least I had finally gotten my way, and my Annamite section was approved, after which the teeny-weeny Vietnamese woman, tears in her eyes, thanked us on behalf of all her people, saying that should I ever go to Australia, whence, pooling pennies, they had sent her to Rio, I'd get a royal reception and be treated to kangaroo-ear stew. I bought myself nothing of Brazilian manufacture but a jar of talcum powder, because, roaming around the city, I had chafed tender tissue.

The best were our night exchanges with Ulrich at the bar, where a local thumper extracted from a keyboard, with feeling, "La Comparsita" and "El Choclo" (the real name of which is known in Russia as "The Argentine Tango"), but failed miserably with "Colonel Bogey." The reason—his southern, different, sentimental (though not devoid of brutality) temperament: no knack for cold negation. During one of our conversations—about the devil knows what—Karl Krauss, I think—my Nordic charge—well, let's call her Stella Polaris—joined us, and ten minutes later, not getting the drift and raving mad because of that, started gushing something for which I nearly punched her in the nose. It's illuminating to watch a little beast wake up in a person, a beast dormant under normal circumstances. With Stella, it was evidently a skunk, and it was extremely absorbing to watch the little weasel rouse itself inside a creature who, just one hour before, had been rustling thoroughly documented papers and uttering Latinate sentences into a mike, *urbi et orbi*. I recall a charming straw-colored dress with a dark blue pattern on it, and a bright red gown in the morning—and the rabid hatred of an animal that begins to realize that it is an animal at 2 a.m. Well, it wouldn't be evolution if it didn't swing back and forth. The tango's twangs, a few couples whispering in the dark, sweet schnapps, and a puzzled look on Ulrich's face. The rascal was no doubt pondering where it would be better to land now—in his salvaged marriage, or with Samantha, who had a natural crush on the educated European.

At the conclusion of the big event, the city fathers threw a reception with liquor and petits fours at the Cultural Center, which, for all its avant-garde architecture, was light-years away from Rio. On the way there, and even more so in the chartered bus on the way back, the polygon slowly began changing its contours, thanks to M.S., who proved to be a true ethnographer, laying siege to one of the local interpreter girls. Then delegates started leaving. The Nordic Star betook herself to the Land of Silver, and I arrived in the lobby too late to say goodbye to her. The triangle (Ulrich, his spouse, and S.) were heading for Bahia, and then up the Amazon River, and from there—to Cuzco. The intoxicated Germans went homeward, and I, without a buck, clutching at my chest, with a broken pulse, to my own place of residence. The night before, the Portuguese guy (who had dragged us to some local ritual that he tried to sell as voodoo but that in effect was a regular pagan version of mass purification in a working-class—and nightmarish at that—neighborhood: clotted vegetation, monotonous wailing from a catatonic choir, and all this in a school auditorium, with holy lithographs, warm Coca-Cola, horrible sore-barnacled dogs, and no cab in sight for return), with his skinny, tall, and jealous wife, went to some peninsula known to him only, since he spoke the local tongue, where healers do miracles restoring potency. Though every country is nothing but a continuation of space, there is in these Third World places a certain specific despair, their own particular hopelessness; the mass debilitation carried out in other parts by state security is ensured here by poverty.

What it boils down to is that I didn't see the place. I wonder whether I even saw what I remember myself looking at. Cardiac cases perhaps shouldn't be allowed to travel by air precisely for this reason: their perceptive ability is clouded as it is by their internal state. To say the least, their focus is elsewhere. But who can resist a round-trip offer, especially if the destination is exotic. On the other hand, a round trip is an awful psychological trap: the return portion robs you of any chance of psychological investment in the place. The best outcome of such travel is a snapshot of your sweet self against some corny backdrop, and indeed Stella Polaris and I took several pictures of each other in the Botanical Garden. Still, the camera was hers. Which spares me at least one more, albeit small, indignity, removing thus one more, perhaps the last, proof of my ever having been to Brazil.

Have I? Was I really there? In the end, I think I should say yes—if only because it makes no difference whatsoever whether I was there or not, and it's always better to admit your own insignificance than to deny it. There are no objective criteria to judge the value of one's life, to begin with; but nothing diminishes it more than its exposure to extraordinary vistas and big crowds. In short, to space. In the end, perhaps that's why one travels, why one rubs one's pupils, shoulders, and navels against strangers. Perhaps the name of the whole game is humility, and fatigue setting into the bone is that virtue's true voice. At any rate, this is the voice that tells me that I've been to Brazil. There is no other trace. Even those four hundred bucks are by now all spent by the thief; even the Annamite writers in Australia have gotten used to the legitimacy of their gatherings and have by now, I imagine, the appropriate stationery. It's strange to partake in something that results in the uncertainty of recollection, but to ask for more would be pure hubris.

Likewise, nothing of value escaped from under my pen: no immortal lyric. One wishes one could produce something on the spot, like a journalist or a painter, but one is seldom that lucky, and I wasn't. Behind *nulla dies sine linea* looms the realization that one has gobbled up at lunch more than one earns in a week. The solution lies in inventing an idiom that would allow production on a daily basis (like Berryman's *Dream Songs* or Lowell's *History*), though there is the threat of becoming a chatterbox. Well, guilt is a better vehicle in this business of scribbling than confidence. And, I guess, a better tenor, too. In any case, among the notes that survived the trip there are several stanzas of a Rio Samba: doggerel, really, but some rhymes aren't so bad:

Come to Rio, oh come to Rio.
Grow a mustache and change your bio.
Here the rich get richer, the poor get poorer,
here each old man is a *Sturmbahnführer*.

Come to Rio, oh come to Rio.
There is no other city with such brio.
There are phones by Siemens, and even Jews
drive around like crazy in VWs.

Come to Rio, oh come to Rio.
Here Urania rules and no trace of Clio.

Buildings ape Corbusier's beehive-cum-waffle,
though this time you can't blame this on the Luftwaffe.

Come to Rio, oh come to Rio.
Here every bird sings "O sole mio."
So do fish when caught, so do proud snow geese
in midwinter here, in Portuguese.

Come to Rio, oh come to Rio.
It's the Third World all right, so they still read Leo
Trotsky, Guevara, and other sirens;
still, the backwardness spares them the missile silos.

Come to Rio, oh come to Rio.
If you come in duo, you may leave in trio.
If you come alone, you'll leave with a zero
in your thoughts as valuable as one cruzeiro.

This, of course, could have been written without my leaving
Manhattan. As quite a lot of far better stuff was written, even
by me. Guilt, as I said, is a better vehicle. Still, I've dipped
myself into the southern Atlantic and in general insinuated
my body into what until then was just a high-school geography lesson. *Ergo sum.*

I was also entertained there by a local pharmacist, a
native of Yugoslavia who had fought either against the Germans or against the Italians, and who was clutching at his
chest almost as often as I was. As it happened, he had read
almost everything I'd penned; he promised to get me a Baby
Hermès with my favorite typeface, and he treated at a *chur-
rascaria* at the Leblon beach. When I meet people like him,
I feel like an impostor, because what they think I am does
not exist (from the moment I finished writing what they just
finished reading). What exists is a haunted lunatic trying

hard not to hurt anyone—because the main thing is not literature but the ability not to cause pain to anyone; but instead of owning up to this, I babble something about Kantemir, Derzhavin, and the like, while they listen with an open mouth, as if there were something else in the world besides despair, neurosis, and the fear of going up in smoke any second. But perhaps even official messengers of Russian culture—of a certain age especially—feel the same way, particularly when they drag their bones across all kinds of Mogadishus and Ivory Coasts. Because everywhere there is dust, rusty soil, twisted chunks of decaying metal, unfinished buildings, the swarthy multitudes of the local population for whom you mean nothing, just like for your own. Sometimes, far away, you can see the blue shine of the sea.

No matter which way journeys begin, they always end identically: in one's own corner, in one's own bed, falling into which you forget what has already become the past. It is unlikely I will ever find myself again in that country and in that hemisphere, but at least, upon my return, my bed is even more "mine," and for a person who buys furniture instead of inheriting it, this is enough to detect a sense of purpose in the most pointless meanderings.

1978

(Translated, from the Russian, by Alexander Sumerkin and the author)

Altra Ego

~

I

The idea of the poet as an inveterate Don Giovanni is of relatively recent coinage. Like many concepts enjoying great currency in the popular imagination, it appears to be a by-product of the Industrial Revolution, which, through its quantum leaps in human accumulation and literacy, gave birth to the very phenomenon of the popular imagination. To put it differently, this image of the poet appears to owe more to the public success of Lord Byron's *Don Juan* than to its author's own romantic record—awe-inspiring perhaps, but unavailable to the public at the time. Besides, for every Byron we always get a Wordsworth.

As the last period of social coherence and its attendant philistinism, the nineteenth century is responsible for the bulk of notions and attitudes we entertain or are guided by today. In poetry, that century squarely belongs to France; and perhaps the expansive gesturing and exotic affinities of the French Romantics and Symbolists contributed to the dim view of the poet no less than the general lowbrow notion of the French as certified immoralists. On the whole, underneath this bad-mouthing of poets lies the instinctive desire of every social order—be it a democracy, autocracy, theocracy, ideocracy, or bureaucracy—to compromise or belittle the authority of poetry, which, apart from rivaling that of the state, hoists a question mark over the individual himself, over his achievements and mental security, over his very significance. In that respect the nineteenth century simply joined the club: when it comes to poetry, every bourgeois is a Plato.

II

Antiquity's attitude toward a poet was, however, by and large both more exalted and more sensible. That had to do as much with polytheism as with the fact that the public had to rely on poets for entertainment. Save for mutual sniping—usual in the literary trade of any age—disparaging treatment of poets in antiquity is rare. On the contrary, poets were revered as figures of divine proximity: in the public imagination they stood somewhere between soothsayers and demigods. Indeed, deities themselves were often their audience, as is evidenced by the myth of Orpheus.

Nothing could be further from Plato than this myth, which is also particularly illuminating about antiquity's view of a poet's sentimental integrity. Orpheus is no Don Giovanni. So distraught is he by the death of his wife, Eurydice, that his lamentations rend the ears of the Olympians, who grant him permission to go down into the netherworld to bring her back. That nothing comes of this trip (followed in poetry by similar descents in Homer, Virgil, and, above all, in Dante) only proves the intensity of the poet's feeling for his beloved, as well, of course, as the ancients' grasp of the nitty-gritty of guilt.

III

As much as the subsequent fate of Orpheus (he was torn apart by a crowd of angry maenads for his refusal—because of his vow of chastity, made in mourning for Eurydice—to submit himself to their bared charms), this intensity points up the monogamous nature of at least this poet's passion. Although, unlike the monotheists of later periods, the ancients didn't put much of a premium on monogamy, it should be noted that they didn't run to the opposite extreme either, and reserved fidelity as the particular virtue of their premier poet. In general, apart from the beloved, the only feminine presence on a poet's agenda in antiquity was that of his Muse.

The two would overlap in the modern imagination; in antiquity they didn't because the Muse was hardly corporeal. The daughter of Zeus and Mnemosyne (the goddess of memory), she had nothing palpable about her; the only way she would reveal herself to a mortal, particularly a poet, was through her voice: by dictating to him this or that line. In other words, she was the voice of the language; and what a poet actually listens to, what really does dictate to him the next line, is the language. And it is presumably the language's own gender in Greek (*glossa*) that accounts for the Muse's femininity.

With the same allusive consequences, the noun for language is feminine in Latin, French, Italian, Spanish, and German. In English, however, language is an "it"; in Russian it is "he." Yet whatever language's gender happens to be, a poet's attachment to it is monogamous, for a poet, by trade at least, is a monoglot. It could even be argued that all one's capacity for fidelity gets spent on one's Muse, as is implied in the Byronic version of the poet's romantic program—but that would be true only if one's language were indeed one's choice. As it is, language is the given, and knowledge of which hemisphere of the brain pertains to the Muse would be of value only if one could control that part of one's anatomy.

IV

The Muse, therefore, is not an alternative to the beloved but precedes her. In fact, as an "older woman," the Muse, née language, plays a decisive part in the sentimental development of a poet. She is responsible not only for his emotional makeup but often for the very choice of his object of passion and the manner of its pursuit. It is she who makes him fanatically single-minded, turning his love into an equivalent of her own monologue. What amounts in sentimental matters to obstinacy and obsession is essentially the dictate of the Muse, whose choice is always of an aesthetic origin and discards alternatives. In a manner of speaking, love is always a monotheistic experience.

Christianity, of course, hasn't failed to capitalize on this. Yet what really binds a religious mystic to a pagan sensualist, Gerard Manley Hopkins to Sextus Propertius, is emotional absolutism. The intensity of that emotional absolutism is such that at times it overshoots anything that lies near, and often one's very target. As a rule, the nagging, idiosyncratic, self-referential, persistent voice of the Muse takes a poet beyond imperfect and perfect unions alike, beyond utter disasters and paroxysms of happiness—at the expense of reality, with or without a real, reciprocating girl in it. In other words, the pitch gets higher for its own sake, as if the language propels a poet, especially a romantic, whence it came, where in the beginning there was a word, or a discernible sound. Hence many a broken marriage, hence many a lengthy poem, hence poetry's metaphysical affinities, for every word wants to return to where it came from, if only as an echo, which is the mother of rhyme. Hence, too, the reputation of the poet as a rake.

V

Among the many agents of the public's spiritual debilitation, it is the voyeuristic genre of biography that takes the cake. That there are far more ruined maidens than immortal lyrics seems to give pause to nobody. The last bastion of realism, biography is based on the breathtaking premise that art can be explained by life. To follow this logic, *The Song of Roland* should have been penned by Bluebeard (well, by Gilles de Rais, at least) and *Faust* by Frederick of Prussia—or, if you like him better, Humboldt.

What a poet has in common with his less articulate fellows is that his life is hostage to his métier, not the other way around. And it is not just that he gets paid for his words (seldom and meagerly): the point is that he also pays for them (often horrifically). It is the latter that creates confusion and spawns biographies, because this payment takes the form not only of indifference; ostracism, imprisonment, exile, oblivion, self-disgust, uncertainty, remorse, madness; a variety of addictions is also acceptable currency. These things are obviously describable. They are, however, not the cause of one's penmanship but its effect. To put it crassly, in order to make his work sell, as well as to avoid cliché, our poet continually has to get where nobody has ever been before —mentally, psychologically, or lexically. Once he gets there, he discovers that indeed there's nobody about, save perhaps the word's original meaning or that initial discernible sound.

This takes its toll. The longer he is at it—at uttering something hitherto unutterable—the more idiosyncratic his conduct becomes. Revelations and insights obtained by him in the process may lead him either to an upsurge of hubris or—more likely—to a deepening of his humility before the force that he surmises behind those insights and revelations. He may also be afflicted by a belief that, older and more viable than anything, language imparts to him, its mouth-piece, its wisdom and the knowledge of the future alike. No matter how gregarious or humble he is by nature, this sort of thing boxes him even further out of the social context, which desperately tries to reclaim him by running its com-mon denominator through his groin.

VI

This is done on account of the Muse's alleged femininity (even when the poet happens to be a woman). The real reason, though, is that art survives life, and this unpalatable realization lies behind the *lumpen* desire to subordinate the former to the latter. The finite always mistakes the perma-nent for the infinite and nurtures designs upon it. That, of course, is the permanent's own fault, for it cannot help at times behaving like the finite. Even the most misogynistic or misanthropic poet produces a spate of love lyrics, if only as a token of allegiance to the guild, or as an exercise. This is enough to occasion research, textual exegesis, psychoan-alytical interpretation, and whatnot. The general scheme goes like this: the femininity of the Muse presupposes the masculinity of the poet. The masculinity of the poet presup-poses the femininity of the lover. Ergo: the lover is the Muse, or could be called that. Another ergo: a poem is the subli-mation of the author's erotic urges and should be treated as such. Simple.

That Homer must have been fairly frail by the time he wrote the *Odyssey* and that Goethe, when he got to the second part of *Faust*, definitely was, is of no consequence.

What, on the whole, should we do with epic poets? And how can one sublimating so much remain a rake? Since we seem to be saddled with the term, perhaps it would be civilized to assume that both artistic *and* erotic activities are expressions of one's creative energy, that *both* are a sublimation. As for the Muse, that angel of language, that "older woman," it would be best if biographers and the public left her alone, and if they can't they should at least remember that she is older than any lover or mother, and that her voice is more implacable than the mother tongue. She's going to dictate to a poet no matter where, how, or when he lives, and if not to this poet, then to the next one—partly because living and writing are different occupations (that's what the two different verbs are for) and to equate them is more absurd than to separate them, for literature has a richer past than any individual, whatever his pedigree.

VII

"To a man, a girl's visage is of course a visage of his soul," wrote a Russian poet, and that's what lies behind the exploits of Theseus or St. George, the quests of Orpheus and Dante. The sheer cumbersomeness of those undertakings bespeaks a motive other than lust alone. In other words, love is a metaphysical affair whose goal is either accomplishing or liberating one's soul: winnowing it from the chaff of existence. That is and always has been the core of lyric poetry.

A maiden, in short, is one's soul's stand-in, and one zeroes in on her precisely because one is not given an alternative, save perhaps in a mirror. In the era we call modern, both a poet and his public have grown accustomed to short takes. Still, even in this century there have been enough exceptions whose thoroughness in treating the subject rivals that of Petrarch. One can cite Akhmatova, one can cite Montale, one can cite the "dark pastorals" of Robert Frost or Thomas Hardy. These are quests for the soul, in the form of lyric poetry. Hence the singularity of the addressee and the stability of the manner, or style. Often the career of a poet, if he lives long enough, emerges as a genre variation on a single theme, helping us to distinguish the dancer from the dance—in this case, a love poem from love as such. If a poet dies young, the dancer and the dance tend to merge. This leads to an awful terminological confusion and bad press for the participants, not to mention their purpose.

VIII

If only because a love poem is more often than not an applied art (i.e., it's written to get the girl), it takes an author to an emotional and, quite likely, a linguistic extreme. As a result, he emerges from such a poem knowing himself—his psychological and stylistic parameters—better than before, which explains the popularity of the genre among its practitioners. Also, sometimes the author gets the girl.

Practical application notwithstanding, what makes love lyrics abound is simply that they are a product of sentimental necessity. Triggered by a particular addressee, this necessity may stay proportionate to that addressee, or develop an autonomous dynamic and volume, prompted by the centrifugal nature of language. The consequence of the latter may be either a cycle of love poems addressed to the same person or a number of poems fanning out, as it were, in different directions. The choice here—if one can speak of choice where necessity is at work—is not so much moral or spiritual as stylistic, and depends on a poet's longevity. And here's where a stylistic choice—if one can speak of choice where chance and the passage of time are at play—starts to smell of spiritual consequences. For ultimately a love lyric, by necessity, is a narcissistic affair. It is a statement, however imaginative, of the author's own feeling, and as such it amounts to a self-portrait rather than to one of his beloved or her world. Were it not for sketches, oils, miniatures, or snapshots, having read a poem, we often wouldn't have known what—or more to the point, whom—it was all about. Even provided with them, we don't learn much about the beauties they depict, save that they looked different from their bards and that not all of them qualify in *our* eyes as beauties. But then a picture seldom complements words, or vice versa. Besides, images of souls and magazine covers are bound to have different standards. For Dante, at least, the notion of beauty was contingent on the beholder's ability to discern in the human face's oval just seven letters comprising the term *Homo Dei*.

IX

The crux of the matter is that their actual appearances are irrelevant and were not supposed to be registered. What was supposed to be registered is the spiritual accomplishment which is the ultimate proof of the poet's existence. A picture is a bonus only to him, perhaps to her; to a reader it is practically a minus, for it subtracts from the imagination. For a poem is a mental affair: for its reader as much as for its author. "Her" portrait is the poet's state conveyed through his tune and choice of words; a reader would be a fool to settle for less. What matters about "her" is not her particularity but her universality. Don't try to find her snapshot and position yourself next to it: it won't work. Plain and simply, a love lyric is one's soul set in motion. If it's good, it may do the same to you.

It is otherness, therefore, that provides the metaphysical opportunity. A love lyric may be good or bad but it offers its writer an extension of himself—or, if a lyric is exceptionally good, or an affair is long, self-negation. What is the Muse up to while this is going on? Not much, since a love lyric is dictated by existential necessity and necessity doesn't care much about the quality of articulation. As a rule, love lyrics are done fast and don't undergo much revision. But once a metaphysical dimension is attained, or at least once self-negation is attained, one indeed can tell the dancer from the dance: a love lyric from love and, thus, from a poem about, or informed by, love.

X

Now, a poem about love doesn't insist on the author's own reality and seldom employs the word "I." It is about what a poet is not, about what he perceives as different from himself. If it is a mirror, it is a small one, and placed too far away. To recognize oneself in it requires, apart from humility, a lens whose power of resolution doesn't distinguish between observing and being mesmerized. A poem about love can have for its subject practically anything: the girl's features, ribbons in her hair, the landscape behind her house, the passage of clouds, starry skies, some inanimate object. It may have nothing to do with the girl; it can describe an exchange between two or more mythic characters, a wilted bouquet, snow on the railroad platform. The readers, though, will know that they are reading a poem informed by love thanks to the intensity of attention paid to this or that detail of the universe. For love is an attitude toward reality—usually of someone finite toward something infinite. Hence, the intensity caused by the sense of the provisional nature of one's possessions. Hence, that intensity's need for articulation. Hence, its quest for a voice less provisional than one's own. And in walks the Muse, that older woman, meticulous about possessions.

XI

Pasternak's famous exclamation "Great god of love, great god of details!" is poignant precisely because of the utter insignificance of the sum of these details. A ratio could no doubt be established between the smallness of the detail and the intensity of attention paid to it, as well as between the latter and one's spiritual accomplishment, because a poem—any poem, regardless of its subject—is in itself an act of love, not so much of an author for his subject as of language for a piece of reality. If it is often tinged with an elegiac air, with the timbre of pity, this is so because it is the love of the greater for the lesser, of the permanent for the transitory. This surely doesn't affect a poet's romantic conduct, since he, a physical entity, identifies himself more readily with the provisional than with the eternal. All he may know is that when it comes to love, art is a more adequate form of expression than any other; that on paper one can reach a higher degree of lyricism than on bedroom linen.

Were it otherwise, we would have far less art on our hands. The way martyrdom or sainthood prove not so much the substance of a creed as the human potential for belief, so love poetry speaks for art's ability to overshoot reality— or to escape it entirely. Perhaps the true measure of this kind of poetry is precisely its inapplicability to reality, the impossibility of translating its sentiment into action for want of physical equivalence to abstract insight. The physical world must take offense at this kind of criterion. But, then, it has photography—not quite an art yet, but capable of arresting the abstract in flight, or at least in progress.

XII

And a while ago, in a small garrison town in the north of Italy, I chanced on an attempt to do precisely this: to depict poetry's reality by means of the camera. It was a small exhibition consisting of photographs of thirty or so great twentieth-century poets' beloveds—wives, mistresses, concubines, boys, men. It started in fact with Baudelaire and ended with Pessoa and Montale; next to each beloved, a famous lyric was attached, in its original language and in translation. A fortunate idea, I thought, shuffling past the glass-covered stands that contained the black-and-white full faces, profiles, and three-quarter profiles of bards and of what amounted to their own or their languages' destinies. There they were—a flock of rare birds caught in the net of that gallery, and one could indeed regard them as art's points of departure from reality, or better still, as reality's means of transportation toward that higher degree of lyricism, toward a poem. (After all, for one's fading and generally moribund features, art is another kind of future.)

Not that the women (and some men) depicted there lacked the psychological, visual, or erotic qualities required to forge a poet's happiness: on the contrary, they appeared sufficiently if variously endowed. Some were wives, others mistresses and lovers, still others lingered in a poet's mind while their appearance in his quarters may have been rather fleeting. Of course, given the mind-boggling variety of what nature can paint into a human oval, one's choice of a beloved appears arbitrary. The usual factors—genetic, historical, social, aesthetic—narrow the range, for the poet as for everyone else. Yet perhaps the particular prerequisite for a poet's choice is the presence in that oval of a certain nonfunctional air, an air of ambivalence and open-endedness, echoing, as it were, in flesh and blood the essence of his endeavor.

That's what such epithets as "enigmatic," "dreamy," or "otherworldly" normally struggle to denote, and what accounts for the preponderance in that gallery of visually aleatoric blondes over the excessive precision of brunettes. By and large, at any rate, this characteristic, vague as it is, did apply to the birds of passage caught in that particular net. Conscious of the camera or taken unawares, those faces appeared to carry in one way or another a common expression of being elsewhere, or having their mental focus somewhat blurred. The next moment, of course, they would be energetic, alert, supine, lascivious, bearing a child or eloping with a friend, bloody-minded or suffering a bard's infidelity—in short, more definite. For an instant of exposure, though, they were their tentative, indefinite selves, which, like a poem in progress, didn't yet have a next line or, very often, a subject. Also like poems, they were never finished: they were only abandoned. In short, they were drafts.

It is mutability, then, that animates a face for a poet, that reverberates almost palpably in Yeats's famous lines:

> How many loved your moments of glad grace,
> And loved your beauty with love false or true,
> But one man loved the pilgrim soul in you,
> And loved the sorrows of your changing face.

That a reader can empathize with these lines proves him to be as susceptible to the appeal of mutability as the poet. More exactly, the degree of his lyrical appreciation here is the degree to which he is removed from that very mutability, the degree to which he is confined to the definite: features or circumstances or both. With the poet, he discerns in that changing oval far more than just the seven letters of *Homo Dei*; he discerns there the entire alphabet, in all its combinations, i.e., the language. That is how in the end the Muse perhaps indeed becomes feminine, how she gets photographed. The Yeats quatrain sounds like a moment of recognition of one form of life in another: of the poet's own vocal cords' tremolo in his beloved's mortal features, or uncertainty in uncertainty. To a vibrating voice, in other words, everything tentative and faltering is an echo, promoted at times to an *alter ego* or, as gender would have it, to an *altra ego*.

XIII

Gender imperatives notwithstanding, let's keep in mind that an *altra ego* is no Muse. Whatever solipsistic depths a carnal union may avail him, no poet ever mistakes his voice for its echo, the inner for the outer. The prerequisite of love is the autonomy of its object, preferably within arm's reach. The same goes for an echo that defines the range of one's voice. Those depicted in the exhibition—women and, moreover, men—were not themselves Muses, but their good stand-ins, inhabiting this side of reality and sharing with the older women their language. They were (or ended up being) other people's wives; actresses and dancers, schoolteachers, divorcées, nurses; they had a social station and thus could be defined, while the Muse's main trait—let me repeat it—is that she is undefinable. They were neurotic or serene, promiscuous or strict, religious or cynical, great dressers or slovenly, highly sophisticated or barely literate. Some of them couldn't care less for poetry and would embrace a common cad more eagerly than an ardent admirer. On top of that, they lived in different lands, though at about the same time, spoke different tongues, and didn't know of each other. In short, nothing bound them together save that something they said or did at a certain moment triggered and set in motion the machinery of language, and it rolled along, leaving behind on paper "the best words in the best possible order." They were not Muses, because they made the Muse, the older woman, speak.

Caught in the gallery's net, I thought, these birds of bards' paradise had at least got their proper identification, if not actual rings. Like their bards, most of them were gone now, and gone were their guilty secrets, moments of triumph, substantial wardrobes, protracted malaises, and peculiar affinities. What remained was a song owing to the birds' capacity to flutter off no less than to the bards' to chirp, yet outlasting both—the way it will outlast its readers, who, for the moment of reading at least, share in a song's afterlife.

XIV

Herein lies the ultimate distinction between the beloved and the Muse: the latter doesn't die. The same goes for the Muse and the poet: when he's gone, she finds herself another mouthpiece in the next generation. To put it another way, she always hangs around a language and doesn't seem to mind being mistaken for a plain girl. Amused by this sort of error, she tries to correct it by dictating to her charge now pages of *Paradiso*, now Thomas Hardy's poems of 1912–13; that is, those where the voice of human passion yields to that of linguistic necessity—but apparently to no avail. So let's leave her with a flute and a wreath of wildflowers. This way at least she might escape a biographer.

1990

How to Read a Book

~

The idea of a book fair in the city where, a century ago, Nietzsche lost his mind has, in its own turn, a nice ring to it. A Möbius strip (commonly known as a vicious circle), to be precise, for several stalls in this book fair are occupied by the complete or selected works of this great German. On the whole, infinity is a fairly palpable aspect of this business of publishing, if only because it extends a dead author's existence beyond the limits he envisioned, or provides a living author with a future which we all prefer to regard as unending.

On the whole, books are indeed less finite than ourselves. Even the worst among them outlast their authors— mainly because they occupy a smaller amount of physical space than those who penned them. Often they sit on the shelves absorbing dust long after the writer himself has turned into a handful of dust. Yet even this form of the future is better than the memory of a few surviving relatives or friends on whom one cannot rely, and often it is precisely the appetite for this posthumous dimension which sets one's pen in motion.

Delivered at the opening of the first book fair in Turin, Italy, in May 1988.

So as we toss and turn these rectangular objects in our hands—those in octavo, in quarto, in duodecimo, etc., etc.—we won't be terribly amiss if we surmise that we fondle in our hands, as it were, the actual or potential urns with our returning ashes. After all, what goes into writing a book—be it a novel, a philosophical treatise, a collection of poems, a biography, or a thriller—is, ultimately, a man's only life: good or bad but always finite. Whoever said that to philosophize is an exercise in dying was right in more ways than one, for by writing a book nobody gets younger.

Nor does one become any younger by reading one. Since this is so, our natural preference should be for good books. The paradox, however, lies in the fact that in literature, as nearly everywhere, "good" is not an autonomous category: it is defined by its distinction from "bad." What's more, in order to write a good book, a writer must read a great deal of pulp—otherwise he won't be able to develop the necessary criteria. That's what may constitute bad literature's best defense at the Last Judgment; that's also the *raison d'être* of the proceedings in which we take part today.

Since we are all moribund, and since reading books is time-consuming, we must devise a system that allows us a semblance of economy. Of course, there is no denying the possible pleasure of holing up with a fat, slow-moving, mediocre novel; still, we all know that we can indulge ourselves in that fashion only so much. In the end, we read not for reading's sake but to learn. Hence the need for concision, condensation, fusion—for the works that bring the human predicament, in all its diversity, into its sharpest possible focus; in other words, the need for a shortcut. Hence, too—as a by-product of our suspicion that such shortcuts exist (and they do, but about that later)—the need for some compass in the ocean of available printed matter.

The role of that compass, of course, is played by literary criticism, by reviewers. Alas, its needle oscillates wildly. What is north for some is south (South America, to be precise) for others; the same goes in an even wilder degree for east and west. The trouble with a reviewer is (minimum) threefold: (a) he can be a hack, and as ignorant as ourselves; (b) he can have strong predilections for a certain kind of writing or simply be on the take with the publishing industry; and (c) if he is a writer of talent, he will turn his review writing into an independent art form—Jorge Luis Borges is a case in point—and you may end up reading reviews rather than the books themselves.

In any case, you find yourselves adrift in the ocean, with pages and pages rustling in every direction, clinging to a raft whose ability to stay afloat you are not so sure of. The alternative, therefore, would be to develop your own taste, to build your own compass, to familiarize yourself, as it were, with particular stars and constellations—dim or bright but always remote. This, however, takes a hell of a lot of time, and you may easily find yourself old and gray, heading for the exit with a lousy volume under your arm. Another alternative—or perhaps just a part of the same—is to rely on hearsay: a friend's advice, a reference caught in a text you happen to like. Although not institutionalized in any fashion (which wouldn't be such a bad idea), this kind of procedure is familiar to all of us from a tender age. Yet this, too, proves to be poor insurance, for the ocean of available literature swells and widens constantly, as this book fair amply testifies: it is yet another tempest in that ocean.

So where is one's terra firma, even though it may be

but an uninhabitable island? Where is our good man Friday, let alone a Cheetah?

Before I come up with my suggestion—nay! what I perceive as being the only solution for developing sound taste in literature—I'd like to say a few words about this solution's source, i.e., about my humble self—not because of my personal vanity, but because I believe that the value of an idea is related to the context in which it emerges. Indeed, had I been a publisher, I'd be putting on my books' covers not only their authors' names but also the exact age at which they composed this or that work, in order to enable their readers to decide whether the readers care to reckon with the information or the views contained in a book written by a man so much younger—or, for that matter, so much older—than themselves.

The source of the suggestion to come belongs to the category of people (alas, I can no longer use the term "generation," which implies a certain sense of mass and unity) for whom literature has always been a matter of some hundred names; to the people whose social graces would make Robinson Crusoe or even Tarzan wince; to those who feel awkward at large gatherings, do not dance at parties, tend to find metaphysical excuses for adultery, and are finicky about discussing politics; the people who dislike themselves far more than their detractors do; who still prefer alcohol and tobacco to heroin or marijuana—those who, in W. H. Auden's words, "one will not find on the barricades and who never shoot themselves or their lovers." If such people occasionally find themselves swimming in their blood on the floor of prison cells or speaking from a platform, it is because they rebel against (or, more precisely, object to) not some particular injustice but the order of the world as a whole. They have no illusions about the objectivity of the views they put forth; on the contrary, they insist on their unpardonable subjectivity right from the threshold. They act in this fashion, however, not for the purpose of shielding themselves from possible attack: as a rule, they are fully aware of the vulnerability pertinent to their views and the positions they defend. Yet—taking the stance somewhat opposite to Darwinian—they consider vulnerability the primary trait of living matter. This, I must add, has less to do with masochistic tendencies, nowadays attributed to almost every man of letters, than with their instinctive, often firsthand knowledge that extreme subjectivity, prejudice, and indeed idiosyncrasy are what help art to avoid cliché. And the resistance to cliché is what distinguishes art from life.

Now that you know the background of what I am about to say, I may just as well say it: The way to develop good taste in literature is to read poetry. If you think that I am speaking out of professional partisanship, that I am trying to advance my own guild interests, you are mistaken: I am no union man. The point is that being the supreme form of human locution, poetry is not only the most concise, the most condensed way of conveying the human experience; it also offers the highest possible standards for any linguistic operation—especially one on paper.

The more one reads poetry, the less tolerant one becomes of any sort of verbosity, be it in political or philosophical discourse, in history, social studies, or the art of fiction. Good style in prose is always hostage to the precision, speed, and laconic intensity of poetic diction. A child of epitaph and epigram, conceived, it appears, as a shortcut to any conceivable subject matter, poetry is a great disciplinarian to prose. It teaches the latter not only the value of each word but also the mercurial mental patterns of the species, alternatives to linear composition, the knack of omitting the self-evident, emphasis on detail, the technique of anticlimax. Above all, poetry develops in prose that appetite for metaphysics which distinguishes a work of art from mere *belles lettres*. It must be admitted, however, that in this particular regard, prose has proven to be a rather lazy pupil.

Please, don't get me wrong: I am not trying to debunk prose. The truth of the matter is that poetry simply happens to be older than prose and thus has covered a greater distance. Literature started with poetry, with the song of a nomad that predates the scribblings of a settler. And although I have compared somewhere the difference between poetry and prose to that between the air force and the infantry, the suggestion that I make now has nothing to do with either hierarchy or the anthropological origins of literature. All I am trying to do is to be practical and spare your eyesight and brain cells a lot of useless printed matter. Poetry, one might say, has been invented for just this purpose—for it is synonymous with economy. What one should do, therefore, is recapitulate, albeit in miniature, the process that took place in our civilization over the course of two millennia. It is easier than you might think, for the body of poetry is far less voluminous than that of prose. What's more, if you are concerned mainly with contemporary literature, then your job is indeed a piece of cake. All you have to do is arm yourselves for a couple of months with the works of poets in your mother tongue, preferably from the first half of this century. I suppose you'll end up with a dozen rather slim books, and by the end of the summer you will be in great shape.

If your mother tongue is English, I might recommend to you Robert Frost, Thomas Hardy, W. B. Yeats, T. S. Eliot, W. H. Auden, Marianne Moore, and Elizabeth Bishop. If the language is German, Rainer Maria Rilke, Georg Trakl, Peter Huchel, and Gottfried Benn. If it is Spanish, Antonio Machado, Federico García Lorca, Luis Cernuda, Rafael Alberti, Juan Ramón Jiménez, and Octavio Paz will do. If the language is Polish—or if you know Polish (which would be to your great advantage, because the most extraordinary poetry of this century is written in that language)—I'd like to mention to you the names of Leopold Staff, Czeslaw Milosz, Zbigniew Herbert, and Wisława Szymborska. If it is French, then of course Guillaume Apollinaire, Jules Supervielle, Pierre Reverdy, Blaise Cendrars, some of Paul Eluard, a bit of Aragon, Victor Segalen, and Henri Michaux. If it is Greek, then you should read Constantine Cavafy, George Seferis, Yannis Ritsos. If it is Dutch, then it should be Martinus Nijhoff, particularly his stunning "Awater." If it is Portuguese, you should read Fernando Pessoa and perhaps Carlos Drummond de Andrade. If the language is Swedish, read Gunnar Ekelöf, Harry Martinson, Tomas Tranströmer. If it is Russian, it should be, to say the least, Marina Tsvetaeva, Osip Mandelstam, Anna Akhmatova, Boris Pasternak, Vladislav Khodasevich, Velemir Khlebnikov, Nikolai Klyuev. If it is Italian, I don't presume to submit any name to this audience, and if I mention Quasimodo, Saba, Ungaretti, and Montale, it is simply because I have long wanted to acknowledge my personal, private gratitude and debt to these four great poets whose lines influenced my life rather crucially, and I am glad to do so while standing on Italian soil.

If after going through the works of any of these, you drop a book of prose picked from the shelf, it won't be your fault. If you continue to read it, that will be to the author's credit; that will mean that this author has indeed something to add to the truth about our existence as it was known to these few poets just mentioned; this would prove at least that this author is not redundant, that his language has an independent energy or grace. Or else, it would mean that reading is your incurable addiction. As addictions go, it is not the worst one.

Let me draw a caricature here, for caricatures accentuate the essential. In this caricature I see a reader whose two hands are occupied with holding open books. In the left, he holds a collection of poems; in the right, a volume of prose. Let's see which he drops first. Of course, he may fill both his palms with prose volumes, but that will leave him with self-negating criteria. And, of course, he may also ask what distinguishes good poetry from bad, and where is his guarantee that what he holds in his left hand is indeed worth bothering with.

Well, for one thing, what he holds in his left hand will be, in all likelihood, lighter than what he holds in the right. Second, poetry, as Montale once put it, is an incurably semantic art, and chances for charlatanism in it are extremely low. By the third line a reader will know what sort of thing he holds in his left hand, for poetry makes sense fast and the quality of language in it makes itself felt immediately. After three lines he may glance at what he has in the right.

This is, as I told you, a caricature. At the same time, I believe, this might be the posture many of you will unwittingly assume at this book fair. Make sure, at least, that the books in your hands belong to different genres of literature. Now, this shifting of eyes from left to right is, of course, a maddening enterprise; still, there are no horsemen on the streets of Turin any longer, and the sight of a cabbie flogging his animal won't aggravate the state you will be in when you leave these premises. Besides, a hundred years hence, nobody's insanity will matter much to the multitudes whose number will exceed by far the total of little black letters in all the books at this book fair put together. So you may as well try the little trick I've just suggested.

In Praise of Boredom

But should you fail to keep your kingdom
And, like your father before you come
Where thought accuses and feeling mocks,
Believe your pain . . .

—W. H. Auden, *"Alonso to Ferdinand"*

A substantial part of what lies ahead of you is going to be claimed by boredom. The reason I'd like to talk to you about it today, on this lofty occasion, is that I believe no liberal arts college prepares you for that eventuality; Dartmouth is no exception. Neither humanities nor science offers courses in boredom. At best, they may acquaint you with the sensation by incurring it. But what is a casual contact to an incurable malaise? The worst monotonous drone coming from a lectern or the eye-splitting textbook in turgid English is nothing in comparison to the psychological Sahara that starts right in your bedroom and spurns the horizon.

Known under several aliases—anguish, ennui, tedium, doldrums, humdrum, the blahs, apathy, listlessness, stolidity, lethargy, languor, accidie, etc.—boredom is a complex phenomenon and by and large a product of repetition. It would seem, then, that the best remedy against it would be constant inventiveness and originality. That is what you, young and newfangled, would hope for. Alas, life won't sup-

Delivered as a commencement address at Dartmouth College, in July 1989.

ply you with that option, for life's main medium is precisely repetition.

One may argue, of course, that repeated attempts at originality and inventiveness are the vehicle of progress and—in the same breath—civilization. As benefits of hindsight go, however, this one is not the most valuable. For should we divide the history of our species by scientific discoveries, not to mention ethical concepts, the result will not be in our favor. We'll get, technically speaking, centuries of boredom. The very notion of originality or innovation spells out the monotony of standard reality, of life, whose main medium—nay, idiom—is tedium.

In that, it—life—differs from art, whose worst enemy, as you probably know, is cliché. Small wonder, then, that art, too, fails to instruct you as to how to handle boredom. There are few novels about this subject; paintings are still fewer; and as for music, it is largely nonsemantic. On the whole, art treats boredom in a self-defensive, satirical fashion. The only way art can become for you a solace from boredom, from the existential equivalent of cliché, is if you yourselves become artists. Given your number, though, this prospect is as unappetizing as it is unlikely.

But even should you march out of this commencement in full force to typewriters, easels, and Steinway grands, you won't shield yourselves from boredom entirely. If repetitiveness is boredom's mother, you, young and newfangled, will be quickly smothered by lack of recognition and low pay, both chronic in the world of art. In these respects, writing, painting, composing music are plain inferior to working for a law firm, a bank, or even a lab.

Herein, of course, lies art's saving grace. Not being lucrative, it falls victim to demography rather reluctantly. For if, as we've said, repetition is boredom's mother, demography (which is to play in your lives a far greater role than any discipline you've mastered here) is its other parent. This may sound misanthropic to you, but I am more than twice your age, and I have lived to see the population of our globe double. By the time you're my age, it will have quadrupled, and not exactly in the fashion you expect. For instance, by the year 2000 there is going to be such cultural and ethnic rearrangement as to challenge your notion of your own humanity.

That alone will reduce the prospects of originality and inventiveness as antidotes to boredom. But even in a more monochromatic world, the other trouble with originality and inventiveness is precisely that they literally pay off. Provided that you are capable of either, you will become well off rather fast. Desirable as that may be, most of you know firsthand that nobody is as bored as the rich, for money buys time, and time is repetitive. Assuming that you are not heading for poverty—for otherwise you wouldn't have entered college—one expects you to be hit by boredom as soon as the first tools of self-gratification become available to you.

Thanks to modern technology, those tools are as numerous as boredom's synonyms. In light of their function— to render you oblivious to the redundancy of time—their abundance is revealing. Equally revealing is the function of your purchasing power, toward whose increase you'll walk out of this commencement ground through the click and whirr of some of those instruments tightly held by your parents and relatives. It is a prophetic scene, ladies and gentlemen of the class of 1989, for you are entering the world where recording an event dwarfs the event itself—the world of video, stereo, remote control, jogging suit, and exercise machine to keep you fit for reliving your own or someone else's past: canned ecstasy claiming raw flesh.

Everything that displays a pattern is pregnant with boredom. That applies to money in more ways than one, both to the banknotes as such and to possessing them. That is not to bill poverty, of course, as an escape from boredom—although St. Francis, it would seem, has managed exactly that. Yet for all the deprivation surrounding us, the idea of new monastic orders doesn't appear particularly catchy in this era of video-Christianity. Besides, young and newfangled, you are more eager to do good in some South Africa or other than next door, keener on giving up your favorite brand of soda than on venturing to the wrong side of the tracks. So nobody advises poverty for you. All one can suggest is to be a bit more apprehensive of money, for the zeros in your accounts may usher in their mental equivalents.

As for poverty, boredom is the most brutal part of its misery, and the departure from it takes more radical forms: of violent rebellion or drug addiction. Both are temporary, for the misery of poverty is infinite; both, because of that infinity, are costly. In general, a man shooting heroin into his vein does so largely for the same reason you buy a video: to dodge the redundancy of time. The difference, though, is that he spends more than he's got, and that his means of escape become as redundant as what he is escaping from faster than yours. On the whole, the difference in tactility between a syringe's needle and a stereo's push button roughly corresponds to that between the acuteness and dullness of time's impact upon the have-nots and the haves. In short, whether rich or poor, sooner or later you will be afflicted by this redundancy of time.

Potential haves, you'll be bored with your work, your friends, your spouses, your lovers, the view from your window, the furniture or wallpaper in your room, your thoughts, yourselves. Accordingly, you'll try to devise ways of escape. Apart from the self-gratifying gadgets mentioned before, you may take up changing jobs, residence, company, country, climate; you may take up promiscuity, alcohol, travel, cooking lessons, drugs, psychoanalysis.

In fact, you may lump all these together; and for a while that may work. Until the day, of course, when you wake up in your bedroom amid a new family and a different wallpaper, in a different state and climate, with a heap of bills from your travel agent and your shrink, yet with the same stale feeling toward the light of day pouring through your window. You'll put on your loafers only to discover they're lacking bootstraps to lift yourself out of what you recognize. Depending on your temperament or the age you are at, you will either panic or resign yourself to the familiarity of the sensation; or else you'll go through the rigmarole of change once more.

Neurosis and depression will enter your lexicon; pills, your medical cabinet. Basically, there is nothing wrong about turning life into the constant quest for alternatives, into leap-frogging jobs, spouses, surroundings, etc., provided you can afford the alimony and jumbled memories. This predicament, after all, has been sufficiently glamorized on screen and in Romantic poetry. The rub, however, is that before long this quest turns into a full-time occupation, with your need for an alternative coming to match a drug addict's daily fix.

There is yet another way out of it, however. Not a better one, perhaps, from your point of view, and not necessarily secure, but straight and inexpensive. Those of you who have read Robert Frost's "Servant to Servants" may remember a line of his: "The best way out is always through." So what I am about to suggest is a variation on the theme.

When hit by boredom, go for it. Let yourself be crushed by it; submerge, hit bottom. In general, with things unpleasant, the rule is, the sooner you hit bottom, the faster you surface.

The idea here, to paraphrase another great poet of the English language, is to exact full look at the worst. The reason boredom deserves such scrutiny is that it represents pure, undiluted time in all its repetitive, redundant, monotonous splendor.

In a manner of speaking, boredom is your window on time, on those properties of it one tends to ignore to the likely peril of one's mental equilibrium. In short, it is your window on time's infinity, which is to say, on your insignificance in it. That's what accounts, perhaps, for one's dread of lonely, torpid evenings, for the fascination with which one watches sometimes a fleck of dust aswirl in a sunbeam, and somewhere a clock tick-tocks, the day is hot, and your willpower is at zero.

Once this window opens, don't try to shut it; on the contrary, throw it wide open. For boredom speaks the language of time, and it is to teach you the most valuable lesson in your life—the one you didn't get here, on these green lawns—the lesson of your utter insignificance. It is valuable to you, as well as to those you are to rub shoulders with. "You are finite," time tells you in a voice of boredom, "and whatever you do is, from my point of view, futile." As music to your ears, this, of course, may not count; yet the sense of futility, of limited significance even of your best, most ardent actions is better than the illusion of their consequences and the attendant self-aggrandizement.

For boredom is an invasion of time into your set of values. It puts your existence into its perspective, the net result of which is precision and humility. The former, it must be noted, breeds the latter. The more you learn about your own size, the more humble and the more compassionate you become to your likes, to that dust aswirl in a sunbeam or already immobile atop your table. Ah, how much life went into those flecks! Not from your point of view but from theirs.

You are to them what time is to you; that's why they look so small. And do you know what the dust says when it's being wiped off the table?

> "Remember me,"
> whispers the dust.

Nothing could be farther away from the mental agenda of any of you, young and newfangled, than the sentiment expressed in this two-liner of the German poet Peter Huchel, now dead.

I've quoted it not because I'd like to instill in you affinity for things small—seeds and plants, grains of sand or mosquitoes—small but numerous. I've quoted these lines because I like them, because I recognize in them myself, and, for that matter, any living organism to be wiped off from the available surface. " 'Remember me,' whispers the dust." And one hears in this that if we learn about ourselves from time, perhaps time, in turn, may learn something from us. What would that be? That inferior in significance, we best it in sensitivity.

This is what it means—to be insignificant. If it takes will-paralyzing boredom to bring this home, then hail the boredom. You are insignificant because you are finite. Yet the more finite a thing is, the more it is charged with life, emotions, joy, fears, compassion. For infinity is not terribly lively, not terribly emotional. Your boredom, at least, tells you that much. Because your boredom is the boredom of infinity.

Respect it, then, for its origins—as much perhaps as for your own. Because it is the anticipation of that inanimate infinity that accounts for the intensity of human sentiments, often resulting in a conception of a new life. This is not to say that you have been conceived out of boredom, or that the finite breeds the finite (though both may ring true). It is to suggest, rather, that passion is the privilege of the insignificant.

So try to stay passionate, leave your cool to constellations. Passion, above all, is a remedy against boredom. Another one, of course, is pain—physical more so than psychological, passion's frequent aftermath; although I wish you neither. Still, when you hurt you know that at least you haven't been deceived (by your body or by your psyche). By the same token, what's good about boredom, about anguish and the sense of the meaninglessness of your own, of everything else's existence, is that it is not a deception.

You also might try detective novels or action movies—something that leaves you where you haven't been verbally/visually/mentally before—something sustained, if only for a couple of hours. Avoid TV, especially flipping the channels: that's redundancy incarnate. Yet should those remedies fail, let it in, "fling your soul upon the growing gloom." Try to embrace, or let yourself be embraced by, boredom and anguish, which anyhow are larger than you. No doubt you'll find that bosom smothering, yet try to endure it as long as you can, and then some more. Above all, don't think you've goofed somewhere along the line, don't try to retrace your steps to correct the error. No, as the poet said, "Believe your pain." This awful bear hug is no mistake. Nothing that disturbs you is. Remember all along that there is no embrace in this world that won't finally unclasp.

If you find all this gloomy, you don't know what gloom is. If you find this irrelevant, I hope time will prove you right. Should you find this inappropriate for such a lofty occasion, I will disagree.

I would agree with you had this occasion been celebrating your staying here; but it marks your departure. By tomorrow you'll be out of here, since your parents paid only for four years, not a day longer. So you must go elsewhere, to make your careers, money, families, to meet your unique fates. And as for that elsewhere, neither among stars and in the tropics nor across the border in Vermont is there much awareness of this ceremony on the Dartmouth Green. One wouldn't even bet that the sound of your band reaches White River Junction.

You are exiting this place, members of the class of 1989. You are entering the world, which is going to be far more thickly settled than this neck of the woods and where you'll be paid far less attention than you have been used to for the last four years. You are on your own in a big way. Speaking of your significance, you can quickly estimate it by pitting your 1,100 against the world's 4.9 billion. Prudence, then, is as appropriate on this occasion as is fanfare.

I wish you nothing but happiness. Still, there is going to be plenty of dark and, what's worse, dull hours, caused as much by the world outside as by your own minds. You ought to be fortified against that in some fashion; and that's what I've tried to do here in my feeble way, although that's obviously not enough.

For what lies ahead is a remarkable but wearisome journey; you are boarding today, as it were, a runaway train. No one can tell you what lies ahead, least of all those who remain behind. One thing, however, they can assure you of is that it's not a round trip. Try, therefore, to derive some comfort from the notion that no matter how unpalatable this or that station may turn out to be, the train doesn't stop there for good. Therefore, you are never stuck—not even when you feel you are; for this place today becomes your past. From now on, it will only be receding for you, for that train is in constant motion. It will be receding for you even when you feel that you are stuck . . . So take one last look at it, while it is still its normal size, while it is not yet a photograph. Look at it with all the tenderness you can muster, for you are looking at your past. Exact, as it were, the full look at the best. For I doubt you'll ever have it better than here.

Profile of Clio

❧

I never thought it would come to this, to my speaking on history. But as concessions to one's age go, a lecture on the subject appears inevitable. An invitation to deliver it suggests not so much the value of the speaker's views as his perceptible moribundity. "He is history" goes the disparaging remark, referring to a has-been, and it is the proximity of an individual to this status that turns him, sometimes in his own eyes, into a sage. After all, those to whom we owe the very notion of history—the great historians as well as their subjects—are the dead. In other words, the closer one gets to one's future, i.e., to the graveyard, the better one sees the past.

I accept this. The recognition of mortality gives birth to all sorts of insights and qualifiers. History, after all, is one of those nouns that can't do without epithets. Left to its own devices, history stretches from our own childhood all the way back to the fossils. It may stand simultaneously for the past in general, the recorded past, an academic discipline, the quality of the present, or the implication of a continuum. Every culture has its own version of antiquity; so does every century; so should, I believe, every individual. Consensus

Delivered as the Huizinga Lecture at the University of Leiden in 1991.

on this noun's definition is, therefore, unthinkable and, come to think of it, unnecessary. It is always used loosely as an antonym to the present and is defined by the context of discourse. Given my age as well as my métier, I should be interested in those antonyms, in each one of them. At my age and in my line of work, the less palpable a notion, the more absorbing it is.

If we have anything in common with antiquity, it is the prospect of nonbeing. This alone can engender the study of history, as perhaps it did, because what history is all about is absence, and absence is always recognizable—much more so than presence. Which is to say that our interest in history, normally billed as the quest for a common denominator, for the origins of our ethics, is, in the first place, an eschatological, and therefore anthropomorphic, and therefore narcissistic, affair. This is proved by all sorts of revisionist quarrels and bickerings that abound in this field, thus recalling a model arguing with an artist over her depiction— or a bunch of artists in front of an empty canvas.

Further proof of this is our predilection for reading— and the historians' for producing—the lives of Caesars, pharaohs, satraps, kings, and queens. These have nothing to do with the common denominator, and often not much with ethics either. We go in for this sort of reading because of the central position that we believe we occupy in our own reality, because of the illusion of the individual's paramount consequence. To that one must add that, like biographies, those lives are, stylistically speaking, the last bastions of realism, since in this genre stream-of-consciousness and other avant-garde hopscotch techniques won't do.

The net result is the expression of uncertainty that bedevils every portrait of history. That's what the model fights over with the artist, or the artists among themselves. For the model—let us call her Clio—may think herself, or her agents, more resolute and clear-cut than the way historians paint her. Yet one can understand historians projecting their own ambiguities and subtleties upon their subject: in the light—or rather, the dark—of what awaits them, they don't wish to seem like simpletons. Generally known for their longevity, historians, by showing scruple and doubt, turn their discipline into a kind of insurance policy.

Whether he realizes it or not, the historian's predicament is to be transfixed between two voids: of the past that he ponders and of the future for whose sake he ostensibly does this. For him, the notion of nonbeing gets doubled. Perhaps the voids even overlap. Unable to handle both, he strives to animate the former, since by definition the past, as a source of personal terror, is more controllable than the future.

His opposite number, then, should be the religious mystic or the theologian. Admittedly, the structuring of the afterlife involves a greater degree of rigidity than that of the pre-life. What makes up for this difference, however, is their respective quests for causality, the common denominator, and the ethical consequences for the present—so much so that in a society in which the authority of the church is in decline, and the authority of philosophy and the state are negligible or nonexistent, it falls precisely to history to take care of ethical matters.

In the end, of course, the choice that one's eschatological proclivity makes between history and religion is determined by temperament. Yet regardless of the commandments of one's bile, or whether one is retrospective, introspective, or prospective by nature, the inalienable aspect of either pursuit is the anxiety of its validity. In this respect, the fondness of all creeds for citing their pedigree and their general reliance on historical sources is particularly worth noting. For when it comes to the burden of proof, history, unlike religion, has nobody to turn to but itself.

(Also, unlike creeds, history to its credit stops cold at geology, thus demonstrating a degree of honesty and its potential for turning into a science.)

This makes history, I believe, a more dramatic choice. An escape route trying to prove every step of the way that it is an escape route? Perhaps, but we judge the effectiveness of our choices not so much by their results as by their alternatives. The certitude of your existence's discontinuity, the certitude of the void, makes the uncertainties of history a palpable proposition. In fact, the more uncertain it is, the greater its burden of proof, the better it quells your eschatological dread. Frankly, it is easier for an effect to handle the shock of its inconsequence, easier to face the unavoidable void, than the apparent lack of its cause (for instance, when one's progenitors are gone).

Hence that vagueness in the looks of Clio, whether she is decked out in ancient or in fairly modern garb. Yet it becomes her, not least because of her femininity, which makes her more attractive to the eye than any bearded Pantocrator. It should also be noted that, younger though she is than her sister Urania (who, being the Muse of Geography, curbs many of history's motions significantly), Clio is still older than *any* being. As large as one's appetite for infinity may be, this is a good match for the life everlasting, should it go in for numerical expression. What's particularly unpalatable about death is that it negates numbers.

So it is as Clio's admirer that I stand before you today, not as a connoisseur of her works, let alone as her suitor. Like anyone of my age, I may also claim the status of her witness; but by neither temperament nor métier am I prepared to generalize about her deportment. The métier especially conspires against my expanding on any—particularly any absorbing—subject. It trains one, albeit not always successfully, to make one's utterances succinct, sometimes to the point of appearing hermetic and losing either one's audience or, more often, the subject itself. So should you find some of what is to follow too breezy or inconclusive, you'll know whom to blame. It's Euterpe.

Now, Clio of course also has a knack for brevity, which she displays in a murder or in an epitaph. Those two genres alone give the lie to Marx's famous adage about history occurring first as tragedy, then as farce. For it is always a different man who gets murdered; it is always a tragedy. Not to mention that once we're employing theatrical terminology, we shouldn't stop at farce: there is also vaudeville, musical, theater of the absurd, soap opera, and so on. One should be very careful about metaphors when dealing with history, not only because they often breed either unwarranted cynicism (like the example I just quoted) or groundless enthusiasm, but also because they obscure—almost without exception—the singular nature of every historical occurrence.

For Clio is the Muse of Time, as the poet said, and in time nothing happens twice. Perhaps the most pernicious aspect of that theatrical metaphor is that it ushers into one's mind the sense of being a spectator, of observing from the stalls what transpires on the stage, be it a farce or a tragedy. Even if such a state of affairs were really possible, that in itself would be a tragedy: that of complicity; that is, a tragedy of the ethical kind. The truth, however, is that history does not provide us with distance. It does not distinguish between the stage and the audience, which it often lacks, since murder, for one thing, is almost synonymous with the absence of witnesses. Let me quote the poet's—W. H. Auden's — invocation of Clio a bit more fully:

Clio,
Muse of Time, but for whose merciful silence
Only the first step would count and that
Would always be murder . . .

Since everything that happens in time happens only once, we, in order to grasp what has occurred, have to identify with the victim, not with the survivor or the onlooker. As it is, however, history is an art of the onlookers, since the victims' main trait is their silence, for murder renders them speechless. If our poet is referring to the story of Cain and Abel, then history is always Cain's version. The reason for putting this so drastically is to assert the distinction between fact and its interpretation, which we fail to make when we say "history."

This failure leads to our belief that we can learn from history, and that it has a purpose, notably ourselves. For all our fondness for causality and hindsight, this assumption is monstrous, since it justifies many an absence as paving the way to our own presences. Had they not been bumped off, this benefit of hindsight tells us, it would be somebody else sitting here at our table, not exactly ourselves. Our interest in history, in that case, would be plain prurience, tinged perhaps with gratitude.

And perhaps that's exactly what it is, which would put us on a somewhat bland ethical diet; but then we were never gluttonous that way to begin with (for we accept the erasure of our predecessors to the point at which we should perhaps take history out of the humanities altogether and place it squarely with the natural sciences). The other option is to distinguish between fact and description, treating each historical event as Clio's unique appearance in human quarters, triggered not by our formal logic but by her own arbitrary will. The drawback in this case is that, placing as high a premium on rationality and linear thought as we do, we may panic, and either collapse as ethical beings or, more likely, dash for a further Cartesian rigidity.

None of this is desirable or satisfactory. To accept history as a rational process governed by graspable laws is impossible, because it is often too carnivorous. To regard it as an irrational force of incomprehensible purpose and appetite is equally unacceptable, and for the same reason: it acts on our species. A target cannot accept a bullet.

Characteristically, the voice of our instinct for self-preservation comes out as a cry: What are we to tell our young? Because we are the products of linear thought, we believe that history, whether it is a rational process or an irrational force, is to dog the future. Linear thinking, to be sure, is a tool of the instinct for self-preservation; and in the conflict between this instinct and our eschatological predilection, it is the former that always wins. It is a Pyrrhic victory, but what matters is the battle itself, and our notion of the future amounts to an extension of our own present. For we know that every bullet flies in from the future, which, in order to arrive, has to wipe out the obstacle of the present. That's what our notion of history is for, that's why interpretation is preferred to fact, that's why the irrational version is always dismissed.

It is hard to argue with an instinct; in fact, it is futile. We simply crave the future, and history is here to make that claim, or the future itself, legitimate. If indeed we care so much about what we are to tell the young, the following should be done. First, we should define history as a summary either of known events or of their interpretations. In all likelihood, we'll settle for the latter, since every event's name is itself an interpretation. Since interpretations are unavoidable, the second step should be the publication of a chronological canon of world history, in which every event would be supplied with a minimum number of interpretations—say, conservative, Marxist, Freudian, structuralist. This may result in an unwieldy encyclopedia, but the young about whom we seem to worry so much will at least be provided with a multiple choice.

Apart from enabling them to think more enterprisingly, such a canon will render Clio more stereoscopic, and thus more easily recognizable in a crowd or a drawing room. For portraits in profile, three-quarters, or even full face (down to the last pore, in the manner of the Annales school) invariably obscure what one may hold behind one's back. This sort of thing lowers one's guard, and this is how history usually finds us: with our guard down.

The main attraction of such a canon is that it would convey to the young the atemporal and arrhythmic nature of Clio. The Muse of Time cannot, by definition, be held hostage to one's homemade chronology. It's quite possible that from time's own point of view the murder of Caesar and World War II occurred simultaneously, in reverse order, or not at all. By throwing many interpretations at any given event simultaneously, we may not hit the jackpot, but we will develop a better grasp of the slot machine itself. The cumulative effect of using such a canon may have peculiar consequences for our psyche; but it surely will improve our defenses, not to mention our metaphysics.

Every discourse on history's meaning, laws, principles, and whatnot is but an attempt to domesticate time, a quest for predictability. This is paradoxical, because history nearly always takes us by surprise. Come to think of it, predictability is precisely what precedes a shock. Given the toll it normally takes, a shock can be regarded as a sort of bill one pays for comforts. The benefit of hindsight waxing metaphysical will explain this preference as an echo of time's own tick-tock monotony. Regrettably, time also has a tendency to sound shrill, and all we've got to echo that with is mass graves.

In this sense, the more one learns history, the more liable one is to repeat its mistakes. It's not that many a Napoleon wants to emulate Alexander the Great; it's just that rationality of discourse implies the rationality of its subject. While the former may be possible, the latter is not. The net result of this sort of thing is self-deception, which is fine and absorbing for a historian but is often lethal for at least a part of his audience. The case of the German Jews is a good example, and perhaps I should dwell on it a bit. Above all, however, what tricks us into making mistakes by learning from history is our growing numbers. One man's meat may prove to be a thousand men's poison, or else it may prove not to be enough. The current discourse on the origins of black slavery is a good illustration.

For if you are black, unemployed, live in a ghetto, and shoot drugs, the precision with which your well-heeled religious leader or prominent writer apportions the blame for the origins of black slavery, or the vividness with which they depict the nightmare it was, does little to alter your plight. It may even cross your mind that were it not for that nightmare, neither they nor you would be here now. Perhaps this sounds preferable, but the genetic scramble in such a case would be unlikely to end in oneself. Anyhow, what you need now is a job, also some help to kick the habit. A historian won't help you with either. In fact, he dilutes your focus by supplanting your resolve with anger. In fact, it may cross your mind—well, it crosses mine—that the entire discourse on who's to blame might be simply a white man's ploy to prevent you from acting as radically as your condition requires. Which is to say, the more you learn from history, the less efficiently you are likely to act in the present.

As a data bank for human negative potential, history has no rival (save, perhaps, the doctrine of original sin, which is, come to think of it, that data's succinct summary). As a guide, history invariably suffers from numerical inferiority, since history, by definition, doesn't procreate. As a mental construct, it is also invariably subject to the unwitting fusion of its data with our perception of it. This leaves history as a naked force—an incoherent, nonetheless convincing, animistic notion; between a natural phenomenon and Divine Providence; an entity that leaves a trail. As we proceed, we better give up our high Cartesian pretenses and stick to this vague animistic notion for want of anything more clear-cut.

Let me repeat: whenever history makes her move, she catches us unawares. And since the general purpose of every society is the safety of all its members, it must first postulate the total arbitrariness of history, and the limited value of any recorded negative experience. Second, it must postulate that, although all its institutions will strive to obtain the greatest measure of safety for all its members, this very quest for stability and security effectively turns society into a sitting duck. And third, that it would, therefore, be prudent for society as a whole, as for its members individually, to develop patterns of motional irregularity (ranging from erratic foreign policy to mobile habitats and shifting residences) to make it difficult for a physical enemy or a metaphysical enemy to take aim. If you don't wish to be a target, you've got to move. "Scatter," said the Almighty to His chosen people, and at least for a while they did.

One of the greater historical fallacies that I absorbed with my high-school ink was the idea that man evolved from a nomad to a settler. Such a notion, echoing rather nicely both the intent of the authoritarian state and the realm's own highly pronounced agrarian makeup, immobilizes one completely. For nailing one down, it is second only to the physical comforts of a city dweller, whose brainchild this notion actually is (and so is the bulk of historical, social, and political theories of the last two centuries: they are all the products of city boys, all are essentially urban constructs).

Let us not go overboard: it is obvious that, for a human animal, settled existence is preferable and, given our growing numbers, inevitable. Yet it is quite possible to imagine a settled man hitting the road when his settlement is sacked by invaders or destroyed by an earthquake, or when he hears the voice of his God promising him a different place. It is equally possible to imagine him doing so when he detects danger. (Isn't God's promise an articulation of a danger?) And so a settled man gets moving, becomes a nomad.

It is easier for him to do this if his mind is not stamped all over with evolutionary and historical taboos; and as far as we know, the ancient historians, to their great credit, produced none. Becoming a nomad again, a man could think of himself as imitating history, since history, in his eyes, was itself a nomad. With the advent of Christian monotheism, however, history had to get civilized, which it did. In fact, it became a branch of Christianity itself, which is, after all, a creed of community. It even allowed itself to be subdivided into B.C. and A.D., turning the chronology of the B.C. period into a countdown, from the fossils on, as though those who lived in that period were subtracting their age from birth.

I'd like to add here—because I may not have another opportunity—that one of the saddest things that ever transpired in the course of our civilization was the confrontation between Greco-Roman polytheism and Christian monotheism, and its known outcome. Neither intellectually nor spiritually was this confrontation really necessary. Man's metaphysical capacity is substantial enough to allow for the creeds' coexistence, not to mention fusion. The case of Julian the Apostate is a good example, and so is the case of the Byzantine poets of the first five centuries A.D. Poets on the whole provide the best proof of the compatibility, because the centrifugal force of verse often takes them well beyond the confines of either doctrine, and sometimes beyond both. Were the polytheism of the Greeks and Romans and the monotheism of the Christians really that incompatible? Was it necessary to throw out of the window so much of B.C.'s intellectual achievement? (To facilitate the Renaissance later?) Why did what could have been an addition become an alternative? Could it be true that the God of Love could not stomach Euripides or Theocritus, and if He couldn't, then what kind of stomach did He have? Or was it really, to use the modern parlance, all about power, about taking over the pagan temples to show who was in charge?

Perhaps. But the pagans, though defeated, had in their pantheon a Muse of History, thereby demonstrating a better grasp of its divinity than their victors. I am afraid that there is no similar figure, no comparable reach, in the entire well-charted passage from Sin to Redemption. I am afraid that the fate of the polytheistic notion of time at the hands of Christian monotheism was the first leg of humanity's flight from a sense of the arbitrariness of existence into the trap of historical determinism. And I am afraid that it is precisely this universalism in hindsight that reveals the reductive nature of monotheism—reductive by definition.

> That we've broken their statues,
> that we've driven them out of their temples,
> doesn't mean at all that the gods are dead . . .

So wrote a Greek poet, Constantine Cavafy, two thousand years after the reduction of history from—let's think of the young in this room!—stereo to mono. And let us hope that he is right.

And yet even before history got secularized—in order to become merely scientific—the damage was done: the upper hand that was gained by historical determinism in the course of those two thousand years gripped the modern conscience tightly and, it seems, irreversibly. The distinction between time and chronology was lost: first by historians, then by their audience. One can't blame either of them, since the new creed, having grabbed the places of pagan worship, shanghaied time's metaphysics, too. And here I must go back to where I sidetracked myself with my own aside, to nomads and settlers.

"Scatter," said God to His chosen people; and for a long time they did. That was actually the second time He spoke to them about moving. Both times they obeyed, albeit reluctantly. The first time, they had been on the road for forty years; the second time, it took them a bit longer, and in a manner of speaking, they are still in progress. The drawback of being in progress for so long is that you start to believe in progress: if not in your own, then in history's. It is about the latter that I'd like to comment here, on one of its recent examples; but first I must issue a few disclaimers.

The historical literature about the fate of Jews in this century is vast, and one shouldn't aspire to add anything qualitatively new to it. What prompts the following remarks is precisely the abundance of that history, not its want. More pointedly, the reason for these remarks is a few books on the subject that recently came my way. They all deal with the whats and the whys of the wrong that was done to the Jews by the Third Reich; and they are all written by professional historians. Like many books before them, they are rich in information and hypothesis; moreover, like many that will no doubt come after them, they are stronger on objectivity than on passion. This, one should hope, expresses the authors' professionalism as historians rather than the distance from these events accorded to the authors by their own age. Objectivity, of course, is the motto of every historian, and that's why passion is normally ruled out—since, as the saying goes, it blinds.

One wonders, however, whether a passionate response, in such a context, wouldn't amount to a greater human objectivity, for disembodied intelligence carries no weight. Moreover, one wonders whether in such a context the absence of passion is nothing but a stylistic device to which writers resort in order to emulate the historian or, for that matter, the modern cultural stereotype, a cool, thin-lipped, soft-spoken character inhabiting the silver screen for the better part of the century in a sleuthing or slaying capacity. If that's the case—and all too often the imitation is too convincing to feel otherwise—then history, which used to be the source of ethical education in society, has indeed come full circle.

In the end, however, most of these thin-lipped folk of the silver screen pull the trigger. A modern historian doesn't do anything of the sort, and he would cite science as the explanation for his reserve. In other words, the quest for objectivity of interpretation takes precedence over the sentiments caused by what is interpreted. One wonders, then, what is the significance of interpretation: Is history simply an instrument for measuring how far we can remove ourselves from events, a sort of anti-thermometer? And does it exist independently, or only insofar as historians come and go, i.e., solely for their sake?

I'd rather let these questions hang for a while; otherwise I'll never get through with my disclaimers, let alone with what they are meant to precede. To begin with, I'd like to point out that the following remarks are in no way motivated by my identification with the victims. Of course, I am a Jew: by birth, by blood, but not—alas, perhaps—by upbringing. That would be enough for a sense of affinity, except that I was born when they, those Jews, were dying, and I was not very cognizant of their fate until quite late into my teens, being pretty much absorbed by what was happening to my race, and to many others, in my own country, which had just defeated Germany, losing in the process some 20 million of its own. In other words, I had plenty to identify with as it was.

Now, I mention this not because I have caught the bug of historical objectivity. On the contrary, I speak from a position of strong subjectivity. As a matter of fact, I wish it were greater, since for me what happened to the Jews in the Third Reich is not history: their annihilation overlapped with the burgeoning of my existence. I enjoyed the dubious comfort of being a witless babe, bubbling sweet bubbles while they were going up in smoke in the crematoria and the gas chambers of what is known these days as Eastern or Central Europe, but what I and some friends of mine still regard as Western Asia. I am also cognizant that, had it not been for those 20 million dead Russians, I could have identified with the Jewish victims of the Third Reich in more ways than one.

So if I sometimes peruse books on this subject, I do it largely for egotistical reasons: to get a more stereoscopic picture of what amounts to my life, of the world in which I found myself a half century ago. Because of the close, indeed overlapping parallelism of the German and Soviet political systems, and because the penal iconography of the latter is rather scarce, I stare at the piles of corpses in my life's background with, I believe, a double intensity. How, I ask myself, did they get there?

The answer is breathtakingly simple: because they were there. In order to become a victim, one ought to be present at the scene of the crime. In order to be present at the scene of the crime, one ought either to disbelieve its probability or to be unable or unwilling to flee the premises. Of the three, it is the last, I'm afraid, that played the major role.

The origins of this unwillingness to move are worth pondering. This has been done many times over, yet less than the origins of the crime. This is so partly because the origins of the crime appear, to historians, to be an easier proposition. It is all ascribed to German anti-Semitism, whose lineage is habitually traced, with varying degrees of enterprise, to Wagner, Luther, and further down to Erasmus, the Middle Ages, and generally to the Jews-versus-gentiles business. Some historians are prepared to take their audience all the way back to dark Teutonic urges, straight into Valhalla. Others are content with the aftermath of World War I, the Peace of Versailles, and Jewish "usury" against the backdrop of Germany's economic collapse. Still others lump all these things together, adding at times an interesting wrinkle, such as linking the virulence of the Nazis' anti-Jewish propaganda, rich in vermin imagery and references to Jewish hygienic habits, to the history of epidemics and their relatively small toll among the Jews in comparison to the main ethnic stock.

They are Lamarckians, these historians; they are not Darwinists. They appear to believe that affiliation to a creed can be passed on genetically (thus approximating one of Judaism's main tenets), that the same goes for attendant prejudices, intellectual patterns, and so on. They are biological determinists moonlighting as historians. Hence a straight line out of Valhalla into the bunker.

Had the line been that straight, however, the bunker could have been averted. The history of a nation, like the history of an individual, consists more of what's forgotten than of what's remembered. As a process, history is not so much an accretion as a loss: otherwise we wouldn't need historians in the first place. Not to mention that the ability to retain doesn't translate itself into the ability to predict. Whenever this is done—by a philosopher or a political thinker—the translation almost invariably turns into a blueprint for a new society. The rise, the crescendo, and the fall of the Third Reich, as much as those of the Communist system in Russia, was not averted precisely because it was not expected.

The question is, can the translation be blamed for the quality of the original? The answer, I am tempted to say, is yes; and let me succumb to this temptation. Both the German and the Russian versions of socialism sprang from the same late-nineteenth-century philosophical root, which used the shelves of the British Museum for fuel and Darwinian thought for a model. (Hence their subsequent confrontation, which wasn't a battle between good and evil but a clash of two demons—a family feud, if you will.)

An earlier fertilizer, of course, was the splendid French showing in the eighteenth century, which kept the Germans flat on their back militarily and intellectually long enough to develop a national inferiority complex, which took the form of German nationalism and the idea of German *Kultur*. With its incoherence of elevation, German Romantic idealism, initially a *cri de coeur*, pretty soon turned into a *cri de guerre,* especially during the Industrial Revolution, since the British were better at it.

Consider, then, Russia, which had even less to show for itself than Germany, and not only in the eighteenth century. It was a case of an inferiority complex squared, since it proceeded to emulate Germany in every conceivable—no, available—manner, producing along the way its own Slavophiles and the notion of a specifically Russian soul, as though the Almighty distributed souls geographically. To put it cutely, the *cri de coeur* and the *cri de guerre* merged in the Russian ear into *le dernier cri;* and it was out of an inferiority complex, out of provincialism—always keen on the latest—that Lenin set out to read Marx, not out of a perceived necessity. Capitalism in Russia, after all, was just raising its first smokestacks; the country was predominantly agrarian.

But then you can hardly reproach either one of them for not reading other philosophers—say, Vico. The mental pattern of the epoch was linear, sequential, evolutionary. One falls into that pattern unwittingly, tracing a crime to its origins rather than to its purpose. Yeah, we are that kind of hound: we would rather sniff out ethics than demography. The real paradox of history is that its linear pattern, a product of the self-preservation instinct, dulls this very instinct. Be that as it may, however, both the German and the Russian versions of socialism were informed by precisely this pattern, by the principle of historical determinism echoing, after a fashion, the quest for the Just City.

Literally so, one must add. For the chief trait of the historical determinist is his disdain for the peasantry, and the setting of his sights on the working class. (That is why in Russia they still refuse to decollectivize agriculture, putting—literally, again—the cart before the horse.) A by-product of the Industrial Revolution, the socialist idea was essentially an urban construct, generated by deracinated minds that identified society with the city. Small wonder, then, that this brainchild of mental *lumpen*, maturing with an enviable logic into the authoritarian state, amplified the basest properties of the urban lower middle class, anti-Semitism first of all.

This had little to do with the religious or cultural histories of Germany or Russia, which couldn't be more different. For all the vehemence of Luther's rhetoric, I honestly doubt that his largely illiterate audience bothered much about the substance of his ecclesiastical distinctions; and as for Russia, Ivan the Terrible in his correspondence with the runaway Prince Kurbsky proudly and sincerely proclaimed himself a Jew and Russia, Israel. (On the whole, had religious matters really been the root of modern anti-Semitism, its ugliest head would have been not German but Italian, Spanish, or French.) And so for German revolutionary thought of the nineteenth century, no matter how wildly it oscillated on the subject of the Jewish expulsion or Jewish emancipation, the legal result, in 1871, was the latter.

Now, first and foremost, what happened to the Jews in the Third Reich had to do with the creation of a brand-new state, a new social and existential order. The thousand-year-long Reich had a distinctly millenarian, fin-de-siècle ring to it—a bit premature, perhaps, since the siècle was only the nineteenth. But postwar Germany's political and economic rubble was a time as good as any for starting from scratch. (And history, as we remarked, doesn't set much store by human chronology.) Hence the emphasis on youth, the cult of the young body, the purity-of-the-race spiel. Social utopianism meets blond bestia.

The offspring of such an encounter, naturally, was social bestiality. For nothing could be less utopian than an Orthodox—or even an emancipated and secularized—Jew; and nothing could be less blond. One way to build something new is to raze the old, and the New Germany was that sort of project. The atheistic, future-bound, thousand-year-long Reich couldn't regard three-thousand-year-old Judaism as anything but an obstacle and an enemy. Chronologically, ethically, and aesthetically, anti-Semitism just came in handy; the aim was larger than the means—larger, I am tempted to add, than the targets. The aim was nothing less than history, nothing less than remaking the world in Germany's image; and the means were political. Presumably their concreteness, as well as that of their targets, was what made the aim less abstract. For an idea, the attraction of its victim lies in the latter's helping it to acquire mortal features.

The question is, Why didn't they run? They didn't run because, first, the dilemma of exodus versus assimilation was not new, and fairly recently, only a few generations before, in 1871, it seemed to have been solved by the emancipation laws. Second, because the Weimar Republic's constitution was still binding and the air of its freedoms was still in their lungs, as well as in their pockets. Third, because the Nazis at the time could be regarded as an understandable discomfort, as a party of reconstruction, and their anti-Semitic outbursts as a by-product of that reconstruction's hardship, of its straining muscle. After all, they were the National Socialist Workers Party, and the swastika-clutching eagle could be seen as a provisional phoenix. Any one of these three reasons taken separately would be sufficient not to flee the premises; but the inertia of assimilation, of integration, lumped them all together. The general idea, I imagine, was to huddle together and wait until it all blew over.

But history is not a force of nature, if only because its toll is usually much higher. Correspondingly, one can take out no insurance policy against history. Even the apprehensiveness of a people with a long record of persecution turned out to be a lousy premium: its funds were insufficient, at least for a Deutschebank. The claim submitted by both the doctrine of historical determinism and by the creed-sponsored mental climate of Providence's general benevolence could be settled only in human flesh. Historical determinism translated itself into a determination of extermination; and the notion of Providence's general benevolence, into a patient waiting for a Storm Trooper. Wouldn't it have been better to benefit less from civilization and become a nomad?

The dead would say yes, though one can't be certain. The living will certainly cry, No! The ethical ambiguity of the latter response could be glossed over, were it not based on the false perception that what happened in the Third Reich was unique. It wasn't. What took twelve years in Germany lasted for seventy in Russia, and the toll—in Jews and non-Jews—was almost exactly five times higher. With a little industry, one may presumably establish the same ratio for revolutionary China, Cambodia, Iran, Uganda, and so on: the ethnicity of human loss makes no difference. But if one is loath to continue with this line of reasoning, it is because the similarity is too obvious for one's liking, and because it is too easy to commit the common methodological error of promoting this similarity to the rank of admissible evidence for a subsequent law.

The only law of history, I am afraid, is chance. The more ordered the life of a society or an individual, the more chance gets elbowed out. The longer this goes on, the greater the accumulation of disfranchised chance, and the likelier, one would think, that chance will claim its own. One should not attribute a human property to an abstract idea, but "Remember that the fire and the ice/Are never more than one step away/From a temperate city; it is/But a moment to either," said the poet, and we must heed this warning, now that the temperate city has grown too big.

As the spelling out of the laws of history goes, this one is the closest. And if history is to be admitted into the ranks of science, which it craves, it should be aware of the nature of its inquiry. The truth about things, should it exist, is likely to have a very dark side. Given the humans' status as new-comers, i.e., given the world's precedence, the truth about things is bound to be unhuman. Thus any inquiry into that truth amounts to a solipsistic exercise, varying only in intensity and industry. In this sense, scientific findings (not to mention the language to which they resort) that point toward human inconsequence are closer to that truth than the conclusions of modern historians. Perhaps the invention of the atom bomb is closer to it than the invention of penicillin. Perhaps the same applies to any state-sponsored form of bestiality, particularly to wars and genocidal policies, as well as to spontaneous national and revolutionary movements. Without such awareness, history will remain a meaningless safari for historians of theological bent or theologians with historical proclivities, ascribing to their trophies a human likeness and a divine purpose. But humanity of inquiry is not likely to render its subject human.

The best reason for being a nomad is not the fresh air but the escape from the rationalist theory of society based on the rationalist interpretation of history, since the rationalist approach to either is a blithely idealistic flight from human intuition. A nineteenth-century philosopher could afford it. You can't. If one can't become a nomad physically, one should at least become one mentally. You can't save your skin, but you can try for your mind. One should read history the way one reads fiction: for the story, for the characters, for the setting. In short, for its diversity.

In our minds we do not usually hook up Fabrizio del Dongo and Raskolnikov, David Copperfield and Natasha Rostova, Jean Valjean and Clelia Conti, though they belong to roughly the same period of the same century. We don't do this because they are not related; and neither are centuries, except perhaps dynastically. History is essentially a vast library filled with works of fiction that vary in style more than in subject. Thinking of history in a larger manner is pregnant with our own self-aggrandizement; with readers billing themselves as authors. Cataloguing these volumes, let alone trying to link them to one another, can be done only at the expense of reading them; in any case, at the expense of our own wits.

Besides, we read novels rather erratically; when they come our way, or vice versa. We are guided in this activity by our tastes as much as by the circumstances of our leisure. Which is to say, we are nomads in our reading. The same should apply to history. We should simply keep in mind that linear thinking, while it is *de rigueur* for the historian's trade—a narrative device, a trope—it is, for his audience, a trap. It is awful to fall into the trap individually, but it is a catastrophe when it happens collectively.

An individual, a nomadic individual especially, is more on the lookout for danger than the collectivity. The former can turn 360 degrees; the latter can look in only one direction. One of the greatest joys of a nomad, of an individualist, is in structuring history in one's own personal fashion—in cobbling one's own antiquity, one's own Middle Ages or Renaissance in a chronological or achronological, wholly idiosyncratic order: in making them one's own. That is really the only way to inhabit the centuries.

We should remember that rationalism's greatest casualty was individualism. We should be careful with the supposedly dispassionate objectivity of our historians. For objectivity does not mean indifference, nor does it mean an alternative to subjectivity. It is, rather, the sum total of subjectivities. As murderers, victims, or bystanders, men in the final analysis always act individually, subjectively; and they and their deeds should be judged likewise.

This robs us of a certitude, of course, but the less of that the better. Uncertainty keeps an individual on guard, and is generally less bloodthirsty. Of course, all too often, it makes him agonize. But it is better to agonize than to organize. On the whole, uncertainty is more true to life itself; the only certain thing about which is that we are present in it. Again, the main trait of history, and of the future, is our absence, and one cannot be certain of something one was never a part of.

Hence that vague look on the face of the Muse of Time. It is because so many eyes have stared at her with uncertainty. Also, because she has seen so much energy and commotion, whose true end only she knows. And ultimately, because she knows that had she stared back openly, she would have rendered her suitors blind, and she is not without vanity. It is partly owing to this vanity, but mainly to the fact that she has nowhere else in this world to go, that on occasion, with that vague look on her face, she walks into our midst and makes us absent.

Speech at the Stadium

∿

Life is a game with many rules but no referee. One learns how to play it more by watching it than by consulting any book, including the Holy Book. Small wonder, then, that so many play dirty, that so few win, that so many lose.

At any rate, if this place is the University of Michigan, Ann Arbor, Michigan, that I remember, it's fairly safe for me to assume that you, its graduates, are even less familiar with the Good Book than those who sat on these benches, let's say, sixteen years ago, when I ventured afield here for the first time.

To my eye, ear, and nostril, this place looks like Ann Arbor; it goes blue—or feels blue—like Ann Arbor; it smells like Ann Arbor (though I must admit that there is less marijuana in the air now than there used to be, and that causes momentary confusion for an old Ann Arbor hand). It seems to be, then, Ann Arbor, where I spent a part of my life—the best part for all I know—and where, sixteen years ago, your predecessors knew next to nothing about the Bible.

If I remember my colleagues well, if I know what's

Delivered as a commencement address at the University of Michigan, Ann Arbor, in 1988.

happening to university curricula all over the country, if I am not totally oblivious to the pressures the so-called modern world exerts upon the young, I feel nostalgic for those who sat in your chairs a dozen or so years ago, because some of them at least could cite the Ten Commandments and still others even remembered the names of the Seven Deadly Sins. As to what they've done with that precious knowledge of theirs afterward, as to how they fared in the game, I have no idea. All I can hope for is that in the long run one is better off being guided by rules and taboos laid down by someone totally impalpable than by the penal code alone.

Since your run is most likely to be fairly long, and since being better off and having a decent world around you is what you presumably are after, you could do worse than to acquaint yourselves with those commandments and that list of sins. There are just seventeen items altogether, and some of them overlap. Of course, you may argue that they belong to a creed with a substantial record of violence. Still, as creeds go, this one appears to be the most tolerant; it's worth your consideration if only because it gave birth to the society in which you have the right to question or negate its value.

But I am not here to extol the virtues of any particular creed or philosophy, nor do I relish, as so many seem to, the opportunity to snipe at the modern system of education or at you, its alleged victims. To begin with, I don't perceive you as such. After all, in certain fields your knowledge is immeasurably superior to mine or anyone's of my generation. I regard you as a bunch of young, reasonably egotistical souls on the eve of a very long journey. I shudder to contemplate its length, and I ask myself in what way I could possibly be of use to you. Do I know something about life that could be of help or consequence to you, and if I do, is there a way to pass this information on to you?

The answer to the first question is, I suppose, yes—not

so much because a person of my age is entitled to outfox any of you at existential chess as because he is, in all probability, tired of quite a lot of the stuff you are still aspiring to. (This fatigue alone is something the young should be advised on as an attendant feature of both their eventual success and their failure; this sort of knowledge may enhance their savoring of the former as well as a better weathering of the latter.) As for the second question, I truly wonder. The example of the aforementioned commandments may discourage any commencement speaker, for the Ten Commandments themselves were a commencement address—literally so, I must say. But there is a transparent wall between the generations, an ironic curtain, if you will, a see-through veil allowing almost no passage of experience. At best, some tips.

Regard, then, what you are about to hear as just tips—of several icebergs, if I may say so, not of Mount Sinai. I am no Moses, nor are you biblical Jews; these are a few random jottings scribbled on a yellow pad somewhere in California—not tablets. Ignore them if you wish, doubt them if you must, forget them if you can't help it: there is nothing imperative about them. Should some of it now or in the time to be come in handy to you, I'll be glad. If not, my wrath won't reach you.

1. Now, and in the time to be, I think it will pay for you to zero in on being precise with your language. Try to build and treat your vocabulary the way you are to treat your checking account. Pay every attention to it and try to increase your earnings. The purpose here is not to boost your bedroom eloquence or your professional success—although those, too, can be consequences—nor is it to turn you into parlor sophisticates. The purpose is to enable you to articulate yourselves as fully and precisely as possible; in a word, the purpose is your balance. For the accumulation of things

not spelled out, not properly articulated, may result in neurosis. On a daily basis, a lot is happening to one's psyche; the mode of one's expression, however, often remains the same. Articulation lags behind experience. That doesn't go well with the psyche. Sentiments, nuances, thoughts, perceptions that remain nameless, unable to be voiced and dissatisfied with approximations, get pent up within an individual and may lead to a psychological explosion or implosion. To avoid that, one needn't turn into a bookworm. One should simply acquire a dictionary and read it on the same daily basis—and, on and off, books of poetry. Dictionaries, however, are of primary importance. There are a lot of them around; some of them even come with a magnifying glass. They are reasonably cheap, but even the most expensive among them (those equipped with a magnifying glass) cost far less than a single visit to a psychiatrist. If you are going to visit one nevertheless, go with the symptoms of a dictionary junkie.

2. Now, and in the time to be, try to be kind to your parents. If this sounds too close to "Honor thy mother and father" for your comfort, so be it. All I am trying to say is, try not to rebel against them, for, in all likelihood, they will die before you do, so you can spare yourselves at least this source of guilt if not of grief. If you must rebel, rebel against those who are not so easily hurt. Parents are too close a target (so, by the way, are sisters, brothers, wives, or husbands); the range is such that you can't miss. Rebellion against one's parents, for all its I-won't-take-a-single-penny-from-you, is essentially an extremely bourgeois sort of thing, because it provides the rebel with the ultimate in comfort, in this case, mental comfort: the comfort of one's convictions. The later you hit this pattern, the later you become a mental bourgeois; i.e., the longer you stay skeptical, doubtful, intellectually

uncomfortable, the better it is for you. On the other hand, of course, this not-a-single-penny business makes practical sense, because your parents, in all likelihood, will bequeath all they've got to you, and the successful rebel will end up with the entire fortune intact—in other words, rebellion is a very efficient form of savings. The interest, though, is crippling; I'd say, bankrupting.

3. Try not to set too much store by politicians—not so much because they are dumb or dishonest, which is more often than not the case, but because of the size of their job, which is too big even for the best among them, by this or that political party, doctrine, system, or a blueprint thereof. All they or those can do, at best, is to diminish a social evil, not eradicate it. No matter how substantial an improvement may be, ethically speaking it will always be negligible, because there will always be those—say, just one person—who won't profit from this improvement. The world is not perfect; the Golden Age never was or will be. The only thing that's going to happen to the world is that it will get bigger, i.e., more populated while not growing in size. No matter how fairly the man you've elected will promise to cut the pie, it won't grow in size; as a matter of fact, the portions are bound to get smaller. In light of that—or, rather, in dark of that— you ought to rely on your own home cooking, that is, on managing the world yourselves—at least that part of it that lies within your reach, within your radius. Still, in doing this, you must also prepare yourselves for the heartrending realization that even that pie of yours won't suffice; you must prepare yourselves that you're likely to dine as much in disappointment as in gratitude. The most difficult lesson to learn here is to be steady in the kitchen, since by serving this pie just once you create quite a lot of expectations. Ask yourself whether you can afford a steady supply of those

pies, or would you rather bargain on a politician? Whatever the outcome of this soul-searching may be—however much you think the world can bet on your baking—you might start right away by insisting that those corporations, banks, schools, labs, and whatnot where you'll be working, and whose premises are heated and policed round the clock anyway, permit the homeless in for the night, now that it's winter.

4. Try not to stand out, try to be modest. There are too many of us as it is, and there are going to be many more, very soon. Thus climbing into the limelight is bound to be done at the expense of the others who won't be climbing. That you must step on somebody's toes doesn't mean you should stand on their shoulders. Besides, all you will see from that vantage point is the human sea, plus those who, like you, have assumed a similarly conspicuous—and very precarious at that—position: those who are called rich and famous. On the whole, there is always something faintly unpalatable about being better off than one's likes, and when those likes come in billions, it is more so. To this it should be added that the rich and famous these days, too, come in throngs, that up there on the top it's very crowded. So if you want to get rich or famous or both, by all means go ahead, but don't make a meal of it. To covet what somebody else has is to forfeit your uniqueness; on the other hand, of course, it stimulates mass production. But as you are running through life only once, it is only sensible to try to avoid the most obvious clichés, limited editions included. The notion of exclusivity, mind you, also forfeits your uniqueness, not to mention that it shrinks your sense of reality to the already-achieved. Far better than belonging to any club is to be jostled by the multitudes of those who, given their income and their appearance, represent—at least theoretically—un-

limited potential. Try to be more like them than like those who are not like them; try to wear gray. Mimicry is the defense of individuality, not its surrender. I would advise you to lower your voice, too, but I am afraid you will think I am going too far. Still, keep in mind that there is always somebody next to you, a neighbor. Nobody asks you to love him, but try not to hurt or discomfort him much; try to tread on his toes carefully; and should you come to covet his wife, remember at least that this testifies to the failure of your imagination, to your disbelief in—or ignorance of—reality's unlimited potential. Worse comes to worse, try to remember how far away—from the stars, from the depths of the universe, perhaps from its opposite end—came this request not to do it, as well as this idea of loving your neighbor no less than yourself. Maybe the stars know more about gravity, as well as about loneliness, than you do; coveting eyes that they are.

5. At all costs try to avoid granting yourself the status of the victim. Of all the parts of your body, be most vigilant over your index finger, for it is blame-thirsty. A pointed finger is a victim's logo—the opposite of the V sign and a synonym for surrender. No matter how abominable your condition may be, try not to blame anything or anybody: history, the state, superiors, race, parents, the phase of the moon, childhood, toilet training, etc. The menu is vast and tedious, and this vastness and tedium alone should be offensive enough to set one's intelligence against choosing from it. The moment that you place blame somewhere, you undermine your resolve to change anything; it could be argued even that that blame-thirsty finger oscillates as wildly as it does because the resolve was never great enough in the first place. After all, victim status is not without its sweetness. It commands compassion, confers distinction, and whole nations and con-

tinents bask in the murk of mental discounts advertised as the victim's conscience. There is an entire victim culture, ranging from private counselors to international loans. The professed goal of this network notwithstanding, its net result is that of lowering one's expectations from the threshold, so that a measly advantage could be perceived or billed as a major breakthrough. Of course, this is therapeutic and, given the scarcity of the world's resources, perhaps even hygienic, so for want of a better identity, one may embrace it—but try to resist it. However abundant and irrefutable is the evidence that you are on the losing side, negate it as long as you have your wits about you, as long as your lips can utter "No." On the whole, try to respect life not only for its amenities but for its hardships, too. They are a part of the game, and what's good about a hardship is that it is not a deception. Whenever you are in trouble, in some scrape, on the verge of despair or in despair, remember: that's life speaking to you in the only language it knows well. In other words, try to be a little masochistic: without a touch of masochism, the meaning of life is not complete. If this is of any help, try to remember that human dignity is an absolute, not a piecemeal notion; that it is inconsistent with special pleading, that it derives its poise from denying the obvious. Should you find this argument a bit on the heady side, think at least that by considering yourself a victim you but enlarge the vacuum of irresponsibility that demons or demagogues love so much to fill, since a paralyzed will is no dainty for angels.

6. The world you are about to enter and exist in doesn't have a good reputation. It's been better geographically than historically; it's still far more attractive visually than socially. It's not a nice place, as you are soon to find out, and I rather doubt that it will get much nicer by the time you leave it.

Still, it's the only world available: no alternative exists, and if one did, there is no guarantee that it would be much better than this one. It is a jungle out there, as well as a desert, a slippery slope, a swamp, etc.—literally—but what's worse, metaphorically, too. Yet, as Robert Frost has said, "The best way out is always through." He also said, in a different poem, though, that "to be social is to be forgiving." It's with a few remarks about this business of getting through that I would like to close.

Try not to pay attention to those who will try to make life miserable for you. There will be a lot of those—in the official capacity as well as the self-appointed. Suffer them if you can't escape them, but once you have steered clear of them, give them the shortest shrift possible. Above all, try to avoid telling stories about the unjust treatment you received at their hands; avoid it no matter how receptive your audience may be. Tales of this sort extend the existence of your antagonists; most likely they are counting on your being talkative and relating your experience to others. By himself, no individual is worth an exercise in injustice (or for that matter, in justice). The ratio of one-to-one doesn't justify the effort: it's the echo that counts. That's the main principle of any oppressor, whether state-sponsored or autodidact. Therefore, steal, or still, the echo, so that you don't allow an event, however unpleasant or momentous, to claim any more time than it took for it to occur.

What your foes do derives its significance or consequence from the way you react. Therefore, rush through or past them as though they were yellow and not red lights. Don't linger on them mentally or verbally; don't pride yourself on forgiving or forgetting them—worse come to worse, do the forgetting first. This way you'll spare your brain cells a lot of useless agitation; this way, perhaps, you may even save those pigheads from themselves, since the prospect of being forgotten is shorter than that of being forgiven. So flip the channel: you can't put this network out of circulation, but at least you can reduce its ratings. Now, this solution is not likely to please angels, but then again, it's bound to hurt demons, and for the moment that's all that really matters.

I had better stop here. As I said, I'll be glad if you find what I've said useful. If not, it will show that you are equipped far better for the future than one would expect from people of your age. Which, I suppose, is also a reason for rejoicing—not for apprehension. In either case—well equipped or not—I wish you luck, because what lies ahead is no picnic for the prepared and the unprepared alike, and you'll need luck. Still, I believe that you'll manage.

I'm no gypsy; I can't divine your future, but it's pretty obvious to any naked eye that you have a lot going for you. To say the least, you were born, which is in itself half the battle, and you live in a democracy—this halfway house between nightmare and utopia—which throws fewer obstacles in the way of an individual than its alternatives.

Last, you've been educated at the University of Michigan, in my view the best school in the nation, if only because sixteen years ago it gave a badly needed break to the laziest man on earth, who, on top of that, spoke practically no English—to yours truly. I taught here for some eight years; the language in which I address you today I learned here; some of my former colleagues are still on the payroll, others retired, and still others sleep the eternal sleep in the earth of Ann Arbor that now carries you. Clearly this place is of extraordinary sentimental value for me; and so it will become, in a dozen years or so, for you. To that extent, I *can* divine your future; in that respect, I know you will manage, or, more precisely, succeed. For feeling a wave of warmth coming over you in a dozen or so years at the mention of this town's name will indicate that, luck or no luck, as human beings you've succeeded. It's this sort of success I wish to you above all in the years to come. The rest depends on luck and matters less.

Collector's Item

❧

If you sit long on the bank of the river, you may
see the body of your enemy floating by.

—*Chinese proverb*

I

Given the lunacy this piece deals with, it ought to be written
in a language other than English. The only option available
to me, however, is Russian, which is the very source of the
lunacy in question. Who needs tautology? Besides, several
of the assertions I am going to make are, in their turn, quite
loony, and best checked by a language that has a reputation
for being analytical. Who wants to have his insights ascribed
to the vagaries of some highly inflected language? Nobody,
perhaps, save those who keep asking what language I think
or dream in. One dreams in dreams, I reply, and thinks in
thoughts. A language gets into the picture only when one
has to make those things public. This, of course, gets me
nowhere. Still (I persevere), since English isn't my mother
tongue, since my grip on its grammar isn't that tight, my
thoughts, for example, could get quite garbled. I sure hope
that they don't; at any rate, I can tell them from dreams.
And believe it or not, dear reader, this sort of quibbling,
which normally gets one nowhere, brings you straight to the
core of our story. For no matter how its author solves his
dilemma, no matter what language he settles for, his very

ability to choose a language makes him, in your eyes, suspect; and suspicions are what this piece is all about. Who is he, you may wonder about the author, what is he up to? Is he trying to promote himself to the status of a disembodied intelligence? If it were only you, dear reader, inquiring about the author's identity, that would be fine. The trouble is, he wonders about his identity himself—and for the same reason. Who are you, the author asks himself in two languages, and gets startled no less than you would upon hearing his own voice muttering something that amounts to "Well, I don't know." A mongrel, then, ladies and gentlemen, this is a mongrel speaking. Or else a centaur.

II

This is the summer of 1991, August. That much at least is certain. Elizabeth Taylor is about to take her eighth walk down the aisle, this time with a blue-collar boy of Polish extraction. A serial killer with cannibalistic urges is apprehended in Milwaukee; the cops find three hard-boiled skulls in his fridge. Russia's Great Panhandler makes his rounds in London with cameras zeroing in, as it were, on his empty tin. The more it changes, the more it stays the same: like the weather. And the more it tries to stay the same, the more it changes: like a face. And judging by the "weather," this could easily be 1891. On the whole, geography (European geography in particular) leaves history very few options. A country, especially a large one, gets only two. Either it's strong or it's weak. Fig. 1: Russia. Fig. 2: Germany. For most of the century, the former tried to play it big and strong (at what cost is another matter). Now its turn has come to be weak: by the year 2000 it will be where it was in 1900, and about the same perimeter. The latter, Germany, will be there, too. (At long last it dawned on the descendants of

Wotan that saddling their neighbors with debt is a more stable and less costly form of occupation than sending in troops.) The more it changes, the more it stays the same. Still, you can't tell time by weather. Faces are better: the more one tries to stay the same, the more it changes. Fig. 1: Miss Taylor's. Fig. 2: one's own. The summer of 1991, then, August. Can one tell a mirror from a tabloid?

III

And here is one such, of humble strikebreaking origins. Actually it is a literary paper, *The London Review of Books* by name, which came into existence several years ago when *The* (London) *Times* and its *Literary Supplement* went on strike for a few months. In order not to leave the public without literary news and the benefits of liberal opinion, *LRB* was launched and evidently blossomed. Eventually *The Times* and its *Literary Supplement* resumed operation, but *LRB* stayed afloat, proof not so much of the growing diversity of reading tastes as of burgeoning demography. No individual I know subscribes to both papers, unless he is a publisher. It's largely a matter of one's budget, not to mention one's attention span or one's plain loyalty. And I wonder, for instance, which one of these—the latter, I should hope—prevented me from purchasing a recent issue in a small Belsize Park bookstore, where I and my young lady ventured the other day on our way to the movies. Budgetary considerations as well as my attention span—alarming as it may be of late—must be ruled out: the most recent issue of the *LRB* sat there on the counter in full splendor, its cover depicting a blown-up postal stamp: unmistakably of Soviet origin. This sort of thing has been enough to catch my eye since I was twelve. In its own turn, the stamp depicted a bespectacled man with silver, neatly parted hair. Above and underneath the face, the stamp's legend, in now-fashionable Cyrillic, went as follows: *Soviet Secret Agent Kim Philby (1912–1988)*. He looked indeed like Alec Guinness, with a touch perhaps of Trevor Howard. I reached into my pocket for two one-pound coins, caught the salesboy's friendly glance, adjusted my vocal cords for some highly pitched, civilized "May I have . . . ," and then turned 90 degrees and walked out of the store. I must add that I didn't do it abruptly, that I managed to send the boy at the counter a "just changed my mind" nod and to collect, with the same nod, my young lady.

IV

As we had some time to kill before the show, we went into a nearby café. "What's the matter with you?" my young comrade-in-arms asked me once we sat down. "You look like . . ." I didn't interrupt her. I knew how I felt and actually wondered what it might look like. "You look, you look . . . sideways," she continued hesitantly, tentatively, since English wasn't her mother tongue either. "You look as if you can't face the world any longer, can't look straight in the world's eye," she managed finally. "Something like that," she added, just in case, to widen the margin of error. Well, I thought, one is always a greater reality for others than for oneself, and vice versa. What are we here for but to be observed. If that's what "it" really looks like from the outside, then I am doing fine—and so, perhaps, is the bulk of the human race. For I felt like throwing up, like a great deal of barf was welling up in my throat. Still, while I wasn't puzzled by the sensation, I was surprised by its intensity. "What's the matter?" asked my young lady. "What's wrong?" And now, dear reader, after trying to figure out who the author of this piece is and what its timing, we've got to find out also who its audience is. Do you remember, dear reader, who Kim Philby was and what he did? If you do, then you are around fifty and thus, in a manner of speaking, on your way out. What you are going to hear, therefore, will be of little import to you, still of lesser comfort. Your game is up, you are too far gone; this stuff won't change anything for you. If, on the other hand, you've never heard of Kim Philby, this means that you are in your thirties, life lies ahead, all this is ancient history and of no possible use or entertainment value for you, unless you are some sort of a spy buff. So? So where does all this leave our author, the question of his identity still hanging? Can a disembodied intelligence rightfully expect to find an able-bodied audience? I say, Hardly, and I say, Who gives a damn.

V

All of this leaves our author at the close of the twentieth century with a very bad taste in his mouth. That, of course, is to be expected in a mouth that is in its fifties. But let's stop being cute with each other, dear reader, let's get down to business. Kim Philby was a Briton, and he was a spy. He worked for the British Intelligence Service, for MI5 or MI6, or both—who cares about all that arcana and whatever it stands for—but he spied for the Russians. In the parlance of the trade, he was a mole, though we are not going to use that lingo here. I am not a spy buff, not an aficionado of that genre, and never was; neither in my thirties nor even in my fifties, and let me tell you why. First, because espionage provides a good plot but seldom palatable prose. In fact, the upsurge of spy novels in our time is the by-product of modernism's emphasis on texture, which left literature in practically all European languages absolutely plotless: the reaction was inevitable but, with few exceptions, equally execrable.

Still, aesthetic objections are of little consequence to you, dear reader, aren't they, and that in itself tells the time as accurately as the calendar or a tabloid. Let's try ethics, then, on which everyone seems to be an expert. I, for one, have always regarded espionage as the vilest human pursuit, mainly, I guess, because I grew up in a country the advancement of whose fortunes was inconceivable to its natives. To do that, one indeed had to be a foreigner; and that's perhaps why the country took such pride in its cops, fellow travelers, and secret agents, commemorating them in all manner of ways, from stamps to plaques to monuments. Ah, all those Richard Sorges, Pablo Nerudas, and Hewlett Jonsons, and so on, all that pulp of our youth! Ah, all those flicks shot in Latvia or in Estonia for the "Western" backdrop! A foreign surname and the neon lettering of HOTEL (always put vertically, never horizontally), sometimes the screeching brakes of a Czech-made motorcar. The goal was not so much verisimilitude or suspense as the legitimization of the system by the exploits on its behalf outside it. You could get a bar scene with a little combo toiling in the background, you could get a blonde with a tin-can taffeta skirt and a decent nose job looking positively non-Slavic. Two or three of our actors, too, looked sufficiently gaunt and lanky, the emphasis being always on a thoroughbred beak. A German-sounding name for a spy was better than a French one, a French one was better than a Spanish one, a Spanish one was better than an Italian one (come to think of it, I can't recall a single Italian Soviet secret agent). The English were tops, but hard to come by. In any case, neither English landscapes nor street scenes were ever attempted on our big screens, as we lacked vehicles with steering wheels on the right. Ah, those were the days—but I've digressed.

VI

Who cares what country one grows up in, and whether it colors one's view of espionage? Too bad if it does, because then one is robbed of a source of entertainment—perhaps not of the most delectable kind, but entertainment nonetheless. In view of what surrounds us, not to mention what lies ahead, this is barely forgivable. Dearth of action is the mother of the motion picture. And if one indeed loathes spies, there still remains spy-catching, which is as engrossing as it is righteous. What's wrong with a little paranoia, with a bit of manifest schizophrenia? Isn't there something recognizable and therefore therapeutic to their paperback and Bakelite video versions? And what's any aversion, including this aversion toward spies, if not a hidden neurosis, an echo of some childhood trauma? First therapy, then ethics.

VII

The face of Kim Philby on that stamp. The face of the late Mr. Philby, Esq., of Brighton, Sussex, or of Welwyn Garden, Herts., or of Ambala, India—you name it. The face of an Englishman in the Soviet employ. The pulp writer's dream come true. Presumably, the rank of general, if the poor sod cared for such trifles; presumably, highly decorated, maybe a Hero of the Soviet Union. Though the snapshot used for the stamp shows none of that. Here he appears in his civvies, which is what he donned for most of his life: the dark coat and the tie. The medals and the epaulets were saved for the red velvet cushion of a soldier's funeral, if he had one. Which I think he did, his employers being suckers for top-secret solemnity. Many moons ago, reviewing a book about a chum of his for the *TLS*, I suggested that, considering his service to the Soviet state, this now aging Moscow denizen should be buried in the Kremlin wall. I mention this since I've been told that he was one of the few *TLS* subscribers in Moscow. He ended up, though, I believe, in the Protestant cemetery, his employers being sticklers for propriety, albeit posthumously. (Had Her Majesty's government been handling these matters, it could hardly have done better.) And now I feel little pangs of remorse. I imagine him interred, clad in the same coat and tie shown on the stamp, wearing this disguise—or was it a uniform?—in death as in life. Presumably he left some instructions concerning this eventuality, although he couldn't have been fully certain whether they would be followed. Were they? And what did he want on his tombstone? A line of English poetry, perhaps? Something like "And death shall have no dominion"? Or did he prefer a matter-of-fact "Soviet Secret Agent Kim Philby (1912–1988)"? And did he want it in Cyrillic?

VIII

Back to hidden neurosis and childhood trauma, to therapy and ethics. When I was twenty-four, I was after a girl, and in a big way. She was slightly older than I, and after a while I began to feel that something was amiss. I sensed that I was being deceived, perhaps even two-timed. It turned out, of course, that I wasn't wrong, but that was later. At the time I simply grew suspicious, and one evening I decided to track her down. I hid myself in an archway across the street from her building, waited there for about an hour, and when she emerged from her poorly lit entrance, I followed her for several blocks. I was tense with excitement, but of an unfamiliar nature. At the same time, I felt vaguely bored, as I knew more or less what I might discover. The excitement grew with every step, with every evasive action I took; the boredom stayed at the same level. When she turned to the river, my excitement reached its crescendo, and at that point I stopped, turned around, and headed for a nearby café. Later I would blame my abandoning the chase on my laziness and reproach myself, especially in the light—or, rather, in the dark—of this affair's denouement, playing an Actaeon to the dogs of my own hindsight. The truth was less innocent and more absorbing. The truth was that I stopped because I had discovered the nature of my excitement. It was the joy of a hunter pursuing his prey. In other words, it was something atavistic, primordial. This realization had nothing to do with ethics, with scruples, taboos, or anything of the sort. I had no problem with conferring upon the girl the status of prey. It's just that I hated being the hunter. A matter of temperament, perhaps? Perhaps. Perhaps had the world been subdivided into the four humors, or at least boiled down to four humor-based political parties, it would be a better place. Yet I think that one's resistance to turning into a hunter, the ability to spot and to control the hunting impulse, has to do with something more basic than temperament, upbringing, social values, received wisdom, ecclesiastical affiliation, or one's concept of honor. It has to do with the degree of one's evolution, with the species' evolution, with reaching the stage marked by one's inability to regress. One loathes spies not so much because of their low rung on the evolutionary ladder as because betrayal invites you to descend.

IX

Dear reader, if this sounds to you like an oblique way of bragging about one's own virtues, so be it. Virtue, after all, is far from being synonymous with survival; duplicity is. But you will accept, dear reader, won't you, that there is a hierarchy between love and betrayal. And you also know that it is the former that ushers in the latter, not vice versa. What's worse, you know that the latter outlasts the former. So there is not much to brag about, even when you are absolutely smitten or besotted, is there? If one is not a Darwinist, if one still sticks to Cuvier, it is because lower organisms seem to be more viable than complex ones. Look at moss, look at algae. I understand that I am out of my depth here. All I am trying to say is that to an advanced organism duplicity is, at worst, an option; for a lower one, however, it is the means of survival. In this sense, spies don't choose to be spies any more than a lizard chooses its pigmentation: they just can't do any better. Duplicity, after all, is a form of mimicry; it is this particular animal's maximum. One could argue with this proposition if spies spied for money, but the best of them do it out of conviction. In their pursuit, they are driven by excitement, better yet by instinct unchecked by boredom. For boredom interferes with instinct. Boredom is the mark of a highly evolved species; a sign of civilization, if you will.

X

Whoever it was who ordered this stamp's issue was no doubt making a statement. Especially given the current political climate, the warming of East–West relations and all. The decision must have been made on high, in the Kremlin's own hallowed chambers, since the Foreign Ministry would have been up in arms against it, not to mention the Ministry of Finances, such as they are. You don't bite the hand that feeds you. Or do you? You do if your teeth are those of the CSS—the Committee for State Security (a.k.a. the KGB)— which is larger than both those ministries to begin with, not only in the number of employees, but in the place it occupies in the conscience and the subconscious of the powerful and the powerless alike. If you are that big, you may bite any hand you like and, for that matter, throats, too. You may do it for several reasons. Out of vanity: to remind the jubilant West of your existence. Or out of inertia: you're used to biting that hand anyway. Or out of nostalgia for the good old days, when your diet was rich in the enemy's protein because you had a constant supply of it in your compatriots. Still, for all the grossness of the CSS's appetite, one senses behind this stamp initiative a particular individual: the head of a directorate, or perhaps his deputy, or just a humble case officer who came up with the idea. He might simply have revered Philby, or wanted to get ahead in his department; or on the contrary, he may have been approaching retirement and, like many people of that generation, truly believed in the didactic value of a postage stamp. None of these things contradicts the others. They are fully compatible: vanity, inertia, nostalgia, reverence, careerism, naïveté; and the brain of the CSS's average employee is as good a place for their confluence as any, including a computer. What's puzzling about this stamp, however, is the promptness with which it has been issued: only two years after Mr. Philby's demise. His shoes, as well as the gloves that he always wore on account of a skin allergy, were, so to speak, still warm. Issuing a stamp in any country takes a hell of a lot of time, and normally it is preceded by national recognition of its subject. Even if one skips this requirement (the man was, after all, a secret agent), the speed with which the stamp was produced is amazing, given the thick of bureaucratic hurdles it ought to have gone through. It obviously didn't; it was evidently rushed into production. Which leaves you with this sense of personal involvement, of an individual will behind this four-centimeter-square piece of paper. And you ask yourself about the motive behind that will. And you understand that somebody wanted to make a statement. *Urbi et orbi,* as it were. And, as a part of the orbis, you wonder what sort of statement that was.

XI

The answer is: menacing and spiteful; also profoundly provincial. One judges an undertaking, I'm afraid, by its result. The stamp subjects the late Mr. Philby to the ultimate ignominy, to the final slight: it proclaims a Briton to be Russia's own, not so much in spirit—what's so special about that?—but precisely in body. No doubt Philby asked for that. He spied for the Soviet Union for a good quarter of a century. For another quarter of a century he simply lived in the Soviet Union, and wasn't entirely idle either. On top of that, he died there and was interred in Russian soil. The stamp is essentially his tombstone's replica. Also, we shouldn't discount the possibility that he might have been pleased by his masters' posthumous treatment: he was stupid enough, and secrecy is a hotbed of vanity. He could even have approved (if not initiated himself) the stamp project. Yet one can't help feeling some violation here, something deeper than the desecration of a grave: a violation that is elemental. He was, after all, a Briton, and the Brits are used to dying in odd places. What's revolting about this stamp is its proprietary sentiment; it's as though the earth that swallowed the poor sod licks its lips with profound satisfaction and says, He is mine. Or else it licks the stamp.

XII

Such was the statement that a humble case officer, or a bunch of them at CSS, wished to make, and did, and that a liberal literary paper of humble strikebreaking origins has found so amusing. Well, let's say point taken. What should be done about it, if anything? Should we try to disinter the unholy remains and bring them back to Britain? Should we petition the Soviet government or offer it a large sum? Or should Her Majesty's Postmaster issue perhaps a counterstamp, with a legend something like *English Traitor Kim Philby, 1912–1988*, in English, of course, and see whether some Russian paper reprints it? Should we try to retrieve the idea of this man, despite himself, from the collective psyche of his masters? And anyway who are these "we" who provide your author, dear reader, with such rhetorical comfort? No, nothing of the sort could, or for that matter should, be done. Philby belongs there, body and soul. Let him rot in peace. But what one—and I emphasize this "one"—can do, and therefore should do, is rob the aforementioned collective psyche of its ownership of that unholy relic, rob it of the comfort it thinks it enjoys. And in fact it's easy to do this. For, in spite of himself, Kim Philby wasn't theirs. Considering where we are today, and especially where Russia is, it is obvious that, for all its industry, cunning, human toil, and investment of time and currency, the Philby enterprise was a bust. Were he a British double agent, he couldn't inflict a greater damage on the system whose fortunes he was actually trying to advance. But double or triple, he was a British agent through and through, for the bottom line of his quite extraordinary effort is a sharp sense of futility. Futility is so hideously British. And now for the fun part.

XIII

In the few spy novels that I read as a child, the role of the postage stamp was as grand as the item itself was small, and would yield only to that of a torn photograph, the appearance of the other half of which often would clinch the plot. On the stamp's sticky side, a spy in those novels would convey in his chicken scrawl, or on a microfilm, the secret message to his master, or vice versa. The Philby stamp is thus a fusion of the torn man with the medium-is-the-message principle; as such, it is a collector's item. To this we might add also that the priciest things in the stamp-collecting world are those issued by political or geographical ephemera—by short-lived or defunct states, negligible potentates or specks of land. (The most-sought-after item in my childhood, I recall, was a stamp from Pitcairn Island—a British colony, as it happens, in the South Pacific.) So, to use this philatelist logic, the issue of the Philby stamp appears to be a cry from the Soviet Union's future. At any rate, there is something in its future that, in the guise of the CSS, asks for that. Actually, this is a fine time for philatelists, and in more ways than one. One can even speak of philatelist justice here— the way one speaks of poetic license. For half a century ago, when the CSS warriors were deporting people from the Baltic states that the U.S.S.R. invaded and rendered defunct, it was precisely philatelists who clinched the list of social categories subject to removal. (In fact, the list ended with the Esperantists, the philatelists being the penultimate category. There were, if memory serves me right, sixty-four such categories; the list began with the leaders and active members of political parties, followed by university professors, journalists, teachers, businessmen, and so on. It came with a highly detailed set of instructions as to how to separate the provider from his family, children from their mothers, and so forth, down to the actual wording of sentences like "Your daddy went to get hot water from the station boiler." The whole thing was rather well thought through and signed by CSS General Serov. I saw the document with my own eyes; the country of application was Lithuania.) This, perhaps, is the source of a retiring case officer's belief in the didactic power of a stamp. Well, nothing pleases the tired eyes of an impartial observer so much as the sight of things coming full circle.

XIV

Let's not dismiss, though, the didactic powers of the stamp. This one at least could have been issued to encourage the CSS's present and future employees, and was no doubt distributed among the former for free, a modest fringe benefit. As for the latter, one can imagine the stamp doing rather well with a young recruit. The establishment is big on visuals, on iconography, its monitoring abilities being justly famous for their omniscience, not to mention omnivorousness. When it comes to didactic purposes, especially among its own brethren, the organization readily goes the extra mile. When Oleg Penkovsky, a GRU man who betrayed Soviet military secrets to the British in the 1960s, was finally caught, the establishment (or so I was told) filmed his execution. Strapped to a stretcher, Penkovsky is wheeled into the Moscow city crematorium's chamber. An attendant opens the furnace door and two other attendants start to push the stretcher and its contents into the roaring furnace; the flame is already licking the screaming man's soles. At this point a voice comes over the loudspeaker, interrupting the procedure, because another body is scheduled for this time slot. Screaming but unable to kick, Penkovsky is pulled back; another body arrives and, after a small ceremony, is pushed into the furnace. The voice comes over the loudspeaker again: now it's Penkovsky's turn, and in he goes. A small but effective skit. Beats Beckett hands down, boosts morale, and can't be forgotten: it brands your wits. A kind of stamp, if you will: for intramural correspondence.

XV

Before we set out for the fun part in earnest, dear reader, let me say this: There is a distinction between the benefit of hindsight and having lived long enough to see heads' tails. This is not a disclaimer; quite the contrary, most of your author's assertions are borne out by his life, and if they are wrong, then he blew it, at least partially. Still, even if they are accurate, a good question remains. Is he entitled to pass judgment upon those who are no longer around—who have lost? Outlasting your opponent gives you the sense of membership in a victorious majority, of having played your cards right. Aren't you then applying the law retroactively? Aren't you punishing the poor buggers under a code of conscience foreign to them and to their times? Well, I am not troubled by this, and for three reasons. First, because Kim Philby kicked the bucket at the ripe age of seventy-six; as I write this, I am still twenty-six years behind him in the game, my catching-up prospects being very dim. Second, because what he believed in for most of his life, allegedly to its very end, has been utter garbage to me at least since the age of sixteen, though no benefit of foresight can be claimed here, let alone obtained. Third, because the baseness of the human heart and the vulgarity of the human mind never expire with the demise of their most gifted exponents. What I must disclaim, however, is any pretense to expertise in the field I am wading through. As I say, I am no spy buff. Of Philby's life, for instance, I know only the bare bones, if that. I've never read his biography, in English or in Russian, nor do I expect I ever will. Of the options available to a human being, he chose the most redundant one: to betray one set of people to another. This sort of subject is not worthy of study; intuition will suffice. I am also not terribly good with dates, though I normally try to check them. So the reader should decide for himself at this stage whether he is going to proceed with this stuff any further. I certainly will. I suppose I should bill the following as a fantasy. Well, it isn't.

XVI

On Marchember umpteenth, nineteen filthy-fine, in Brooklyn, New York, agents of the FBI arrested a Soviet spy. In a small apartment filled with photo equipment, on a floor strewn with microfilm, stood a little middle-aged man with beady eyes, an aquiline profile, and a balding forehead, his Adam's apple moving busily: he was swallowing a scrap of paper containing some top-secret information. Otherwise the man offered no resistance. Instead, he proudly declared: "I am Colonel of the Red Army Rudolf Abel, and I demand to be treated as such in accordance with the Geneva Convention." Needless to say, the tabloids went ape, in the States and all over the place. The colonel was tried, got donkey years, and was locked up, if I remember correctly, in Sing Sing. There he mostly played pool. In nineteen sissy-through or thereabouts, he was exchanged at Checkpoint Charlie in Berlin for Gary Powers, the unlucky U-2 pilot who made headlines for the last time just a few years ago when he went down again, this time near L.A., in a helicopter, and for good. Rudolf Abel returned to Moscow, retired, and made no headlines, save that he became the most feared pool shark in Moscow and its vicinity. He died in nineteen-cementy and was buried, with scaled-down military honors, at Novodevichye Cemetery in Moscow. No stamp was issued for him. Or was one? I may have missed it. Or the British literary paper of humble origin missed it. Perhaps he didn't earn a stamp: what's four years in Sing Sing to a lifelong record? And besides, he wasn't a foreigner, just another displaced native. In any case, no stamp for Rudolf Abel, just a tomb-stone.

XVII

But what do we read on this tombstone? We read: *Willie Fischer, a.k.a. Rudolf Abel, 1903–1971*, in Cyrillic, of course. Now, that's a bit too long for a stamp's legend, but not for us. (Ah, dear reader, look at what we've got here: spies, stamps, cemeteries, tombstones! But wait, there's more: poets, painters, assassinations, exiles, Arab sheikhs, murder weapons, stolen cars, and more stamps!) But let's try to make this long story short. Once upon a time—in 1936–39 in Spain, to be precise—there were two men: Willie Fischer and Rudolf Abel. They were colleagues and they were close friends. So close that other employees of the same enterprise called them "Fischerabel." But nothing unto-ward, dear reader, they were simply inseparable, partly be-cause of the work they did. They were a team. The enterprise for which they toiled was the Soviet intelligence outfit that handled the messy side of the Spanish Civil War's business. That's the side where you find bullet-riddled bodies miles away from the trenches. Anyway, the outfit's boss was a fellow by the name of Orlov, who prior to his Spanish as-signment headed the entire Soviet counterintelligence op-eration for Western Europe out of an office in the Soviet Embassy in the French capital. We'll play with him later—or, as the case may be, he will play with us. For the moment let's say that Orlov was very close with Fischerabel. Not as close as they were with each other, but very close. Nothing untoward there either, since Orlov was married. He was just the boss, and Fischerabel were his right and his left hand at once. Both hands were dirty.

XVIII

But life is cruel, it separates even the best of friends. In 1939 the Spanish Civil War is ending, and Fischerabel and Orlov part ways. They check out of the Hotel Nacional in Madrid, where the entire operation was run, and travel— some by air, some by boat, still others by the submarine that carried the Spanish Gold Reserve, which was handed over to the Soviets by Juan Negrín, the Republican government's Finance Minister—in opposite directions. Orlov disappears into thin air. Fischerabel return to Moscow and continue to work for the old establishment, filing reports, training new recruits—the kind of thing that field men do when they are out of the field. In 1940, when Rudolf Abel gets transferred to the Far East, where trouble is brewing on the Mongolian border, he makes a wrong move and gets killed. Then comes World War II. Throughout it Willie Fischer remains in Moscow, trains more recruits—this time perhaps with greater gusto, since German is his father tongue—but he generally feels fallen by the wayside, bypassed for promotion, aging. This fretful state of affairs ends only in nineteen faulty-ape, when he's suddenly taken out of mothballs and given a new assignment. "The kind of assignment," he remarks cryptically on the eve of his departure to one of his former sidekicks from the old Spanish days, "the kind of assignment that a field man's entire life is the preparation for." Then he takes off. The next time his pals hear of him is x years later when, nabbed by the feds in that Brooklyn apartment, good old Willie sings, "I am Colonel of the Red Army Rudolf Abel, and I demand . . ."

XIX

Of the many virtues available to us, dear reader, patience is best known for being rewarded. In fact, patience is an integral part of every virtue. What's virtue without patience? Just good temper. In a certain line of work, however, that won't pay. It may, in fact, be deadly. A certain line of work requires patience, and a hell of a lot of it. Perhaps because it is the only virtue detectable in a certain line of work, those engaged in it zero in on patience with a vengeance. So bear with us, dear reader. Consider yourself a mole.

XX

The twang of a guitar, the sound of a shot fired in a poorly lit alley. It's Spain, shortly before the end of the Civil War (not ending through neglect on the part of Orlov's good offices, of course, but in Moscow they may see things differently). On this night Orlov has been summoned to see a certain official from Moscow aboard a ship lying at anchor in Barcelona. As the head of Soviet intelligence in Spain, he reports only to Stalin's own secretariat: directly. Orlov senses a trap and runs. He grabs his wife, takes the elevator down, tells a bellboy in the lobby to get him a taxi. Cut. Panorama of the ragged Pyrenees, roar of a two-engine airplane. Cut. Next morning in Paris, sound of an accordion, panorama of, say, the Place de la Concorde. Cut. An office in the Soviet Embassy on the rue de Varenne. Stalin's whiskers above the door of a Mosler safe flung wide open; a pin-striped wrist with cuffs stuffing a satchel with French banknotes and files. Cut. Blackout.

XXI

Sorry, no close-ups. Orlov's disappearing act offers none. Still, if one stares at the blackout intently enough, one can make out a letter. This letter is addressed to Comrade Stalin, and it says something to the effect that he, Orlov, now severs his links with godless Communism and its hateful, criminal system; that he and his wife choose freedom, and should a single hair fall from the heads of their aging parents, who are still in the clutches of this system, then he, Orlov, will spill *urbi et orbi* all the dirty top-secret beans in his possession. The letter goes into an envelope, the address on that envelope is that of the offices of *Le Monde*, or maybe *Figaro*. At any rate, it's in Paris. Then the pen dips into the ink pot again: another letter. This one is to Leon Trotsky, and it goes something like this: I, the undersigned, am a Russian merchant who just escaped with my life from the Soviet Union via Siberia to Japan. While in Moscow and staying in a hotel, I overheard, by pure chance, a conversation in the next room. The subject was an attempt on your life, and through the crack in the door I even managed to espy your would-be assassin. He is young, tall, and speaks perfect Spanish. I thought it my duty to warn you. The letter is signed with an alias, but Don Levin, the Trotsky scholar and biographer, has positively identified its author as Orlov, and if I am not mistaken, the scholar has received Orlov's personal confirmation. This letter is postmarked Nagasaki and the address on it is in Mexico City. It, too, however ends up in a local tabloid (*La Prensa Latina? El País?*), since Trotsky, still smarting from the second attempt on his life (in the course of which his American secretary was murdered by a would-be world-famous muralist—David Alfaro Siqueiros—with the assistance of a would-be world-famous, indeed a Nobel Prize–winning, poet, Pablo Neruda), habitually forwards all threats and warnings he receives to the press. And Orlov must be aware of this, if only because for the last three years he has been in the habit of perusing quite a few periodicals in Spanish. While having his coffee, say. In the lobby of the Nacional, or in his suite there on the sixth floor.

XXII

Where he used to entertain all sorts of people. Including Ramón Mercader, Trotsky's third and successful assassin. Who was simply Orlov's employee, much the same as Fischerabel, working for the same outfit. So if Orlov really wanted to warn Trotsky, he could have told him a lot more about Ramón Mercader than that he was young, tall, handsome, and spoke perfect Spanish. Yet the reason for the second letter was not Trotsky; the reason was the first letter, whose addressee wasn't Stalin. To put it more neatly, the Stalin letter, printed in *Le Monde*, addressed the West, while the Trotsky letter, though it went literally to the Western Hemisphere, addressed the East. The purpose of the first was to win Orlov good standing abroad, preferably in the intelligence community. The second was a letter home, informing his pals in Moscow headquarters that he was not spilling the beans, though he could: about Mercader, for instance. So they, the pals, could go ahead with the Trotsky job if they cared to. (They did, though no tear should be shed, since Trotsky, who drowned the only genuine Russian Revolution that ever took place—the Kronstadt Uprising—in blood, wasn't any better than the spawn of hell who ordered his assassination. Stalin, after all, was an opportunist. Trotsky was an ideologue. The mere thought that they could have swapped places makes one wince.) Moreover, should the authorship of the second letter ever come to light, as it did in Don Levin's research, it could only enhance Orlov's credentials as a true anti-Stalinist. Which is precisely what he wasn't. He had no ideological or any other disagreement with Stalin. He was simply running for his dear life, so he threw the dogs a bone to munch on. They munched on it for a couple of decades.

XXIII

Blackout. Time for the credits. Ten years ago an émigré Russian publishing house in France published a book called *A Hunter Upside Down*. The title suggests one of those cartoon puzzles in which you have to look for the hidden figures: hunters, rabbits, farmers, birds, and so on. The author's name was Victor Henkin. He was Willie Fischer's sidekick from the good old Spanish days, and the Fischerabel story is what the book is all about, although it aims to be an autobiography. Some of the Orlov tidbits also hail from there. The book should have been a hit, if only because people in the know on the longer side of the Atlantic still believed that they had Rudolf Abel. By the same token, they still believed that Orlov, who had joined them, truly worked for that side whose decorations one may see proudly displayed on his chest in one of Orlov's rare close-ups, in a book published with great fanfare in the States well after Orlov's death in 1972. But no fanfare for Henkin's book. When an American publisher tried to get a contract for it, he ran into a copyright wall. There were also some minor scandals over alleged plagiarism in the German or French edition, it was in the courts, and for all I know Henkin lost. Now he works for a radio station in Munich that broadcasts into Russia—almost the flip side of the job he had for donkey's years at Radio Moscow broadcasting in French. Or else he is retired. A Russian émigré, with a highly checkered record . . . Not trustworthy,

presumably paranoid . . . Living in the past, ill-tempered
. . . Still, he is free now, he's got the right papers. He can
go to the Gare de Lyon, board a train, and just like fifty
years ago, after a nightlong journey, he can arrive in Madrid,
the city of his youth and adventure. All he has to do is to
cross the large station square and he'll be standing in front
of the Nacional; he could do it with his eyes closed. Still
with his eyes closed, he can enter a lobby that teemed fifty
years ago with Orlovs, Fischers, Abels, Hemingways, Phil-
bys, Orwells, Mercaders, Malrauxs, Negríns, Ehrenburgs,
and lesser lights like himself: with all those who have taken
part in our story thus far or to whom we, one way or another,
owe credit. Should he open his eyes, however, he'll discover
that the Nacional is closed. It's been closed, according to
some—mostly the young—for the last ten years; according
to others, for the last fifty. Neither the young nor the old
seem to know who pays the property tax, but maybe in Spain
they do things differently.

XXIV

And in case you think, dear reader, that we've forgotten
him, let's extract Kim Philby from the crowd in the lobby,
and let's ask him what he's doing there. "I'm with the paper,
actually," we'll hear. "Covering the war." Let's press him as
to whose side he's on, and let's imagine that, just for an
instant, he'll talk straight. "Switching at the moment. Orders." He may as well motion slightly upward with his chin,
toward the sixth floor of the Nacional. For I am absolutely
convinced that it was Orlov who told Kim Philby in 1937 in
Madrid or thereabouts to change his tune in *The Times* from
pro-Republican to pro-Franco, for reasons of deeper cover.
If, as the story goes, Philby was meant to be a long shot
aimed at the *sancta sanctorum* of British intelligence, he had

better go pro-Fascist. It's not that Orlov foresaw which way
the Spanish show might go, though he could have had an
inkling; he simply thought, or knew, that Philby should be
played for keeps. And he could think this way, or know this,
only if he was privy to the file that the Russians by then had
on Philby, who was recruited in 1933, or to the actual recruitment of Philby. The first is certain, the second is possible. In any case, Orlov knew Philby personally, which is
what he tried to tell the hapless FBI man who interviewed
him in 1944, in Iowa, I think, where he then dwelled, having
emigrated to the United States from Canada. At that point,
it seems, Orlov was finally ready to spill the beans; but the
FBI man paid no attention to the mention of some Englishman with a stutter who worked for the Soviet Union, which,
on top of everything, was at that time an American ally. So
Orlov decided not to press this any further, and Kim Philby
headed for the stamp.

XXV

With these beans still intact in his hippothalamus on the one
hand, and on the other having penned a couple of novels
filled with the standard field-man yarn, but of the Russian
variety, Orlov was no doubt of some interest to the budding
CIA in the late 1940s. I have no idea, dear reader, who
approached whom: I haven't studied Orlov's life or its available record. Not my line of work. I am not even an amateur;
I am just piecing all these things together in my spare time,
not out of curiosity even but to quell the sensation of utter
disgust caused by the sight of that literary paper's cover.
Self-therapy, then, and who cares about sources so long as
it works. At any rate, regardless of who approached whom,
Orlov seems to have been retained by the CIA from the
1950s onward. Whether he was on the payroll or just free-

lancing is hard to say; but to judge by his decorations, as well as by the marginal evidence of his subsequent penmanship, it's a fair assumption. Most likely, he was engaged by the agency in an advisory capacity; nowadays this sort of thing is called consultancy. A good question would be whether the fellows back in Moscow knew of his new affiliation. Assuming, for Orlov's sake, that he didn't notify them himself, for that would still be suicidal, and assuming that the newly born agency couldn't be penetrated—if only for the sake of definitions—the fellows in Moscow were in the dark. Still, they had reason to believe that Orlov was around, if only as an aspiring thriller writer. As they had no news of him for a couple of decades, they may have wondered. And when you wonder, you imagine the worst. In a certain line of work, it's only prudent. They might even have wanted to check.

XXVI

And they had the wherewithal. So they took it out of mothballs and put it in place. Still, they were in no hurry. Not until nineteen filthy-fine, that is. Then they suddenly felt pressed. And on Marchember umpteenth, Willie Fischer gets himself arrested in Brooklyn, New York, by those FBI men and declares, *urbi et orbi*: I am Rudolf Abel. And the tabloids go ape, in the States and all over the place. And Orlov doesn't squeak. Evidently he doesn't want to see his old pal again.

XXVII

What was so special about nineteen filthy-fine, you may ask, and why was it imperative now to check the state of the beans in Orlov's hippothalamus? Even if they were still all there, hadn't they gone stale and useless? And who says old pals must be seen? Well, dear reader, brace yourself for loony assertions. For now we are going to show you, in a big way, that we haven't forgotten our subject. Now we are cooking literally with oil.

XXVIII

Contrary to popular demonology, the foreign policy of the Soviet Union was, from the beginning of its existence, always opportunistic. I am using this term in its literal, not its derogatory, sense. Opportunism is the core of any foreign policy, regardless of the degree of confidence a state may have in itself. It means the use of opportunity: objectively present, imagined, or created. For most of its sorry history, the Soviet Union remained a highly insecure customer, traumatized by the circumstances of its birth, its deportment vis-à-vis the rest of the world fluctuating between caution and hostility. (Nobody fitted the width of that margin better than Molotov, Stalin's Foreign Minister.) As a consequence, the Soviet Union could afford only objectively present opportunities. Which it seized, notably in 1939, grabbing the Baltic states and half of Poland, as offered to Stalin by Hitler, and in the final stages of the war, when the Soviet Union found itself in possession of Eastern Europe. As for the opportunities imagined—the 1928 march on Warsaw, the 1936–39 adventure in Spain, and the 1940 Finnish campaign—the Soviet Union paid dearly for these flights of fancy (though in the case of Spain it was reimbursed with the country's gold reserve). The first to pay, of course, was the General Staff, almost entirely beheaded by 1941. Yet the worst consequence of all these fantasies, I suppose, was that the Red Army's performance against a handful of Finnish troops made Hitler's temptation to attack Russia absolutely irresistible.

The real price for the pleasure of playing with imagined opportunities was the total number of divisions assigned to Operation Barbarossa.

XXIX

Victory in the war didn't change Soviet foreign policy much, since the spoils of war hardly matched the gigantic human and industrial losses the war inflicted. The scale of the devastation was extraordinary; the main postwar cry was reconstruction. This was carried out mainly by means of stripping the conquered territories of their technology and transplanting it into the U.S.S.R. Psychologically satisfactory, this, however, could not put the nation ahead industrially. The country remained a second- or third-rate power, its only claim to consequence being its sheer size and its military machine. Formidable and state-of-the-art as the latter tried to be, the comfort the nation could derive from it was largely of the narcissistic sort, given the cumulative strength of its supposed adversaries and the emergence of nuclear weapons. What really fell under the onslaught of that machine, however, was the Soviet Union's foreign policy—its options defined, as it were, by its legions. To this reversal of Clausewitz one must add the growing rigidity of a state apparatus petrified by the fear of personal responsibility and imbued with the notion that the first word and the last word on all matters, above all on matters of foreign policy, belonged to Stalin. Under the circumstances, diplomatic initiatives, let alone attempts at creating opportunities, were unthinkable. What's more, the distinction between a created opportunity and an imagined one can be galling. It takes a mind accustomed to the dynamics of a well-heeled economy (to the accumulation of wealth, surplus production, and so on) to tell one from another. If you are short on that sort of expertise, you may confuse the one thing for the other. And well into the 1950s, the Soviet Union was short on it. It still is.

XXX

And yet in the late 1950s the Soviet Union undertakes something rather spectacular, something that leaves you with the sense that, with the death of Stalin in 1953, Soviet foreign policy comes to life. After the Suez debacle in the autumn of 1956, the U.S.S.R. undertakes an unusually well-coordinated and well-sustained push toward the eastern Mediterranean and North Africa. This departure is as sudden as it is successful. Its goal, as hindsight avails us, is control of the Middle East, or, more pointedly, of its oil fields. The logic behind this move is simple and fairly Marxist: whoever controls energy resources controls production. In other words, the idea is to bring the Western industrial democracies to their knees. Whether to do it directly, by sending troops into the region, or by proxy, by supporting the local Arab regimes and turning them pro-Soviet, is, for the moment, a matter of circumstance and logistics; the proxy option is obviously preferable. And initially this works: a number of Arab states in the region go pro-Soviet, and so fast that one may think that these societies were ripe for Communist ideology, or at least accustomed to that sort of discourse. They were not. The few existing CP cells in King Farouk's Egypt, for instance, were wiped out under Nasser entirely, their members turned into cellmates or dangled from the rope. An even greater Marxist dearth marked—still does—the rest of the Islamic world, east and west of Cairo: the culture of the Book won't abide another one, especially one written by a Jew. Still, the first Soviet steps in the region met with success, the degree of which could be explained only by the newcomer's recourse to some sort of network within those societies, and with access to all its levels. Such a network couldn't be of German origin (not even in Egypt), since Reinhard Gehlen, the postwar head of West German intelligence, sold his entire file cabinet in the late 1940s to the United States. Nor could it be the French, who were a marginal presence in the region to begin with, and then fiercely loyal to France. That left the local pro-British element, presumably taking its cue—in the vacuum left by the master race's withdrawal—from some local resident (stationed, say, in Beirut). Out of nostalgia, perhaps, out of the hope for the empire's return. At any rate, it certainly wasn't the novelty of the Russian version of the infidel that nearly delivered the region to the Soviets in the late 1950s; it was a created opportunity.

XXXI

Imagine this blueprint on a drawing board somewhere in Moscow thirty-five or forty years ago. It says: There is a vacuum left in the Middle East by the British. Fill it up. Support new Arab leaders: one by one, or bundle them together into some sort of confederation, say, into a United Arab Republic or League. Give them arms, give them anything. Drive them into debt. Tell them that they can pay you back if they hike their oil prices. Tell them that they can be unreasonable about that, that you'll back them up all the way; and you've got nukes. In no time, the West cries uncle, the Arabs get rich, and you control the Arabs. You become top dog, as befits the first socialist country in the world. As for how to get your foot in the door, it's all taken care of. You'll get along with these guys just fine, they don't like Jews either.

XXXII

And imagine this blueprint being not of your own manufacture. For it simply could not have been. In order to conceive of it, you would have to be acquainted with the region, and intimately so. You ought to know who is who there, what this sheikh or that colonel is up to, his pedigree and hangups. In Moscow and its vicinity, there is nobody with that sort of data. Furthermore, you ought to know about oil revenues, the market, its fluctuations, stocks, this or that industrial democracy's annual intake of crude, tankers' fleets, refineries, stuff like that. There is nobody acquainted with this sort of thing on your staff, or moonlighting elsewhere either. And even if to imagine that such a fellow existed, a doctrinaire Marxist and a bookworm, with the clearance to read Western periodicals—even if such a fellow existed, and came up with such a blueprint, he would have to have a godfather in the Politburo to place this blueprint on the drawing board; and placing it there would give that member of the Politburo an edge that his colleagues wouldn't tolerate for a split second. Ultimately this plan could not have been conceived by a Russian, if only because Russia herself has oil; actually plenty of it. You don't regard as a source of energy something you waste. Had it been homemade, this blueprint would never have seen the light of day. Besides, it's too damn close to an imagined opportunity. The very reason that it is on your drawing board, though, is that it has nothing to do with the native imagination. That alone should be enough to qualify it as a created opportunity. For it comes from without, and its main attraction is that it is foreign-made. To members of the Soviet Politburo in the 1950s, this blueprint was what blue jeans are to their kids. They liked it very much. Still, they wanted to check the label. And they had the wherewithal.

XXXIII

And while they are checking the label, dear reader, let me give you something straight, without the author's interference. Harold Adrian Russell Philby, "Kim" to his chums in England and especially in Russia, where this nickname rang no Kipling bell, being instead a brand-new Soviet name, popular especially in the 1930s, since it was the acronym of Kommunisticheskii Internatsional Molodezhi (Communist International of Youth), was born in Ambala, India, in—as the stamp rightly says—1912. His daddy was Harry St. John Philby, a great English Arabist and explorer who subsequently converted to Islam and became an adviser to King Ibn Saud of guess which country. The boy was educated at Westminster and Trinity College, Cambridge, where he read history and economics and was a member of the Apostles. After Cambridge he freelanced for various London publications, and in this capacity he went in 1937 to Spain to cover the Civil War and later on was taken up by *The Times*, for which he covered the initial stages of World War II. That's essentially what was known about the twenty-eight-year-old man by 1940, when he was employed by MIG, the counterintelligence branch of the fabled British SIS, and given the job of handling anti-Communist counterespionage matters. Presumably at his own request. During the war years he moves rapidly through the ranks, gets stationed in Istanbul, and becomes, in 1946, the head of Soviet counterintelligence. That's a big job, which he abandons only three years later, having been posted as first secretary of the British Embassy in Washington, that is, as chief liaison officer between the SIS and the CIA, where, among other things, he becomes a close friend of James Angleton, the CIA's head of counterintelligence. On the whole, it is a marvelous career. The man is awarded the OBE for his wartime services, he is greatly respected by the Foreign Office and the gentlemen of the press, and is groomed to become the head of the SIS. That, essentially, is what was known to his peers and his superiors about this thirty-nine-year-old man in 1951, when something rather untoward occurs. Two of his old pals, way back from Cambridge days, Guy Burgess and Donald Maclean, turn out to be Soviet spies and flee to the Soviet Union. What's worse, a suspicion lurks in the heads of people-in-the-know on both sides of the Atlantic that it was Philby who warned them off. He is investigated, nothing is proved, doubt persists, and he is asked to resign. Life is cruel, the best of pals can bring you down. Such was the verdict of many, including the Foreign Office. He resumes his journalistic career—after all, he is still in his forties—but the inquiries continue. Some people just don't give up. In 1955 Harold Macmillan, then the British Foreign Secretary, in a statement before the Commons, fully exonerates Philby of any wrongdoing. His slate wiped clean, Philby obtains, through the Foreign Office's misty-eyed assistance, the job of foreign correspondent for *The Economist* and *The Observer* in Beirut, whereto he sails in 1956, never to see the chalk cliffs of Sussex again.

XXXIV

It's three years later that the fellows in Moscow click their tongues, admiring the blueprint. Still, they want to check the label. For what is a clean slate to some is the writing on the wall to others. They figure that the Brits couldn't get any goods on a Brit because they were searching the Brits; they were doomed because they were engaged in a tautology. For the job of a mole is to outsmart the natives. As for the Russian end—should they ever gain access to it, which is highly unlikely—it would reveal nothing either. The identity of a mole, especially a mole so highly placed, wouldn't be known even to the case officer running him, it would be only a code name or a bunch of digits at best. That's as much as even the most knowledgeable defector can tell you, not to mention the fact that he would be defecting straight into the arms of the SIS counterintelligence section, and guess who is in charge of that. The only two people who might know his identity would be the present Soviet head of counterintelligence, and that far no Brit could ever go, or the counterintelligence officer who recruited the man initially. A sergeant, by definition, is older than his recruit, and since we are talking here about the 1950s, that sergeant should by now be either dead or indeed running the whole Soviet counterintelligence show. Most likely, though, he is dead, since the best way to protect the recruit's identity is to kill the sergeant. Still, in 1933, when a twenty-one-year-old Cambridge graduate was recruited, things were not as watertight as they are now in the 1950s, when we are checking the label, and the good old—no, dead—sergeant might have said something to his superior (who was presumably dead, too: those purges of the state security apparatus in the late 1930s were not for nothing) or had a witness to the recruitment, or the poor young witless recruit himself might have rubbed shoulders with somebody who later went bad. After all, his choice of pals is what brought him down, though for a while they delivered all the comings and goings of the Anglo-American Atomic Energy Commission. (Good flies on the wall they were, but now look at them coming here to roost!) Let bygones be bygones, of course; but if we are to carry out this blueprint, we need something tighter than an exoneration by Harold Macmillan—bless his heart—in the Commons, we need complete immunity for our man against any whistleblowers. No surprises, no voices from the past, no skeletons in the closet. So who are those guys he might have rubbed shoulders with before they went bad? Where are their death certificates?

XXXV

And they can't find Orlov's. And Willie Fischer sings his world-famous Abel lyric. And Orlov doesn't want to see his old pal. And they conclude that he is either dead or not suicidal. And so they move into the Middle East, into Egypt, Syria, Yemen, Iraq, Libya; they seize the created opportunity. They shower new Arab leaders with planeloads and shiploads of military surplus, advisers, and whatnot; they drive those nations into debt. And the advisers advise the leaders to hike oil prices to pay them back. And the leaders do just that: by high margins and with impunity, backed by this new set of infidels with nukes. And the West starts to kowtow and cry "UN"—but that's just the first syllable of "uncle." And now the faithful, the fidel and the infidel, hate the Jews together. It all works just like the man said it would.

XXXVI

But life is cruel, and one day the new oil-producing pals get greedy. They create a cartel, OPEC by name, and start filling up their own coffers. They put the squeeze on the West, but not for our sake! They also quarrel among themselves. Anyhow, they get richer than their old masters, not to mention us. That wasn't in the blueprint. The architect of our Middle East policy, the son of King Ibn Saud's adviser, an observer and economist to boot, our great and unexposed— well, technically speaking—secret agent should have been able to foresee this turn of events! Thus far everything went according to the plan: he delivered, and now this. Well, he better tell us what to do next. Basically, we need him here now, on a day-to-day basis. Anyway, it's safer for him here in Moscow; fewer temptations as well. He can concentrate better. It ain't Beirut.

XXXVII

It certainly was much colder. At least for the spy who came in from the warmth. At long last. Actually, exactly thirty years after he was recruited. Whatever that means, except that he is fifty-one years old now and has to start a new life. Which, after all, isn't that hard, since the local lads go out of their privileged ways to assist you; and besides, at fifty-one no life is that new, no country is that foreign. Especially if you have spied for that country all your adult life. And especially if you did it not for money but out of conviction. So the place should be familiar to you, at least mentally. For it's the conviction that is your home, your ultimate comfort: you blow all your life savings on furnishing it. If the world around you is poor and colorless, then you stuff this place with all manner of mental candelabra and Persian carpets. If that world used to be rich in texture, then you'll settle for mental monochrome, for a few abstract chairs.

XXXVIII

And, as we are on our last leg, dear suffering reader, let's get a bit anachronistic. There is a certain type of Englishman who appreciates frugality and inefficiency: the one who nods contentedly at a stalled elevator or at one boy being caned for another boy's prank. He recognizes botch and bungle the way one recognizes one's relatives. He recognizes himself in a peeling, wobbly railing, damp hotel sheets, slovenly trees in a soot-laden window, bad tobacco, the smelly carriage of a delayed train, bureaucratic obstacles, indecision and sloth, impotent shrugs; certainly in poorly cut serge clothes, in gray. So he loves Russia; mainly from a distance, as he cannot afford the trip except perhaps later in life, in his fifties or sixties, when he retires. And he'd do a lot for Russia, for his inefficient yet dramatic, soulful, *Doctor Zhivago*–like (the movie, not the book) Russia, where the twentieth century hasn't yet set its Goodyear tire, where his childhood still continues. He doesn't want his Russia to go American. He wants her to stay intense and awkward, in brown woolen stockings with broad pink garters: no nylons, and please no pantyhose. It is his equivalent of rough trade, of the working-class lads for whom his old Cambridge pals will be prowling London pubs for the rest of their lives. He is straight, though; and it's Russia for him, if it's not Germany or Austria.

XXXIX

And if Russia is Communist, so much the better. Especially if it is 1933 and Germany is out of the question. And if somebody with a slight accent asks you to work for Russia, and you are just twenty-one, you say yes, because it's unlike anything else, and it sounds subversive. If school teaches you anything, it is to belong to a party, or at least to a club, and to form a cell. The CP is just another Apostles, a sort of frat, and it preaches brotherhood. At any rate, you go for what your pals do, and to them "the world proletariat" conjures up rough trade on a grand scale. And in a while you hear that slight accent again and you are asked to do a job —nothing big, though faintly foul. And you do it, and now the slight accent has the goods on you. If he is smart, the next time he asks you to do something, he doesn't mention the world proletariat, he mentions Russia. Because you won't do it, say, for India, though India, technically speaking, is part of the world, not to mention the proletariat. Fifty years ago social fiction was still ethnocentric, and so were spies. More Chekhov for you, then; more of Constance Garnett's Tolstoy on the train ride to Spain, for it's the time. It is also the place. A bright young thing can sample that brotherhood here: its blood, lice, hope, despair, defeat, apathy. Instead, he hangs around in the lobby of the Nacional, sees some scum upstairs, and is told—to his secret relief, no doubt— to switch sides, for the sake of the greater good. That's how a bright young thing learns about the big picture, a.k.a. the future. The next time he hears the slight accent he knows it is a voice from the future. The accent will be different, since the first slightly accented throat has already been cut for the bright young thing's eventual safety; and if that throat had a beloved, she's already digging the permafrost of her twenty-five-year sentence in the Russian Far East, against the majestic snowy backdrop of a would-be Zhivago movie. Yet by the time the voice from the future enters your ear, there is World War II on your hands, Russia is an ally, and the SIS wants you to take part in the war effort. The big picture barges into view, and you ask for a Russian job. And since you are a gentleman, you are welcomed to it by senior gentlemen who can be identified as such, however, mainly by which door they push in a loo. Well, not even then.

XL

So you know the country where you end up thirty years later at the ripe age of fifty-one. Full of beans, no doubt, but past your prime. Ah, the chalk cliffs of Sussex! Ah, the accursed island! Ah, the whole Pax Britannica! They'll pay dearly for ruining such a brilliant career, for putting a clever man out to grass at the apogee of his ascent! A clever man knows how to get even with an empire: by using another empire. Never the twain shall meet. That's what makes a big picture grow bigger. Not a tooth for a tooth but a mouthful for a tooth! Perhaps the greatest satisfaction of every spy is the thought that he is playing Fate, that it's he who pulls strings. Or else cuts them. He fashions himself after Clotho, or perhaps after Arachne. A *deus in machina* that runs on petrol, he may not even catch the irony of being situated in Mazoutny Lane— well, not initially. At any rate, *deus* or deuce, controlling oil fields is a greater game than betraying the secrets of British intelligence to the Russians. There is not much left to betray in London anyway, whereas here the stakes are huge. The entire world order is at stake. Whoever wins here, it will be *his* victory. He, an observer and economist to boot, didn't read *Das Kapital* and *The Seven Pillars of Wisdom* for nothing. Not to mention that the victory will be Russia's, since what can you expect of democracies: no resolve. Imagine Russia, his slovenly brown-woolen-stockings-cum-pink-garters-clad Russia, as the world's master, and not because of the nukes or the ballistic missiles only: imagine her, soulful and slothful, with all the Arabian peninsula's oil revenues under her pillow—uncertain, Chekhovian, anti-rationalist! A far better master (nay, mistress) of the world than his own Cartesian West, so easy to fool, himself being a good example. And should worse come to worse, should it be not Russia but some local, some sheikh or dictator, it's fine by him, too. In fact, Daddy would be proud of him if it should all go to the Saudis.

XLI

And there it went, practically all of it. So much of it, in any case, that it should be the Saudis issuing this stamp, not the Russians. Well, perhaps one day they will. Or the Iraqis, or the Iranians. Whoever is to master the oil monopoly should issue the stamp. Ah, Muslims, Muslims! Where would they be now, were it not for the Soviet foreign policy of the 1960s and 1970s; that is, were it not for the late Mr. Philby? Imagine them unable to purchase a Kalashnikov, let alone a rocket launcher. They'd be unfit for the front page, they wouldn't make even the backdrop for a pack of camels . . . Ah, but life is cruel, and beneficiaries don't remember their benefactors; nor, for that matter, do victims remember the villain. And perhaps they shouldn't. Perhaps the origins of good and bad are better off remaining obscured—especially the latter. Does it really matter what clouds the godhead: the concept of dialectical materialism or the Prophet's turban? Can we tell one from the other? In the final analysis, there is no hierarchy between the cherry orchard and the triviality of the sand; it is only a matter of preference. For men, as well as for their money. Money, evidently, lacks a conscience of its own, and the jackpot goes to the desert simply out of its kinship for multitudes. On the whole, like a certain kind of Englishman, money has an eastward longing, if only because that realm is extremely populous. A secret agent, then, is but an early bird, a big bank's harbinger. And if he settles there, in the East, and goes native, helped along by local liquor or a willing maiden, well, so what? Have Noah's pigeons returned? Ah, dear reader, imagine a letter sent today or in the near future from Moscow to Riyadh. What do you think it will contain? A birthday greeting, vacation plans, news of a loss in the family, complaints about the cold climate? No, more likely a request for money. Say, for an investment in the well-being of Riyadh's fellow Muslims on Soviet territory. And it will be written in English, this letter, and it won't be worth perlustration. A postmaster, perhaps, having glanced at its return address, may lift the crescent of the eyebrow obscured by his traditional headgear, but after a momentary hesitation he'll shove this envelope into an appropriate slot: an envelope with a Philby stamp on it.

XLII

A glum thought, nods the exhausted reader. But wouldn't things have come to this juncture anyway, even without our English friend's assistance? Sure they would have, given the so-called dynamics of the modern world, which means the population explosion and the industrial gluttony of the West. These two would suffice; no need for a third party, let alone for an individual agency. At best, our English friend just articulated what was in the air or, as it were, afoot. Other than that, he was utterly insignificant. Sooner or later this was bound to happen, Kim or no Kim, Russia or no Russia. Well, without Russia perhaps it would have taken a touch longer, but so what. Individuals are incidental, it's all economics, isn't it? In this sense, even if an individual exists, he doesn't. Sounds a bit solipsistic, in a Marxist way; but our English friend would be the first to appreciate that. After all, historical necessity was his motto, his credo, his occasional rebuke to pangs of conscience. And after that, for all the professional hazards of one's trade, a belief in the imminent triumph of one's cause is safe betting, isn't it? (What if your cause triumphs in your lifetime, eh?) At any rate, from the standpoint of historical necessity, our man was of no use, at best he was redundant. For the objective of history was to make the Arabs rich, the West poor, and the Russians bob and bubble in limbo. This is what the bottom line says in that true bel canto of necessity, and who is the author to argue with it? A penny, then, for our friend's sense of mission; but not much more for the author's flight of fancy either. Anyway, what are his sources?

XLIII

"Sources?" shrugs the author contemptuously. Who needs them? Who can trust sources? And since when? And does the reader realize what he is getting into by suspecting his author of being wrong, not to mention by proving it? Aren't you afraid, dear reader, that your successful refutation of the author's little theory might boil down to an inescapable conclusion on your part that the dark brown substance in which you find yourself up to your nostrils in the world today is immanent, preordained on high, at the very least sponsored by Mother Nature? Do you really need that? Whereas the author aims to spare you this anguish by proving that the aforementioned substance is of human manufacture. In this respect, your author is a true humanist. No, dear reader, you don't need sources. Neither sources nor tributaries of defectors' evidence; not even electronic precipitation raining onto your lap from the satellite-studded heaven. With our sort of flow, all you need is an estuary, a mouth really; and beyond that, a sea with the bottom line for a horizon. Well, that much you've already seen.

XLIV

Nobody, though, knows the future. Least of all those who believe in historical determinism; and next to them, spies and journalists. Perhaps that's why the former often disguise themselves as the latter. Of course, when it comes to the future, any occupation is good cover. Still, information gathering beats them all, since any bit of information, including a secret one, is generated by the past: almost by definition, information deals with *faits accomplis*. Be it a new bomb, a planned invasion, or a shift in policy, you can learn only about what has already happened, what has already taken place. The paradox of espionage is that the more you know about your adversary, the more your own development is stunted, since this knowledge forces you into trying to catch up with him, to thwart his efforts. He keeps you occupied by altering your own priorities. The better your spies, therefore, the more you fall into dependence on what you learn. You are not acting any longer: you are reacting. This maroons you in the past, with little access to the present and none to the future. Well, not to a future of your own design, let alone your own making. Imagine the Soviets not stealing American atomic secrets and thus spending the last four decades with no nukes to brandish. It could have been a different country; not much more prosperous, perhaps, given the doctrine, but at least the fiasco that we have recently witnessed might have occurred much earlier. If worse came to worse, they might have built a viable version of their socialism. But when you steal something, the catch possesses you, or at least your faculties. Considering the industry of our English friend and his pals, it went far beyond faculties; both hands of their Russian fence were, for quite some time, too busy to build socialism, they were hoarding goods. It could be argued that by betraying the empire in such volume, the boys, in fact, served the empire in a far more substantial manner than its most ardent standard-bearers. For the wealth of secret intelligence passed to the Soviets by the Cambridge class of 1931 mesmerized its recipients to the point of making at least their foreign policy thoroughly contingent on the harvest yielded by their own plants. For the men in Moscow Center, it's been like reading the Sunday papers nonstop seven days a week instead of doing the dishes or taking the kids to the zoo.

XLV

So you can't say it was all in vain, dear reader, can you?
Even though you may be as tired of the subject as the author
himself. Let's claim fatigue, dear reader, and reach no conclusion, and spare ourselves the distrust, not to say the ac-
rimony. On the whole, there is nothing wrong with intricacy
of thought except that it's always achieved at the expense of
thought's depth. Let's get into your Japanese Toyota, which
doesn't consume a lot of the Arab oil product, and go for a
meal. Chinese? Vietnamese? Thai? Indian? Mexican? Hungarian? Polish? The more we bungle abroad, the more varied
our diet. Spanish? Greek? French? Italian? Perhaps the only
good thing about the dead spies was that they had a choice.
But as I write this, the news comes over the wireless that
the Soviet Union is no more Armenian, then? Uzbek? Ka-
zakh? Estonian? For some reason, we don't feel like eating
at home tonight. We don't want to eat English.

XLVI

Why should one bother so much about dead spies? Why
can't one contain the repulsion that rises at the sight of a
literary magazine's cover? Isn't this an overreaction? What's
so new about someone's belief that a just society exists elsewhere, so special about this old Rousseauish lunacy, enacted
or not? Every epoch and every generation is entitled to its
own utopia, and so was Philby's. Sure, the ability to cling
to that sort of garbage beyond the age of down payment (not
to mention the age of retirement) is puzzling, but one can
easily put this down to temperament or to some organic
disorder. A Catholic, a lapsed Catholic especially, can appreciate the predicament, and make a meal out of it if he is
a writer; and so can a heathen. Or did I feel queasy simply

because of the violation of scale, because of the printing enlargement of something small, a stamp really, as a result of which the perforation line takes on the dimension of a cloth fringe: a hanky's, a pillowcase's, a bedspread's, a petticoat's? Maybe I have a problem with fringed linen—a childhood trauma again? The day was hot and for a moment it felt like the enlargement of the stamp on the magazine's cover would go on and on, and envelop Belsize Park, Hampstead, and keep growing, larger and larger. A vision, you know. Too much reading of surrealist poets. Or else too many placards with the Politburo members' faces on the old retina—and the man on the stamp looks like one of them, for all his resemblances to Alec Guinness and Trevor Howard. Plus, of course, the Cyrillic . . . enough to get dizzy. But it wasn't like that. There was no vision. There was just a face, of the kind you wouldn't pay attention to were it not for the caption, which, apart from anything else, was in Cyrillic. At that moment I regretted that I knew Russian. I stood there groping for an English word to shield my wits from the familiarity that the Cyrillic letters exuded. As is often the case with mongrels, I couldn't come up with the right word instantly, and so I turned and left the store. I only remembered the word well outside, but because of what it was, I couldn't get myself back to the store to buy the issue. The word was "treachery."

XLVII

A wonderful word, that. It creaks like a board laid over a chasm. Onomatopoeically, it beats ethics. It has all the euphony of a taboo. For the ultimate boundary of a tribe is its language. If a word doesn't stop you, then a tribe isn't yours. Its vowels and its sibilants don't trigger your instincts, don't send your nerve cells into revulsion, don't make you wince.

Which is to say, your command of this tribe's language is just a matter of mimicry. Which, in turn, points at your belonging to a different evolutionary order. Sublingual or supralingual, at least as regards the language that contains the word "treachery." Which is to prevent the sudden reversal of a bone to jelly. Which is to say, evolution never ends: it still continues. *The Origin of Species* ain't the end of the road; at best a milestone. Which is to say, not all people are people. Might as well add this stamp to the Shells and Mollusks series. It's still a seabed.

XLVIII

You can only enlarge a stamp, you can't reduce it. That is, you can, but reduction will serve no purpose. That is the self-defense of small items, or, if you will, their *raison d'être*. They can only be enlarged. That is, if you are in the graphics department of a literary paper of humble strikebreaking origins. "Blow it up," says the editor, and you cheerfully trot off to the lab. Can't reduce it, can you? Simply wouldn't cross your mind. Nowadays just push a button and it either grows or shrinks. To life-size, or to the size of a louse. Push it once more and the louse is gone. Extinct. Not what the editor asked for, though. He wants it life-size: large. The size of his fantasy, if not his dilemma. "Would you buy this man a drink or shake hands with him?" The old English pickle, except now it's grown chic, with perhaps a touch of retro to it. Ah, these days you push a button and the whole mental swamp gets heaving and gurgling, from the Pas de Calais to the Bering Strait, from the 1930s onward. For that's what history is for the generation currently active: for lapsed Catholics, editors in chief, and the like. For nowadays everything is chic and retro: this isn't the fin-de-siècle for nothing.

There is little to look forward to save your bank statement. Whom would you spy for nowadays if you had access to secret information, if you still ached to defy your class or your country? For the Arabs? For the Japanese? Whose plant, let alone mole, could you be? The village has gone truly global; there is a dearth of allegiance, a dearth of affinity. Ay, you can't betray Europe to Asia any longer, or, I'm afraid, the other way around. It's goodbye to conviction, goodbye to the good old godless Communism. From now on, it's all nostalgia for you, old boy, all retro. From your baggy pants to the matte black of your video, stereo, or dashboard echoing the burnished steel of a gun barrel. That's about how radical, how chic it's going to be: in Europe, but in Asia, too. So go ahead, blow up that louse from the 1950s, for reducing it might rob you of your emotional history. What would you be without that, without a big-time traitor never caught and never recanting in your past? Just a cipher in tax-bracket hell, not dissimilar to that of the old wretch when he still drew his salary in pounds. Go ahead and blow it up; pity it can't be made three-dimensional. Pity, too, that you have no idea, as you are pressing "enlarge," that in less than three weeks the whole thing on whose behalf your man toiled all his life will go bust.

XLIX

In a dream. A cross between a meadow and a communal garden somewhere in Kensington, with a fountain or a statue in the middle of it. A sculpture, anyway. Modern, but not very modern. Abstract, with a big hole in the center and a few strings across it: like a guitar but less feminine. Gray. Sort of like by Barbara Hepworth, but made of discarded thoughts and unfinished sentences. Lacelike. On the plinth there is an inscription: *To Beloved Spider. Grateful Cobwebs.*

L

Twangs of balalaika, the crackle of atmospherics. A hand fiddling with an eye-blinking wireless. It's Moscow, Russia, anytime between 1963 and 1988. More atmospherics and balalaika. Then the first bars of "Lilli" Burter and an upright female voice: "This is the BBC World Service. The news. Read to you by . . ." In her thirties, perhaps. Well-scrubbed face, almost no makeup. A chiffon blouse. White. And a cardigan. Most likely beige, the tea-cum-milk color. A broadcloth skirt, knee-high. Black or dark blue, like the evening sky outside. Or maybe it's gray; but knee-high. Knee-high knee-high knee-high. And then there is a slip. Oh my oh my oh my. Another Boeing is blown up in a desert. Pol Pot, Phnom Penh. Mister—a split-second pause—Mugabe. Knee-high. Main thing, the lace. Fragile and intricate like circumlocution. Minuscule dotty flowers. That never see the light of day. And that's why they are so white. Oh blast! Sihanouk, Pinochet, Rudi Deutchke. Chile, Chile, Chile, Chile. Dotty little pansies smothered to death by light-brown tights from a shop in Islington. That's what the world came down to. From the step-by-step approach, from the silks/flesh/garter/bingo system to the either/or of pantyhose. Détente, SYGINT, ICBMs. New tricks, but the dog's too old. For these, and for the old ones, too. Well, looks like. And going to end up here after all. Pity. Can't win them all, can you? Another whiskey, then. "The main points again . . ." In her thirties, if you ask me, and on the plump side. Dinnertime anyway. Methuselah fancies dotty little pansies. Methuselah fancies . . . All that matters in this life is that

cobwebs outlive the spider. How does that thingummy—
Tyutchev's! Tyutchev is the name—lyric go?

> We are not given to appraise
> In whom or how our word may live on.
> And we are vouchsafed oblivion
> The way we once were given grace.

Dushenka! Dushenka! What's for dinner? "Ah, dahrleeng, I
thought we would eat English tonight. Boiled beef."

1991

An Immodest Proposal

❧

About an hour ago, the stage where I stand now as well as your seats were quite empty. An hour hence, they will be empty again. For most of the day, I imagine, this place stays empty; emptiness is its natural state. Had it been endowed with consciousness of its own, it would regard our presence as a nuisance. This is as good an illustration as any of one's significance, in any case; certainly of the significance of our gathering. No matter what brings us here, the ratios are not in our favor. Pleased as we may be with our number, in spatial terms it is of infinitesimal consequence.

This is true, I think, of any human assembly; but when it comes to poetry, it rings a special bell. For one thing, poetry, the writing or the reading of it, is an atomizing art; it is far less social than music or painting. Also, poetry has a certain appetite for emptiness, starting, say, with that of infinity. Mainly, though, because historically speaking the ratio of poetry's audience to the rest of society is not in the former's favor. So we should be pleased with one another, if only because our being here, for all its seeming insignif-

Delivered at the Library of Congress, October 1991.

icance, is a continuation of that history which, by some accounts floating around this town, has ended.

Throughout what we call recorded history, the audience for poetry does not appear to have exceeded 1 percent of the entire population. The basis for this estimate is not any particular research but the mental climate of the world that we live in. In fact, the weather has been such that, at times, the quoted figure seems a bit generous. Neither Greek nor Roman antiquity, nor the glorious Renaissance, nor the Enlightenment provides us with an impression of poetry commanding huge audiences, let alone legions or battalions, or of its readership being vast.

It never was. Those we call the classics owe their reputations not to their contemporaries but to their posterity. This is not to say that posterity is the quantitative expression of their worth. It just supplies them, albeit retroactively and with some effort, with the size of readership to which they were entitled from the beginning. As it was, their actual circumstances were by and large fairly narrow; they courted patrons or flocked to the courts pretty much in the same way poets today go to the universities. Obviously that had to do with the hope of largesse, but it was also the quest for an audience. Literacy being the privilege of the few, where else could a poet find a sympathetic ear or an attentive eye for his lines? The seat of power was often the seat of culture; and its diet was better, the company was less monochrome and more tender than elsewhere, including the monastery.

Centuries passed. Seats of power and seats of culture parted ways, it seems for good. That, of course, is the price you pay for democracy, for the rule of the people, by the people, and for the people, of whom still only 1 percent reads poetry. If a modern poet has anything in common with his Renaissance colleague, it is in the first place the paltry distribution of his work. Depending on one's temperament, one may relish the archetypal aspects of this predicament— pride oneself in being the means of carrying on the hallowed tradition, or derive a similar degree of comfort from one's so-well-precedented resignation. There is nothing more psychologically rewarding than linking oneself to the glories of the past, if only because the past is more articulate than the present, not to mention the future.

A poet can always talk himself out of a jam; after all, that's his métier. But I am here to speak not about the predicament of the poet, who is never, in the final analysis, a victim. I am here to speak about the plight of his audience: about your plight, as it were. Since I am paid this year by the Library of Congress, I take this job in the spirit of a public servant, not in any other. So it is the audience for poetry in this country that is my concern; and it is the public servant in me who finds the existing ratio of 1 percent appalling and scandalous, not to say tragic. Neither my temperament nor the chagrin of an author over his own dismal sales has anything to do with this appraisal.

The standard number of copies of a first or second collection by any poet in this country is something between 2,000 and 10,000 (and I speak of the commercial houses only). The latest census that I've seen gives the population of the United States as approximately 250 million. This means that a standard commercial publishing house, printing this or that author's first or second volume, aims at only .001 percent of the entire population. To me, this is absurd.

What stood for centuries in the way of the public's access to poetry was the absence of press and the limitation of literacy. Now both are practically universal, and the aforementioned ratio is no longer justifiable. Actually, even if we are to go by that 1 percent, it should result in publishers printing not 2,000 to 10,000 copies of a poet's collection but 2.5 million. Do we have that many readers of poetry in this country? I believe that we do; in fact, I believe that we have a lot more than that. Just how many could be determined, of course, through market research, but that is precisely what should be avoided.

For market research is restrictive by definition. So is any sociological breakdown of census figures into groups, classes, and categories. They presuppose certain binding characteristics pertaining to each social group, ushering in their prescribed treatment. This leads, plain and simple, to a reduction of people's mental diet, to their intellectual segregation. The market for poetry is believed to be those with a college education, and that's whom a publisher targets. The blue-collar crowd is not supposed to read Horace, nor the farmer in his overalls Montale or Marvell. Nor, for that matter, is the politician expected to know by heart Gerard Manley Hopkins or Elizabeth Bishop.

This is dumb as well as dangerous. More about that later. For the moment I'd like to assert only that the distribution of poetry should not be based on market criteria, since any such estimate, by definition, shortchanges the existing potential. When it comes to poetry, the net result of market research, for all its computers, is distinctly medieval. We are all literate, therefore everybody is a potential reader of poetry: it is on this assumption that the distribution of books should be based, not on some claustrophobic notion of demand. For in cultural matters, it is not demand that creates supply, it is the other way around. You read Dante because he wrote the *Divine Comedy*, not because you felt the need for him: you would not have been able to conjure either the man or the poem.

Poetry must be available to the public in far greater

volume than it is. It should be as ubiquitous as the nature that surrounds us, and from which poetry derives many of its similes; or as ubiquitous as gas stations, if not as cars themselves. Bookstores should be located not only on campuses or main drags but at the assembly plant's gates also. Paperbacks of those we deem classics should be cheap and sold at supermarkets. This is, after all, a country of mass production, and I don't see why what's done for cars can't be done for books of poetry, which take you quite a bit further. Because you don't want to go a bit further? Perhaps; but if this is so, it's because you are deprived of the means of transportation, not because the distances and the destinations that I have in mind don't exist.

Even to sympathetic ears, I suppose, all this may sound a bit loony. Well, it isn't; it also makes perfect economic sense. A book of poetry printed in 2.5 million copies and priced at, say, two dollars, will in the end bring in more than 10,000 copies of the same edition priced at twenty dollars. You may encounter, of course, a problem of storage, but then you'll be compelled to distribute as far and wide as the country goes. Moreover, if the government would recognize that the construction of your library is as essential to your inner vocation as business lunches are to the outer, tax breaks could be made available to those who read, write, or publish poetry. The main loser, of course, would be the Brazilian rain forest. But I believe that a tree facing the choice between becoming a book of poems or a bunch of memos may well opt for the former.

A book goes a long way. Overkill in cultural matters is not an optional strategy, it is a necessity, since selective cultural targeting spells defeat no matter how well one's aim is taken. Fittingly, then, without having any idea whom it is in particular that I am addressing at the moment, I would like to suggest that with the low-cost technology currently available, there is now a discernible opportunity to turn this nation into an enlightened democracy. And I think this opportunity should be risen to before literacy is replaced with videocy.

I recommend that we begin with poetry, not only because this way we would echo the development of our civilization—the song was there before the story—but also because it is cheaper to produce. A dozen titles would be a decent beginning. The average poetry reader's bookshelf contains, I believe, somewhere between thirty and fifty collections by various authors. It's possible to put half of it on a single shelf, or a mantelpiece—or if worse comes to worse, on the windowsill—of every American household. The cost of a dozen poetry paperbacks, even at their current price, would amount at most to one-fourth the price of a television set. That this is not done has to do not with the absence of a popular appetite for poetry but with the near-impossibility of whetting this appetite: with the unavailability of books.

In my view, books should be brought to the doorstep like electricity, or like milk in England: they should be considered utilities, and their cost should be appropriately minimal. Barring that, poetry could be sold in drugstores (not least because it might reduce the bill from your shrink). At the very least, an anthology of American poetry should be found in the drawer in every room in every motel in the land, next to the Bible, which will surely not object to this proximity, since it does not object to the proximity of the phone book.

All this is doable, in this country especially. For apart from anything else, American poetry is this country's greatest patrimony. It takes a stranger to see some things clearly. This is one of them, and I am that stranger. The quantity of verse that has been penned on these shores in the last century and a half dwarfs the similar enterprise of any literature and, for that matter, both our jazz and our cinema, rightly adored throughout the world. The same goes, I daresay, for its quality, for this is a poetry informed by the spirit of personal responsibility. There is nothing more alien to American poetry than those great Continental specialties: the sensibility of the victim with its wildly oscillating, blame-thirsty finger; the incoherence of elevation; the Promethean affectations and special pleading. To be sure, American verse has its vices—too many a parochial visionary, a verbose neurotic. But it is extremely tempering stuff, and sticking with the 1 percent distribution method robs this nation of a natural resource of endurance, not to mention a source of pride.

Poetry, by definition, is a highly individualistic art; in a sense, this country is its logical abode. At any rate, it is only logical that in this country this individualistic tendency has gone to its idiosyncratic extreme, in modernists and traditionalists alike. (In fact, this is what gave birth to modernists.) To my eye as well as my ear, American poetry is a relentless nonstop sermon on human autonomy; the song of the atom, if you will, defying the chain reaction. Its general tone is that of resilience and fortitude, of exacting the full look at the worst and not blinking. It certainly keeps its eyes wide open, not so much in wonderment, or poised for a revelation, as on the lookout for danger. It is short on consolation (the diversion of so much European poetry, especially Russian); rich and extremely lucid in detail; free of nostalgia for some Golden Age; big on hardihood and escape. If one looked for its motto, I would suggest Frost's line from "A Servant to Servants": "The best way out is always through."

If I permit myself to speak about American poetry in such a wholesale manner, it is not because of its body's strength and vastness but because my subject is the public's access to it. In this context it must be pointed out that the old adage about a poet's role in, or his duty to, his society puts the entire issue upside down. If one can speak of the social function of somebody who is essentially self-employed, then the social function of a poet is writing, which he does not by society's appointment but by his own volition. His only duty is to his language, that is, to write well. By writing, especially by writing well, in the language of his society, a poet takes a large step toward it. It is society's job to meet him halfway, that is, to open his book and to read it.

If one can speak of any dereliction of duty here, it's not on the part of the poet, for he keeps writing. Now, poetry is the supreme form of human locution in any culture. By failing to read or listen to poets, a society dooms itself to inferior modes of articulation—of the politician, or the salesman, or the charlatan—in short, to its own. It forfeits, in other words, its own evolutionary potential, for what distinguishes us from the rest of the animal kingdom is precisely the gift of speech. The charge frequently leveled against poetry—that it is difficult, obscure, hermetic, and whatnot —indicates not the state of poetry but, frankly, the rung of the evolutionary ladder on which society is stuck.

For poetic discourse is continuous; it also avoids cliché and repetition. The absence of those things is what speeds up and distinguishes art from life, whose chief stylistic device, if one may say so, is precisely cliché and repetition, since it always starts from scratch. It is no wonder that society today, chancing on this continuing poetic discourse, finds itself at a loss, as if boarding a runaway train. I have remarked elsewhere that poetry is not a form of entertainment, and in a certain sense not even a form of art, but our anthropological, genetic goal, our linguistic, evolutionary beacon. We seem to sense this as children, when we absorb and remember verses in order to master language. As adults, however, we abandon this pursuit, convinced that we have mastered it. Yet what we've mastered is but an idiom, good enough perhaps to outfox an enemy, to sell a product, to get laid, to earn a promotion, but certainly not good enough to cure anguish or cause joy. Until one learns to pack one's sentences with meanings like a van or to discern and love in the beloved's features a "pilgrim soul"; until one becomes aware that "No memory of having starred / Atones for later disregard, / Or keeps the end from being hard"—until things like that are in one's bloodstream, one still belongs among the sublinguals. Who are the majority, if that's a comfort.

If nothing else, reading poetry is a process of terrific linguistic osmosis. It is also a highly economical form of mental acceleration. Within a very short space a good poem covers enormous mental ground, and often, toward its finale, provides one with an epiphany or a revelation. That happens because in the process of composition a poet employs—by and large unwittingly—the two main modes of cognition available to our species: Occidental and Oriental. (Of course both modes are available whenever you find frontal lobes, but different traditions have employed them with different degrees of prejudice.) The first puts a high premium on the rational, on analysis. In social terms, it is accompanied by man's self-assertion and generally is exemplified by Descartes's *"Cogito ergo sum."* The second relies mainly on intuitive synthesis, calls for self-negation, and is best represented by the Buddha. In other words, a poem offers you a sample of complete, not slanted, human intelligence at work. This is what constitutes the chief appeal of poetry, quite apart from its exploiting rhythmic and euphonic properties of the language which are in themselves quite revelatory. A poem, as it were, tells its reader, "Be like me." And at the moment of reading you become what you read, you become the state of the language which is a poem, and its epiphany or its revelation is yours. They are still yours once you shut the book, since you can't revert to not having had them. That's what evolution is all about.

Now, the purpose of evolution is the survival neither of the fittest nor of the defeatist. Were it the former, we would have to settle for Arnold Schwarzenegger; were it the latter, which ethically is a more sound proposition, we'd have to make do with Woody Allen. The purpose of evolution, believe it or not, is beauty, which survives it all and generates truth simply by being a fusion of the mental and the sensual. As it is always in the eye of the beholder, it can't be wholly embodied save in words: that's what ushers in a poem, which is as incurably semantic as it is incurably euphonic.

No other language accumulates so much of this as does English. To be born into it or to arrive in it is the best boon that can befall a man. To prevent its keepers from full access to it is an anthropological crime, and that's what the present system of the distribution of poetry boils down to. I don't rightly know what's worse, burning books or not reading them; I think, though, that token publishing falls somewhere in between. I am sorry to put this so drastically, but when I think of the great works by the poets of this language bulldozed into neglect, on the one hand, and then consider the mind-boggling demographic vista, on the other, I feel that we are on the verge of a tremendous cultural backslide. And it is not the culture I am worried about, or the fate of the great or not-so-great poets' works. What concerns me is that man, unable to articulate, to express himself adequately, reverts to action. Since the vocabulary of action is limited, as it were, to his body, he is bound to act violently, extending his vocabulary with a weapon where there should have been an adjective.

In short, the good old quaint ways should be abandoned. There should be a nationwide distribution of poetry, classic and contemporary. It should be handled privately, I suppose, but supported by the state. The age group it should be aiming at is fifteen and up. The emphasis should be on the American classics; and as to who or what should be printed, that should be decided by a body of two or three people in the know, that is, by the poets. The academics, with their ideological bickering, should be kept out of it, for nobody has the authority to prescribe in this field on any grounds other than taste. Beauty and its attendant truth are not to be subordinated to any philosophical, political, or even ethical doctrine, since aesthetics is the mother of ethics and not the other way around. Should you think otherwise, try to recall the circumstances in which you fall in love.

What should be kept in mind, however, is that there is a tendency in society to appoint one great poet per period, often per century. This is done in order to avoid the responsibility of reading others, or for that matter the chosen one, should you find his or her temperament uncongenial. The fact is that at any given moment in any literature there are several poets of equal gravity and significance by whose lights you can go. In any case, whatever their number, in the end it corresponds to the known temperaments, for it can't be otherwise: hence their differences. By grace of language, they are there to provide society with a hierarchy or a spectrum of aesthetic standards to emulate, to ignore, to acknowledge. They are not so much role models as mental shepherds, whether they are cognizant of it or not—and it's better if they are not. Society needs all of them; and should the project I am speaking of ever be embarked on, no preferences should be shown to any one of them. Since on these heights there is no hierarchy, the fanfare should be equal.

I suspect that society settles just for one, because one is easier to dismiss than several. A society with several poets for its secular saints would be harder to rule, since a politician would have to offer a plane of regard, not to mention a level of diction, matching at least the one offered by poets: a plane of regard and a level of diction which no longer could be viewed as exceptional. But such a society would be perhaps a truer democracy than what we've known thus far. For the purpose of democracy is not democracy itself: that would be redundant. The purpose of democracy is its enlightenment. Democracy without enlightenment is at best a well-policed jungle with one designated great poet in it for its Tarzan.

It's the jungle that I am talking about here, not Tarzans. For a poet to sink into oblivion is not such an extraordinary drama; it comes with the territory: he can afford it. Unlike society, a good poet always has the future, and his poems, in a manner of speaking, are an invitation for us to sample it. And the least—perhaps the best—thing that can be said about us is that we are the future of Robert Frost, Marianne Moore, Wallace Stevens, Elizabeth Bishop: to name just a few . . . Every generation living on the earth is the future —more exactly, a part of the future of those who are gone, but of poets in particular, because when we read their work we realize that they knew us, that the poetry that preceded us is essentially our gene pool. This calls not for reverence; this calls for reference.   .

I repeat: A poet is never a loser; he knows that others will come in his stead and pick up the trail where he left it. (In fact, it's the swelling number of others, energetic and vocal, clamoring for attention, that drive him into oblivion.)

He can take this, as well as being regarded as a sissy. It is society that cannot afford to be oblivious, and it is society that—compared with the mental toughness of practically any poet—comes out a sissy and a loser. For society, whose main strength is that of reproducing itself, to lose a poet is like having a brain cell busted. This impairs one's speech, makes one draw a blank where an ethical choice is to be made; or it barnacles speech with qualifiers, turns one into an eager receptacle for demagoguery or just pure noise. The organs of reproduction, however, are not affected.

There are few cures for hereditary disorders (undetectable, perhaps, in an individual, but striking in a crowd), and what I'm suggesting here is not one of them. I just hope that this idea, if it catches on, may slow down somewhat the spread of our cultural malaise to the next generation. As I said, I took this job in the spirit of public service, and maybe being paid by the Library of Congress in Washington has gone to my head. Perhaps I fancy myself as a sort of Surgeon General slapping a label onto the current packaging of poetry. Something like *This Way of Doing Business Is Dangerous to the National Health*. The fact that we are alive does not mean that we are not sick.

It's often been said—first, I think, by Santayana—that those who don't remember history are bound to repeat it. Poetry doesn't make such claims. Still, it has some things in common with history: it employs memory, and it is of use for the future, not to mention the present. It certainly cannot reduce poverty, but it can do something for ignorance. Also, it is the only insurance available against the vulgarity of the human heart. Therefore, it should be available to everyone in this country and at a low cost.

Fifty million copies of an anthology of American poetry for two dollars a copy can be sold in a country of 250 million. Perhaps not at once, but gradually, over a decade or so, they will sell. Books find their readers. And if they will not sell, well, let them lie around, absorb dust, rot, and disintegrate. There is always going to be a child who will fish a book out of the garbage heap. I was such a child, for what it's worth; so, perhaps, were some of you.

A quarter of a century ago, in a previous incarnation in Russia, I knew a man who was translating Robert Frost into Russian. I got to know him because I saw his translations: they were stunning poems in Russian, and I wanted to become acquainted with the man as much as I wanted to see the originals. He showed me a hardcover edition (I think it was by Holt), which fell open onto the page with "Happiness Makes Up in Height for What It Lacks in Length." Across the page went a huge, size-twelve imprint of a soldier's boot. The front page of the book bore the stamp STALAG #3B," which was a World War II concentration camp for Allied POWs somewhere in France.

Now, there is a case of a book of poems finding its reader. All it had to do was to be around. Otherwise it couldn't be stepped on, let alone picked up.

Letter to a President

჻

Dear Mr. President,

I've decided to write this letter to you because we have something in common: we both are writers. In this line of work, one weighs words more carefully, I believe, than elsewhere before committing them to paper or, for that matter, to the microphone. Even when one finds oneself engaged in a public affair, one tries to do one's best to avoid catchwords, Latinate expressions, all manner of jargon. In a dialogue, of course, or with two or more interlocutors around, that's difficult, and may even strike them as pretentiousness. But in a soliloquy or in a monologue it is, I think, attainable, though, of course, one always tailors one's diction to one's audience.

We have something else in common, Mr. President, and that is our past in our respective police states. To put it less grandly: our prisons, that shortage of space amply made up for by an abundance of time, which, sooner or later, renders one, regardless of one's temperament, rather contemplative. You spent more time in yours, of course, than

Published in The New York Review of Books *in response to a lecture by Mr. Havel that appeared in the May 27, 1993, issue of that publication.*

I in mine, though I started in mine long before the Prague Spring. Yet in spite of my nearly patriotic belief that the hopelessness of some urine-reeking cement hole in the bowels of Russia awakens one to the arbitrariness of existence faster than what I once pictured as a clean, stuccoed solitary in civilized Prague, as contemplative beings, I think, we might be quite even.

In short, we were pen pals long before I conceived of this letter. But I conceived of it not because of the literalness of my mind, or because our present circumstances are quite different from those of the past (nothing can be more natural than that, and one is not obliged to remain a writer forever: not any more so than to stay a prisoner). I've decided to write this letter because a while ago I read the text of one of your most recent speeches, whose conclusions about the past, the present, and the future were so different from mine that I thought one of us must be wrong. And it is precisely because the present and the future—and not just your own or your country's but the global one—were involved that I decided to make this an open letter to you. Had the issue been only the past, I wouldn't have written you this letter at all, or if I had, I'd have marked it "Personal."

The speech of yours that I read was printed in *The New York Review of Books* and its title was "The Post-Communist Nightmare." You begin by reminiscing about a time when you would be avoided in the street by your friends and acquaintances, since in those days you were on dangerous terms with the state and under police surveillance. You proceed to explain the reasons for their avoiding you and suggest, in the usual, grudge-free manner for which you are justly famous, that to those friends and acquaintances you constituted an inconvenience; and "inconveniences"—you cite the conventional wisdom—"are best avoided." Then for most of your speech you describe the post-Communist reality (in Eastern Europe and by implication in the Balkans) and equate the deportment of the democratic world vis-à-vis that reality to avoiding an inconvenience.

It is a wonderful speech, with a great many wonderful insights and a convincing conclusion; but let me go to your starting point. It occurs to me, Mr. President, that your famous civility benefited your hindsight here rather poorly. Are you so sure you were avoided by those people then and there for reasons of embarrassment and fear of "potential persecution" only, and not because you were, given the seeming stability of the system, written off by them? Are you sure that at least some of them didn't simply regard you as a marked, doomed man on whom it would be foolish to waste much time? Don't you think that instead of, or as well as, being inconvenient (as you insist), you were also a convenient example of the wrong deportment and thus a source of considerable moral comfort, the way the sick are for the healthy majority? Haven't you imagined them saying to their wives in the evening, "I saw Havel today in the street. He's had it." Or do I misjudge the Czech character?

That they were proven wrong and you right matters little. They wrote you off in the first place because even by the standards of our half of the century you were not a martyr. Besides, don't we all harbor a certain measure of guilt, totally unrelated to the state, of course, but nonetheless palpable? So whenever the arm of the state reaches us, we regard it vaguely as our comeuppance, as a touch of the blunt but nevertheless expected tool of Providence. That's, frankly, the main *raison d'être* behind the institution of police, plain-clothed or uniformed, or at least behind our general inability to resist an arrest. One may be perfectly convinced that the state is wrong, but one is seldom confident of one's own virtue. Not to mention that it is the same arm that locks one up and sets one free. That's why one is seldom surprised at being avoided when one gets released, and doesn't expect a universal embrace.

Such expectations, under such circumstances, would be disappointed, because nobody wants to be reminded of the murky complexity of the relations between guilt and getting one's comeuppance, and in a police state providing such a reminder is what heroic deportment is largely about. It alienates one from others, as any emphasis on virtue does; not to mention that a hero is always best observed from a distance. In no small measure, Mr. President, you were avoided by the people you've mentioned precisely because for them you were a sort of test tube of virtue confronting evil, and they didn't interfere with the experiment, since they had their doubts about both. As such, you again were a convenience, because in the police state absolutes compromise each other since they engender each other. Haven't you imagined those prudent people saying to their wives in the evening: "I saw Havel today in the street. He's too good to be true." Or do I misjudge the Czech character again?

That they were proven wrong and you right, I repeat, matters little. They wrote you off at the time because they were guided by the same relativism and self-interest that I suppose helps them to make a go of it now, under the new dispensation. And as a healthy majority, they no doubt had a significant part in your velvet revolution, which, after all, asserts, the way democracy always does, precisely self-interest. If such is the case, and I'm afraid it is, they've paid you back for their excessive prudence, and you preside now over a society which is more theirs than yours.

There is nothing wrong with that. Besides, things might easily have gone the other way: for you, that is; not for them (the revolution was so velvet because the tyranny itself by that time was more woolen than ironclad—otherwise I wouldn't have this privilege of commenting upon your speech). So all I'm trying to suggest is that by introducing the notion of inconvenience you quite possibly misspoke, for self-interest is always exercised at the expense of others, whether it's done by individuals or by nations. A better notion would be the vulgarity of the human heart, Mr. President; but then you wouldn't be able to bring your speech to a ringing conclusion. Certain things come with a pulpit, though one should resist them, writer or no writer. As I am not faced with your task, I'd like to take your argument now where, I think, it could perhaps have gone. I wonder if you'll disagree with the result.

"For long decades," your next paragraph begins, "the chief nightmare of the democratic world was Communism. Today —three years after it began to collapse like an avalanche—it would seem as though another nightmare has replaced it: post-Communism." Then you describe in considerable detail the existing modes of the democratic world's response to the ecological, economic, political, and social catastrophes unraveling where previously one perceived a smooth cloth. You liken these responses to those toward your "inconvenience" and suggest that such a position leads "to a turning away from reality, and ultimately, to resigning oneself to it. It leads to appeasement, even to collaboration. The consequences of such a position may even be suicidal."

It is here, Mr. President, that I think your metaphor fails you. For neither the Communist nor the post-Communist nightmare amounts to an inconvenience, since it helped, helps, and for quite some time will help the democratic world to externalize evil. And not the democratic world only. To quite a few of us who lived in that nightmare, and especially those who fought it, its presence was a source of considerable moral comfort. For one who fights or resists

evil almost automatically perceives oneself as good and skips
self-analysis. So perhaps it's time—for us and for the world
at large, democratic or not—to scrub the term "Communism" from the human reality of Eastern Europe so one can
recognize that reality for what it was and is: a mirror.

For that is what human evil always is. Geographic names
or political terminology provides not a telescope or a window
but the reflection of ourselves: of human negative potential.
The magnitude of what took place in our parts of the world,
and over two-thirds of a century, cannot be reduced to "Communism." Catchwords, on the whole, lose more than they
retain, and in the case of tens of millions killed and the lives
of entire nations subverted, a catchword simply won't do.
Although the ratio of executioners to victims favors the latter,
the scale of what happened in our realm suggests, given its
technological backwardness at the time, that the former, too,
run in the millions, not to mention the complicity of millions
more.

Homilies are not my forte, Mr. President; besides, you
are a convert. It's not for me to tell you that what you call
"Communism" was a breakdown of humanity and not a political problem. It was a human problem, a problem of our
species, and thus of a lingering nature. Neither as a writer
nor, moreover, as a leader of a nation should you use terminology that obscures the reality of human evil—terminology, I should add, invented by evil to obscure its own
reality. Nor should one refer to it as a nightmare, since that
breakdown of humanity wasn't a nocturnal affair, not in our
hemisphere, to say the least.

To this day, the word "Communism" remains a convenience, for an -ism suggests a *fait accompli*. In Slavic
languages especially, an -ism, as you know, suggests the
foreignness of a phenomenon, and when a word containing
an -ism denotes a political system, the system is perceived

as an imposition. True, our particular -ism wasn't conceived on the banks of the Volga or the Vltava, and the fact that it blossomed there with a unique vigor doesn't bespeak our soil's exceptional fertility, for it blossomed in different latitudes and extremely diverse cultural zones with equal intensity. This suggests not so much an imposition as our -ism's rather organic, not to say universal, origins. One should think, therefore, that a bit of self-examination—on the part of the democratic world as well as our own—is in order, rather than ringing calls for mutual "understanding." (What does this word mean, anyway? What procedure do you propose for this understanding? Under the auspices of the UN, perhaps?)

And if self-examination is unlikely (why should what's been avoided under duress be done at leisure?), then at least the myth of imposition should be dispelled, since, for one thing, tank crews and fifth columns are biologically indistinguishable. Why don't we simply start by admitting that an extraordinary anthropological backslide has taken place in our world in this century, regardless of who or what triggered it? That it involved masses acting in their self-interest and, in the process of doing so, reducing their common denominator to the moral minimum? And that the masses' self-interest—stability of life and its standards, similarly reduced—has been attained at the expense of other masses, albeit numerically inferior? Hence the number of the dead.

It is convenient to treat these matters as an error, as a horrendous political aberration, perhaps imposed upon human beings from an anonymous elsewhere. It is even more convenient if that elsewhere bears a proper geographical or foreign-sounding name, whose spelling obscures its utterly human nature. It was convenient to build navies and defenses against that aberration—as it is convenient to dismantle those defenses and those navies now. It is convenient,

I must add, to refer to these matters in a civil manner, Mr. President, from a pulpit today, although I don't question for a minute the authenticity of your civility, which, I believe, is your very nature. It was convenient to have around this living example of how not to run things in this world and supply this example with an -ism, as it is convenient to supply it nowadays with "know-how" and a "post-." (And one easily envisions our -ism, embellished with its post-, conveniently sailing on the lips of dimwits into the future.)

For it would be truly inconvenient—for the cowboys of the Western industrial democracies specifically—to recognize the catastrophe that occurred in Indian territory as the first cry of mass society: a cry, as it were, from the world's future, and to recognize it not as an -ism but as a chasm suddenly gaping in the human heart, to swallow up honesty, compassion, civility, justice, and, thus satiated, presenting to the still democratic outside a reasonably perfect, monotonous surface.

Cowboys, however, loathe mirrors—if only because there they may recognize the backward Indians more readily than they would in the open. So they prefer to mount their high horses, scan the Indian-free horizons, deride the Indians' backwardness, and derive enormous moral comfort from being regarded as cowboys—first of all, by the Indians.

As one who has been likened often to a philosopher-king, you can, Mr. President, appreciate better than many how much all that happened to our "Indian nation" harks back to the Enlightenment, with its idea (from the Age of Discovery, actually) of a noble savage, of man being inherently good but habitually ruined by bad institutions; with its belief that improvement of those institutions will restore man to his initial goodness. So to the admission previously made or hoped for, one should add, I suppose, that it's precisely the accomplishment of the "Indian" in perfecting those institutions that brought them to that project's logical end: the police state. Perhaps the manifest bestiality of this achievement should suggest to the "Indians" that they must retreat some way into the interior, that they should render their institutions a bit less perfect. Otherwise they may not get the "cowboys' " subsidies for their reservations. And perhaps there is indeed a ratio between man's goodness and the badness of institutions. If there isn't, maybe somebody should admit that man isn't that good.

Isn't this the juncture at which we find ourselves, Mr. President—or at least you do? Should "Indians" embark on imitating "cowboys," or should they consult the spirits about other options? May it be that the magnitude of the tragedy that befell them is in itself a guarantee that it won't happen again? May their grief and their memory of what happened in their parts create a greater egalitarian bond than free enterprise and a bicameral legislature? And if they should draft a constitution anyway, maybe they should start by recognizing themselves and their history for the better part of this century as a reminder of Original Sin.

It's not such a heady concept, as you know. Translated into common parlance, it means that man is dangerous. Apart from being a footnote to our beloved Jean-Jacques, this principle may allow us to build—if not elsewhere, then at least in our realm, so steeped in Fourier, Proudhon, and Blanc at the expense of Burke and Tocqueville—a social order resting on a less self-flattering basis than was our habit, and perhaps with less disastrous consequences. This also may qualify as man's "new understanding of himself, of his limitations and his place in the world" you call for in your speech.

"We must discover a new relationship to our neighbors, and to the universe," you say toward the end of your speech, "and its metaphysical order, which is the source of the moral order." The metaphysical order, Mr. President, should it really exist, is pretty dark, and its structural idiom is its parts' mutual indifference. The notion that man is dangerous runs, therefore, closest to that order's implications for human morality. Every writer is a reader, and if you scan your library's shelves, you must realize that most of the books you've got there are about either betrayal or murder. At any rate, it seems more prudent to build society on the premise that man is evil rather than the premise of his goodness. This way at least there is the possibility of making it safe psychologically, if not physically (but perhaps that as well), for most of its members, not to mention that its surprises, which are inevitable, might be of a more pleasant nature.

Maybe the real civility, Mr. President, is not to create illusions. "New understanding," "global responsibilities," "pluralistic metaculture" are not much better at the core than the retrospective utopias of the latter-day nationalists or the entrepreneurial fantasies of the *nouveaux riches*. This sort of stuff is still predicated on the premise, however qualified, of man's goodness, of his notion of himself as either a fallen or a possible angel. This sort of diction befits, perhaps, the innocents, or demagogues, running the affairs of industrial democracies, but not you, who ought to know the truth about the condition of the human heart.

And you are, one would imagine, in a good position not only to convey your knowledge to people but also to cure that heart condition somewhat: to help them to become like yourself. Since what made you the way you are was not your penal experience but the books you've read. I'd suggest, for starters, serialization of some of those books in the country's major dailies. Given the population figure of Czechia, this can be done, even by decree, although I don't think your parliament would object. By giving your people Proust, Kafka, Faulkner, Platonov, Camus, or Joyce, you may turn at least one nation in the heart of Europe into a civilized people.

That may do more good for the future of the world than emulating cowboys. Also, it would be a real post-Communism, not the doctrine's meltdown, with the attendant "hatred of the world, self-affirmation at all costs, and the unparalleled flourishing of selfishness" that dog you now. For there is no other antidote to the vulgarity of the human heart than doubt and good taste, which one finds fused in works of great literature, as well as your own. If man's negative potential is best manifested by murder, his positive potential is best manifested by art.

Why, you may ask, don't I make a similar crackpot suggestion to the President of the country of which I am a citizen? Because he is not a writer; and when he is a reader, he often reads trash. Because cowboys believe in law, and reduce democracy to people's equality before it: i.e., to the well-policed prairie. Whereas what I suggest to you is equality before culture. You should decide which deal is better for your people, which book it is better to throw at them. If I were you, though, I'd start with your own library, because apparently it wasn't in law school that you learned about moral imperatives.

Yours sincerely,
Joseph Brodsky

On Grief and Reason

❧

I

I should tell you that what follows is a spinoff of a seminar given four years ago at the Collège International de Philosophie, in Paris. Hence a certain breeziness to the pace; hence, too, the paucity of biographical material—irrelevant, in my view, to the analysis of a work of art in general, and particularly where a foreign audience is concerned. In any case, the pronoun "you" in these pages stands for those ignorant of or poorly acquainted with the lyrical and narrative strengths of the poetry of Robert Frost. But, first, some basics.

Robert Frost was born in 1874 and died in 1963, at the age of eighty-eight. One marriage, six children; fairly strapped when young; farming, and, later, teaching jobs in various schools. Not much traveling until late in his life; he mostly resided on the East Coast, in New England. If biography accounts for poetry, this one should have resulted in none. Yet he published nine books of poems; the second one, *North of Boston*, which came out when he was forty, made him famous. That was in 1914.

After that, his sailing was a bit smoother. But literary

fame is not exactly popularity. As it happens, it took the Second World War to bring Frost's work to the general public's notice. In 1943, the Council on Books in Wartime distributed fifty thousand copies of Frost's "Come In" to United States troops stationed overseas, as a morale-builder. By 1955, his *Selected Poems* was in its fourth edition, and one could speak of his poetry's having acquired national standing.

It did. In the course of nearly five decades following the publication of *North of Boston*, Frost reaped every possible reward and honor an American poet can get; shortly before Frost's death, John Kennedy invited him to read a poem at the Inauguration ceremony. Along with recognition naturally came a great deal of envy and resentment, a substantial contribution to which emerged from the pen of Frost's own biographer. And yet both the adulation and resentment had one thing in common: a nearly total misconception of what Frost was all about.

He is generally regarded as the poet of the countryside, of rural settings—as a folksy, crusty, wisecracking old gentleman farmer, generally of positive disposition. In short, as American as apple pie. To be fair, he greatly enhanced this notion by projecting precisely this image of himself in numerous public appearances and interviews throughout his career. I suppose it wasn't that difficult for him to do, for he had those qualities in him as well. He was indeed a quintessential American poet; it is up to us, however, to find out what that quintessence is made of, and what the term "American" means as applied to poetry and, perhaps, in general.

In 1959, at a banquet thrown in New York on the occasion of Robert Frost's eighty-fifth birthday, the most prominent literary critic at that time, Lionel Trilling, rose and, goblet in hand, declared that Robert Frost was "a terrifying poet." That, of course, caused a certain stir, but the epithet was well chosen.

Now, I want you to make the distinction here between terrifying and tragic. Tragedy, as you know, is always a *fait accompli*, whereas terror always has to do with anticipation, with man's recognition of his own negative potential—with his sense of what he is capable of. And it is the latter that was Frost's forte, not the former. In other words, his posture is radically different from the Continental tradition of the poet as tragic hero. And that difference alone makes him— for want of a better term—American.

On the surface, he looks very positively predisposed toward his surroundings—particularly toward nature. His fluency, indeed, his "being versed in country things" alone can produce this impression. However, there is a difference between the way a European perceives nature and the way an American does. Addressing this difference, W. H. Auden, in his short essay on Frost (perhaps the best thing on the poet), suggests something to the effect that when a European conceives of confronting nature, he walks out of his cottage or a little inn, filled with either friends or family, and goes for an evening stroll. If he encounters a tree, it's a tree made familiar by history, to which it's been a witness. This or that king sat underneath it, laying down this or that law—something of that sort. A tree stands there rustling, as it were, with allusions. Pleased and somewhat pensive, our man, refreshed but unchanged by that encounter, returns to his inn or cottage, finds his friends or family absolutely intact, and proceeds to have a good, merry time. Whereas when an American walks out of his house and encounters a tree it is a meeting of equals. Man and tree face each other in their respective primal power, free of references: neither has a past, and as to whose future is greater, it is a toss-up. Basically, it's epidermis meeting bark. Our man returns to his cabin in a state of bewilderment, to say the least, if not in actual shock or terror.

Now, this is obviously a romantic caricature, but it accentuates the features, and that's what I am after here. In any case, the second point could be safely billed as the gist of Robert Frost's nature poetry. Nature for this poet is neither friend nor foe, nor is it the backdrop for human drama; it is this poet's terrifying self-portrait. And now I am going to start with one of his poems, which appears in the 1942 volume *A Witness Tree*. I am about to put forth my views and opinions about his lines without any concern for academic objectivity, and some of these views will be pretty dark. All I can say in my defense is (a) that I do like this poet enormously and I am going to try to sell him to you as he is, and (b) that some of that darkness is not entirely mine: it is his lines' sediment that has darkened my mind; in other words, I got it from him.

II

COME IN

As I came to the edge of the woods,
Thrush music—hark!
Now if it was dusk outside,
Inside it was dark.

Too dark in the woods for a bird
By sleight of wing
To better its perch for the night,
Though it still could sing.

The last of the light of the sun
That had died in the west
Still lived for one song more
In a thrush's breast.

Far in the pillared dark
Thrush music went—
Almost like a call to come in
To the dark and lament.

But no, I was out for stars:
I would not come in.
I meant not even if asked,
And I hadn't been.

Let's look at "Come In." A short poem in short meter—
actually, a combination of trimeter with dimeter, anapest
with iamb. The stuff of ballads, which by and large are all
about gore and comeuppance. So, up to a certain point, is
this poem. The meter hints as much. What are we dealing
with here? A walk in the woods? A stroll through nature?
Something that poets usually do? (And if yes, by the way,
then why?) "Come In" is one of many poems written by
Frost about such strolls. Think of "Stopping by Woods on a
Snowy Evening," "Acquainted with the Night," "Desert
Places," "Away!," and so forth. Or else think of Thomas
Hardy's "The Darkling Thrush," with which this poem has
a distinct affinity. Hardy was also very fond of lonely strolls,
except most of his had a tendency to wind up in a
graveyard—since England was settled long ago, and more
thickly, I guess.

To begin with, we again have a thrush. And a bird, as
you know, is very often a bard, since, technically speaking,

both sing. So as we proceed we should bear in mind that our poet may be delegating certain aspects of his psyche to the bird. Actually, I firmly believe that these two birds are related. The difference is only that it takes Hardy sixteen lines to introduce his in a poem, whereas Frost gets down to business in the second line. On the whole, this is indicative of the difference between the Americans and the British— I mean in poetry. Because of a greater cultural heritage, a greater set of references, it usually takes much longer for a Briton to set a poem in motion. The sense of echo is stronger in his ear, and thus he flexes his muscle and demonstrates his facility before he gets down to his subject. Normally, that sort of routine results in a poem's being as big on exposition as on the actual message: in long-windedness, if you will—though, depending on who is doing the job, this is not necessarily a shortcoming.

Now, let's do it line by line. "As I came to the edge of the woods" is a fairly simple, informative job, stating the subject and setting the meter. An innocent line, on the surface, wouldn't you say? Well, it is, save for "the woods." "The woods" makes one suspicious, and, with that, "the edge" does, too. Poetry is a dame with a huge pedigree, and every word comes practically barnacled with allusions and associations. Since the fourteenth century, the woods have given off a very strong smell of *selva oscura*, and you may recall what that *selva* led the author of *The Divine Comedy* into. In any case, when a twentieth-century poet starts a poem with finding himself at the edge of the woods there is a reasonable element of danger—or, at least, a faint suggestion of it. The edge, in its very self, is sufficiently sharp.

Maybe not; maybe our suspicions are unfounded, maybe we are just paranoid and are reading too much into this line. Let's go to the next one, and we shall see:

> As I came to the edge of the woods,
> Thrush music—hark!

Looks like we've goofed. What could be more innocuous than this antiquated, Victorian-sounding, fairy-tale-like "hark"? A bird is singing—listen! "Hark" truly belongs in a Hardy poem, or in a ballad; better yet, in a jingle. It suggests a level of diction at which nothing untoward could be conveyed. The poem promises to proceed in a comforting, melodious way. That's what you're thinking, anyway, after hearing "hark": that you're going to have some sort of description of the music made by the thrush—that you are getting into familiar territory.

But that was a setup, as the following two lines show. It was but an exposition, crammed by Frost into two lines. Abruptly, in a fairly indecorous, matter-of-fact, non-melodious, and non-Victorian way, the diction and the register shift:

> Now if it was dusk outside,
> Inside it was dark.

It's "now" that does this job of leaving very little room for any fancy. What's more, you realize that the "hark" rhymes with "dark." And that that "dark" is the condition of "inside," which could allude not only to the woods, since the comma sets that "inside" into sharp opposition to the third line's "outside," and since the opposition is given you in the fourth line, which makes it a more drastic statement. Not to mention that this opposition is but the matter of substitution of just two letters: of putting *ar* instead of *us* between *d* and *k*. The vowel sound remains essentially the same. What we've got here is the difference in just one consonant.

There is a slight choking air in the fourth line. That has to do with its distribution of stresses, different from the first dimeter. The stanza contracts, as it were, toward its end, and the caesura after "inside" only underscores that "inside" 's isolation. Now, while I am offering you this deliberately slanted reading of this poem, I'd like to urge you to pay very close attention to its every letter, every caesura, if only because it deals with a bird, and a bird's trills are a matter of pauses and, if you will, characters. Being predominantly monosyllabic, English is highly suitable for this parroting job, and the shorter the meter, the greater the pressure upon every letter, every caesura, every comma. At any rate, that "dark" literally renders the "woods" as *la selva oscura*.

With the memory of what that dark wood was entry to, let's approach the next stanza:

> Too dark in the woods for a bird
> By sleight of wing
> To better its perch for the night,
> Though it still could sing.

What do you think is happening here? A British or a Continental—or, for that matter, a properly American—innocent would still reply that it is about a bird singing in the evening, and that it is a nice tune. Interestingly, he would be right, and it is on this sort of rightness that Frost's reputation rests. In fact, though, this stanza, in particular, is extremely dark. One could argue that the poem considers something rather unpleasant, quite possibly a suicide. Or, if not suicide—well, death. And, if not necessarily death, then—at least, in this stanza—the notion of the afterlife.

In "Too dark in the woods for a bird," a bird, alias bard, scrutinizes "the woods" and finds them too dark. "Too" here echoes—no! harks back to—Dante's opening lines in *The Divine Comedy*: our bird/bard's assessment of that *selva* differs from the great Italian's. To put it plainly, the afterlife is darker for Frost than it is for Dante. The question is why, and the answer is either because he disbelieves in the whole thing or because his notion of himself makes him, in his mind, slated for damnation. Nothing in his power can improve his eventual standing, and I'd venture that "sleight of wing" could be regarded as a reference to last rites. Above all, this poem is about being old and pondering what is next. "To better its perch for the night" has to do with the possibility of being assigned elsewhere, not just to hell—the night here being that of eternity. The only thing the bird/bard has to show for himself is that it/he "still could sing."

"The woods" are "too dark" for a bird because a bird is too far gone at being a bird. No motion of its soul, alias "sleight of wing," can improve its eventual fate in these "woods." Whose woods these are I think we know: one of their branches is where a bird is to end up anyway, and a "perch" gives a sense of these woods' being well structured: it is an enclosure—a sort of chicken coop, if you will. Thus, our bird is doomed; no last-minute conversion ("sleight" is a conjuring term) is feasible, if only because a bard is too old for any quick motion of the hand. Yet, old though he is, he still can sing.

And in the third stanza you have that bird singing: you have the song itself, the last one. It is a tremendously expansive gesture. Look at how every word here postpones the next one. "The last"—caesura—"of the light"—caesura—"of the sun"—line break, which is a big caesura—"That had died"—caesura—"in the west." Our bird/bard traces the last of the light to its vanished source. You almost hear in this line the good old "Shenandoah," the song of going West. Delay and postponement are palpable here.

"The last" is not finite, and "of the light" is not finite, and "of the sun" is not. What's more, "that had died" itself is not finite, though it should have been. Even "in the west" isn't. What we've got here is the song of lingering: of light, of life. You almost see the finger pointing out the source and then, in the broad circular motion of the last two lines, returning to the speaker in "Still lived"—caesura—"for one song more"—line break—"In a thrush's breast." Between "The last" and "breast" our poet covers an extraordinary distance: the width of the continent, if you will. After all, he describes the light, which is still upon him, the opposite of the darkness of the woods. The breast is, after all, the source of any song, and you almost see here not so much a thrush as a robin; anyhow, a bird singing at sunset: it lingers on the bird's breast.

And here, in the opening lines of the fourth stanza, is where the bird and the bard part ways. "Far in the pillared dark / Thrush music went." The key word here is "pillared," of course: it suggests a cathedral interior—a church, in any case. In other words, our thrush flies into the woods, and you hear his music from within, "almost like a call to come in / To the dark and lament." If you want, you may replace "lament" with "repent": the effect will be practically the same. What's being described here is one of the choices before our old bard this evening: the choice he does not make. The thrush has chosen that "sleight of wing" after all. It is bettering its perch for the night; it accepts its fate, for lament is acceptance. You could plunge yourself here into a maze of ecclesiastical distinctions—Frost's essential Protestantism, etc. I'd advise against it, since a stoic posture befits believers and agnostics alike; in this line of work, it is practically inescapable. On the whole, references (religious ones especially) are not to be shrunk to inferences.

"But no, I was out for stars" is Frost's usual deceptive

maneuver, projecting his positive sensibility: lines like that are what earned him his reputation. If he was indeed "out for stars," why didn't he mention that before? Why did he write the whole poem about something else? But this line is here not solely to deceive you. It is here to deceive—or, rather, to quell—himself. This whole stanza is. Unless we read this line as the poet's general statement about his presence in this world—in the romantic key, that is, as a line about his general metaphysical appetite, not to be quenched by this little one-night agony.

> I would not come in.
> I meant not even if asked,
> And I hadn't been.

There is too much jocular vehemence in these lines for us to take them at face value, although we should not omit this option, either. The man is shielding himself from his own insights, and he gets grammatically as well as syllabically assertive and less idiomatic—especially in the second line, "I would not come in," which could be easily truncated into "I *won't* come in." "I meant not even if asked" comes off with a menacing resoluteness, which could amount to a statement of his agnosticism were it not for the last line's all too clever qualifier: "And I hadn't been." This is indeed a sleight of hand.

Or else you can treat this stanza and, with it, the whole poem as Frost's humble footnote or postscript to Dante's *Commedia*, which ends with "stars"—as his acknowledgment of possessing either a lesser belief or a lesser gift. The poet here refuses an invitation into darkness; moreover, he questions the very call: "*Almost* like a call to come in . . ." One shouldn't make heavy weather of Frost's affinity with Dante, but here and there it's palpable, especially in the poems dealing with dark nights of the soul—for instance, in "Acquainted with the Night." Unlike a number of his illustrious contemporaries, Frost never wears his learning on his sleeve—mainly because it is in his bloodstream. So "I meant not even if asked" could be read not only as his refusal to make a meal of his dreadful apprehension but also as a reference to his stylistic choice in ruling out a major form. Be that as it may, one thing is clear: without Dante's *Commedia*, this poem wouldn't have existed.

Still, should you choose to read "Come In" as a nature poem, you are perfectly welcome to it. I suggest, though, that you take a longer look at the title. The twenty lines of the poem constitute, as it were, the title's translation. And in this translation, I am afraid, the expression "come in" means "die."

III

While in "Come In" we have Frost at his lyrical best, in "Home Burial" we have him at his narrative best. Actually, "Home Burial" is not a narrative; it is an eclogue. Or, more exactly, it is a pastoral—except that it is a very dark one. Insofar as it tells a story, it is, of course, a narrative; the means of that story's transportation, though, is dialogue, and it is the means of transportation that defines a genre. Invented by Theocritus in his idylls, refined by Virgil in the poems he called eclogues or bucolics, the pastoral is essentially an exchange between two or more characters in a rural setting, returning often to that perennial subject, love. Since the English and French word "pastoral" is overburdened with happy connotations, and since Frost is closer to Virgil than to Theocritus, and not only chronologically, let's follow Virgil and call this poem an eclogue. The rural setting is here, and so are the two characters: a farmer and his wife, who may qualify as a shepherd and a shepherdess, except that it is two thousand years later. So is their subject: love, two thousand years later.

To make a long story short, Frost is a very Virgilian poet. By that, I mean the Virgil of the *Bucolics* and the *Georgics*, not the Virgil of the *Aeneid*. To begin with, the young Frost did a considerable amount of farming—as well as a lot of writing. The posture of gentleman farmer wasn't all posture. As a matter of fact, until the end of his days he kept buying farms. By the time he died, he had owned, if I am not mistaken, four farms in Vermont and New Hampshire. He knew something about living off the land—not less, in any case, than Virgil, who must have been a disastrous farmer, to judge by the agricultural advice he dispenses in the *Georgics*.

With few exceptions, American poetry is essentially Virgilian, which is to say contemplative. That is, if you take four Roman poets of the Augustan period, Propertius, Ovid, Virgil, and Horace, as the standard representatives of the four known humors (Propertius' choleric intensity, Ovid's sanguine couplings, Virgil's phlegmatic musings, Horace's melancholic equipoise), then American poetry—indeed, poetry in English in general—strikes you as being by and large of Virgilian or Horatian denomination. (Consider the bulk of Wallace Stevens's soliloquies, or the late, American Auden.) Yet Frost's affinity with Virgil is not so much temperamental as technical. Apart from frequent recourse to disguise (or mask) and the opportunity for distancing oneself that an invented character offers to the poet, Frost and Virgil have in common a tendency to hide the real subject matter of their dialogues under the monotonous, opaque sheen of their respective pentameters and hexameters. A poet of extraordinary probing and anxiety, the Virgil of the *Eclogues* and the *Georgics* is commonly taken for a bard of love and country pleasures, just like the author of *North of Boston*.

To this it should be added that Virgil in Frost comes to you obscured by Wordsworth and Browning. "Filtered" is perhaps a better word, and Browning's dramatic monologue is quite a filter, engulfing the dramatic situation in solid Victorian ambivalence and uncertainty. Frost's dark pastorals are dramatic also, not only in the sense of the intensity of the characters' interplay but above all in the sense that they are indeed theatrical. It is a kind of theater in which the author plays all the roles, including those of stage designer, director, ballet master, etc. It's he who turns the lights off, and sometimes he is the audience also.

That stands to reason. For Theocritus' idylls, like nearly all Augustan poetry, in their own right are but a compression of Greek drama. In "Home Burial" we have an arena reduced to a staircase, with its Hitchcockian banister. The opening line tells you as much about the actors' positions as about their roles: those of the hunter and his prey. Or, as you'll see later, of Pygmalion and Galatea, except that in this case the sculptor turns his living model into stone. In the final analysis, "Home Burial" is a love poem, and if only on these grounds it qualifies as a pastoral.

But let's examine this line and a half:

> He saw her from the bottom of the stairs
> Before she saw him.

Frost could have stopped right here. It is already a poem, it is already a drama. Imagine this line and a half sitting on the page all by itself, in minimalist fashion. It's an extremely loaded scene—or, better yet, a frame. You've got an enclosure, the house, with two individuals at cross— no, diverse—purposes. He's at the bottom of the stairs;

she's at the top. He's looking up at her; she, for all we know thus far, doesn't register his presence at all. Also, you've got to remember that it's in black and white. The staircase dividing them suggests a hierarchy of significances. It is a pedestal with her atop (at least, in his eyes) and him at the bottom (in our eyes and, eventually, in hers). The angle is sharp. Place yourself here in either position—better in his —and you'll see what I mean. Imagine yourself observing, watching somebody, or imagine yourself being watched. Imagine yourself interpreting someone's movements—or immobility—unbeknownst to that person. That's what turns you into a hunter, or into Pygmalion.

Let me press this Pygmalion business a bit further. Scrutiny and interpretation are the gist of any intense human interplay, and of love in particular. They are also the most powerful source of literature: of fiction (which is by and large about betrayal) and, above all, of lyric poetry, where one is trying to figure out the beloved and what makes her/him tick. And this figuring out brings us back to the Pygmalion business quite literally, since the more you chisel out and the more you penetrate the character, the more you put your model on a pedestal. An enclosure—be it a house, a studio, a page—intensifies this pedestal aspect enormously. And, depending on your industry and on the model's ability to cooperate, this process results either in a masterpiece or in a disaster. In "Home Burial" it results in both. For every Galatea is ultimately a Pygmalion's self-projection. On the other hand, art doesn't imitate life but infects it.

So let's watch the deportment of the model:

> She was starting down,
> Looking back over her shoulder at some fear.
> She took a doubtful step and then undid it
> To raise herself and look again.

On the literal level, on the level of straight narrative, we have the heroine beginning to descend the steps with her head turned to us in profile, her glance lingering on some frightful sight. She hesitates and interrupts her descent, her eyes still trained, presumably, on the same sight: neither on the steps nor on the man at the bottom. But you are aware of yet another level present here, aren't you?

Let's leave that level as yet unnamed. Each piece of information in this narrative comes to you in an isolated manner, within a pentameter line. The isolation job is done by white margins framing, as it were, the whole scene, like the silence of the house; and the lines themselves are the staircase. Basically, what you get here is a succession of frames. "She was starting down" is one frame. "Looking back over her shoulder at some fear" is another; in fact, it is a close-up, a profile—you see her facial expression. "She took a doubtful step and then undid it" is a third: again a close-up—the feet. "To raise herself and look again" is a fourth—full figure.

But this is a ballet, too. There is a minimum of two *pas de deux* here, conveyed to you with a wonderful euphonic, almost alliterative precision. I mean the *ds* in this line, in "doubtful" and in "undid it," although the *ts* matter also. "Undid it" is particularly good, because you sense the spring in that step. And that profile in its opposition to the movement of the body—the very formula of a dramatic heroine —is straight out of a ballet as well.

But the real *faux pas de deux* starts with "He spoke / Advancing toward her." For the next twenty-five lines, a conversation occurs on the stairs. The man climbs them as he speaks, negotiating mechanically and verbally what separates them. "Advancing" bespeaks self-consciousness and apprehensiveness. The tension grows with the growing prox-imity. However, the mechanical and, by implication, phys-ical proximity is more easily attained than the verbal—i.e., the mental—and that's what the poem is all about. " 'What is it you see / From up there always?—for I want to know' " is very much a Pygmalion question, addressed to the model on the pedestal: atop the staircase. His fascination is not with what he sees but with what he imagines it conceals—what he has placed there. He invests her with mystery and then rushes to uncloak it: this rapacity is always Pyg-malion's double bind. It is as though the sculptor found himself puzzled by the facial expression of his model: she "sees" what he does not "see." So he has to climb to the pedestal himself, to put himself in her position. In the po-sition of "up there always"—of topographical (vis-à-vis the house) and psychological advantage, where he put her him-self. It is the latter, the psychological advantage of the cre-ation, that disturbs the creator, as the emphatic " 'for I want to know' " shows.

The model refuses to cooperate. In the next frame ("She turned and sank upon her skirts at that"), followed by the close-up of "And her face changed from terrified to dull," you get that lack of cooperation plain. Yet the lack of co-operation here *is* cooperation. The less you cooperate, the more you are a Galatea. For we have to bear in mind that the woman's psychological advantage is in the man's self-projection. He ascribes it to her. So by turning him down she only enhances his fantasy. In this sense, by refusing to cooperate she plays along. That's basically her whole game here. The more he climbs, the greater is that advantage; he pushes her into it, as it were, with every step.

Still, he is climbing: in "he said to gain time" he does, and also in

> "What is it you see?"
> Mounting until she cowered under him.
> "I will find out now—you must tell me, dear."

The most important word here is the verb "see," which we
encounter for the second time. In the next nine lines, it will
be used four more times. We'll get to that in a minute. But
first let's deal with this "mounting" line and the next. It's a
masterly job here. With "mounting," the poet kills two birds
at once, for "mounting" describes both the climb and the
climber. And the climber looms even larger, because the
woman "cowers"—i.e., shrinks under him. Remember that
she looks "at some fear." "Mounting" versus "cowered" gives
you the contrast, then, between their respective frames, with
the implicit danger contained in his largeness. In any case,
her alternative to fear is not comfort. And the resoluteness
of " 'I will find out now' " echoes the superior physical mass,
not alleviated by the cajoling "dear" that follows a remark
—" 'you must tell me' "—that is both imperative and conscious of this contrast.

> She, in her place, refused him any help,
> With the least stiffening of her neck and silence.
> She let him look, sure that he wouldn't see,
> Blind creature; and awhile he didn't see.
> But at last he murmured, "Oh," and again, "Oh."
>
> "What is it—what?" she said.
>   "Just that I see."
> "You don't," she challenged. "Tell me what it is."
>
> "The wonder is I didn't see at once."

And now we come to this verb "see." Within fifteen lines it's been used six times. Every experienced poet knows how risky it is to use the same word several times within a short space. The risk is that of tautology. So what is it that Frost is after here? I think he is after precisely that: tautology. More accurately, nonsemantic utterance. Which you get, for instance, in " 'Oh,' and again, 'Oh.' " Frost had a theory about what he called "sentence-sounds." It had to do with his observation that the sound, the tonality, of human locution is as semantic as actual words. For instance, you overhear two people conversing behind a closed door, in a room. You don't hear the words, yet you know the general drift of their dialogue; in fact, you may pretty accurately figure out its substance. In other words, the tune matters more than the lyrics, which are, so to speak, replaceable or redundant. Anyway, the repetition of this or that word liberates the tune, makes it more audible. By the same token, such repetition liberates the mind—rids you of the notion presented by the word. (This is the old Zen technique, of course, but, come to think of it, finding it in an American poem makes you wonder whether philosophical principles don't spring from texts rather than the other way around.)

The six "see"s here do precisely that. They exclaim rather than explain. It could be "see," it could be "Oh," it could be "yes," it could be any monosyllabic word. The idea is to explode the verb from within, for the content of the actual observation defeats the process of observation, its means, and the very observer. The effect that Frost tries to create is the inadequacy of response when you automatically repeat the first word that comes to your tongue. "Seeing" here is simply reeling from the unnameable. The least seeing our hero does is in " 'Just that I see,' " for by this time the verb, having already been used four times, is robbed of its "observing" and "understanding" meaning (not to mention the fact—draining the word even further of content—that we readers are ourselves still in the dark, still don't know what there is to see out that window). By now, it is just sound, denoting an animal response rather than a rational one.

This sort of explosion of bona-fide words into pure, nonsemantic sounds will occur several times in the course of this poem. Another happens very soon, ten lines later. Characteristically, these explosions occur whenever the players find themselves in close physical proximity. They are the verbal—or, better yet, the audial—equivalents of a hiatus. Frost directs them with tremendous consistency, suggesting his characters' profound (at least, prior to this scene) incompatibility. "Home Burial" is, in fact, the study of that, and on the literal level the tragedy it describes is the characters' comeuppance for violating each other's territorial and mental imperatives by having a child. Now that the child is lost, the imperatives play themselves out with vehemence: they claim their own.

IV

By standing next to the woman, the man acquires her vantage point. Because he is larger than she, and also because this is *his* house (as line 23 shows), where he has lived, presumably, most of his life, he must, one imagines, bend somewhat to put his eyes on her line of vision. Now they are next to each other, in an almost intimate proximity, on the threshold of their bedroom, atop the stairs. The bedroom has a window; a window has a view. And here Frost produces the most stunning simile of this poem, and perhaps of his entire career:

"The wonder is I didn't see at once.
I never noticed it from here before.

I must be wonted to it—that's the reason.
The little graveyard where my people are!
So small the window frames the whole of it.
Not so much larger than a bedroom, is it?
There are three stones of slate and one of marble,
Broad-shouldered little slabs there in the sunlight
On the sidehill. We haven't to mind *those.*
But I understand: it is not the stones,
But the child's mound—"

" 'The little graveyard where my people are!' " generates an air of endearment, and it's with this air that " 'So small the window frames the whole of it' " starts, only to tumble itself into " 'Not so much larger than a bedroom, is it?' " The key word here is "frames," because it doubles as the window's actual frame and as a picture on a bedroom wall. The window hangs, as it were, on the bedroom wall like a picture, and that picture depicts a graveyard. "Depicting," though, means reducing to the size of a picture. Imagine having that in your bedroom. In the next line, though, the graveyard is restored to its actual size and, for that reason, equated with the bedroom. This equation is as much psychological as it is spatial. Inadvertently, the man blurts out the summary of the marriage (foreshadowed in the grim pun of the title). And, equally inadvertently, the "is it?" invites the woman to agree with this summary, almost implying her complicity.

As if that were not enough, the next two lines, with their stones of slate and marble, proceed to reinforce the simile, equating the graveyard with the made-up bed, with its pentametrically arranged pillows and cushions—populated by a family of small, inanimate children: "Broad-shouldered little slabs." This is Pygmalion unbound, on a rampage. What we have here is the man's intrusion into the woman's mind, a violation of her mental imperative—if you will, an ossification of it. And then this ossifying hand—petrifying, actually—stretches toward what's still raw, palpably as well as in her mind:

> "But I understand: it is not the stones,
> But the child's mound—"

It's not that the contrast between the stones and the mound is too stark, though it is; it is his ability—or, rather, his attempt—to articulate it that she finds unbearable. For, should he succeed, should he find the words to articulate her mental anguish, the mound will join the stones in the "picture," will become a slab itself, will become a pillow of their bed. Moreover, this will amount to the total penetration of her inner sanctum: that of her mind. And he is getting there:

> "Don't, don't, don't,
> don't," she cried.

> She withdrew, shrinking from beneath his arm
> That rested on the banister, and slid downstairs;
> And turned on him with such a daunting look,
> He said twice over before he knew himself:
> "Can't a man speak of his own child he's lost?"

The poem is gathering its dark force. Four "don't"s are that nonsemantic explosion, resulting in hiatus. We are so much in the story line now—up to the eyebrows—that we may forget that this is still a ballet, still a succession of frames, still an artifice, stage-managed by the poet. In fact, we are about to take sides with our characters, aren't we? Well, I suggest we pull ourselves out of this by our eyebrows and think for a moment about what it all tells us about our poet. Imagine, for instance, that the story line has been drawn from experience—from, say, the loss of a firstborn. What does all that you've read thus far tell you about the author, about his sensibility? How much he is absorbed by the story and—what's more crucial—to what degree he is free from it?

Were this a seminar, I'd wait for your answers. Since it is not, I've got to answer this question myself. And the answer is: He is very free. Dangerously so. The very ability to utilize—to play with—this sort of material suggests an extremely wide margin of detachment. The ability to turn this material into a blank-verse, pentameter monotone adds another degree to that detachment. To observe a relation between a family graveyard and a bedroom's four-poster—still another. Added up, they amount to a considerable degree of detachment. A degree that dooms human interplay, that makes communication impossible, for communication requires an equal. This is very much the predicament of Pygmalion vis-à-vis his model. So it's not that the story the poem tells is autobiographical but that the poem is the author's self-portrait. That is why one abhors literary biography—because it is reductive. That is why I am resisting issuing you with actual data on Frost.

Where does he go, you may ask, with all that detachment? The answer is: into utter autonomy. It is from there that he observes similarities among unlike things, it is from there that he imitates the vernacular. Would you like to meet Mr. Frost? Then read his poems, nothing else; otherwise, you are in for criticism from below. Would you like to be him? Would you like to become Robert Frost? Perhaps one should be advised against such aspirations. For a sensibility like this, there is very little hope of real human congeniality, or conjugality either; and, actually, there is very little romantic dirt on him—of the sort normally indicative of such hope.

This is not necessarily a digression, but let's get back to the lines. Remember the hiatus, and what causes it, and remember that this is an artifice. Actually, the author himself reminds you of it with

> She withdrew, shrinking from beneath his arm
> That rested on the banister, and slid downstairs.

It is still a ballet, you see, and the stage direction is incorporated into the text. The most telling detail here is the banister. Why does the author put it here? First, to reintroduce the staircase, which we might by now have forgotten about, stunned by the business of ruining the bedroom. But, secondly, the banister prefigures her sliding downstairs, since every child uses banisters for sliding down. "And turned on him with such a daunting look" is another stage direction.

> He said twice over before he knew himself:
> "Can't a man speak of his own child he's lost?"

Now, this is a remarkably good line. It has a distinctly vernacular, almost proverbial air. And the author is definitely aware of how good it is. So, both trying to underscore its effectiveness and to obscure his awareness of it, he emphasizes the unwittingness of this utterance: "He said twice over before he knew himself." On the literal, narrative level, we have the man stunned by the woman's gaze, the daunting look, and groping for words. Frost was awfully good with those formulaic, quasi-proverbial one-liners. "For to be social is to be forgiving" (in "The Star-Splitter"), or "The best way out is always through" ("A Servant to Servants"), for example. And a few lines later you are going to get yet another one. They are mostly pentametric; iambic pentameter is very congenial to that sort of job.

This whole section of the poem, from " 'Don't, don't, don't, don't' " on, obviously has some sexual connotations, of her turning the man down. That's what the story of Pygmalion and his model is all about. On the literal level, "Home Burial" evolves along similar "hard to get" lines. However, I don't think that Frost, for all his autonomy, was conscious of that. (After all, "North of Boston" shows no acquaintance with Freudian terminology.) And, if he was not, this sort of approach on our part is invalid. Nevertheless, we should bear some of it in mind as we are embarking on the bulk of this poem:

> "Not you!—Oh, where's my hat? Oh, I don't need it!
> I must get out of here. I must get air.—
> I don't know rightly whether any man can."

> "Amy! Don't go to someone else this time.
> Listen to me. I won't come down the stairs."
> He sat and fixed his chin between his fists.
> "There's something I should like to ask you, dear."

> "You don't know how to ask it."
>   "Help me, then."

> Her fingers moved the latch for all reply.

V

What we've got here is the desire to escape: not so much the man as the enclosure of the place, not to mention the subject of their exchange. Yet the resolution is incomplete, as the fidgeting with the hat shows, since the execution of this desire will be counterproductive for the model as far as being the subject of explication goes. May I go so far as to suggest that that would mean a loss of advantage, not to mention that it would be the end of the poem? In fact, it does end with precisely that, with her exit. The literal level will get into conflict, or fusion, with the metaphorical. Hence " 'I don't know rightly whether any man can,' " which fuses both these levels, forcing the poem to proceed; you don't know any longer who is the horse here, who is the cart. I doubt whether the poet himself knew that at this point. The fusion's result is the release of a certain force, which subordinates his pen, and the best it can do is keep both strands—literal and metaphorical—in check.

We learn the heroine's name, and that this sort of discourse had its precedents, with nearly identical results. Given the fact that we know the way the poem ends, we may judge—well, we may imagine—the character of those occasions. The scene in "Home Burial" is but a repetition. By this token, the poem doesn't so much inform us about their life as replace it. We also learn, from " 'Don't go to someone else this time,' " about a mixture of jealousy and sense of shame felt by at least one of them. And we learn, from " 'I won't come down the stairs' " and from "He sat and fixed his chin between his fists," about the fear of violence present in their physical proximity. The latter line is a wonderful embodiment of stasis, very much in the fashion of Rodin's *Penseur*, albeit with two fists, which is a very telling self-referential detail, since the forceful application of fist to chin is what results in a knockout.

The main thing here, though, is the reintroduction of the stairs. Not only the literal stairs but the steps in "he sat," too. From now on, the entire dialogue occurs on the stairs, though they have become the scene of an impasse rather than a passage. No physical steps are taken. Instead, we have their verbal, or oral, substitute. The ballet ends, yielding to the verbal advance and retreat, which is heralded by " 'There's something I should like to ask you, dear.' " Note again the air of cajoling, colored this time with the recognition of its futility in "dear." Note also the last semblance of actual interplay in " 'You don't know how to ask it.' 'Help me, then' "—this last knocking on the door, or, better yet, on the wall. Note "Her fingers moved the latch for all reply," because this feint of trying for the door is the last physical movement, the last theatrical or cinematic gesture in the poem, save one more latch-trying.

> "My words are nearly always an offense.
> I don't know how to speak of anything
> So as to please you. But I might be taught,
> I should suppose. I can't say I see how.
> A man must partly give up being a man
> With womenfolk. We could have some arrangement
> By which I'd bind myself to keep hands off
> Anything special you're a-mind to name.
> Though I don't like such things 'twixt those that love.
> Two that don't love can't live together without them.
> But two that do can't live together with them."
> She moved the latch a little.

The speaker's hectic mental pacing is fully counterbalanced by his immobility. If this is a ballet, it is a mental one. In fact, it's very much like fencing: not with an opponent or a shadow but with one's self. The lines are constantly taking a step forward and then undoing it. ("She took a doubtful step and then undid it.") The main technical device here is enjambment, which physically resembles descending the stairs. In fact, this back-and-forth, this give-and-take almost gives you a sense of being short of breath. Until, that is, the release that is coming with the formulaic, folksy " 'A man must partly give up being a man / With womenfolk.' "

After this release, you get three lines of more evenly paced verse, almost a tribute to iambic pentameter's proclivity for coherence, ending with the pentametrically triumphant " 'Though I don't like such things 'twixt those that love.' " And here our poet makes another not so subdued dash toward the proverbial: " 'Two that don't love can't live together without them. / But two that do can't live together with them' "—though this comes off as a bit cumbersome, and not entirely convincing.

Frost partly senses that: hence "She moved the latch a little." But that's only one explanation. The whole point of this qualifier-burdened monologue is the explication of its addressee. The man is groping for understanding. He realizes that in order to understand he's got to surrender—if not suspend entirely—his rationality. In other words, he descends. But this is really running down stairs that lead upward. And, partly from rapidly approaching the end of his wits, partly out of purely rhetorical inertia, he summons here the notion of love. In other words, this quasi-proverbial two-liner about love is a rational argument, and that, of course, is not enough for its addressee.

For the more she is explicated, the more remote she gets: the higher her pedestal grows (which is perhaps of specific importance to her now that she is downstairs). It's not grief that drives her out of the house but the dread of being explicated, as well as of the explicator himself. She wants to stay impenetrable and won't accept anything short of his complete surrender. And he is well on the way to it:

> "Don't—don't go.
> Don't carry it to someone else this time.
> Tell me about it if it's something human."

The last is the most stunning, most tragic line, in my view, in the entire poem. It amounts practically to the heroine's ultimate victory—i.e., to the aforementioned rational surrender on the part of the explicator. For all its colloquial air, it promotes her mental operations to supernatural status, thus acknowledging infinity—ushered into her mind by the child's death—as his rival. Against this he is powerless, since her access to that infinity, her absorption by and commerce with it, is backed in his eyes by the whole mythology of the opposite sex—by the whole notion of the alternative being impressed upon him by her at this point rather thoroughly. That's what he is losing her to by staying rational. It is a shrill, almost hysterical line, admitting the man's limitations and momentarily bringing the whole discourse to a plane of regard that the heroine could be at home on—the one she perhaps seeks. But only momentarily. He can't proceed at this level, and succumbs to pleading:

> "Let me into your grief. I'm not so much
> Unlike other folks as your standing there
> Apart would make me out. Give me my chance.
> I do think, though, you overdo it a little.
> What was it brought you up to think it the thing
> To take your mother-loss of a first child
> So inconsolably—in the face of love.
> You'd think his memory might be satisfied—"

He tumbles down, as it were, from the hysterical height of " 'Tell me about it if it's something human.' " But this tumble, this mental knocking about the metrically lapsing stairs, restores him to rationality, with all its attendant qualifiers. That brings him rather close to the heart of the matter—to her taking her " 'mother-loss of a first child / So inconsolably' "—and he evokes the catchall notion of love again, this time somewhat more convincingly, though still tinged with a rhetorical flourish: " 'in the face of love.' " The very word—"love"—undermines its emotional reality, reducing the sentiment to its utilitarian application: as a means of overcoming tragedy. However, overcoming tragedy deprives its victim of the status of hero or heroine. This, combined with the resentment over the explicator's lowering of his explication's plane of regard, results in the heroine's interruption of " 'You'd think his memory might be satisfied—' " with " 'There you go sneering now!' " It's Galatea's self-defense, the defense against the further application of the chiseling instrument to her already attained features.

Because of its absorbing story line, there is a strong temptation to bill "Home Burial" as a tragedy of incommunicability, a poem about the failure of language; and many have succumbed to this temptation. In fact, it is just the reverse: it is a tragedy of communication, for communication's logical end is the violation of your interlocutor's mental imperative. This is a poem about language's terrifying success, for language, in the final analysis, is alien to the sentiments it articulates. No one is more aware of that than a poet; and if "Home Burial" is autobiographical, it is so in the first place by revealing Frost's grasp of the collision between his métier and his emotions. To drive this point home, may I suggest that you compare the actual sentiment you may feel toward an individual in your company and the word "love." A poet is doomed to resort to words. So is the speaker in "Home Burial." Hence, their overlapping in this poem; hence, too, its autobiographical reputation.

But let us take it a step further. The poet here should

be identified not with one character but with both. He is the man here, all right, but he is the woman also. Thus you've got a clash not just of two sensibilities but of two languages. Sensibilities may merge—say, in the act of love; languages can't. Sensibilities may result in a child; languages won't. And, now that the child is dead, what's left is two totally autonomous languages, two non-overlapping systems of verbalization. In short: words. His versus hers, and hers are fewer. This makes her enigmatic. Enigmas are subject to explication, which they resist—in her case, with all she's got. His job, or, more exactly, the job of his language, is, therefore, the explication of her language, or, more exactly, her reticence. Which, when it comes to human interplay, is a recipe for disaster. When it comes to a poem, an enormous challenge.

Small wonder, then, that this "dark pastoral" grows darker with every line; it proceeds by aggravation, reflecting not so much the complexity of the author's mind as words' own appetite for disaster. For the more you push reticence, the greater it gets, having nothing to fall back upon but itself. The enigma thus grows bigger. It's like Napoleon invading Russia and finding that it goes beyond the Urals. Small wonder that this "dark pastoral" of ours has no choice but to proceed by aggravation, for the poet's mind plays both the invading army and the territory; in the end, he can't take sides. It is a sense of the incomprehensible vastness of what lies ahead, defeating not only the notion of conquest but the very sense of progress, that informs both " 'Tell me about it if it's something human' " and the lines that follow " 'There you go sneering now!' ":

> "I'm not, I'm not!
> You make me angry. I'll come down to you.
> God, what a woman!"

A language invading reticence gets no trophy here, save the echo of its own words. All it has to show for its efforts is a good old line that brought it nowhere before:

> "And it's come to this,
> A man can't speak of his own child that's dead."

It, too, falls back on itself. A stalemate.

It's broken by the woman. More exactly, her reticence is broken. Which could be regarded by the male character as success, were it not for what she surrenders. Which is not so much an offensive as a negation of all the man stands for.

> "You can't because you don't know how to speak.
> If you had any feelings, you that dug
> With your own hand—how could you?—his little grave;
> I saw you from that very window there,
> Making the gravel leap and leap in air,
> Leap up, like that, like that, and land so lightly
> And roll back down the mound beside the hole.
> I thought, Who is that man? I didn't know you.
> And I crept down the stairs and up the stairs
> To look again, and still your spade kept lifting.
> Then you came in. I heard your rumbling voice
> Out in the kitchen, and I don't know why,
> But I went near to see with my own eyes.
> You could sit there with the stains on your shoes
> Of the fresh earth from your own baby's grave
> And talk about your everyday concerns.
> You had stood the spade up against the wall
> Outside there in the entry, for I saw it."

"I shall laugh the worst laugh I ever laughed.
I'm cursed. God, if I don't believe I'm cursed."

This is the voice of a very foreign territory indeed: a foreign language. It is a view of the man from a distance he can't possibly fathom, since it is proportionate to the frequency with which the heroine creeps up and down the stairs. Which, in its own right, is proportionate to the leaps of his gravel in the course of his digging the grave. Whatever the ratio, it is not in favor of his actual or mental steps toward her on that staircase. Nor in his favor is the rationale behind her creeping up and down the stairs while he is digging. Presumably, there is nobody else around to do the job. (That they lost their firstborn suggests that they are fairly young and thus not very well off.) Presumably also, by performing this menial task, and by doing it in a particularly mechanical way—as a remarkably skillful mimetic job in the pentameter here indicates (or as is charged by the heroine)—the man is quelling, or controlling, his grief; that is, his movements, unlike the heroine's, are functional.

In short, this is futility's view of utility. For obvious reasons, this view is usually precise and rich in judgment: " 'If you had any feelings,' " and " 'Leap up, like that, like that, and land so lightly / And roll back down the mound beside the hole.' " Depending on the length of observation—and the description of digging runs here for nine lines—this view may result, as it does here, in a sensation of utter disparity between the observer and the observed: " 'I thought, Who is that man? I didn't know you.' " For observation, you see, results in nothing, while digging produces at least a mound, or a hole. Whose mental equivalent in the observer is also, as it were, a grave. Or, rather, a fusion of the man and his purpose, not to mention his instrument. What futility and Frost's pentameter register here above all is rhythm. The heroine observes an inanimate machine. The man in her eye is a gravedigger, and thus her alternative.

Now, the sight of our alternative is always unwelcome, not to say threatening. The closer your view of it, the sharper your general sense of guilt and of a deserved comeuppance. In the mind of a woman who has lost her child, that sense may be fairly sharp. Add to that her inability to translate her grief into any useful action, save a highly agitated creeping up and down, as well as the recognition—and subsequent glorification—of that inability. And add a cross-purpose correspondence between her movements and his: between her steps and his spade. What do you think it would result in? And remember that she is in *his* house, that this is the graveyard where *his* people are. And that he is a gravedigger.

> "Then you came in. I heard your rumbling voice
> Out in the kitchen, and I don't know why,
> But I went near to see with my own eyes."

Note this "and I don't know why," for here she unwittingly drifts toward her own projection. All that she needs now is to check that projection with her own eyes. That is, she wants to make her mental picture physical:

> "You could sit there with the stains on your shoes
> Of the fresh earth from your own baby's grave
> And talk about your everyday concerns.
> You had stood the spade up against the wall
> Outside there in the entry, for I saw it."

So what do you think she sees with her own eyes, and what does that sight prove? What does the frame contain this time? What does she have a close-up of? I am afraid she sees a murder weapon: she sees a blade. The fresh earth stains either on the shoes or on his spade make the spade's edge shine: make it into a blade. And does earth "stain," however fresh? Her very choice of noun, denoting liquid, suggests—accuses—blood. What should our man have done? Should he have taken his shoes off before entering the house? Perhaps. Perhaps he should have left his spade outside, too. But he is a farmer, and acts like one—presumably out of fatigue. So he brings in his instrument—in her eyes, the instrument of death. And the same goes for his shoes, and it goes for the rest of the man. A gravedigger is equated here, if you will, with the reaper. And there are only the two of them in this house.

The most awful bit is "for I saw it," because it emphasizes the perceived symbolism of that spade left standing against the wall outside there in the entry: for future use. Or as a guard. Or as an unwitting *memento mori*. At the same time, "for I saw it" conveys the capriciousness of her perception and the triumph of somebody who cannot be fooled, the triumph of catching the enemy. It is futility in full bloom, engulfing and absorbing utility into its shadow.

> "I shall laugh the worst laugh I ever laughed.
> I'm cursed. God, if I don't believe I'm cursed."

This is practically a nonverbal recognition of defeat, coming in the form of a typical Frostian understatement, studded with tautological monosyllables quickly abandoning their semantic functions. Our Napoleon or Pygmalion is completely routed by his creation, who still keeps pressing on.

> "I can repeat the very words you were saying:
> 'Three foggy mornings and one rainy day
> Will rot the best birch fence a man can build.'

> Think of it, talk like that at such a time!
> What had how long it takes a birch to rot
> To do with what was in the darkened parlor?"

Now, this is where our poem effectively ends. The rest is simply denouement, in which our heroine goes rambling on in an increasingly incoherent fashion about death, the world being evil, uncaring friends, and feeling alone. It is a rather hysterical monologue, whose only function, in terms of the story line, is to struggle toward a release for what has been pent up in her mind. It does not, and in the end she resorts to the door, as though only landscape were proportionate to her mental state and thus could be of solace.

And, quite possibly, it is. A conflict within an enclosure—a house, say—normally deteriorates into tragedy, because the rectangularity of the place itself puts a higher premium on reason, offering emotion only a straitjacket. Thus in the house the man is the master not only because the house is his but because—within the context of the poem—rationality is his. In a landscape, "Home Burial' "s dialogue would have run a different course; in a landscape, the man would be the loser. The drama would perhaps be even greater, for it's one thing when the house sides with a character, and another when the elements do so. In any case, that's why she is trying for the door.

So let's get back to the five lines that precede the denouement—to this business of rotting birches. "Three foggy mornings and one rainy day / Will rot the best birch fence a man can build," our farmer is quoted as saying, sitting there in the kitchen, clods of fresh earth on his shoes and the spade standing up there in the entry. One may ascribe this phrase again to his fatigue and to the next task in store for him: building a little fence around the new grave. However, since this is not a public but a family graveyard, the fence he mentioned might indeed be one of his everyday concerns, something else he has to deal with. And presumably he mentions it to take his mind off what he has just finished doing. Still, for all his effort, the mind is not entirely taken, as the verb "rot" indicates: the line contains the shadow of the hidden comparison—if a fence rots so quickly in the damp *air*, how quickly will a little coffin rot in earth damp enough to leave "stains" on his shoes? But the heroine once again resists the encompassing gambits of language— metaphor, irony, litotes—and goes straight for the literal meaning, the absolute. And that's what she jumps on in " 'What had how long it takes a birch to rot / To do with what was in the darkened parlor?' " What is remarkable here is how diverse their treatment of the notion of rotting is. While he is talking about a "birch fence," which is a clear deflection, not to mention a reference to something above the ground, she zeroes in on "what was in the darkened parlor." It's understandable that, being a mother, she concentrates—that Frost makes her concentrate—on the dead child. Yet her way of referring to it is highly roundabout, even euphemistic: "what was in." Not to mention that she refers to her dead child as a "what," not a "who." We don't learn his name, and for all we know, he didn't have much of a life after his birth. And then you should note her reference to the grave: "the darkened parlor."

Now, with "darkened parlor," the poet finishes his portrait of the heroine. We have to bear in mind that this is a rural setting, that the heroine lives in "his" house—i.e., that she came here from without. Because of its proximity to rot, this darkened parlor, for all its colloquial currency, sounds noticeably oblique, not to say arch. To the modern ear it has an almost Victorian ring, suggesting a difference of sensibilities bordering on class distinction.

I think you will agree that this is not a European poem.

Not French, not Italian, not German, not even British. I also can assure you that it is not Russian at all. And, in terms of what American poetry is like today, it is not American, either. It's Frost's own, and he has been dead for over a quarter of a century now. Small wonder, then, that one rambles on about his lines at such length, and in strange places, though he no doubt would wince at being introduced to a French audience by a Russian. On the other hand, he was no stranger to incongruity.

So what was it that he was after in this, his very own poem? He was, I think, after grief and reason, which, while poison to each other, are language's most efficient fuel—or, if you will, poetry's indelible ink. Frost's reliance on them here and elsewhere almost gives you the sense that his dipping into this ink pot had to do with the hope of reducing the level of its contents; you detect a sort of vested interest on his part. Yet the more one dips into it, the more it brims with this black essence of existence, and the more one's mind, like one's fingers, gets soiled by this liquid. For the more there is of grief, the more there is of reason. As much as one may be tempted to take sides in "Home Burial," the presence of the narrator here rules this out, for while the characters stand, respectively, for reason and for grief, the narrator stands for their fusion. To put it differently, while the characters' actual union disintegrates, the story, as it were, marries grief to reason, since the bond of the narrative here supersedes the individual dynamics— well, at least for the reader. Perhaps for the author as well. The poem, in other words, plays fate.

I suppose it is this sort of marriage that Frost was after, or perhaps the other way around. Many years ago, on a flight from New York to Detroit, I chanced upon an essay by the poet's daughter printed in the American Airlines in-flight magazine. In that essay Lesley Frost says that her father and her mother were co-valedictorians at the high school they both attended. While she doesn't recall the topic of her father's speech on that occasion, she remembers what she was told was her mother's. It was called something like "Conversation as a Force in Life" (or "the Living Force"). If, as I hope, someday you find a copy of *North of Boston* and read it, you'll realize that Elinor White's topic is, in a nutshell, the main structural device of that collection, for most of the poems in *North of Boston* are dialogues—are conversations. In this sense, we are dealing here—in "Home Burial," as elsewhere in *North of Boston*—with love poetry, or, if you will, with poetry of obsession: not that of a man with a woman so much as that of an argument with a counterargument— of a voice with a voice. That goes for monologues as well, actually, since a monologue is one's argument with oneself; take, for instance, "To be or not to be . . ." That's why poets so often resort to writing plays. In the end, of course, it was not the dialogue that Robert Frost was after but the other way around, if only because by themselves two voices amount to little. Fused, they set in motion something that, for want of a better term, we may just as well call "life." This is why "Home Burial" ends with a dash, not with a period.

HOME BURIAL

He saw her from the bottom of the stairs
Before she saw him. She was starting down,
Looking back over her shoulder at some fear.
She took a doubtful step and then undid it
To raise herself and look again. He spoke
Advancing toward her: "What is it you see

From up there always?—for I want to know."
She turned and sank upon her skirts at that,
And her face changed from terrified to dull.
He said to gain time: "What is it you see?"
Mounting until she cowered under him.
"I will find out now—you must tell me, dear."
She, in her place, refused him any help,
With the least stiffening of her neck and silence.
She let him look, sure that he wouldn't see,
Blind creature; and awhile he didn't see.
But at last he murmured, "Oh," and again, "Oh."

"What is it—what?" she said.
                                    "Just that I see."
"You don't," she challenged. "Tell me what it is."

"The wonder is I didn't see at once.
I never noticed it from here before.
I must be wonted to it—that's the reason.
The little graveyard where my people are!
So small the window frames the whole of it.
Not so much larger than a bedroom, is it?
There are three stones of slate and one of marble,
Broad-shouldered little slabs there in the sunlight
On the sidehill. We haven't to mind *those*.
But I understand: it is not the stones,
But the child's mound—"
                                    "Don't, don't, don't,
    don't," she cried.

She withdrew, shrinking from beneath his arm
That rested on the banister, and slid downstairs;
And turned on him with such a daunting look,

He said twice over before he knew himself:
"Can't a man speak of his own child he's lost?"

"Not you!—Oh, where's my hat? Oh, I don't need it!
I must get out of here. I must get air.—
I don't know rightly whether any man can."

"Amy! Don't go to someone else this time.
Listen to me. I won't come down the stairs."
He sat and fixed his chin between his fists.
"There's something I should like to ask you, dear."

"You don't know how to ask it."
                                  "Help me, then."

Her fingers moved the latch for all reply.

"My words are nearly always an offense.
I don't know how to speak of anything
So as to please you. But I might be taught,
I should suppose. I can't say I see how.
A man must partly give up being a man
With womenfolk. We could have some arrangement
By which I'd bind myself to keep hands off
Anything special you're a-mind to name.
Though I don't like such things 'twixt those that love.
Two that don't love can't live together without them.
But two that do can't live together with them."
She moved the latch a little. "Don't—don't go.
Don't carry it to someone else this time.
Tell me about it if it's something human.
Let me into your grief. I'm not so much
Unlike other folks as your standing there

Apart would make me out. Give me my chance.
I do think, though, you overdo it a little.
What was it brought you up to think it the thing
To take your mother-loss of a first child
So inconsolably—in the face of love.
You'd think his memory might be satisfied—"

"There you go sneering now!"

                                        "I'm not, I'm not!
You make me angry. I'll come down to you.
God, what a woman! And it's come to this,
A man can't speak of his own child that's dead."

"You can't because you don't know how to speak.
If you had any feelings, you that dug
With your own hand—how could you?—his little grave;
I saw you from that very window there,
Making the gravel leap and leap in air,
Leap up, like that, like that, and land so lightly
And roll back down the mound beside the hole.
I thought, Who is that man? I didn't know you.
And I crept down the stairs and up the stairs
To look again, and still your spade kept lifting.
Then you came in. I heard your rumbling voice
Out in the kitchen, and I don't know why,
But I went near to see with my own eyes.
You could sit there with the stains on your shoes
Of the fresh earth from your own baby's grave
And talk about your everyday concerns.
You had stood the spade up against the wall
Outside there in the entry, for I saw it."

"I shall laugh the worst laugh I ever laughed.
I'm cursed. God, if I don't believe I'm cursed."

"I can repeat the very words you were saying:
'Three foggy mornings and one rainy day
Will rot the best birch fence a man can build.'
Think of it, talk like that at such a time!
What had how long it takes a birch to rot
To do with what was in the darkened parlor?
You *couldn't* care! The nearest friends can go
With anyone to death, comes so far short
They might as well not try to go at all
No, from the time when one is sick to death,
One is alone, and he dies more alone.
Friends make pretense of following to the grave,
But before one is in it, their minds are turned
And making the best of their way back to life
And living people, and things they understand.
But the world's evil. I won't have grief so
If I can change it. Oh, I won't. I won't!"

"There, you have said it all and you feel better.
You won't go now. You're crying. Close the door.
The heart's gone out of it: why keep it up?
Amy! There's someone coming down the road!"

"*You*—oh, you think the talk is all. I must go—
Somewhere out of this house. How can I make you—"

"If—you—do!" She was opening the door wider.
"Where do you mean to go? First tell me that.
I'll follow and bring you back by force. I *will!*—"

If this poem is dark, darker still is the mind of its maker, who plays all three roles: the man, the woman, and the narrator. Their equal reality, taken separately or together, is still inferior to that of the poem's author, since "Home Burial" is but one poem among many. The price of his autonomy is, of course, in its coloration, and perhaps what you ultimately get out of this poem is not its story but the vision of its ultimately autonomous maker. The characters and the narrator are, as it were, pushing the author out of any humanly palatable context: he stands outside, denied re-entry, perhaps not coveting it at all. This is the dialogue's—alias the Life Force's—doing. And this particular posture, this utter autonomy, strikes me as utterly American. Hence this poet's monotone, his pentametric drawl: a signal from a far-distant station. One may liken him to a spacecraft that, as the downward pull of gravity weakens, finds itself nonetheless in the grip of a different gravitational force: outward. The fuel, though, is still the same: grief and reason. The only thing that conspires against this metaphor of mine is that American spacecraft usually return.

1994

Homage to
Marcus Aurelius

I

While antiquity exists for us, we, for antiquity, do not. We never did, and we never will. This rather peculiar state of affairs makes our take on antiquity somewhat invalid. Chronologically and, I am afraid, genetically speaking, the distance between us is too immense to imply any causality: we look at antiquity as if out of nowhere. Our vantage point is similar to that of an adjacent galaxy's view of ourselves; it boils down, at best, to a solipsistic fantasy, to a vision. We shouldn't claim more, since nothing is less repeatable than our highly perishable cellular mix. What would an ancient Roman, were he to wake up today, recognize? A cloud on high, blue waves, a woodpile, the horizontality of the bed, the verticality of the wall—but no one by face, even if those he encountered were stark naked. Finding himself in our midst, he at best would have a sensation similar to that of a moon landing, i.e., not knowing what is before him: the future, or the distant past? a landscape or a ruin? These things, after all, have great similarity. Unless, of course, he saw a horseman.

II

The twentieth is perhaps the first century that looks at this statue of a horseman with slight bewilderment. Ours is the century of the automobile, and our kings and presidents drive, or else they are driven. We don't see many horsemen around, save at equestrian shows or races. One exception is perhaps the British consort, Prince Philip, as well as his daughter, Princess Anne. But that has to do not even so much with their royal station as with the name "Philip," which is of Greek origin and means *phil-hippos*: lover of horses. It is so much so that Her Royal Highness was married—until recently—to Captain Mark Phillips of the Royal Guards, an accomplished steeplechaser himself. You may even add to that Prince Charles, the heir to the British crown, an avid polo player. But that would be it. You don't see leaders of democracies or, for that matter, the few available tyrannies, mounted. Not even military commanders receiving parades, of which these days there are fewer and fewer. Horsemen have left our precincts almost entirely. To be sure, we still have our mounted police; and there is perhaps no greater *Schadenfreude* for a New Yorker than to watch one of these Lochinvars in the saddle issuing a traffic ticket to an illegally parked car while his hackney is sniffing at the victim's hood. But when we erect monuments to our leaders and public heroes these days, there are only two feet resting on the pediment. Well, too bad, since a horse used to symbolize quite a lot: empires, virility, nature. Actually, there is a whole etiquette of equestrian statuary, as when a horse, for instance, rears up under the rider, it means that the latter died in battle. If all of its four hooves rest on the pediment, that suggests he died in his four-poster. If one leg is lifted high up in the air, then the implication is that he died of battle-related wounds; if not so high up, that he lived long enough, trotting, as it were, through his existence. You can't do that with a car. Besides, a car, even a Rolls, doesn't bespeak one's uniqueness, nor does it elevate one above the crowd the way a horse does. Roman emperors in particular used to be depicted on horseback not in order to commemorate their preferred mode of transportation but precisely to convey their superiority: their belonging, often by birth, to the equestrian class. In the parlance of the time, "equestrian" presumably meant "high up" or "highborn." An equus, in other words, in addition to carrying an actual rider, was saddled with a lot of allusions. Above all, it could represent the past, if only because it represented the animal kingdom—and that's where the past came from. Maybe this is what Caligula had in mind after all when he introduced his horse to the Senate. Since antiquity seems to have made this connection already. Since it had far more truck with the past than with the future.

III

What the past and the future have in common is our imagination, which conjures them. And our imagination is rooted in our eschatological dread: the dread of thinking that we are without precedence or consequence. The stronger that dread, the more detailed our notion of antiquity or of utopia. Sometimes—actually, all too often—they overlap, as when antiquity appears to possess an ideal order and abundance of virtues, or when the inhabitants of our utopias stroll through their marble well-governed cities clad in togas. Marble is, to be sure, the perennial building material of our antiquity and utopia alike. On the whole, the color white permeates our imagination all the way through its extreme ends, when its version of the past or the future takes a metaphysical or religious turn. Paradise is white, so are ancient Greece and Rome. This predilection is not so much an alternative to the darkness of our fancy's source as a metaphor for our ignorance, or simply a reflection of the material our fancy normally employs for its flight: paper. A crumpled paper ball on its way to the wastebasket could easily be taken for a splinter of a civilization, especially with your glasses off.

IV

I first saw this bronze horseman indeed through a windshield of a taxi some twenty years ago, almost in a previous incarnation. I'd just landed in Rome for the first time, and was on my way to the hotel, where a distant acquaintance of mine had made a reservation. The hotel bore a very un-Roman name: it was called Bolivar. Something equestrian was already in the air, since the great *libertador* is normally depicted atop his rearing horse. Did he die in battle? I couldn't remember. Presently we were stuck in the evening traffic, in what looked like a cross between a railroad station's square and the end of a soccer game. I wanted to ask the driver how far we had to go, but my Italian was good only for "Where are we?" "Piazza Venezia," he blurted, nodding to the left. "Campidoglio," a nod to the right. And with another nod: "Marco Aurelio," followed by what was no doubt an energetic reference to the traffic. I looked to the right. "Marco Aurelio," I repeated to myself, and felt as if two thousand years were collapsing, dissolving in my mouth thanks to the Italian's familiar form of this Emperor's name. Which always had for me an epic, indeed imperial, sway, sounding like a caesura-studded, thundering announcement by history's own majordomo: Marcus!—caesura—Aurelius! The Roman! Emperor! Marcus! Aurelius! This is how I knew him in high school, where the majordomo was our own

stumpy Sarah Isaakovna, a very Jewish and very resigned
lady in her fifties, who taught us history. Yet for all her
resignation, when it came to uttering the names of Roman
emperors, she'd straighten up, assuming an attitude of grandeur, and practically shout, well above our heads, into the
peeling-off stucco of the classroom wall adorned with its
portrait of Stalin: Caius Julius Caesar! Caesar Octavian Augustus! Caesar Tiberius! Caesar Vespasianus Flavius! The
Roman Emperor Antoninus Pius! And then—Marcus Aurelius! It was as though the names were bigger than she
herself, as though they were swelling up from inside to be
released into a far greater space than her own body or, for
that matter, the room, the country, the times themselves
could contain. She reveled in those odd-sounding foreign
names, in their unpredictable succession of vowels and consonants, and that was, frankly, contagious. A child loves this
sort of thing: strange words, strange sounds, and that's why,
I suppose, history is best taught in childhood. At the age of
twelve one may not grasp the intrigue, but a strange sound
suggests an alternative reality. "Marcus Aurelius" certainly
did to me, and that reality proved to be quite vast: larger,
in fact, than that Emperor's own. Now apparently came time
to domesticate that reality; which is why, I suppose, I was
in Rome. "Marco Aurelio, eh?" I said to myself, and turned
to the driver: "Where?" He pointed to the top of a huge
waterfall of marble steps leading uphill, now right in front
of us, and as the car sharply swerved to gain some minuscule
advantage in the sea of traffic, I momentarily beheld a floodlit
pair of horse's ears, a bearded head, and a protruding arm.
Then the sea swallowed us up. Half an hour later, at the
entrance to the Bolivar, my valet pack in one hand, my
money in another, I asked the driver in a sudden surge of
fraternity and gratitude—after all, he was the first person I
had spoken with in Rome and he had also brought me to my

hotel and didn't even overcharge me, or so it seemed—his name. "Marco," he said, and drove off.

V

The most definitive feature of antiquity is our absence. The more available its debris and the longer you stare at it, the more you are denied entry. Marble negates you particularly well, though bronze and papyri don't fall too far behind. Reaching us intact or in fragments, these things strike us, of course, with their durability and tempt us to assemble them, fragments especially, into a coherent whole, but they were not meant to reach us. They were, and still are, for themselves. For man's appetite for the future is as limited as his own ability to consume time, or as grammar, this first casualty of every discourse on the subject of the hereafter, shows. At best, these marbles, bronzes, and papyri were meant to outlast their subjects and their makers, but not themselves. Their existence was functional, which is to say, of limited purpose. Time is no jigsaw puzzle, because it is made up of perishing pieces. And though perhaps objects-inspired, the idea of the afterlife wasn't an option until quite late. Anyhow, what is before us are the leftovers of necessity or vanity, i.e., of considerations always nearsighted. Nothing exists for the future's sake; and the ancients couldn't in nature regard themselves as the ancients. Nor should we bill ourselves as their tomorrow. We won't be admitted into antiquity: it being well inhabited—in fact, overpopulated—as it was. There are no vacancies. No point in busting your knuckles against marble.

VI

If we find the lives of Roman emperors highly absorbing, it is because we are highly self-absorbed creatures. To say the least, we regard ourselves as the centers of our own universes, varying to be sure in width, but universes nonetheless, and as such having centers. The difference between an empire and a family, a network of friends, a web of romantic entanglements, a field of expertise, etc., is a difference in volume, not in structure. Also, because the Caesars are so much removed from us in time, the complexity of their predicament appears to be graspable, shrunk, as it were, by the perspective of two millennia to almost a fairy-tale scale, with its wonders and its naïveté. Our address books are their empires, especially after hours. One reads Suetonius or Aelius or, for that matter, Psellus, for archetypes even if all one runs is a bike shop or a household of two. Somehow it is easier to identify with a Caesar than with a consul, or praetor, or lictor, or slave, even though that is what one's actual station in the modern reality corresponds to. This has nothing to do with self-aggrandizement or aspirations but is due to the understandable attraction of king-size (so to speak), clear-cut versions of compromised virtue, vice, or self-delusion rather than their fuzzy, inarticulate originals next door or, for that matter, in the mirror. That's why, perhaps, one looks at their likenesses, at the marbles especially. For in the end, a human oval can accommodate only so much. You can't have more than two eyes or less than one mouth; surrealism wasn't yet invented and African masks were not yet in vogue. (Or maybe the Romans clung so much to Greek standards precisely because they were.) So in the end you are bound to recognize yourself in one of them. For there is no Caesar without a bust, as there is no swan without a reflection. Clean-shaven, bearded, bald, or well coiffed, they all return a vacant, pupil-free, marble stare, pretty much like that of a passport photo or the mug shot of a criminal. You won't know what they have been up to; and putting these faces to their stories is what, perhaps, makes them indeed archetypal. It also moves them somewhat closer to us, since, being depicted fairly often, they, no doubt, must also have developed a degree of detachment vis-à-vis their physical reality. In any case, to them a bust or a statue was indeed what a photograph is to us, and the most "photographed" person would obviously be a Caesar. There were, of course, others: their wives, senators, consuls, praetors, great athletes or beauties, actors and orators. On the whole, though, judging by what has survived, men were chiseled more often than women, which presumably reflects who controlled the purse as much as the society's ethos. By either standard, a Caesar would be a winner. In the Capitoline Museum you can shuffle for hours through chambers filled up practically to the rafters with rows and rows of marble portraits of Caesars, emperors, dictators, *augusti* hoarded there from all over what used to be the place they ran. The longer one stayed on the job, the more numerous would be one's "photographs." One would be depicted in one's youth, maturity, decrepitude; sometimes the distance between one's busts is no more, it would seem, than a couple of years. It appears that marble portraiture was an industry and, with its calibrations of decay, something of a mortuary one; the rooms strike you in the end as not unlike a library housing an encyclopedia of beheading. It is hard to "read," though, because marble is notoriously blank. In a sense, what it also has in common with photography—or, more accurately, with what photographs used to be—is that it is literally monochrome. For one thing, it renders everyone blond. Whereas in their real lives, some of the models—

Caesars' wives, to say the least, since many of them came from Asia Minor—were not. Yet one is almost grateful to marble for its lack of pigmentation, the way one is grateful to a black-and-white photograph, for it unleashes one's fantasy, one's intuition, so that viewing becomes an act of complicity: like reading.

VII

And there are ways of turning viewing into reading. When I was a boy I used to frequent a big museum in my hometown. It had a vast collection of Greek and Roman marbles, not to mention those by Canova and Thorvaldsen. I'd noticed that, depending on the time of day as well as the season, those carved features would wear different expressions, and I wondered what they would look like after hours. But the museum closed at 6 p.m., presumably because the marbles were not accustomed to electricity. I couldn't do much about that. In general, one can't do much about statues anyway. One can circle around them, squint at them from different angles; but that's that. With busts, though, one can go a bit further, as I discovered inadvertently. One day, staring at the little white face of some early Roman *fanciulla*, I lifted my hand, presumably to smooth my hair, and thus obstructed the single source of light coming to her from the ceiling. At once her facial expression changed. I moved my hand a bit to the side: it changed again. I began moving both my arms rather frantically, casting each time a different shadow upon her features: the face came to life. Eventually, of course, I was interrupted by the shrieks of the guard. He ran toward me, but looking at his screaming face, I thought it less animated than that of a little marble girl from B.C.

VIII

Of all Roman emperors, Marcus Aurelius gets the best press. Historians love him, and so do philosophers. It is to the latter, though, that Marcus Aurelius owes his good standing to this day, since this discipline proved to be more durable than the Roman Empire or the aspects of one's statecraft in it. Actually, historians should be perhaps less enthusiastic about him than they are, because a couple of times he came very close to depriving them of their subject, particularly by designating his son, the really moronic Commodus, to be his heir. But historians are a sturdy lot; they've digested things much harder than Commodus' idea of renaming Rome after himself. They could live with—as well as live in—Commodiopolis and research the history of the Commodian empire. As for philosophers, they were, and some still are, enamored of Marcus Aurelius' *Meditations* perhaps not so much for the depth of its probing as for the respectability the discipline itself gained in the royal embrace. Politics is far more often the pursuit of philosophers than philosophy is the sideline of kings. Besides, for Marcus Aurelius, philosophy was a lot more than a sideline: it was, as we'd say today, a therapy, or, as Boethius put it later, a consolation. He wasn't a great philosopher, nor was he a visionary; not even a sage; his *Meditations* is at once a melancholy and repetitive book. The Stoic doctrine at the time had become a doctrine indeed, and though he did write in Greek, he is no match for Epictetus. Most likely a Roman emperor was drawn to this kind of language out of respect for the doctrine's origins, and also perhaps out of nostalgia, in order not to forget the language of civilized discourse; the language, after all, of his youth and pursuits more noble perhaps than those at hand. Add to that, if you will, possible considerations of secrecy, and the benefit of detachment: the purpose and the method of the discipline itself, enhanced here by the very means of expression. Not to mention that his reign simply happened to coincide with a substantial revival of Greek culture in Rome, the first Renaissance, if you will, owing no doubt to the long era of considerable stability historians dubbed the "Pax Romana." And historians love Marcus Aurelius precisely because he was the last guardian of that Pax. Because his reign effectively and neatly concluded a period of Roman history lasting nearly two centuries that began with Augustus and, to all intents and purposes, ended with our man. They love him because he is the end of the line, and a very coherent one at that: which, for historians, is a luxury. Marcus was a highly conscientious ruler; perhaps because he was appointed to the job—not anointed; because he was adopted into the dynasty, not born to it. And both historians and philosophers love him precisely for carrying out so well the commission for which he thought himself ill suited, and was in fact reluctant to accept. To them, his predicament presumably echoes in some fashion their own: he is, as it were, a model for those who have to go in this life against their calling. In any case, the Roman Empire gained a lot more from his dual loyalty to duty and philosophy than did the Stoic doctrine (which, in its own turn, comes with Marcus to the end of its own line: to ethics). So much so that it's been maintained, often vigorously, that this sort of inner split is a good recipe for ruling. That it's better if one's spiritual yearnings have their own outlet and don't interfere too much with one's actions. This is what the whole philosopher-king business is all about, isn't it? When your metaphysics get short shrift. As for Marcus, however, he dreaded this prospect from the very beginning, dreaded being summoned to Hadrian's court, for all its comforts and bright perspectives. Perhaps precisely because of those; as a true product of the Greek doctrine, all he aspired to was "the camp-bed and skin coverlet." Philosophy for him was a manner of dressing as much as it was a manner of discourse: the texture of existence, not just a mental pursuit. Picture him as a Buddhist monk, then; you won't be much off target, since the "way of life" was the essence of Stoicism as well; emphatically so, we may add. The young Marcus must have been apprehensive of the royal adoption for more reasons than Hadrian's sexual predilections: it meant a wardrobe as different as the accompanying mental diet. That he went for it had to do, one imagines, less with royal pressure than with our man's own misgivings about his intellectual fortitude: apparently it's easier to be a king than a philosopher. Anyhow, it came to pass, and here's a monument. The good question, though, is: To whom? To a philosopher? Or to a king? To both? Perhaps to neither.

IX

A monument is by and large a vertical affair, a symbolic departure from the general horizontality of existence, an antithesis to spatial monotony. A monument never actually departs from this horizontality—well, nothing does—but rather rests upon it, punctuating it at the same time like an exclamation mark. In principle, a monument is a contradiction. In this way, it resembles its most frequent subject: a human being, equally endowed with vertical and horizontal properties, but eventually settling for the latter. The durability of the material a monument is usually made of—marble, bronze, increasingly cast-iron, and now even concrete —highlights the contradictory nature of the undertaking even further, especially if a monument's subject is a great battle, a revolution, or a natural disaster—i.e., an event that took a great toll and was momentary. Yet even if the subject is an abstract ideal or the consequence of a momentous event, there is a detectable clash of time frames and notions of viability, not to mention textures. Perhaps given the material's aspiration for permanence, the best subject for a monument is indeed destruction. Zadkin's statue of bombed-out Rotterdam immediately comes to mind: its verticality is functional, since it points at the catastrophe's very source. Also, what could be more horizontal than the Netherlands? And it occurs to one that the monument owes its genealogy to great planes, to the idea of something being seen from afar—whether in a spatial or a temporal sense. That it is of nomadic origin, for at least in a temporal sense we are all nomads. A man as aware of the futility of all human endeavor as our philosopher-king would be, of course, the first to object to being turned into a public statue. On the other hand, twenty years of what appears to have been practically nonstop frontier combat, taking him all over the place, effectively turned him into a nomad. Besides, here's his horse.

X

The Eternal City is a city of hills, though. Of seven of them, actually. Some are natural, some artificial, but negotiating them is an ordeal in any case, especially on foot and especially in summer, although the adjacent seasons' temperatures don't fall too far behind. Add to that the Emperor's rather precarious health; add to that its not getting any better with age. Hence, a horse. The monument sitting at the top of the Capitoline actually fills up the vacuum left by Marcus' actual mounted figure, which, some two thousand years ago, occupied that space quite frequently, not to say routinely. On the way to the Forum, as the saying goes. Actually, on his way from it. Were it not for Michelangelo's pedestal, the monument would be a footprint. Better yet, a hoofprint. The Romans, superstitious like all Italians, maintain that when the bronze Marcus hits the ground, the end of the world will occur. Whatever the origin of this superstition, it stands to reason if one bears in mind that Marcus' motto was Equanimity. The word suggests balance, composure under pressure, evenness of mental disposition; literally: equation of the animus, i.e., keeping the soul—and thus the world—in check. Give this formula of the Stoic posture a possible misspelling and you'll get the monument's definition: Equinimity. The horseman tilts, though, somewhat, as if leaning toward his subjects, and his hand is stretched out in a gesture that is a cross between a greeting and a blessing. So much so that for a while some insisted that this was not Marcus Aurelius but Constantine, who converted Rome to Christianity. For that, however, the horseman's face is too serene, too free of zeal or ardor, too uninvolved. It is the face of detachment, not of love—and detachment is precisely what Christianity never could manage. No, this is no Constantine, and no Christian. The face is devoid of any sentiment; it is a postscript to passions, and the lowered corners of the mouth bespeak the lack of illusion. Had there been a smile, you could think perhaps of the Buddha; but the Stoics knew too much about physics to toy with the finality of human existence in any fashion. The face shines with the bronze's original gold, but the hair and the beard have oxidized and turned green, the way one turns gray. All thought aspires to the condition of metal; and the bronze denies you any entry, including interpretation or touch. What you've got here, then, is detachment per se. And out of this detachment the Emperor leans toward you slightly, extending his right hand either to greet you or to bless you—which is to say, acknowledge your presence. For where he is, there is no you, and vice versa. The left hand theoretically holds the reins, which are either missing now or were never there in the first place: a horse would obey this rider no matter what.

Especially if it represented Nature. For he represents Reason. The face is clearly of the Antonine dynasty, though he
wasn't born into it but adopted. The hair, the beard, the
somewhat bulging eyes and slightly apoplectic posture are
those of his stepfather turned father-in-law and his very own
son. Small wonder that it is so hard to tell the three of them
apart among the Ostia marbles. But, as we know nowadays,
a period's fashion may easily beat the genes. Remember the
Beatles. Besides, he revered Antoninus Pius enough to emulate him in a variety of ways; his appearance could be simply
that attitude's spin-off. Also, the sculptor, being a contemporary, might have wished to convey the sense of continuum
perceived by the historians of the stepfather's and the step-
son's reigns: a sense that Marcus himself, needless to say,
sought to create. Or else the sculptor just tried to produce
a generic portrait of the era, of the perfect ruler, and what
we've got here is the fusion of the two best emperors the
realm had had since the murder of Domitian—the way he
did the horse, whose identity we don't ponder. In all probability, however, this is the author of the *Meditations* himself: the face and the torso slightly tilted toward his subjects
fit extremely well the text of that melancholy book, which
itself leans somewhat toward the reality of human existence,
in the attitude not so much of a judge as of an umpire. In
this sense this monument is a statue to a statue: it's hard to
picture a Stoic in motion.

XI

The Eternal City resembles a gigantic old brain that long
ago gave up any interest in the world—it being too graspable
a proposition—and settled for its own crevasses and folds.
Negotiating their narrows, where even a thought about yourself is too cumbersome, or their expanses, where the concept

of the universe itself appears puny, you feel like a worn-out needle shuffling the grooves of a vast record—to the center and back—extracting with your soles the tune that the days of yore hum to the present. This is the real His Master's Voice for you, and it turns your heart into a dog. History is not a discipline but something that is not yours—which is the main definition of beauty. Hence, the sentiment, for it is not going to love you back. It is a one-way affair, and you recognize its platonic nature in this city instantly. The closer you get to the object of your desire, the more marble or bronze it gets, as the natives' fabled profiles scatter around like animated coins escaped from some broken terra-cotta jar. It is as though here time puts, between bedsheets and mattress, its own carbon paper—since time mints as much as it types. The moment you leave the Bolivar or the equally smelly yet cheaper Nerva, you hit Foro Trajano with its triumphant column tightly wrapped in conquered Dacians and soaring like a mast above the marble ice floe of broken pillars, capitals, and cornices. Now this is the domain of stray cats, reduced lions in this city of reduced Christians. The huge white slabs and blocks are too unwieldy and random to arrange them in a semblance of order or to drag them away. They are left here to absorb the sun, or to represent "antiquity." In a sense they do; their ill-matching shapes are a democracy, this place is still a forum. And on his way from it, just across the road, beyond pines and cypresses, atop the Capitoline Hill, stands the man who made the fusion of republic and imperial rule probable. He has no company: virtue, like a malady, alienates. For a split second, it is still A.D. 176 or thereabouts, and the brain ponders the world.

XII

Marcus was a good ruler and a lonely man. In his line of work, loneliness, of course, comes with the territory; but he was lonelier than most. *Meditations* gives you a greater taste of that than his correspondence; yet it is just a taste. The meal had many courses and was pretty heavy. To begin with, he knew that his life had been subverted. For the ancients, philosophy wasn't a by-product of life but the other way around, and Stoicism was particularly exacting. Perhaps we should momentarily dispense here with the very word "philosophy," for Stoicism, its Roman version especially, shouldn't be characterized as love for knowledge. It was, rather, a lifelong experiment in endurance, and a man was his own guinea pig: he was not a probing instrument, he was an answering instrument. By the time of Marcus, the doctrine's knowledge was to be lived rather than loved. Its materialist monism, its cosmogony, its logic, and its criterion of truth (the perception that irresistibly compels the subject to assent to it as true) were already in place, and for a philosopher, life's purpose was to prove the validity of this knowledge by applying it to reality till the end of his days. In other words, a Stoic's life was a study in ethics, since ethics buys nothing except osmosis. And Marcus knew that his experiment was interrupted, or qualified, to a degree he himself wouldn't be able to comprehend; worse still, that his findings—provided there were any—could have no application. He believed Plato, but not to this extent. At any rate, he would be the first to square the common good with individual unhappiness, and that's what *Meditations* is perhaps all about: a postscript to *the Republic*. He knew that as a philosopher he was finished: that concentration was out, that all he could hope for was some time for sporadic contemplation. That the best his life would amount to would be a few glimpses of eternity, a true surmise now and then. He accepted that, for the sake of the common good no doubt, but hence *Meditations'* overriding melancholy or, if you will, pessimism—all the more deep because the man definitely suspected that there was rather more to the story. *Meditations* is thus a patchy book, nurtured by interference. It is a disjointed, rambling internal monologue, with occasional flashes of pedantry as well as of genius. It shows you what he might have been rather than what he was: his vector, rather than an attained destination. It appears to have been jotted down amid the hubbub and babel of this or that military campaign, successful as they might have been—by the campfire, indeed, and the soldier's cloak played the Stoic philosopher's body coverlet. In other words, it was done in spite of—or, if you will, against—history, of which his destiny was trying to make him a part. A pessimist he perhaps was, but certainly not a determinist. That's why he was a good ruler, why the mixture of republic and imperial rule under him didn't look like a sham. (One may even argue that the larger democracies of the modern world show an increasing preference for his formula. Good examples are contagious, too; but virtue, as we said, alienates. Not to mention that time, wasting its carbon paper on subjects, seems to have very little left for rulers.) To say the least, he was a good caretaker: he didn't lose what he inherited; and if the empire under him didn't expand, it was just as well; as Augustus said, "Enough is enough." For somebody in charge of an entity so vast and for so long (practically thirty-three years, from A.D. 147, when his father-in-law conferred upon him the powers of emperorship, to his death in A.D. 181 near the would-be Vienna), he has surprisingly little blood on his hands. He would rather pardon than punish those who rebelled against him; those who fought him, he would rather subdue than destroy. The laws he made benefited the most powerless: widows, slaves, juniors, although it must be said that he was the first to introduce the double standard in prosecuting criminal offenses by members of the Senate (the office of special prosecutor was his invention). He used the state's purse sparingly and, being abstemious himself, tried to encourage this in others. On several occasions, when the empire needed money, he sold imperial jewels rather than hit his subjects up for new taxes. Nor did he build anything extravagant, no Pantheon or Colosseum. In the first place, because those already existed; second, because his sojourn in Egypt was quite brief and he didn't go beyond Alexandria, unlike Agrippa and unlike Titus and Hadrian, to have his mind fired up by the gigantic, desert-fitting scale of Egyptian edifices. Besides, he didn't like *circenses* that much, and when he had to attend a show, he is reported to have read or written or been briefed during the performance. It was he, however, who introduced to the Roman Circus the safety net for acrobats.

XIII

Antiquity is above all a visual concept, generated by objects whose age escapes definition. The Latin *antiquus* is essentially a more drastic term for "old," deriving from the equally Latin *ante*, which means "before," and used to be applied presumably to things Greek. "Beforishness," then. As for the Greeks themselves, their *arche* denotes beginning or genesis, the moment when something occurs for the first time. "Firstness," then? Herein, in any case, lies a substantial distinction between the Romans and the Greeks—a distinction owing its existence partly to the Greeks having fewer objects at their disposal to fathom the provenance of, partly to their general predilection for dwelling on origins. The former, in fact, may very well be an explanation for the latter, since next to archaeology there is only geology. As for our own version of antiquity, it eagerly swallows both the Greeks and the Romans, yet, if worse comes to worse, might cite the Latin precedent in its defense. Antiquity to us is a vast chronological jumble, filled with historical, mythical, and divine beings, interrelated among themselves by marble and also because a high percentage of the depicted mortals claim divine descendance or were deified. This last aspect, resulting in the practically identical scant attire of those marbles and in the confusion on our part of attributing fragments (did this splintered arm belong to a mortal or to a deity?), is worth noticing. The blurring of distinctions between mortals and deities was habitual with the ancients, with the Roman Caesars in particular. While the Greeks on the whole were interested in lineage, the Romans were after promotion. The target, however, was the same: Celestial Mansions, yet vanity or boosting the ruler's authority played a rather small part in this. The whole point of identifying with the gods lies not so much in the notion of their omniscience as in the sense that their extreme carnality is fully matched by the extremes of their detachment. To begin with, a ruler's own margin of detachment would make him identify with a god (carnality, of course, would be Nero or Caligula's shortcut). By acquiring a statue, he'd boost that margin considerably, and it's best if it's done in the course of one's lifetime, since marble reduces both the expectations of the subjects and the model's own willingness to deviate from manifest perfection. It sets one free, as it were, and freedom is the province of deities. Putting it very broadly, the marble and mental vista that we call antiquity is a great repository of shed and shredded skins, a landscape after the departure, if you will; a mask of freedom, a jumble of discarded boosters.

XIV

If Marcus indeed hated anything, and was proscriptive about it, that was gladiatorial show. Some say it was because he detested blood sports, so vulgar and non-Greek, because siding with a team would be for him the beginning of partiality. Others insist that it had to do with his wife, Faustina, who, for all her thirteen children—only six survived—was remarkably promiscuous for an empress. Among her numerous affairs, these others single out a particular gladiator who, they claim, was the real father of Commodus. But nature works in mysterious ways; an apple often rolls far from the tree, especially if that tree grows on a slope. Commodus was both a rotten apple and its slope. Actually, as far as the imperial fortunes were concerned, he was a precipice. And perhaps an inability to grasp nature's mysterious ways was the source of Faustina's reputation (though if Marcus had it against the gladiators because of Faustina, he should have proscribed also against sailors, pantomime actors, generals, and so forth). Marcus himself would make light of this. Once, approached with these rumors and the suggestion that he get rid of her, he retorted: "If we send our wife away, we must give back her dowry, too." The dowry here was the empire itself, since Faustina was the daughter of Antoninus Pius. On the whole, he stood by her unswervingly and, judging by the honors he bestowed upon her when she died, perhaps even loved her. She was, it appears, one of those heavy main courses whose taste you barely sample in the *Meditations*. In general, Caesar's wife is beyond reproach and suspicion. And perhaps precisely in order to uphold this attitude as well as to save Faustina's reputation Marcus departed from the nearly two-century-old tradition of selecting an heir to the throne and passed the crown to what he thus asserted to be his own flesh and blood. At any rate, it was

Faustina's. Apparently his reverence for his father-in-law was enormous and he simply couldn't believe that someone in whose veins ran the blood of the Antonines could be all that bad. Or perhaps he regarded Faustina as a force of nature; and nature for a Stoic philosopher was the ultimate authority. If anything, nature taught him indifference and a sense of proportion; otherwise his life would have been pure hell; *Meditations* strings out solipsism like glacial debris. Toward the wrong and atrocious, Marcus was not so much forgiving as dismissive. Which is to say that he was impartial rather than just and that his impartiality was the product not of his mind's fairness but of his mind's appetite for the infinite; in particular, for impartiality's own limits. This would stun his subjects no less than it does his historians, for history is the domain of the partial. And as his subjects chided Marcus for his attitude toward gladiatorial shows, historians jumped on him for his persecution of Christians. It is unclear, of course, how much Marcus was informed about the Christian creed, but it is easy to imagine him finding its metaphysics myopic and its ethics detestable. From a Stoic point of view, a god with whom you trade in virtue to obtain eternal favors wouldn't be worth a prayer. For somebody like Marcus, virtue's value lay precisely in its being a gamble, not an investment. Intellectually, to say the least, he had very little reason to favor the Christians; still less could he do so as a ruler, faced at the time with wars, plague, uprisings—and a disobedient minority. Besides, he didn't introduce new laws against the Christians; those of Hadrian, and those of Trajan before him, were quite enough. It is obvious that, following his beloved Epictetus, Marcus regarded a philosopher, i.e., himself, as the missionary of Divine Providence to mankind, i.e., to his own subjects. You are welcome to quibble with his notion of it; one thing is quite clear, though:

it was far more open-ended than the Christian version. Blessed are the partial, for they shall inherit the earth.

XV

Take white, ocher, and blue; add to that a bit of green and a lot of geometry. You'll get the formula time has picked for its backdrop in these parts, since it is not without vanity, especially once it assumes the shape of history or of an individual. It does so out of its prurient interest in finality, in its reductive ability, if you will, for which it has numerous guises, including the human brain or the human eye. So you shouldn't be surprised, especially if you were born here, to find yourself one day surrounded by the white-cum-ocher, trapezoid square with the white-cum-blue trapeze overhead. The former is human-made (actually, by Michelangelo), the latter is heaven-made, and you may recognize it more readily. However, neither is of use to you, since you are green: the shade of oxidized bronze. And if the cumulus white in the oxygen blue overhead is still preferable to the balustrade's marble calves and well-tanned Tiburtine chests below, it is because clouds remind you of your native antiquity: because they are the future of any architecture. Well, you've been around for nearly two thousand years, and you ought to know. Perhaps they, the clouds, are indeed the only true antiquity there is, if only because among them you are not a bronze.

XVI

Ave, Caesar. How do you feel now, among barbarians? For we are barbarians to you, if only because we speak neither Greek nor Latin. We are also afraid of death far more than you ever were, and our herd instinct is stronger than the one for self-preservation. Sound familiar? Maybe it's our numbers, Caesar, or maybe it's the number of our goods. We sure feel that by dying we stand to lose far more than you ever had, empire or no empire. To you, if I remember correctly, birth was an entrance, death an exit, life a little island in the ocean of particles. To us, you see, it's all a bit more melodramatic. What spooks us, I guess, is that an entrance is always guarded, whereas an exit isn't. We can't conceive of dwindling into particles again: after hoarding so many goods, that's unpalatable. Status's inertia, I guess, or fear of the elemental freedom. Be that as it may, Caesar, you are among barbarians. We are your true Parthians, Marcomanni, and Quadi, because nobody came in your stead, and we inhabit the earth. Some of us go even further, barging into your antiquity, supplying you with definitions. You can't respond, can't bless, can't greet or quell us with your outstretched right hand—the hand whose fingers still remember scribbling your *Meditations*. If that book hasn't civilized us, what will? Perhaps they billed you as the Philosopher-King precisely to dodge its spell by underscoring your uniqueness. For theoretically what's unique isn't valid, Caesar, and you were unique. Still, you were no philosopher-king—you'd be the first to wince at this label. You were what the mixture of power and inquiry made you: a postscript to both, a uniquely autonomous entity, almost to the point of pathology. Hence your emphasis on ethics, for supreme power exempts one from the moral norm practically by definition, and so does supreme knowledge. You got both for the price of one, Caesar; that's why you had to be so bloody ethical. You wrote an entire book to keep your soul in check, to steel yourself for daily conduct. But was it really ethics that you were after, Caesar? Wasn't it your extraordinary appetite for the infinite that drove you to the most minute self-scrutiny, since you considered yourself a fragment, no matter how tiny, of the Whole, of the Universe—and the Universe, you maintained, changes constantly. So whom were you checking, Marcus? Whose morality did you try and, for all I know, manage to prove? Small wonder, then, that you are not surprised to find yourself now among the barbarians; small wonder that you always were far less afraid of them than of yourself—since you were afraid of yourself far more than of death. "Reflect that the chief source of all evils to man," says Epictetus, "as well as of baseness and cowardice, is not death but the fear of death." But you knew also that no man owns his future—or, for that matter, his past. That all one stands to lose by dying is the day when it happens—the day's remaining part, to be precise—and in time's eye, still less. The true pupil of Zeno, weren't you? At any rate, you wouldn't allow the prospect of nonbeing to color your being, Universe or no Universe. The eventual dance of particles, you held, should have no bearing on the animated body, not to mention on its reason. You were an island, Caesar, or at least your ethics were, an island in the primordial and—pardon the expression—postmordial ocean of free atoms. And your statue just marks the place on the map of the species' history where this island once stood: uninhabited, before submerging. The waves of doctrine and of creed—of the Stoic doctrine and the Christian creed—have closed over your head, claiming you as their own Atlantis. The truth, though, is that you never were either's. You were just one of the best men that ever lived, and you were obsessed with your duty because you were obsessed with virtue. Because it's harder to master than the alternative and because, if the universal design had been evil, the world would not exist. Some will point out no doubt that the doctrine and the creed came before and after you, but it's not history that defines the good. To be sure, time, conscious of its monotony, calls forth men to tell its yesterday from its tomorrow. You, Caesar, were good because you didn't.

XVII

I saw him for the last time a few years ago, on a wet winter night, in the company of a stray Dalmatian. I was returning by taxi to my hotel after one of the most disastrous evenings in my entire life. The next morning I was leaving Rome for the States. I was drunk. The traffic moved with the speed one wishes for one's funeral. At the foot of the Capitol I asked the driver to stop, paid, and got out of the car. The hotel was not far away and I guess I intended to continue on foot; instead, I climbed the hill. It was raining, not terribly hard but enough to turn the floodlights of the square—nay! trapeze—into fizzing-off Alka-Seltzer pellets. I hid myself under the conservatory's arcade and looked around. The square was absolutely empty and the rain was taking a crash course in geometry. Presently I discovered I was not alone: a middle-sized Dalmatian appeared out of nowhere and quietly sat down a couple of feet away. Its sudden presence was so oddly comforting that momentarily I felt like offering it one of my cigarettes. I guess this had to do with the pattern of its spots; the dog's hide was the only place in the whole piazza free of human intervention. For a while we both stared at the horseman's statue. "The universal nature out of the universal substance, as if it were wax, now molds the figure of a horse, then melting this down uses the material for a tree, next for a man, next for something else; and each of these things subsists for a very short time. Yet it is no hardship for a box to be broken up, as it was none for it to be nailed together." This is what a boy memorized at the age of fifteen and remembered thirty-five years later. Still, this horse didn't melt down, nor did this man. Apparently the

universal nature was satisfied with this version of its substance and cast it in bronze. And suddenly—presumably
because of the rain and the rhythmic pattern of Michelangelo's pilasters and arches—all got blurred, and against that
blur, the shining statue, devoid of any geometry, seemed to
be moving. Not at great speed, and not out of this place;
but enough for the Dalmatian to leave my side and follow
the bronze progress.

XVIII

As absorbing as Roman antiquity appears to be, perhaps we
should be a bit more careful with our retrospective proclivity.
What if man-made chronology is but a self-fulfilling fallacy,
a means of obscuring the backwardness of one's own intelligence? What if it's just a way of justifying the snail's pace
of the species' evolution? And what if the very notion of such
evolution is a lie? Ultimately, what if this good old sense of
history is just the dormant majority's self-defense against the
alert minority? What if our concept of antiquity, for example,
is but the switching off of an alarm clock? Let's take this
horseman and his book. To begin with, *Meditations* wasn't
written in the second century A.D., if only because its author
wasn't going by the Christian calendar. In fact, the time of
its composition is of no relevance, since its subject is precisely ethics. Unless, of course, humanity takes a special
pride in having wasted fifteen centuries before Marcus' insights were reiterated by Spinoza. Maybe we are just better
at counting than at thinking, or else we mistake the former
for the latter? Why is it that we are always so interested in
knowing when truth was uttered for the first time? Isn't this
sort of archaeology in itself an indication that we are living
a lie? In any case, if *Meditations* is antiquity, it is we who
are the ruins. If only because we believe that ethics has the

future. Well, perhaps our retrospective ability should indeed be reined in somewhat, lest it become all-consuming. For if nothing else, ethics is the criterion of the present—perhaps the only one there is, since it turns every yesterday and tomorrow into now. It is precisely that sort of arrow that at every moment of its flight is immobile. *Meditations* is no existential manual and it wasn't written for posterity. Nor should we, for that matter, be interested in the identity of its author or promote him to the rank of philosopher-king: ethics is an equalizer; thus the author here is Everyman. His concept of duty cannot be attributed to his royal overdose of it, because he wasn't the only emperor around; neither can his resignation of the imperial origin, because one is able to empathize with it quite readily. Nor can we put it down to his philosophic training—and for the same reasons: there were too many philosophers apart from Marcus, and on the other hand, most of us are not Stoics. What if his sense of duty and his resignation were, in the first place, products of his individual temperament, of the melancholic disposition, if one wants to be precise; combined perhaps with the man's aging? There are, after all, only four known humors; so at least the melancholics among us can take this book to heart and skip the bit about the historical perspective nobody possesses anyhow. As for the sanguinics, cholerics, and phlegmatics, they, too, perhaps should admit that the melancholic version of ethics is accommodating enough for them to marvel at its pedigree and chronology. Perhaps short of compulsory Stoic indoctrination, society may profit by making a detectable melancholic streak a prerequisite for anyone aspiring to rule it. To this extent, a democracy can afford what an empire could. And on top of that, one shouldn't call the Stoic acceptance of the perceptible reality resignation. Serenity would be more apt, given the ratio between man and the subjects of his attention, or—as the case may be—vice versa. A grain of sand can't resign itself to the desert; and perhaps what's ultimately good about melancholics is that they seldom get hysterical. By and large, they are quite reasonable, and, "what is reasonable," as Marcus once said, "is consequently social." Did he say this in Greek, to fit your idea of antiquity?

XIX

Of all Roman poets, Marcus knew best and preferred Seneca. Partly because Seneca, too, was of Spanish origin, sickly, and a great statesman; mainly, of course, because he was a Stoic. As for Catullus, Marcus would find him no doubt too hot and choleric. Ovid for him would be licentious and excessively ingenious, Virgil too heavy-handed and perhaps even servile, Propertius too obsessive and passionate. Horace? Horace would seem to be the most congenial author for Marcus, what with his equipoise and attachment to the Greek monody. Yet perhaps our Emperor thought him too quirky, or too diverse and unsteady as well: in short, too much of a poet. In any case, there is almost no trace of Horace in *Meditations*, nor for that matter of the greatest among the Latins, Lucretius—another you would think a natural choice for Marcus. But then perhaps a Stoic didn't want to be depressed by an Epicurean. On the whole, Marcus seems to have been far more fluent in Greek literature, preferring dramatists and philosophers to poets of course, though snatches from Homer, Agathon, and Menander crop up in his book quite frequently. Come to think of it, if anything makes antiquity a coherent concept, it is the volume of its literature. The library of someone like Marcus would contain a hundred or so authors; another hundred perhaps would be hearsay, a rumor. Those were the good old days indeed: antiquity or no antiquity. And even that rumored

writing would be limited to two languages: Greek and Latin.
If you were he, if you were a Roman emperor, would you
in the evening, to take your mind off your cares, read a Latin
author if you had a choice? Even if he was Horace? No; too
close for comfort. You'd pick up a Greek—because that's
what you'd never be. Because a Greek, especially a philosopher, is in your eyes a more genuine item than yourself,
since he knew no Latin. If only because of that, he was less
a relativist than you, who consider yourself practically a mongrel. So if he were a Stoic, you must take heed. You even
may go so far as to take up a stylus yourself. Otherwise you
might not fit into someone's notion of antiquity.

X X

A stray Dalmatian trotting behind the bronze horseman
hears something strange, sounding somewhat familiar but
muffled by rain. He accelerates slightly and, having overtaken the statue, lifts up his muzzle, hoping to grasp what's
coming out of the horseman's mouth. In theory it should be
easy for him, since his Dalmatia was the birthplace of so
many Caesars. He recognizes the language but fails to make
out the accent:

Take heed not to be transformed into Caesar, not to be dipped
in purple dye; for it does happen. Keep yourself therefore simple,
go pure, grave, unaffected, the friend of justice, religious, kind,
affectionate, strong for your proper work. Wrestle to continue to
be the man that Philosophy wished to make you. Reverence the
gods, save men . . .

Let not the future trouble you, for you will come to it, if come
you must, bearing with you the same reason which you are using
now to meet the present.

All things are the same: familiar in experience, transient in time, sordid in their material; all now such as in the days of those whom we have buried.

To leave the company of men is nothing to fear, if gods exist; for they would not involve you in ill . . .

To turn against anything that comes to pass is a separation from nature.

Men have come into the world for the sake of one another. Either instruct them, then, or bear with them.

The universe is change, life is opinion.

Run always the short road, and nature's road is short.

As are your repeated imaginations, so will your mind be, for the soul is dyed by its imaginations.

Love that to which you go back, and don't return to Philosophy as to a schoolmaster, but as a man to the sponge and slave, as another to a poultice, another to fomentation . . .

The mind of the Whole is social.

The noblest kind of retribution is not to become like your enemy.

What doesn't benefit the hive is no benefit to the bee.

On Pain: what we cannot bear removes us from life; what lasts can be borne. The understanding, too, preserves its own tranquillity by abstraction, and the governing self does not grow worse;

but it is for the parts which are injured by pain, if they can, to declare it.

There are three relations. One is to what surrounds you. One to the divine cause from which all things come to pass for all. One to those who live at the same time with you.

Accept without pride, relinquish without struggle.

And then there was nothing else, save the sound of rain crashing on Michelangelo's flagstones. The Dalmatian darted across the square like a piece of unearthed marble. He was heading no doubt for antiquity, and carried in his ears his master's—the statue's—voice:

To acquaint yourself with these things for a hundred years, or for three, is the same.

1994

A Cat's Meow

～

I

I dearly wish I could begin this monologue from afar, or at least preface it with a bunch of disclaimers. However, this dog's ability to learn new tricks is inferior to its tendency to forget old ones. So let me try to cut straight to the bone.

Many things have changed on this dog's watch; but I believe that a study of phenomena is still valid and of interest only as long as it is being conducted from without. The view from within is inevitably distorted and of parochial consequence, its claims to documentary status notwithstanding. A good example is madness: the view of the physician is of greater import than that of his patient.

Theoretically, the same should apply to "creativity"; except that the nature of this phenomenon rules out the possibility of a vantage point for studying it. Here, the very process of observation renders the observer, to put it mildly, inferior to the phenomenon he observes, whether he is positioned without or within the phenomenon. In a manner of

Delivered at a symposium organized by the Foundation for Creativity and Leadership and held in Zermatt, Switzerland, in January 1995.

speaking, the report of the physician here is as invalid as the patient's own ravings.

The lesser commenting upon the greater has, of course, a certain humbling appeal, and at our end of the galaxy we are quite accustomed to this sort of procedure. I hope, therefore, that my reluctance to objectify creativity bespeaks not a lack of humility on my part but precisely the absence of a vantage point enabling me to pronounce anything of value on the subject.

I don't qualify as a physician; as a patient I am too much of a basket case to be taken seriously. Besides, I detest the very term "creativity," and some of this detestation rubs off on the phenomenon this term appears to denote. Even if I were able to shut down the voice of my senses revolting against it, my utterance on the subject would amount at best to a cat's attempt to catch its own tail. An absorbing endeavor, to be sure; but then perhaps I should be meowing.

Given the solipsistic nature of any human inquiry, that would be as honest a response to the notion of creativity as you can get. Seen from the outside, creativity is the object of fascination or envy; seen from within, it is an unending exercise in uncertainty and a tremendous school for insecurity. In either case, a meow or some other incoherent sound is the most adequate response whenever the notion of creativity is invoked.

Let me, therefore, get rid of the panting or bated breath that accompanies this term, which is to say, let me get rid of the term altogether. Webster's Collegiate Dictionary defines creativity as the ability to create, so let me stick to this definition. This way, perhaps, at least one of us will know what he is talking about, although not entirely.

The trouble begins with "create," which is, I believe, an exalted version of the verb "to make," and the same good old Webster's offers us "to bring into existence." The exaltation here has to do presumably with our ability to distinguish between familiar and unprecedented results of one's making. The familiar, thus, is *made*; the unfamiliar, or unprecedented, is *created*.

Now, no honest craftsman or maker knows in the process of working whether he is making or creating. He may be overtaken with this or that incoherent emotion at a certain stage of the process, he may even have an inkling that he is manufacturing something qualitatively new or unique, but the first, the second, and the last reality for him is the work itself, the very process of working. The process takes precedence over its result, if only because the latter is impossible without the former.

The emergence of something qualitatively new is a matter of chance. Hence there is no visual distinction between a maker and a beholder, between an artist and his public. At a reception, the former may stand out in the crowd at best by virtue of his longer hair or sartorial extravagance, but nowadays the reverse may be true as well. In any case, at the completion of the work, a maker may mingle with beholders and even assume their perspective on his work and employ their vocabulary. It is unlikely, however, that upon returning to his study, studio, or, for that matter, lab, he would attempt to rechristen his tools.

One says "I make" rather than "I create." This choice of verb reflects not only humility but the distinction between the guild and the market, for the distinction between making and creating can be made only retroactively, by the beholder. Beholders are essentially consumers, and that's why a sculptor seldom buys another sculptor's works. Any discourse on creativity, no matter how analytical it may turn out to be, is therefore a market discourse. One artist's recognition of another's genius is essentially a recognition of the power of chance and perhaps of the other's industry in producing occasions for chance to invade.

This, I hope, takes care of the "make" part of Webster's definition. Let's address the "ability" part. The notion of ability comes from experience. Theoretically, the greater one's experience, the more secure one may feel in one's ability. In reality (in art and, I would think, science), experience and the accompanying expertise are the maker's worst enemies.

The more successful you've been, the more uncertain you are, when embarking on a new project, of the result. Say, the greater the masterpiece you just produced, the smaller the likelihood of your repeating the feat tomorrow. In other words: the more questionable your ability becomes. The very notion of ability acquires in your mind a permanent question mark, and gradually one begins to regard one's work as a nonstop effort to erase that mark. This is especially true among those engaged in literature, particularly in poetry, which, unlike other arts, is bound to make detectable sense.

But even adorned with an exclamation mark, ability is not guaranteed to spawn masterpieces each time it is applied. We all know plenty of uniquely endowed artists and scientists who produce little of consequence. Dry spells, writer's blocks, and fallow stretches are the companions of practically every known genius, all lamenting about them bitterly, as do much lesser lights. Often a gallery signs up an artist, or an institution a scientist, only to learn how slim the pickings may get.

In other words, ability is not reducible either to skill or to an individual's energy, much less the congeniality of one's surroundings, one's financial predicament, or one's milieu. Had it been otherwise, we would have had by now a far greater volume of masterpieces on our hands than is the case. In short, the ratio of those engaged throughout just this century in art and science to the appreciable results is such that one is tempted to equate ability with chance.

Well, it looks as if chance inhabits both parts of Webster's definition of creativity rather cozily. It is so much so that it occurs to me that perhaps the term "creativity" denotes not so much an aspect of human agency as the property of the material to which this agency now and then is applied; that perhaps the ugliness of the term is, after all, justified, since it bespeaks the pliable or malleable aspects of inanimate matter. Perhaps the One who dealt with that matter first is not called the Creator for nothing. Hence, creativity.

Considering Webster's definition, a qualifier is perhaps in order. Denoting a certain unidentified resistance, "the ability to make" perhaps should be accompanied by a sobering "war on chance." A good question is, of course, what comes first—the material or its maker? For all our professed humility, at our end of the galaxy the answer is obvious and resounds with hubris. The other—and a much better question—is, whose chance are we talking about here, the maker's or the material's?

Neither hubris nor humility will be of much help here. Perhaps in trying to answer this question, we have to jettison the notion of virtue altogether. But then we always have been tempted to do just that. So let's seize this opportunity: not for the sake of scientific inquiry so much as for Webster's reputation.

But I am afraid we need a footnote.

II

Because human beings are finite, their system of causality is linear, which is to say, self-referential. The same goes for their notion of chance, since chance is not cause-free; it is but a moment of interference by another system of causality, however aberrant its pattern, in our own. The very existence of the term, not to mention a variety of epithets accompanying it (for instance, "blind"), shows that our concepts of order and chance are both essentially anthropomorphic.

Had the area of human inquiry been limited to the animal kingdom, that would be fine. However, it's manifestly not so; it's much larger and, on top of that, a human being insists on knowing the truth. The notion of truth, in its own right, is also anthropomorphic and presupposes, on the part of the inquiry's subject—i.e., the world—a withholding of the story, if not outright deception.

Hence a variety of scientific disciplines probing the universe in the most minute manner, the intensity of which—especially of their language—could be likened to torture. In any case, if the truth about things has not been attained thus far, we should put this down to the world's extraordinary resilience rather than to a lack of effort. The other explanation, of course, is truth's absence; an absence that we don't accept because of its drastic consequences for our ethics.

Ethics—or, to put it less grandly but perhaps more pointedly, pure and simple eschatology—as the vehicle of science? Perhaps; at any rate, what human inquiry indeed boils down to is the animate interrogating the inanimate. Small wonder that the results are inconclusive; smaller wonder still that the methods and the language we employ in the process more and more resemble the matter at hand itself.

Ideally, perhaps, the animate and the inanimate should swap places. That, of course, would be to the liking of the dispassionate scientist, who places such a premium on objectivity. Alas, this is not likely to happen, as the inanimate doesn't seem to show any interest in the animate: the world is not interested in its humans. Unless, of course, we ascribe to the world divine provenance, which, for several millennia now, we've failed to demonstrate.

If the truth about things indeed exists, then, given our status as the world's latecomers, that truth is bound to be nonhuman. It is bound to cancel out our notions of causality, aberrant or not, as well as those of chance. The same applies to our surmises as to the world's provenance, be it divine, molecular, or both: the viability of a concept depends on the viability of its carriers.

Which is to say that our inquiry is essentially a highly solipsistic endeavor. For the only opportunity available for the animate to swap places with the inanimate is the former's physical end: when man joins, as it were, matter.

Still, one can stretch matters somewhat by imagining that it is not the inanimate which is under the animate's investigation but the other way around. This rings a certain metaphysical bell, and not so faintly. Of course, it's difficult to build either science or a religion on such a foundation. Still, the possibility shouldn't be ruled out, if only because this option allows our notion of causality to survive intact. Not to mention that of chance.

What sort of interest could the infinite take in the finite? To see how the latter might modify its ethics? But ethics as such contains its opposite. To tax human eschatology further? But the results will be quite predictable. Why would the infinite keep an eye on the finite?

Perhaps out of the infinite's nostalgia for its own finite past, if it ever had one? In order to see how the poor old finite is still faring against overwhelming odds? How close the finite may come to comprehending, with its microscopes, telescopes, and all, with its observatories' and churches' domes, those odds' enormity?

And what would the infinite's response be, should the finite prove itself capable of revealing the infinite's secrets? What course of action might the infinite take, given that its repertoire is limited to the choice between being punitive or benevolent? And since benevolence is something we are less familiar with, what form might it assume?

If it is, let's say, some version of life eternal, a paradise, a utopia where nothing ever ends, what should be done, for instance, about those who never make it there? And if it were possible for us to resurrect them, what would happen to our notion of causality, not to mention chance? Or maybe the opportunity to resurrect them, an opportunity for the living to meet the dead, is what chance is all about? And isn't the finite's chance to become infinite synonymous with the animate becoming inanimate? Is that a promotion?

Or perhaps the inanimate appears to be so only to the eye of the finite? And if there is indeed no difference, save a few secrets thus far not revealed, where, once they get revealed, are we all to dwell? Would we be able to shift from the infinite to the finite and back, if we had a choice? What would the means of transportation between the two be? An injection, perhaps? And once we lose the distinction between the finite and the infinite, would we care where we are? Wouldn't that be, to say the least, the end of science, not to mention religion?

Have you been influenced by Wittgenstein? asks the reader.

Acknowledging the solipsistic nature of human inquiry shouldn't, of course, result in prohibitive legislation limiting that inquiry's scope. It won't work: no law based on the recognition of human shortcomings does. Furthermore, every legislator, especially an unacknowledged one, should be, in turn, aware all the time of the equally solipsistic nature of the very law he is trying to push.

Still, it would be both prudent and fruitful to admit that all our conclusions about the world outside, including those about its provenance, are but reflections, or better yet articulations, of our physical selves.

For what constitutes a discovery or, more broadly, truth

as such, is our recognition of it. Presented with an observation or a conclusion backed by evidence, we exclaim, "Yes, that's true!" In other words, we recognize something that has been offered to our scrutiny as our own. Recognition, after all, is an identification of the reality within with the reality without: an admission of the latter into the former. However, in order to be admitted into the inner sanctum (say, the mind), the guest should possess at least some structural characteristics similar to those of the host.

This, of course, is what explains the considerable success of all manner of microcosmic research, with all those cells and particles echoing nicely our own self-esteem. Yet, humility aside, when a grateful guest eventually reciprocates by inviting his gracious host over to his place, the latter often finds himself quite comfortable in those theoretically strange quarters and occasionally even benefits from a sojourn in the village of Applied Sciences, emerging from it now with a jar of penicillin, now with a tankful of gravity-spurning fuel.

In other words, in order to recognize anything, you've got to have something to recognize it with, something that will do the recognizing. The faculty that we believe does the recognizing job on our behalf is our brain. Yet the brain is not an autonomous entity: it functions only in concert with the rest of our physiological system. What's more, we are quite cognizant of our brain's ability not only to absorb concepts as regards the outside world but to generate them as well; we are also cognizant of that ability's relative dependence on, say, our motor or metabolic functions.

This is enough to suspect a certain parity between the inquirer and the subject of the inquiry, and suspicion is often the mother of truth. That, at any rate, is enough to suggest a perceptible resemblance between what's getting discovered and the discoverer's own cellular makeup. Now that, of course, stands to reason, if only because we are very much of this world—at least according to the admission of our own evolutionary theory.

Small wonder, then, that we are capable of discovering or discerning certain truths about it. This wonder is so small that it occurs to one that "discovery" is quite possibly a misnomer, and so are "recognition," "admission," "identification," etc.

It occurs to one that what we habitually bill as our discoveries are but the projections of what we contain within upon the outside. That the physical reality of the world/nature/you-name-it is but a screen—or, if you like, a wall—with our own structural imperatives and irregularities writ large or small upon it. That the outside is a blackboard or a sounding board for our ideas and inklings about our own largely incomprehensible tissue.

That, in the final analysis, a human being doesn't so much obtain knowledge from the outside as secrete it from within. That human inquiry is a closed-circuit system, where no Supreme Being or alternative system of intelligence can break in. Were they to, they wouldn't be welcome, if only because He, or it, would become one of us, and we have had enough of our kind.

They had better stay in the realm of probability, in the province of chance. Besides, as one of them said, "My kingdom is not of this world." No matter how scandalous probability's reputation is, it won't thrust either one of them into our midst, because probability is not suicidal. Inhabiting our minds for want of a better seat, it surely won't try to destroy its only habitat. And if infinity indeed has us for its audience, probability will certainly try its best to present infinity as a moral perspective, especially with a view to our eventually entering it.

To that end, it may even send in a messiah, since left

to our own devices we have a pretty rough time with the ethics of even our manifestly limited existence. As chance might have it, this messiah may assume any guise, and not necessarily the guise of human likeness. He may, for instance, appear in the form of some scientific idea, in the shape of some microbiological breakthrough predicating individual salvation on a universal chain reaction that would require safety for all in order to achieve eternity for one, and vice versa.

Stranger things have happened. In any case, whatever it is that makes life safer or gives it hope of extension should be regarded as being of supernatural origin, because nature is neither friendly nor hope-inspiring. On the other hand, between science and creeds, one is perhaps better off with science, because creeds have proven too divisive.

All I am trying to suggest is that, chances are, a new messiah, should he really emerge, is likely to know a bit more about nuclear physics or microbiology—and about virology in particular—than we do today. That knowledge, of course, is bound to be of greater use for us here than in the life everlasting, but for the moment, we may still settle for less.

Actually, this could be a good test for probability, for chance in particular, since the linear system of causality takes us straight into extinction. Let's see whether chance is indeed an independent notion. Let's see whether it is something more than just bumping into a movie star in a suburban bar or winning the lottery. Of course, this depends on how much one wins: a big win may come close to personal salvation.

But have you been influenced by Wittgenstein, perseveres the reader.

No, not by Wittgenstein, I reply. Just by Frankenstein. End of footnote.

III

So if we are a part of the natural world (as our cellular makeup suggests), if the animate is an aspect of the inanimate, then chance pertaining to a maker pertains to matter. Perhaps Webster's "ability to create" is nothing more (or less) than matter's attempts to articulate itself. Since a maker (and with him the whole human species) is an infinitesimal speck of matter, the latter's attempts at articulation must be few and far between. Their infrequency is proportionate to the availability of adequate mouthpieces, whose adequacy, i.e., the readiness to perceive an unhuman truth, is known in our parlance as genius. This infrequency is thus the mother of chance.

Now, matter, I believe, comes to articulate itself through human science or human art presumably only under some kind of duress. This may sound like an anthropomorphic fantasy, but our cellular makeup entitles us to this sort of indulgence. Matter's fatigue, its thinning out, or its oversaturation with time are, among a host of other less and more fathomable processes, what further enunciates chance and what is registered by the lab's instruments or by the no less sensitive pen of the lyric poet. In either case, what you get is the ripple effect.

In this sense, the ability to make is a passive ability: a grain of sand's response to the horizon. For it is the sense of an opened horizon that impresses us in a work of art or a scientific breakthrough, isn't it? Anything less than that qualifies not for the unique but for the familiar. The ability to make, in other words, depends on the horizon and not on one's resolve, ambition, or training. To analyze this ability only from our end of the story is therefore erroneous and not terribly rewarding.

"Creativity" is what a vast beach remarks when a grain

of sand is swept away by the ocean. If this sounds too tragic or too grand for you, it means only that you are too far back in the dunes. An artist's or a scientist's notion of luck or chance reflects essentially his proximity to the water or, if you will, to matter.

One can increase one's proximity to it in principle by will; in reality, though, it happens nearly always inadvertently. No amount of research or of caffeine, calories, alcohol, or tobacco consumed can position that grain of sand sufficiently close to the breakers. It all depends on the breakers themselves, i.e., on matter's own timing, which is solely responsible for the erosion of its so-called beach. Hence all this loose talk about divine intervention, breakthroughs, and so forth. Whose breakthrough?

If poetry fares somewhat better in this context, it is because language is, in a manner of speaking, the inanimate's first line of information about itself released to the animate. To put it perhaps less polemically, language is a diluted aspect of matter. By manipulating it into a harmony or, for that matter, disharmony, a poet—by and large unwittingly —negotiates himself into the domain of pure matter—or, if you will, of pure time—faster than can be done in any other line of work. A poem—and above all a poem with a recurrent stanzaic design—almost inevitably develops a centrifugal force whose ever-widening radius lands the poet far beyond his initial destination.

It is precisely the unpredictability of the place of one's arrival, as well perhaps as one's eventual gratitude, that makes a poet regard his ability "to make" as a passive ability. The vastness of what lies ahead rules out the possibility of any other attitude toward one's regular or irregular procedure; it certainly rules out the notion of creativity. There is no creativity vis-à-vis that which instills terror.

Wooing the Inanimate

Four Poems by Thomas Hardy

I

A decade or so ago, a prominent English critic, reviewing in an American magazine a collection of poems by the Irish poet Seamus Heaney, remarked that that poet's popularity in Britain, in its academic circles particularly, is indicative of the English public's stolid reading tastes, and that for all the prolonged physical presence of Messieurs Eliot and Pound on British soil, modernism never took root in England. The latter part of his remark (certainly not the former, since in that country—not to mention that milieu—where everyone wishes the other worse off, malice amounts to an insurance policy) got me interested, for it sounded both wistful and convincing.

Shortly afterward, I had the opportunity to meet that critic in person, and although one shouldn't talk shop at the dinner table, I asked him why he thinks modernism fared so poorly in his country. He replied that the generation of poets which could have wrought the decisive change was wiped out

Delivered to the students enrolled in "Subject Matter in Modern Lyric Poetry" at Mount Holyoke College, fall 1994.

in the Great War. I found this answer a bit too mechanistic, considering the nature of the medium, too Marxist, if you will—subordinating literature too much to history. But then the man was a critic, and that's what critics do.

I thought that there must have been another explanation—if not for the fate of modernism on that side of the Atlantic, then for the apparent viability of formal verse there at the present time. Surely there are plenty of reasons for that, obvious enough to discard the issue altogether. The sheer pleasure of writing or reading a memorable line would be one; the purely linguistic logic of, and need for, meter and rhyme is another. But nowadays one's mind is conditioned to operate circuitously, and at the time, I thought only that a good rhyme is what in the end saves poetry from becoming a demographic phenomenon. At the time, my thoughts went to Thomas Hardy.

Perhaps I wasn't thinking so circuitously, after all, or at least not yet. Perhaps the expression "Great War" triggered something in my memory, and I remembered Thomas Hardy's "After two thousand years of mass / We've got as far as poison-gas." In that case, my thinking was still straight. Or was it perhaps the term "modernism" that triggered those thoughts. In that case . . . A citizen of a democracy shouldn't be alarmed, of course, to find himself belonging to a minority; though he might get irritable. If a century can be compared to a political system, a significant portion of this one's cultural climate could well qualify as a tyranny: that of modernism. Or, to put it more accurately, of what sailed under that pennant. And perhaps my thoughts went to Hardy because at about that time—a decade ago—he habitually began to be billed as a "pre-modernist."

As definitions go, "pre-modernist" is a reasonably flattering one, since it implies that the so defined has paved the road to our just and happy—stylistically speaking—times. The drawback, though, is that it pensions an author off squarely into the past, offering all the fringe benefits of scholarly interest, of course, but robbing him in effect of relevance. The past tense is his equivalent of a silver watch.

No orthodoxy, especially not a new one, is capable of honest hindsight, and modernism is no exception. While modernism itself presumably benefits from applying this epithet to Thomas Hardy, he, I am afraid, does not. In either case, this definition misleads, for Hardy's poetic output, I daresay, has not so much foreshadowed as overshot, and by an awfully wide margin at that, the development of modern poetry. Had T. S. Eliot, for instance, at the time he read Laforgue, read Thomas Hardy instead (as I believe Robert Frost did), the history of poetry in English in this century, or to say the least its present, might be somewhat more absorbing. For one thing, where Eliot needs a handful of dust to perceive terror, for Hardy, as he shows in "Shelley's Skylark," a pinch is enough.

II

All this no doubt sounds to you a touch too polemical. On top of that, you may wonder whom it is that the man in front of you is arguing with. True, the literature on Thomas Hardy the poet is fairly negligible. There are two or three full-length studies; they are essentially doctoral-dissertations-turned-books. There are also two or three biographies of the man, including one he penned himself, though it bears his wife's name on the cover. They are worth reading, especially the last if you believe—as I expect you do—that the artist's life holds the key for the understanding of his work. If you believe the opposite, you won't lose much by giving them a miss, since we are here to address his work.

I am arguing, I suppose, against seeing this poet through the prism of those who came in his stead. First, because, in most cases, those who came in his stead were operating in relative or absolute ignorance of Hardy the poet's existence—on this side of the Atlantic particularly. The very dearth of literature about Hardy the poet is both that ignorance's proof and its present echo. Second, because, on the whole, there is little point in reviewing the larger through the prism of the smaller, however vociferous and numerous; our discipline is no astronomy. Mainly, however, because the presence of Hardy the novelist impairs one's eyesight from the threshold, and no critic I know of can resist the temptation to hitch the prose writer to the poet, with the inevitable diminution of the poems as a consequence—if only because the critic's own medium isn't verse.

So to a critic, the prospect of dealing with Hardy's work should look quite messy. To begin with, if one's life holds the key to one's work, as received wisdom claims, then, in Hardy's case, the question is: Which work? Is this or that mishap reflected in this novel, or in that poem, and why not in both? And if a novel, what then is a poem for? And vice versa? Especially since there are about nine novels and roughly a thousand poems in his corpus. Which of these is, should you wax Freudian, a form of sublimation? And how come one keeps sublimating up to the ripe age of eighty-eight, for Hardy kept writing poems to the very end (his last, tenth collection came out posthumously)? And should one really draw a line between novelist and poet, or isn't it better to lump them together, echoing Mother Nature?

I say, let's separate them. At any rate, that's what we are going to do in this room. To make a long story short, a poet shouldn't be viewed through any prism other than that of his poems. Besides, technically speaking, Thomas Hardy was a novelist for twenty-six years only. And since he wrote poetry alongside his novels, one could argue that he was a poet for sixty years in a row. To say the least, for the last thirty years of his life; after *Jude the Obscure*—his last and, in my view, his greatest novel—received unfavorable notices, he quit fiction altogether and concentrated on poetry. That alone—the thirty years of verse writing—should be enough to qualify him for the status of a poet. After all, thirty years in this field is an average length for one's career, not to mention life.

So let's give Mother Nature short shrift. Let's deal with the poet's poems. Or, to put it differently, let's bear in mind that human artifice is as organic as any natural masterpiece, which, if we are to believe our naturalists, is also a product of tremendous selection. You see, there are roughly two ways of being natural in this world. One is to strip down to one's underthings, or beyond, and get exposed, as it were, to the elements. That would be, say, a Lawrentian approach, adopted in the second half of this century by many a scribbling dimwit —in our parts, I regret to inform you, especially. The other approach is best exemplified by the following four-liner, written by the great Russian poet Osip Mandelstam:

> Rome is but nature's twin, which has reflected Rome.
> We see its civic might, the signs of its decorum
> in the transparent air, the firmament's blue dome,
> the colonnades of groves and in the meadow's forum.

Mandelstam is a Russian, as I said. Yet this quatrain comes in handy because oddly enough it has more to do with Thomas Hardy than anything by D. H. Lawrence, a Brit.

Anyway, at the moment I'd like to go with you through several poems by Mr. Hardy, which by now I hope you have memorized. We'll go through them line by line, so that, apart from whetting your appetite for this poet, you'll be able to see the process of selection that occurs in the course of composition, and that echoes and—if you don't mind my saying so—outshines the similar process described in the *Origin of Species*, if only because the latter's net result is us, not Mr. Hardy's poems. So let me succumb to the perfectly Darwinian, logical as well as chronological temptation to address the poems belonging to the aforementioned thirty-year period, i.e., to the poems written by Thomas Hardy in the second part of his career, which also means in our century: this way, we leave the novelist behind.

III

Thomas Hardy was born in 1840 and died in 1928. His father was a stonemason and could not afford to support him in a scholarly career, apprenticing him instead to a local church architect. He studied Greek and Latin classics on his own, however, and wrote in his off-hours until the success of *Far from the Madding Crowd* allowed him to quit the job at the age of thirty-four. Thus, his literary career, which started in 1871, allows itself to be fairly neatly divided into two almost even parts: into the Victorian and modern periods, since Queen Victoria conveniently dies in 1901. Bearing in mind that both terms are but catchwords, we'll nevertheless use them for reasons of economy, in order to save ourselves some breath. We shouldn't scrutinize the obvious; as regards our poet, the word "Victorian" catches in particular Robert Browning, Matthew Arnold, George Meredith, both Rossettis, Algernon Charles Swinburne, Tennyson of course, and, conceivably, Gerard Manley Hopkins and A. E. Housman. To these you might add Charles Darwin himself, Carlyle, Disraeli, John Stuart Mill, Ruskin, Samuel Butler, Walter Pater. But let's stop here: that should give you the general idea of the mental and stylistic parameters—or pressures—pertinent at the time for our poet. Let's leave

Cardinal Newman out of it, because our man was a biological determinist and agnostic; let's also leave out the Brontë sisters, Dickens, Thackeray, Trollope, Robert Louis Stevenson, and other fiction writers, because they mattered to Mr. Hardy when he was one of them but not, for instance, when he set out to write "The Darkling Thrush," which is our first poem.

> I leant upon a coppice gate
>> When Frost was spectre-gray,
> And Winter's dregs made desolate
>> The weakening eye of day.
> The tangled bine-stems scored the sky
>> Like strings of broken lyres,
> And all mankind that haunted nigh
>> Had sought their household fires.
>
> The land's sharp features seemed to be
>> The Century's corpse outleant,
> His crypt the cloudy canopy,
>> The wind his death-lament.
> The ancient pulse of germ and birth
>> Was shrunken hard and dry,
> And every spirit upon earth
>> Seemed fervourless as I.
>
> At once a voice arose among
>> The bleak twigs overhead
> In a full-hearted evensong
>> Of joy illimited;
> An aged thrush, frail, gaunt, and small,
>> In blast-beruffled plume,
> Had chosen thus to fling his soul
>> Upon the growing gloom.

So little cause for carolings
    Of such ecstatic sound
Was written on terrestrial things
    Afar or nigh around,
That I could think there trembled through
    His happy good-night air
Some blessed Hope, whereof he knew
    And I was unaware.

Now, although this thirty-two-line job is Thomas Hardy's most anthologized poem, it is not exactly the most typical of him, being extremely fluent. And that's why perhaps it's so frequently anthologized; although, save for one line in it, it could have been written by practically anyone of talent and, well, insight. These properties are not so rare in English poetry, at the turn of the century especially. It is a very fluent, very lucid poem; its texture is smooth and its structure is conservative enough to hark back to the ballad; its argument is clear and well sustained. In other words, there is very little here of vintage Hardy; and now is as good a time as any to tell you what vintage Hardy is like.

Vintage Hardy is a poet who, according to his own admission, "abhorred the smooth line." That would sound perverse were it not for six centuries of verse writing predating his, and were it not for somebody like Tennyson breathing down his neck. Come to think of it, his attitude wasn't very dissimilar from that of Hopkins, and the ways they went about it were, I daresay, not that different, either. At any rate, Thomas Hardy is indeed by and large the poet of a very crammed, overstressed line, filled with clashing consonants, yawning vowels; of an extremely crabby syntax and awkward, cumbersome phrasing aggravated by his seemingly indiscriminate vocabulary; of eye/ear/mind-boggling stanzaic designs unprecedented in their never-repeating patterns.

So why push him on us? you may ask. Because all this was deliberate and, in the light of what transpired in the English poetry of the rest of this century, quite prophetic. To begin with, the intended awkwardness of Hardy's lines wasn't just the natural striving of a new poet toward a distinct diction, although it played that role, too. Nor should this roughness of surface be seen only as a rebellion against the tonal loftiness and polish of the post-Romantics. In fact, these properties of the post-Romantics are quite admirable, and the whole thesis that Hardy, or anyone else for that matter, "rebelled against" them should be taken with a grain of salt, if taken at all. I think there is another, more down-to-earth as well as more metaphysical explanation for Hardy's stylistic idiom, which in itself was both down-to-earth and metaphysical.

Well, metaphysics is always down-to-earth, isn't it? The more down-to-earth it is, the more metaphysical it gets, for the things of this world and their interplay are metaphysics' last frontier: they are the language in which matter manifests itself. And the syntax of this language is very crabby indeed. Be that as it may, what Hardy was really after in his verse was, I think, the effect of verisimilitude, the sense of veracity, or, if you will, of authenticity in his speech. The more awkward, he presumably thought, the more true it sounds. Or, at least, the less artful, the more true. Here, perhaps, we should recall that he was also a novelist—though I hope we bring this up for the last time. And novelists think of such things, don't they? Or let's put it a bit more dramatically: he was the kind of man who would think of such things and that's what made him a novelist. However, the man who became a novelist was, before and after that, a poet.

And here we come close to something crucial for our

understanding of Hardy the poet; to our sense of what kind of man he was or, more exactly, what kind of mind he had. For the moment, I am afraid, you have to take my assessment for granted; but I hope that within the next half hour it will be borne out by his lines. So here we go: Thomas Hardy, I think, was an extraordinarily perceptive and cunning man. I say "cunning" here without negative connotations, but perhaps I should say "plotting." For he indeed plots his poems: not like novels, but precisely as poems. In other words, he knows from the threshold what a poem is, what it should be *like*; he has a certain idea of what his lines should add up to. Nearly every one of his works can be fairly neatly dissected into exposition/argument/denouement, not so much because they were actually structured that way as because structuring was instinctive to Hardy. It comes, as it were, from within the man and reflects not so much his familiarity with the contemporary poetic scene as—as is often the case with autodidacts—his reading of the Greek and Roman classics.

The strength of this structuring instinct in him also explains why Hardy never progressed as a stylist, why his manner never changed. Save for the subject matter, his early poems might sit very comfortably in his late collections, and vice versa, and he was rather cavalier with his dates and attributions. His strongest faculty, moreover, was not the ear but the eye, and the poems existed for him, I believe, more as printed than as spoken matter; had he read them aloud, he himself would have stumbled, but I doubt he would have felt embarrassed and attempted improvements. To put it differently, the real seat of poetry for him was in his mind. No matter how public some of his poems seem, they amount to mental pictures of public address rather than ask for actual delivery. Even the most lyrical of his pieces are essentially mental gestures toward what we know as lyricism in poetry, and they stick to paper more readily than they move your lips. It's hard to imagine Mr. Hardy mouthing his lines into a microphone; but then, I believe, microphones hadn't yet been invented.

So why push him on you, you may persist. Because precisely this voicelessness, this audial neutrality, if you will, and this predominance of the rational over emotional immediacy turn Hardy into a prophetic figure in English poetry: that's what its future liked. In an odd way, his poems have the feeling of being detached from themselves, of not so much being poems as maintaining the appearance of being poems. Herein lies a new aesthetics, an aesthetics insisting on art's conventions not for the sake of emphasis or self-assertion but the other way around: as a sort of camouflage, for better merging with the background against which art exists. Such aesthetics expand art's domain and allow it to land a better punch when and where it's least expected. This is where modernism goofed, but let's let bygones be bygones.

You shouldn't conclude, though, because of what I've told you, that Hardy is heady stuff. As a matter of fact, his verse is entirely devoid of any hermetic arcana. What's unique about him is, of course, his extraordinary appetite for the infinite, and it appears that, rather than hampering it, the constraints of convention only whet it more. But that's what constraints do to a normal, i.e., not self-centered, intelligence; and the infinite is poetry's standard turf. Other than that, Hardy the poet is a reasonably easy proposition; you don't need any special philosophical warm-up to appreciate him. You may even call him a realist, because his verse captures an enormous amount of the physical and psychological reality of the time he lived in, of what is loosely called Victorian England.

And yet you wouldn't call him Victorian. Far more than his actual chronology, the aforesaid appetite for the infinite makes him escape this and, for that matter, any definition save that of a poet. Of a man who's got to tell you something about your life no matter where and when he lived his. Except that with Hardy, when you say "poet" you see not a dashing raconteur or a tubercular youth feverishly scribbling in the haze and heat of inspiration but a clear-eyed, increasingly crusty man, bald and of medium height, with a mustache and an aquiline profile, carefully plotting his remorseless, if awkward lines upstairs in his studio, occasionally laughing at the achieved results.

I push him on you in no small part because of that laughter. To me, he casts a very modern figure, and not only because his lines contain a higher percentage of existential truth than his contemporaries', but because of these lines' unmistakable self-awareness. It is as though his poems say to you: Yes, we remember that we are artifacts, so we are not trying to seduce you with our truth; actually, we don't mind sounding a bit quaint. If nevertheless, boys and girls, you find this poet hard going, if his diction appears to you antiquated, keep in mind that the problem may be with you rather than with the author. There is no such thing as antiquated diction, there are only reduced vocabularies. That's why, for example, there is no Shakespeare nowadays on Broadway; apparently the modern audience has more trouble with the bard's diction than the folks at the Globe had. That's progress for you, then; and there is nothing sillier than retrospection from the point of view of progress. And now, off to "The Darkling Thrush."

IV

"The Darkling Thrush" is, of course, a turn-of-the-century poem. But suppose we didn't look at the date beneath it;

suppose we opened a book and read it cold. People normally don't look at the dates beneath poems; on top of that, Hardy, as I said, wasn't all that systematic about dating his work. Imagine, then, reading it cold and catching the date only in the end. What would you say it's all about?

You'd say it's a nature poem, a description of a landscape. On a cold gray winter day a man strolls through a landscape, you would say; he stops and takes in the view. It's a picture of desolation enlivened by the sudden chirping of a bird, and that lifts his spirits. That's what you would say, and you would be right; moreover, that's what the author wants you to think; why, he practically insists on the ordinariness of the scene.

Why? Because he wants you eventually to learn that a new century, a new era—anything new—starts on a gray day, when your spirits are low and there is nothing eye-arresting in sight. That in the beginning there is a gray day, and not exactly a Word. (In about six years you'll be able to check whether or not he was right.) For a turn-of-the-century poem, "The Darkling Thrush" is remarkably unemphatic and devoid of millenarian hoopla. It is so much so that it almost argues against its own chronology; it makes you wonder whether the date wasn't put below the poem afterward, with the benefit of hindsight. And knowing him, one can easily imagine this, for the benefit of hindsight was Hardy's strong suit.

Be that as it may, let's go on with this nature poem, let's fall into his trap. It all starts with "coppice" in the first line. The precision in the naming of this particular type of growth calls the reader's—especially a modern one's—attention to itself, implying the centrality of natural phenomena to the speaker's mind as well as his affinity with them. It also creates an odd sense of security at the poem's opening, since a man familiar with the names of thickets, hedges, and plants can't, almost by definition, be fierce or, in any case, dangerous. That is, the voice we are hearing in the first line is that of nature's ally, and this nature, his diction implies, is by and large human-friendly. Besides, he is leaning on that coppice gate, and a leaning posture seldom bodes even mental aggression; if anything, it's rather receptive. Not to mention that the "coppice gate" itself suggests a nature reasonably civilized, accustomed, almost of its own accord, to human traffic.

The "spectre-gray" in the second line might perhaps put us on alert, were it not for the run-of-the-mill alternation of tetrameters with trimeters, with their balladlike, folk-tune echo, which plays down the ghostliness of "spectre" to the point that we hear "spectrum" more than "spectre," and our mind wanders to the realm of colors rather than homeless souls. What we get out of this line is the sense of controlled melancholy, all the more so since it establishes the poem's meter. "Gray," sitting here in the rhyming position, releases, as it were, the two *e*'s of "spectre" into a sort of exhaling sigh. What we hear is a wistful *eih*, which, together with the hyphen here, turns "shade" into a tint.

The next two lines, "And Winter's dregs made desolate/ The weakening eye of day," clinch, in the same breath, the quatrain pattern which is going to be sustained throughout this thirty-two-line poem and tell you, I am afraid, something about this poet's general view of humanity, or at least of its habitats. The distance between that weakening eye of day, which is presumably the sun, and those winter dregs makes the latter hug, as it were, the ground and take on "Winter' "s implied white or, as the case may be, gray color. I have the distinct feeling that our poet beholds here village dwellings, that we have here a view of a valley, harking back to the old trope of the human spectacle distressing the planets. The dregs, of course, are nothing but residue, what's left when the good stuff has been drunk out of the cup. On top of that, the "Winter's dregs" conjunction gives you a sense of a poet resolutely exiting Georgian diction and standing with both feet in the twentieth century.

Well, at least with one foot, as befits a poem written at the turn of the century. One of the additional pleasures of reading Hardy is observing the constant two-step of the contemporary (which is to say, traditional) and his own (which is to say, modern) diction. Rubbing these things against one another in a poem is how the future invades the present and, for that matter, the past to which the language has grown accustomed. In Hardy, this friction of stylistic tenses is palpable to the point of making you feel that he makes no meal of any, particularly his own, modern, stylistic mode. A really novel, breakthrough line can easily be followed by a succession of jobs so antiquated you may forget their antecedent altogether. Take, for instance, the second quatrain of the first stanza in "The Darkling Thrush":

> The tangled bine-stems scored the sky
> Like strings of broken lyres,
> And all mankind that haunted nigh
> Had sought their household fires.

The relatively advanced imagery of the first line (similar, in fact, to the opening passage in Frost's "Woodpile") quickly deteriorates here into a fin-de-siècle simile that even at the time of this poem's composition would have given off a stale air of pastiche. Why doesn't our poet strive here for fresher diction, why is he settling for obviously Victorian—even Wordsworthian—tropes, why doesn't he try to get ahead of his time—something he is clearly capable of?

First, because poetry is not a rat race yet. Second, because at the moment, the poem is at the stage of exposition.

The exposition of a poem is the most peculiar part, since at this point poets by and large don't know which way the poem will go. Hence, expositions tend to be long, with English poets especially, and in the nineteenth century in particular. On the whole, that side of the Atlantic they have a greater set of references, while over here we've got to look mainly after ourselves. Add to this the pure pleasure of verse writing, of working all sorts of echoes into your texture, and you'll realize that the notion of somebody being "ahead of his time," for all its complimentary ring, is essentially the benefit of hindsight. In the second quatrain of the first stanza, Hardy is squarely behind his time, and he doesn't mind this in the least.

In fact, he loves it. The chief echo here is of the ballad, a term derived from *ballare*, to dance. This is one of the cornerstones of Hardy's poetics. Somebody should calculate the percentage of ballad-based meters in this poet's output; it may easily pass fifty. The explanation for this is not so much young Thomas Hardy's habit of playing the fiddle at country fairs as the English ballad's proclivity for gore and comeuppance, its inherent air of *danse macabre*. The chief attraction of ballad tunes is precisely their dancing—playful, if you insist—denomination, which proclaims from the threshold its artifice. A ballad—and, by extension, a ballad-based meter—announces to the reader: Look, I am not entirely for real; and poetry is too old an art not to use this opportunity for displaying self-awareness. So the prevalence of this sort of tune, in other words, simply coincides—"overlaps" is a better verb—in Hardy with the agnostic's worldview, justifying along the way an old turn of phrase ("haunted nigh") or a trite rhyme ("lyres"/"fires"), except that "lyres" should alert us to the self-referential aspect of the poem.

And as that aspect goes, the next stanza is full of it. It is a fusion of exposition and statement of theme. The end of a century is presented here as the death of a man lying, as it were, in state. To appreciate this treatment better, we have to bear in mind Thomas Hardy's other trade: that of ecclesiastical architect. In that respect, he undertakes here something quite remarkable when he puts the corpse of time into the church of the elements. What makes this undertaking congenial to him in the first place is the fact that the century's sixty years are his own. In a sense, he owns both the edifice and a large portion of its contents. This dual affinity stems not only from the given landscape at the given season but also from his practiced self-deprecation, all the more convincing in a sixty-year-old.

> The ancient pulse of germ and birth
> Was shrunken hard and dry,
> And every spirit upon earth
> Seemed fervourless as I.

That he had some twenty-eight years to go (in the course of which, at the age of seventy-four, he remarried) is of no consequence, as he couldn't be aware of such a prospect. An inquisitive eye may even zero in on "shrunken" and perceive a euphemistic job in that "pulse of germ and birth." That would be both reductive and irrelevant, however, since the mental gesture of this quatrain is far grander and more resolute than any personal lament. It ends with "I," and the gaping caesura after "fervourless" gives this "as I" terrific singularity.

Now the exposition is over, and had the poem stopped here, we'd still have a good piece, the kind of sketch from nature with which the body of many a poet's work swells. For many poems, specifically those that have nature as their subject, are essentially extended expositions fallen short of their objective; sidetracked, as it were, by the pleasure of the attained texture.

Nothing of the sort ever happens in Hardy. He seems always to know what he is after, and pleasure for him is neither a principle nor a valid consideration in verse. He is not big on sonority and orchestrates his lines rather poorly, until it comes to the punch line of the poem, or to the main point the poem is trying to score. That's why his expositions are not particularly mellifluous; if they are—as is the case in "The Darkling Thrush"—it is more by fluke than by intent. With Hardy, the main adventure of a poem is always toward its end. By and large, he gives you the impression that verse for him is but the means of transportation, justified and perhaps even hallowed only by the poem's destination. His ear is seldom better than his eye, but both are inferior to his mind, which subordinates them to its purposes, at times harshly.

So what we've got by now is a picture of utter desolation, of a man and a landscape locked in their respective moribundity. The next stanza offers a key:

> At once a voice arose among
> The bleak twigs overhead
> In a full-hearted evensong
> Of joy illimited;
>
> An aged thrush, frail, gaunt, and small
> In blast-beruffled plume
> Has chosen thus to fling his soul
> Upon the growing gloom.

This is a treasure trove of a stanza for anyone interested in Hardy. Let's take its story line at face value and see what our poet is up to. He is up to showing you an exit out of the previous stanza's dead end. Dead ends can be exited only upward or by backing out. "Arose" and "overhead" tell you the route our poet chooses. He goes for a full-scale elevation here; in fact, for an epiphany, for a complete takeoff with clear-cut ecclesiastical connotations. But what is remarkable about this takeoff is the self-consciousness accompanying the lyrical release of "In a full-hearted evensong/Of joy illimited." This self-consciousness is apparent in the dactylic undercutting you detect in both "evensong" and "illimited": these words come to you prefaced by a caesura and as though exhaled; as though these lines that begin as assertions dissipate in his throat into qualifiers.

This reflects not so much the understandable difficulty an agnostic may have with ecclesiastical vocabulary as Hardy's true humility. In other words, the takeoff of belief is checked here by the gravity of the speaker's reservations as to his right to use these means of elevation. "An aged thrush, frail, gaunt, and small,/In blast-beruffled plume" is, of course, Hardy's self-portrait. Famous for his aquiline profile, with a tuft of hair hovering above his bald pate, he had indeed a birdlike appearance—in his old age especially, judging by the available photographs. ("Gaunt" is his pet word, a signature really, if only because it is so un-Georgian.)

At any rate, the bird here, in addition to behaving like a bard, has his visual characteristics also. This is our poet's ticket into its sentiments, which yields one of the greatest lines in English poetry of the twentieth century.

It turns out that an aged thrush of not particularly fetching appearance

> Had chosen thus to fling his soul
> Upon the growing gloom.

Speaking of choices, "fling" can't be beaten here. Given the implied visual similarity between bird and bard, this two-liner bespeaking a posture toward reality of the one does the same for another. And if one had to define the philosophy underlying this posture, one would end up no doubt oscillating madly between epicurianism and stoicism. Blissfully, for us terminology is not the most pressing issue. Far more pressing is the need to absorb this two-liner into our system, say, for the dark time of the year.

Had the poem stopped here, we would have an extraordinary piece of moral instruction; they are few and far between in poetry but they still do exist. Besides, the superiority of the animal kingdom (birds in particular) in poetry is taken for granted. In fact, the notion of that superiority is one of poetry's most distinctive trappings. What is quite remarkable about "The Darkling Thrush" is that the poet goes practically against this notion, which he himself has bought and is trying to resell in the process of the poem. What's more, by doing this, he almost goes against his most successful lines ever. What is he hoping for? What is he driven by?

Hard to tell, except that perhaps he does not recognize his own success, and what blinds him to it is his metaphysical appetite. Another explanation for why he goes for the fourth stanza here is that appetite's close relative: the sense of symmetry. Those who write formal verse will always prefer four eight-line stanzas to three, and we shouldn't forget the ecclesiastical architect in Hardy. Quatrains could be likened to euphonic building blocks. As such they tend to generate an order that is most satisfactory when it can be divided by four. The sixteen-line exposition naturally—for our poet's mind, ear, and eye—calls for at minimum the same number of lines for the rest.

To put it less idiosyncratically, the stanzaic pattern employed in a poem determines its length as much as—if not more than—its story line. "So little cause for carolings/Of such ecstatic sound" is no less a denouement than the euphonic imperative created by the preceding twenty-four lines, requiring resolution. A poem's length, in other words, is its breath. The first stanza inhales, the second exhales, the third stanza inhales . . . Guess what you need a fourth stanza for? To complete the cycle.

Remember that this is a poem about looking into the future. As such, it has to be balanced. Our man, poet though he is, is not a utopian; nor can he permit himself the posture of a prophet, or that of a visionary. The subject itself, by definition, is too pregnant with imprecision; so what's required of the poet here is sobriety, regardless of whether he is pessimistic or optimistic by temperament. Hence the absolutely remarkable linguistic content of the fourth stanza, with its fusion of legalese ("cause . . . Was written") with modernist detachment ("on terrestrial things") and the quaintly archaic ("Afar or nigh around").

"So little cause for carolings/Of such ecstatic sound/Was written on terrestrial things" betrays not so much the unique bloody-mindedness of our poet as his impartiality to any level of diction he resorts to in a poem. There is something frighteningly democratic in Hardy's whole approach to poetics, and it can be summed up as "so long as it works."

Note the elegiac opening of this stanza, all the more poignant in tone because of the "growing gloom" a line before. The pitch is still climbing up, we are still after an elevation, after an exit from our cul-de-sac. "So little cause" [caesura] "for carolings/Of such ecstatic"—caesura—"sound . . ." "Ecstatic" carries an exclamation, and so, after the caesura, does "sound."

Vocally, this is the highest point in the stanza; even

"whereof he knew/And I was unaware" is several notes—notches—lower. And yet even at this highest point, the poet, we realize, holds his voice in check, because "carolings/Of such ecstatic sound" are what "a full-hearted evensong" comes down to; which is to say, the evaluation of the bird's voice has undergone a demotion, with ecclesiastical diction being supplanted, as it were, by lay parlance. And then comes this terrific "Was written on terrestrial things," whose detachment from any particularity bespeaks presumably the vantage point either of the "weakening eye of day" or, to say the least, of the bird itself, and that's why we have the archaic—which is to say, impersonal—"Afar or nigh around."

The unparticularity and impersonality, however, belong to neither, but rather to their fusion, the crucible being the poet's mind or, if you will, the language itself. Let's dwell on this extraordinary line—"Was written on terrestrial things"—a bit longer, for it crept into this turn-of-the-century poem out of where no poet had ever been before.

The conjunction "terrestrial things" suggests a detachment whose nature is not exactly human. The point of view attained here through the proximity of two abstract notions is, strictly speaking, inanimate. The only evidence of human manufacture is that it is indeed being "written"; and it gives you a sense that language is capable of arrangements that reduce a human being to, at best, the function of a scribe. That it is language that utilizes a human being, not the other way around. That language flows into the human domain from the realm of nonhuman truths and dependencies, that it is ultimately the voice of inanimate matter, and that poetry just registers now and then its ripple effect.

I am far from suggesting that this is what Thomas Hardy was after in this line. Rather, it was what this line was after in Thomas Hardy, and he responded. And as though he was somewhat perplexed by what escaped from under his pen, he tried to domesticate it by resorting to familiarly Victorian diction in "Afar or nigh around." Yet the diction of this conjunction was destined to become the diction of twentieth-century poetry, more and more. It is only two or three decades from "terrestrial things" to Auden's "necessary murder" and "artificial wilderness." For its "terrestrial things" line alone, "The Darkling Thrush" is a turn-of-the-century poem.

And the fact that Hardy responded to the inanimate voice of this conjunction had to do obviously with his being well prepared to heed this sort of thing, not only by his agnosticism (which might be enough), but by practically any poem's vector upward, by its gravitation toward epiphany. In principle, a poem goes down the page as much as it goes up in spirit, and "The Darkling Thrush" adheres to this principle closely. On this course, irrationality is not an obstacle, and the ballad's tetrameters and trimeters bespeak a considerable familiarity with irrationality:

> That I could think there trembled through
> His happy good-night air
> Some blessed Hope, whereof he knew
> And I was unaware.

What brings our author to this "blessed Hope" is above all the centrifugal momentum developed by the amassment of thirty alternating tetrameters and trimeters, requiring either vocal or mental resolution, or both. In this sense, this turn-of-the-century poem is very much about itself, about its composition which—by happy coincidence—gravitates toward its finale the way the century does. A poem, in fact, offers a century its own, not necessarily rational, version of the future, thereby making the century possible. Against all odds, against the absence of "cause."

And the century—which is soon to be over—has gallantly paid this poem back, as we see in this classroom. In any case, as prophecies go, "The Darkling Thrush" has proved to be more sober and accurate than, let's say, "The Second Coming," by W. B. Yeats. A thrush proved a more reliable source than a falcon; perhaps because this thrush showed up for Mr. Hardy some twenty years earlier. Perhaps because monotony is more in tune with time's own idiom than a shriek.

So if "The Darkling Thrush" is a poem about nature, it is so only by half, since both bard and bird are that nature's effects, and only one of them is, to put it coarsely, hopeful. It is, rather, a poem about two perceptions of the same reality, and as such it is clearly a philosophical lyric. There is no hierarchy here between hope and hopelessness, distributed in the poem with notable evenhandedness—certainly not between their carriers, as our thrush, I am tempted to point out, is not "aged" for nothing. It's been around, and its "blessed Hope" is as valid as the absence thereof. The last line's caesura isolating "unaware" is eloquent enough to muffle out regret and bring to the last word an air of assertion. After all, the "blessed Hope" is that for the future; that's why the last word here is spoken by reason.

V

Twelve years later—but still before the Irish bard's beast set out for Bethlehem—the British passenger liner *Titanic* sank on her maiden voyage in the mid-Atlantic after colliding with an iceberg. Over 1,500 lives were lost. That was presumably the first of many disasters the century ushered in by Thomas Hardy's thrush became famous for.

"The Convergence of the Twain" was written barely two weeks after the catastrophe; it was published shortly afterward, on May 14. The *Titanic* was lost on April 14. In other words, the raging controversy over the cause of the disaster, the court case against the company, the shocking survivors' accounts, etc.—all those things were still ahead at the time of this poem's composition. The poem thus amounts to a visceral response on the part of our poet; what's more, the first time it was printed, it was accompanied by a headnote saying "Improvised on the Loss of the *Titanic*."

So, what chord did this disaster strike in Mr. Hardy? "The Convergence of the Twain" is habitually billed by the critical profession either as the poet's condemnation of modern man's self-delusion of technological omnipotence or as the song of his vainglory's and excessive luxury's comeuppance. To be sure, the poem is both. The *Titanic* itself was a marvel of both modern shipbuilding and ostentatiousness. However, no less than in the ship, our poet seems to be interested in the iceberg. And it is the iceberg's generic—triangular—shape that informs the poem's stanzaic design. So does "A Shape of Ice" 's inanimate nature vis-à-vis the poem's content.

At the same time, it should be noted, the triangular shape suggests the ship: by alluding to the standard representation of a sail. Also, given our poet's architectural past, this shape could connote for him an ecclesiastical edifice or a pyramid. (After all, every tragedy presents a riddle.) In verse, the foundation of such a pyramid would be hexameter, whose caesura divides its six feet into even threes: practically the longest meter available, and one Mr. Hardy was particularly fond of, perhaps because he taught himself Greek.

Although his fondness for figurative verse (which comes to us from Greek poetry of the Alexandrian period) shouldn't be overstated, his enterprise with stanzaic patterns was great enough to make him sufficiently self-conscious about the visual dimension of his poems to make such a move. In any case, the stanzaic design of "The Convergence of the Twain" is clearly deliberate, as two trimeters and one hexameter (normally conveyed in English precisely by two trimeters— also the convergence of a twain) show, held together by the triple rhyme.

I

In a solitude of the sea
Deep from human vanity,
And the Pride of Life that planned her, stilly couches she.

II

Steel chambers, late the pyres
Of her salamandrine fires,
Cold currents thrid, and turn to rhythmic tidal lyres.

III

Over the mirrors meant
To glass the opulent
The sea-worm crawls—grotesque, slimed, dumb, indifferent.

IV

Jewels in joy designed
To ravish the sensuous mind
Lie lightless, all their sparkles bleared and black and blind.

V

Dim moon-eyed fishes near
Gaze at the gilded gear
And query: "What does this vaingloriousness down here?"

VI

Well: while was fashioning
This creature of cleaving wing,
The Immanent Will that stirs and urges everything

VII

Prepared a sinister mate
For her—so gaily great—
A Shape of Ice, for the time far and dissociate.

VIII

And as the smart ship grew
In stature, grace, and hue
In shadowy silent distance grew the Iceberg too.

IX

Alien they seemed to be:
No mortal eye could see
The intimate welding of their later history,

X

Or sign that they were bent
By paths coincident
On being anon twin halves of one august event,

XI

Till the Spinner of the Years
Said "Now!" And each one hears,
And consummation comes, and jars two hemispheres.

This is your bona fide occasional poem in the form of a public
address. In fact, it is an oration; it gives you the feeling that
it should be spoken from a pulpit. The opening line—"In a
solitude of the sea"—is extraordinarily spacious, both vocally
and visually, suggesting the width of the sea's horizon and
that degree of elemental autonomy which is capable of perceiving its own solitude.

But if the opening line scans the vast surface, the second
line—"Deep from human vanity"—takes you farther away
from the human sphere, straight into the heart of this utterly
isolated element. In fact, the second line is an invitation for
the underwater journey which is what the first half of the
poem—a lengthy exposition again!—amounts to. Toward the
end of the third line, the reader is well along on a veritable
scuba-diving expedition.

Trimeters are a tricky proposition. They may be rewarding euphonically, but they naturally constrain the content. At the outset of the poem they help our poet to establish
his tonality; but he is anxious to get on with the business of
the poem. For this, he gets the third, quite capacious hexametric line, in which he proceeds indeed in a very busi-
nesslike, bloody-minded fashion:

And the Pride of Life that planned her, stilly couches she.

The first half of this line is remarkable for its pileup of
stresses, no less than for what it ushers in: the rhetorical,
abstract construct which is, on top of that, also capitalized.

Now, the Pride of Life is of course linked syntactically to human vanity, but this helps matters little because (a) human vanity is not capitalized, and (b) it is still more coherent and familiar a concept than the Pride of Life. Furthermore, the two *n*'s in "that planned her" give you a sense of a truly jammed, bottleneck-type diction, befitting an editorial more than a poem.

No poet in his right mind would try to cram all this into half a line: it is barely utterable. On the other hand, as we've noted, there were no mikes. Actually, "And the Pride of Life that planned her," though menaced by its mechanical scansion, can be delivered out loud, to the effect of somewhat unwarranted emphasis; the effort, however, will be obvious. The question is, why does Thomas Hardy do this? And the answer is, because he is confident that the image of the ship resting at the bottom of the sea and the triple rhyme will bail this stanza out.

"Stilly couches she" is indeed a wonderful counterbalance to the unwieldy pileup of stresses ushering it in. The two *l*'s—a "liquid" consonant—in "stilly" almost convey the gently rocking body of the ship. As for the rhyme, it clinches the femininity of the ship, already emphasized by the verb "couches." For the purposes of the poem, this suggestion is indeed timely.

What does our poet's deportment in this stanza and, above all, in its third line tell us about him? That he is a very calculating fellow (at least he counts his stresses). Also, that his pen is driven less by a sense of harmony than by his central idea, and that his triple rhyme is a euphonic necessity second and a structural device first. As rhymes go, what we've got in this stanza is no great shakes. The best that can be said about it is that it is highly functional and reverberates the wonderful fifteenth-century poem sometimes attributed to Dunbar:

> In what estate so ever I be
> *Timor mortis conturbat me* . . .
> "All Christian people, behold and see:
> This world is but a vanity
> And replete with necessity.
> *Timor mortis conturbat me.*"

It's quite possible that these lines indeed set "The Convergence of the Twain" in motion, because it is a poem above all about vanity and necessity, as well, of course, as about fear of death. However, what perturbs the seventy-two-year-old Thomas Hardy in his poem is precisely necessity.

> Steel chambers, late the pyres
> Of her salamandrine fires,
> Cold currents thrid, and turn to rhythmic tidal lyres.

We are indeed on an underwater journey here, and although the rhymes are not getting any better (we encounter our old friend "lyres"), this stanza is striking because of its visual content. We are clearly in the engine room, and the entire machinery is seen quiveringly refracted by water. The word that really stars in this stanza is "salamandrine." Apart from its mythological and metallurgical connotations, this four-syllable-long, lizardlike epithet marvelously evokes the quivering motion of the element directly opposite to water: fire. Extinguished, yet sustained, as it were, by refractions.

"Cold" in "Cold currents thrid, and turn to rhythmic tidal lyres" underscores this transformation; but on the whole, the line is extremely interesting because it arguably contains a hidden metaphor of the very process of composing this poem. On the surface—or, rather, underneath it—we have the movement of the waves approaching the shore (or a bay, or a cove), which looks like the horn of a lyre. Breakers, then, are its played strings. The verb "thrid," being the archaic (or dialect) form of "thread," while conveying the weaving of the sound and meaning from line to line, euphonically also evokes the triangularity of the stanzaic design, which is a triplet. In other words, with the progression from "fire" to "cold" we get here to an artifice that suggests artistic self-consciousness in general and, given the treatment a great tragedy receives in this poem, Hardy's in particular. For, to put it bluntly, "The Convergence of the Twain" is devoid of the "hot" feelings that might seem appropriate, given the volume of human loss. This is an entirely unsentimental job, and in the second stanza our poet reveals somewhat (most likely unwittingly) the way it's done.

> Over the mirrors meant
> To glass the opulent
> The sea-worm crawls—grotesque, slimed, dumb, indifferent.

This is where, I believe, the poem's reputation for social criticism comes from. It is there, of course, but that's the least of it. The *Titanic* was indeed a floating palace. The ballroom, casino, and cabins themselves were built to redefine luxury on the grandest scale, their decor was lavish. To convey this, the poet uses the verb "to glass," which both doubles the opulence and betrays its one-dimensionality: it is glass-deep. However, in the scene Mr. Hardy paints here, he is concerned less, I think, with debunking the rich than with the discrepancy between the intent and the outcome. The sea-worm crawling over the mirror stands in not for the essence of capitalism but for "the opulent" 's opposite.

The succession of negative epithets qualifying that sea-worm tells us quite a lot about Mr. Hardy himself. For in order to know the value of a negative epithet, one should always try applying it to oneself first. Being a poet, not to mention a novelist, Thomas Hardy would have done that more than once. Therefore, the succession of negative epithets here could and should be perceived as reflecting his hierarchy of human wrongs, the gravest being the last on the list. And the last on this list, sitting above all in the rhyming position, is "indifferent." This renders "grotesque, slimed, dumb" as lesser evils. At least from the point of view of this poet, they are; and one can't help thinking that the gravity "indifferent" is burdened with in this context is perhaps self-referential.

> Jewels in joy designed
> To ravish the sensuous mind
> Lie lightless, all their sparkles bleared and black and blind.

Perhaps this is as good a time as any to point to the cinematic, frame-by-frame procedure our poet resorts to here, and the fact that he is doing this in 1912, long before film became a daily—well, nightly—reality. I believe I've said someplace that it was poetry that invented the technique of montage, not Eisenstein. A vertical arrangement of identical stanzas on the page *is* a film. A couple of years ago a salvaging company trying to raise the *Titanic* showed its footage of the ship on TV; it was remarkably close to the matter at hand. Their emphasis was obviously on the contents of the ship's vault, which among other things might have contained a manuscript of Joseph Conrad's most recent novel, which was sent by the author to his American publisher with the ship, since it was to be the speediest mail carrier, among other virtues. The camera circled in the vault area incessantly, attracted by the smell of its riches, but to no avail. Thomas Hardy does a far better job.

"Jewels in joy designed" practically glitters with its *j*'s and *s*'s. So again does, with its swishing and hissing *s*'s, the next line. Yet the most fascinating use of alliteration is on display in the third line, where the ravished, sensuous mind goes flat, as all the line's *l*'s crackle and burst in "sparkles," turning the jewels in "*bl*eared and *bl*ack and *bl*ind" into so many released bubbles rising to the line's end. The alliteration is literally undoing itself in front of our eyes.

It is more rewarding to admire the poet's ingenuity here than to read into this line a sermon on the ephemeral and destructive nature of riches. Even if the latter were his concern, the emphasis would be on the paradox itself rather than the social commentary. Had Thomas Hardy been fifty years younger at the time of the composition of "The Convergence of the Twain," he perhaps might have sharpened the social edge of the poem a bit more, though even this is doubtful. As it was, he was seventy-two years old, fairly well off himself; and among the 1,500 souls lost when the *Titanic* went down, two were his personal acquaintances. However, on his underwater journey, he is not looking for them either.

> Dim moon-eyed fishes near
> Gaze at the gilded gear
> And query: "What does this vaingloriousness down here?"

"Gaze at the gilded gear" has obviously crept into the second line of this stanza by pure alliterative inertia (the author presumably had other word combinations to consider working up the last stanza, and this is just one of the spin-offs), which serves to recapitulate the ship's ostentatiousness. Fish are seen here as if through a porthole, hence the magnifying-glass effect dilating the fish eyes and making them moonlike. Of much greater consequence, however, is this stanza's third line, which concludes the exposition and serves as the springboard for the poem's main business.

"And query: 'What does this vaingloriousness down

here?' " is not only a rhetorical turn setting up the rest of
the poem to provide the answer to the question posed by
the line. It is first of all the recapturing of the oratorical
posture, somewhat diluted by the lengthy exposition. To
achieve that, the poet heightens his diction here, by com-
bining the legalese of "query" with the clearly ecclesiastical
"vaingloriousness." The latter's five-syllable-long hulk marvelously evokes the cumbersomeness of the ship at the sea's
bottom. Apart from this, though, both the legalese and the
ecclesiastical clearly point to a stylistic shift and a change of
the whole discourse's plane of regard.

> Well: while was fashioning
> This creature of cleaving wing,
> The Immanent Will that stirs and urges everything
>
> Prepared a sinister mate
> For her—so gaily great—
> A Shape of Ice, for the time far and dissociate.

Now, "Well" here both disarms and signals a regroup-
ing. It's a colloquial conceit, designed both to put the audience a bit off guard—should "vaingloriousness" have put
it on alert—and to pump some extra air into the speaker's
lungs as he embarks on a lengthy, extremely loaded period.
Resembling somewhat the speech mannerisms of our fortieth
President, "Well" here indicates that the movie part of the
poem is over and now the discourse begins in earnest. It
appears that the subject, after all, is not submarine fauna
but Mr. Hardy's—as well as poetry's very own, ever since
the days of Lucretius—concept of causality.

"Well: while was fashioning/This creature of cleaving
wing" informs the public—syntactically, above all—that we
are beginning from afar. More important, the subordinate

clause preceding the Immanent Will statement exploits to the hilt the ship's gender designation in our language. We've got three words here with increasingly feminine connotations, whose proximity to each other adds up to an impression of deliberate emphasis. "Fashioning" could have been a fairly neutral reference to shipbuilding were it not qualified by "this creature," with its overtones of particular fondness, and were "this creature" itself not side-lit by "cleaving." There is more of "cleavage" in "cleaving" than of "cleaver," which, while denoting the movement of the ship's prow through the water, also echoes a type of sail with its whiteness, resembling a blade. In any case, the conjunction of "cleaving wing"—and "wing" itself especially, sitting here in the rhyming position—pitches the line sufficiently high for Mr. Hardy to usher in a notion central to his entire mental operation, that of "The Immanent Will that stirs and urges everything."

Hexameter gives this notion's skeptical grandeur full play. The caesura separates the formula from the qualifier in the most natural way, letting us fully appreciate the almost thundering reverberations of consonants in "Immanent Will," as well as the resolute assertiveness "that stirs and urges everything." The latter is all the more impressive thanks to the reserve in the line's dactyls—which borders, in fact, on hesitation—detectable in "everything." Third in the stanza, this line is burdened with the inertia of resolution, and gives you a feeling the entire poem has been written for the sake of this statement.

Why? Because if one could speak of Mr. Hardy's philosophical outlook (if one can speak about a poet's philosophy at all, since, given the omniscient nature of language alone, such discourse is doomed to be reductive by definition), one would have to admit that the notion of Immanent Will was paramount to it. Now, it all harks back to Schopenhauer, with whom the sooner you get acquainted the better—not so much for Mr. Hardy's sake as for your own. Schopenhauer will save you quite a trip; more exactly, his notion of the Will, which he introduced in his *The World as Will and Idea*, will. Every philosophical system, you see, can easily be charged with being essentially a solipsistic, if not downright anthropomorphic, endeavor. By and large they all are, precisely because they are *systems* and thus imply a varying—usually quite high—degree of rationality of overall design. Schopenhauer escapes this charge with his Will, which is his term for the phenomenal world's inner essence; better yet, for a ubiquitous nonrational force and its blind, striving power operating in the world. Its operations are devoid of ultimate purpose or design and are not many a philosopher's incarnations of rational or moral order. In the end, of course, this notion can also be charged with being a human self-projection. Yet it can defend itself better than others with its horrific, meaningless omniscience, permeating all forms of struggle for existence but voiced (from Schopenhauer's point of view, presumably only echoed) by poetry alone. Small wonder that Thomas Hardy, with his appetite for the infinite and the inanimate, zeroed in on this notion; small wonder that he capitalizes it in this line, for whose sake one may think the entire poem was written.

It wasn't:

> Prepared a sinister mate
> For her—so gaily great—
> A Shape of Ice, for the time far and dissociate.

For if you give four stars to that line, how are you to rank "A Shape of Ice, for the time far and dissociate"? Or, for that matter, "a sinister mate"? As conjunctions go, it is so far ahead of 1912! It's straight out of Auden. Lines like that are invasions of the future into the present, they are whiffs of the Immanent Will themselves. The choice of "mate" is absolutely marvelous, since apart from alluding to "shipmate," it again underscores the ship's femininity, sharpened even further by the next trimeter: "For her—so gaily great—"

What we are getting here, with increasing clarity, is not so much collision as a metaphor for romantic union as the other way around: the union as a metaphor for the collision. The femininity of the ship and the masculinity of the iceberg are clearly established. Except that it is not exactly the iceberg. The real mark of our poet's genius is in his offering a circumlocution: "A Shape of Ice." Its menacing power is directly proportionate to the reader's ability to fashion that shape according to his own imagination's negative potential. In other words, this circumlocution—actually, its letter *a* alone—insinuates the reader into the poem as an active participant.

Practically the same job is performed by "for the time far and dissociate." Now, "far" as an epithet attached to time is commonplace; any poet could do it. But it takes Hardy to use in verse the utterly unpoetic "dissociate." This is the benefit of the general stylistic nonchalance of his we commented on earlier. There are no good, bad, or neutral words for this poet: they are either functional or not. This could be put down, of course, to his experience with prose, were it not for his frequently stated abhorrence of the smooth, "jewelled line."

And "dissociate" is about as unglittering as it is functional. It bespeaks not only the Immanent Will's farsightedness but time's own disjointed nature: not in the Shakespearean but in the purely metaphysical—which is to say, highly perceptible, tactile, mundane—sense. The latter is what makes any member of the audience identify with the disaster's participants, placing him or her within time's atomizing domain. What ultimately saves "dissociate," of course, is its being rhymed, with the attendant aspect of resolution moreover, in the third, hexametric line.

Actually, in the last two stanzas, the rhymes get better and better: engaging and unpredictable. To appreciate "dissociate" fully, perhaps, one should try reading the stanza's rhymes vertically, column-wise. One would end up with "mate—great—dissociate." This is enough to give one a shudder, and this is far from being gratuitous, since the succession clearly emerged in the poet's mind before the stanza was finished. In fact, this succession was precisely what allowed him to finish the stanza, and to do it the way he did.

> And as the smart ship grew
> In stature, grace, and hue
> In shadowy silent distance grew the Iceberg too.

And so it emerges that we are dealing with the betrothed. With the feminine smart ship engaged early on to a Shape of Ice. A construction to nature. Almost a brunette to a blonde. Something was growing in Plymouth docks toward that which was growing "In shadowy silent distance" somewhere in the North Atlantic. The hushed, conspiratorial "shadowy silent distance" underscores the secretive, intimate character of this information, and the stresses falling almost mechanically on each word in this stanza sort of echo time's measured pace—the pace of this maid's and her mate's advancement toward one another. For it is that pace that makes the encounter inevitable, not the pair's individual features.

What also makes their approach inexorable is the excess of rhyme in this stanza. "Grew" creeps into the third line, making this triplet contain four rhymes. That could be regarded, of course, as a cheap effect, were it not for the rhyme's sound. "Grew—hue—too" has, as a euphonic referent, the word "you," and the second "grew" triggers the reader's realization of his/her involvement in the story, and not as its addressee only.

> Alien they seemed to be:
> No mortal eye could see
> The intimate welding of their later history . . .

In the euphonic context of the last four stanzas, "Alien" comes as an exclamation, its wide-open vowels being like the last cry of the doomed before submitting to the unavoidable. It's like "not guilty" on the scaffold, or "I don't love him" before the altar: pale face turned to the public. And the altar it is, for "welding" as well as "history" in the third line sound like homonyms for "wedding" and "destiny." So "No mortal eye could see" is not so much the poet's bragging about being privy to the workings of causality as the voice of a Father Lorenzo.

> Or sign that they were bent
> By paths coincident
> On being anon twin halves of one august event . . .

Again, no poet in his right mind, unless his is Gerard Manley Hopkins's, would stud a line with stresses in such a hammering manner. And not even Hopkins would dare to use in verse "anon" like this. Is this our old friend Mr. Hardy's abhorrence of the smooth line, reaching here a degree of perversity? Or a further attempt to obscure, with this Middle English equivalent of "at once," a "mortal eye" 's ability to see what he, the poet, sees? An elongation of the perspective? Going for those coincident paths of origin? His only concession to the standard view of the disaster? Or just a heightening of the pitch, the way "august" does, in view of the poem's finale, to pave the way for the Immanent Will's saying its piece:

> Till the Spinner of the Years
> Said "Now!" And each one hears,
> And consummation comes, and jars two hemispheres.

"Everything" that the Immanent Will "stirs and urges" presumably includes time. Hence the Immanent Will's new billing: "Spinner of the Years." This is a bit too personified for the abstract notion's abstract good, but we may put this down to the ecclesiastical architect's inertia in Hardy. He comes uncomfortably close here to equating the meaningless with the malevolent, whereas Schopenhauer pushes precisely the blind mechanistic—which is to say, nonhuman—nature of that Will, whose presence is recognized by all forms of existence, both animate and inanimate, through stress, conflict, tension, and, as in the case at hand, through disaster.

This, in the final analysis, is what lies behind his poetry's quite ubiquitous predilection for the dramatic anecdote. The nonhumanity of the ultimate truth about the phenomenal world fires up his imagination the way female beauty does many a Lothario's. A biological determinist, on the one hand, he eagerly, as it were, embraces Schopenhauer's notion not only because it amounts in his mind to the source of completely unpredictable and otherwise unaccountable occurrences (unifying thus the "far and dissociate") but also, one suspects, to account for his own "indifference."

You could bill him as a rational irrationalist, of course, but that would be a mistake, since the concept of Immanent Will is not irrational. No, quite the contrary. It is highly uncomfortable, not to say menacing, perhaps; but that is a different matter altogether. Discomfort shouldn't be equated with irrationality any more than rationality with comfort. Still, this is the wrong place for nit-picking. One thing is clear: the Immanent Will for our poet has the status of Supreme Entity, bordering on that of Prime Mover. Fittingly, then, it speaks in monosyllables; fittingly, also, it says, "Now."

The most fitting word in this last stanza, however, is, of course, "consummation," since the collision occurred at night. With "consummation" we have the marital union trope seen, as it were, to the end. "Jars," with its allusion to broken earthenware, is more this trope's residue than its enhancement. It is a stunning verb here, making the two hemispheres, which the "maiden" voyage of the *Titanic* was supposed to connect, into two clashing convex receptacles. It looks as if it was precisely the notion of "maiden" that struck the chord of our poet's "lyre" first.

VI

The question is why, and the answer arrives in the form of a cycle of poems written by Mr. Hardy a year after "The Convergence of the Twain," the famous *Poems of 1912–13*. As we are about to embark on discussing one of them, let's bear in mind that the feminine ship was lost and that the masculine Shape of Ice survived the encounter. That the remarkable lack of sentimentality, warranted in principle by both the genre and the subject of the poem, could be attributed to our poet's inability to identify here with the loser, if only because of the ship's gender.

Poems of 1912–13 was occasioned by the poet's loss of his wife of thirty-eight years, Emma Lavinia Gifford, who died on November 27, 1912, eight months after the *Titanic* disaster. Twenty-one pieces in all, these poems amount to the Shape of Ice's meltdown.

To make a long story short, the marriage was long and unhappy enough to give "The Convergence of the Twain" its central metaphor. It was also sufficiently solid to make at least one of its participants regard himself as a plaything of the Immanent Will, and, as such playthings go, a cold one. Had Emma Hardy outlived her husband, this poem would stand as a remarkable, albeit oblique, monument to the morose equilibrium of their dissociate lives, to the low temperature of the poet's heart.

The sudden death of Emma Hardy shattered this equilibrium. In a manner of speaking, the Shape of Ice suddenly found itself on its very own. In another manner of speaking, *Poems of 1912–13* is essentially this Iceberg's lament for the vanished ship. As such, it is a meticulous reconstruction of the casualty; the by-product, naturally, of an excruciating self-examination rather than a metaphysical quest for the tragedy's origins. After all, no casualty can be redeemed by exposing its causality.

That's why this cycle is essentially retrospective. To make a long story still shorter, its heroine is not Emma Hardy, the wife, but precisely Emma Lavinia Gifford, the bride: a maiden. The poems look at her through the dim prism of thirty-eight years of marriage, through the foggy hard crystal of Emma Hardy herself. If this cycle has a hero, it is the past with its happiness or, to put it a bit more accurately, with its promise of happiness.

As human predicaments go, the story is sufficiently common. As a subject for elegiac poetry, the loss of the beloved is common as well. What makes *Poems of 1912–13* slightly unusual at the outset is not only the age of the poet and his heroine but the sheer number of poems and their formal variety. A characteristic feature with elegies occasioned by someone's demise is their tonal, to say the least, metric uniformity. In the case of this cycle, however, we have a remarkable metric diversity, which points to the possibility that craftsmanship was a no lesser issue for the poet here than the issue itself.

A psychological explanation for this variety might be, of course, that it has to do with our poet's grief searching for an adequate form of expression. Still, the formal intricacy of the twenty-one attempts made in that direction suggests a greater pressure behind this cycle than pure grief or, for that matter, any single sentiment. So let us take a look at perhaps the least stanzaically enterprising among these poems and try to find out what's going on.

YOUR LAST DRIVE

Here by the moorway you returned,
And saw the borough lights ahead
That lit your face—all undiscerned
To be in a week the face of the dead,
And you told of the charm of that haloed view
That never again would beam on you.

And on your left you passed the spot
Where eight days later you were to lie,
And be spoken of as one who was not;
Beholding it with a heedless eye
As alien from you, though under its tree
You soon would halt everlastingly.

I drove not with you . . . Yet had I sat
At your side that eve I should not have seen
That the countenance I was glancing at
Had a last-time look in the flickering sheen,

Nor have read the writing upon your face,
"I go hence soon to my resting-place;

"You may miss me then. But I shall not know
How many times you visit me there,
Or what your thoughts are, or if you go
There never at all. And I shall not care.
Should you censure me I shall take no heed,
And even your praises no more shall need."

True: never you'll know. And you will not mind.
But shall I then slight you because of such?
Dear ghost, in the past did you ever find
The thought "What profit," move me much?
Yet abides the fact, indeed, the same,—
You are past love, praise, indifference, blame.

"Your Last Drive" is the second in the cycle and, according to the date underneath, was written less than a
month after Emma Hardy's death, i.e., when the shock of
her departure was very fresh. Ostensibly an evocation of her
returning home in the evening from a routine outing that
proved to be her last, the poem for its first two stanzas
appears to explore the paradox of the interplay between
motion and stasis. The carriage carrying the heroine past
the place where she shortly will be buried seems to arrest the poet's imagination as a metaphor either of mobility's
myopic vision of immobility or of space's disregard for either.
In any case, the mental input in these stanzas is somewhat
larger than the sentimental one, though the latter comes
first.

More accurately, the poem strays from the emotional
into the rational, and rather quickly so. In this sense, it is
indeed vintage Hardy, for the trend is seldom the reverse

with him. Besides, every poem is a means of transportation by definition, and this one is only more so, since metrically at least it is about a means of transportation. With its iambic tetrameter and the shifting caesura that makes its fifth line slide into an anapest, its stanza wonderfully conveys the tilting movement of a horse-driven carriage, and the closing couplets mimic its arrival. As is inevitable with Hardy, this pattern is sustained throughout the poem.

We first see the features of the cycle's heroine lit—most likely dimly—by "the borough lights ahead." The lighting here is more cinematic than poetic; nor does the word "borough" heighten the diction much—something you would expect when it comes to the heroine's appearance. Instead, a line and a half are expended on stressing—literally, and with a touch of tautological relish—her lack of awareness of the impending transformation into being "the face of the dead." In effect, her features are absent; and the only explanation for our poet's not grabbing this opportunity to depict them is the prospect of the cycle already existing in his head (although no poet is ever sure of his ability to produce the next poem). What's present of her, however, in this stanza is her speech, echoed in "And you told of the charm of that haloed view." One hears in this line her "It's charming," and conceivably, "Such a halo!" as she was by all accounts a churchgoing woman.

The second stanza sticks to the "moorway" topography no less than to the chronology of events. Apparently the heroine's outing occurred one week—perhaps slightly less —before she died, and she was interred on the eighth day at this place, apparently to her left as she drove home by the moorway. Such literalness may owe here to the poet's deliberately reining in his emotion, and "spot" suggests a conscious deflation. It is certainly in keeping with the notion of a carriage trundling along, supported, as it were, by leaf-springs of tetrameters. Yet knowing Hardy's appetite for detail, for the mundane, one may as well assume that no special effort was applied here and no special significance was sought. He simply registers the pedestrian manner in which an absurdly drastic change has taken place.

Hence the next line, which is the highest point in this stanza. In "And be spoken of as one who was not," one detects the sense not so much of loss or unbearable absence as that of all-consuming negation. "One who was not" is too resolute for comfort or, for that matter, for discomfort, and negation of an individual is what death is all about. Therefore, "Beholding it with a heedless eye/As alien from you" is not a scolding but rather an admission of the appropriate response. With ". . . though under its tree/You soon would halt everlastingly" the carriage and the exposition part of the poem indeed come to a halt.

Essentially, the central theme of these two stanzas is their heroine's lack of any inkling or premonition of her approaching end. This could be perceived as a remarkable expectation indeed, were it not for her age. Besides, although throughout the cycle the poet insists on the suddenness of Emma Hardy's demise, it's obvious from other sources that she was afflicted with several ailments, including a mental disorder. But presumably there was something about her that made him convinced of her durability; perhaps that had to do with his notion of himself as the Immanent Will's plaything.

And although many would regard the third stanza's opening as heralding the theme of guilt and remorse that the same many would detect in the whole cycle, "I drove not with you" is just a restatement of that premonition's requirement; worse comes to worse, of his probable failure

at obtaining it. The next line and a half postulate quite resolutely that probability, ruling out grounds for the speaker's
self-reproach on that account. Yet for the first time, true
lyricism creeps into the poem: first through the ellipsis, secondly through "Yet had I sat/At your side that eve" (which
is, of course, a reference to his not being at her side at
the moment of death). It takes over in full force with "That
the countenance I was glancing at," where all the consonants of "countenance" vibrate, giving you a passenger's
silhouette swaying from side to side because of the carriage's movement, seen against the light. The treatment
again is quite cinematic, the film being black-and-white.
One could throw "*flick*ering" into the bargain, were it not
1912.

And were it not for the starkness of "Had a last-time
look" (still, perceptions often run ahead of technology, and
as we said earlier, montage wasn't invented by Eisenstein).
This starkness both enhances and shatters the almost loving
tentativeness of "the countenance I was glancing at," betraying the poet's eagerness to escape a reverie for the truth,
as though the latter is more rewarding.

A reverie he certainly escapes, but he pays for that with
the monstrous next line: with recalling the heroine's actual
features in "Nor have read the writing upon your face." The
reference here, obviously, is to the writing upon the wall,
whose inescapable equation with the heroine's appearance
tells us enough about the state of the union prior to her
death. What informs this equation is his sense of her impenetrability, and that's what the poem was all about thus
far, since this impenetrability applies to the past about as
much as it does to the future, and it's a quality she happens
to share with the future generally. Thus his reading of Emma's equivalent of "*Mene, Mene, Tekel, Upharsin*" here is
no fantasy.

"I go hence soon to my resting-place;

"You may miss me then. But I shall not know
How many times you visit me there,
Or what your thoughts are, of if you go
There never at all. And I shall not care.
Should you censure me I shall take no heed,
And even your praises no more shall need."

And here is our heroine, verbatim. Because of the deftly blended tenses, this is a voice from beyond the grave as much as from the past. And it is relentless. With every next sentence, she takes away what she has given a sentence before. And what she gives and takes is obviously his humanity. This way she reveals herself to be indeed a good match for her poet. There is a strong echo of marital argument in these lines, the intensity of which overcomes completely the listlessness of the verse. It gets much louder here and drowns the sound of the carriage wheels on the cobblestones. To say the least, dead, Emma Hardy is capable of invading her poet's future to the point of making him defend himself.

What we have in this stanza is essentially an apparition. And although the cycle's epigraph—"Traces of an old flame"—is taken from Virgil, this particular passage bears a very close resemblance, both in pitch and substance—to the famous elegy by Sextus Propertius, from his "Cynthia Monobiblos." The last two lines in this stanza, in any case, sound like a good translation of Cynthia's final plea: "And as for your poems in my honor, burn them, burn them!"

The only escape from such negation is into the future, and that's the route our poet takes: "True: never you'll know." That future, however, should be fairly distant, since its foreseeable part, the poet's present, is already occupied. Hence, "And you will not mind" and "But shall I then slight you because of such?" Still, with that escape comes—in this last stanza's first line especially—a piercing recognition of the ultimate parting, of the growing distance. Characteristically, Hardy handles this line with terrific reserve, allowing only a sigh to escape in the caesura and a slight elevation of pitch in "mind." Yet the suppressed lyricism bursts into the open and claims its own in "Dear ghost."

He indeed addresses an apparition, but one that's free of any ecclesiastical dimension. This is not a particularly mellifluous form of address, which alone convinces one of its literalness. He is not searching here for a tactful alternative. (What could there be instead? The meter, allotting him here only two syllables, rules out "Dear Emma"; what then, "Dear friend"?) A ghost she is, and not because she is dead, but because though less than a physical reality she is far more than just a memory: she is an entity he can address, a presence—or absence—he is familiar with. It's not the inertia of marriage but of time itself—thirty-eight years of it—that solidifies into a substance: what may be, he feels, only hardened by his future, which is but another increment of time.

Hence, "Dear ghost." Thus designated, she can almost be touched. Or else "ghost" is the ultimate in detachment. And for somebody who ran the whole gamut of attitudes available to one human being vis-à-vis another, from pure love to total indifference—"ghost" offers one more possibility, if you will, a postscript, a sum total. "Dear ghost" is uttered here indeed with an air of discovery and of summary, which is what, in fact, the poem offers two lines later: "Yet abides the fact, indeed, the same,—/You are past love, praise, indifference, blame." This describes not only the condition of a ghost but also a new attitude attained by the poet —an attitude that permeates the cycle of *Poems 1912–13* and without which that cycle wouldn't be possible.

This finale's enumeration of attitudes is tactically similar to "The Convergence of the Twain" 's "grotesque, slimed, dumb, indifferent." Yet while it is propelled by similar self-deprecating logic, it adds up not to the reductive ("choose one") precision of analysis but to an extraordinary emotional summary that redefines the genre of funeral elegy no less than that of love poetry itself. Immediate as the former, "Your Last Drive" amounts, on account of its finale, to a much-delayed postscript, rarely encountered in poetry, to what love amounts to. Such a summary is obviously the minimal requirement for engaging a ghost in a dialogue, and the last line has an engaging, indeed somewhat flirtatious air. Our old man is wooing the inanimate.

VII

Every poet learns from his own breakthroughs, and Hardy, with his professed tendency to "exact a full look at the worst," seems to profit in, and from, *Poems of 1912–13* enormously. For all its riches of detail and topographical reference, the cycle has an oddly universal, almost impersonal quality, since it deals with the extremes of the emotional spectrum. "A full look at the worst" is well matched by a full look at the best, with very short shrift given to the mean. It is as though a book were being riffled through from the end to the beginning before being shelved.

It never got shelved. A rationalist more than an emotionalist, Hardy, of course, saw the cycle as an opportunity to rectify what many and in part he himself regarded as a lyrical deficiency in his poetry. And true enough, *Poems of 1912–13* does constitute a considerable departure from his pattern of graveyard musing, grand on metaphysics and yet usually rather bland sentimentally. That's what accounts for the cycle's enterprising stanzaic architecture, but above all for its zeroing in on the initial stage of his marital union: on meeting a maiden.

In theory, that encounter ensures an upsurge of positive sentiment, and at times it does. But it was so long ago that the optic of intro- and retrospection often proves insufficient. As such it gets unwittingly replaced by the lens habitually employed by our poet for pondering his beloved infinities, Immanent Wills, and all, exacting a full look at the worst.

It seems he's got no other instruments anyway: whenever faced with a choice between a moving or a drastic utterance, he normally goes for the latter. This may be attributed to certain aspects of Mr. Hardy's character or temperament; a more appropriate attribution would be to the métier itself.

For poetry for Thomas Hardy was above all a tool of cognition. His correspondence as well as his prefaces to various editions of his work are full of disclaimers of a poet's status; they often emphasize the diaristic, commentary role his poetry had for him. I think this can be taken at face value. We should bear in mind also that the man was an autodidact, and autodidacts are always more interested in the essence of what they are learning than its actual data. When it comes to poetry, this boils down to an emphasis on revelatory capacity, often at the expense of harmony.

To be sure, Hardy went to extraordinary lengths to master harmony, and his craftsmanship often borders on the exemplary. Still, it is just craftsmanship. He is no genius at harmony; his lines seldom sing. The music available in his poems is a mental music, and as such it is absolutely unique. The main distinction of Thomas Hardy's verse is that its formal aspects—rhyme, meter, alliteration, etc.—are precisely the aspects standing in attendance to the driving force of his thought. In other words, they seldom generate that force; their main job is to usher in an idea and not to obstruct its progress.

I suppose if asked what he values more in a poem—the insight or the texture—he would cringe, but ultimately he would give the autodidact's reply: the insight. This is, then, the criterion by which one is to judge his work, and this cycle in particular. It is the extension of human insight that he sought in this study of the extremes of estrangement and attachment, rather than pure self-expression. In this sense, this pre-modernist was without peer. In this sense also, his poems are indeed a true reflection of the métier itself, whose operational mode, too, is the fusion of the rational and the intuitive. It could be said, however, that he turned the tables somewhat: he was intuitive about his work's substance; as for his verse's formal aspects, he was excessively rational.

For that he paid dearly. A good example of this could be his "In the Moonlight," written a couple of years later but in a sense belonging to *Poems of 1912–13*—if not necessarily thematically, then by virtue of its psychological vector.

"O lonely workman, standing there
In a dream, why do you stare and stare
At her grave, as no other grave there were?

"If your great gaunt eyes so importune
Her soul by the shine of this corpse-cold moon
Maybe you'll raise her phantom soon!"

"Why, fool, it is what I would rather see
Than all the living folk there be;
But alas, there is no such joy for me!"

"Ah—she was one you loved, no doubt,
Through good and evil, through rain and drought,
And when she passed, all your sun went out?"

"Nay: she was the woman I did not love,
Whom all the others were ranked above,
Whom during her life I thought nothing of."

Like an extremely high percentage of Hardy's verse, the poem seems to hark back to the folk ballad, with its use of dialogue and its element of social commentary. The mock romantic opening and the nagging lapidary tone of triplets —not to mention the poem's very title—suggest a polemical aspect to "In the Moonlight" when viewed within the contemporary poetic discourse. The poem is obviously a "variation on a theme" frequent enough in Hardy's own work in the first place.

The overtones of social commentary, usually fairly sharp in a ballad, are somewhat muted here, though not entirely. Rather, they are subordinated to the psychological thrust of the poem. It is extremely shrewd of the poet to make precisely a "workman," and not the urbane, sneering passerby the carrier of the loaded, terrifying insight revealed in the last stanza. For normally a crisis-ridden conscience in literature is the property of the educated classes. Here, however, it is an uncouth, almost plebeian "workman" who weighs in with at once the most menacing and the most tragic admission Hardy's verse ever made.

Yet although the syntax here is fairly clear, the meter sustained, and the psychology powerful, the poem's texture undermines its mental achievement with its triple rhyme, warranted neither by the story line nor, what's worse, its own quality. In short, the job is expert but not particularly rewarding. We get the poem's vector, not its target. But as far as the truth about the human heart is concerned, this vector may be enough. That's what the poet, one imagines, has told himself on this and on many other occasions. For the full look at the worst blinds you to your own appearance.

VIII

Blissfully, Hardy lived long enough not to be trapped by either his achievements or his failures. Therefore, we may concentrate on his achievements, perhaps with an additional sense of their humanity or, if you will, independent of it. Here's one of them, a poem called "Afterwards." It was written somewhere around 1917, when quite a lot of people all over the place were busy doing each other in and when our poet was seventy-seven years old.

When the Present has latched its postern behind my tremulous
stay,
    And the May month flaps its glad green leaves like wings,
Delicate-filmed as new-spun silk, will the neighbours say,
    "He was a man who used to notice such things"?

If it be in the dusk when, like an eyelid's soundless blink,
    The dewfall-hawk comes crossing the shades to alight
Upon the wind-warped upland thorn, a gazer may think,
    "To him this must have been a familiar sight."

If I pass during some nocturnal blackness, mothy and warm,
    When the hedgehog travels furtively over the lawn,
One may say, "He strove that such innocent creatures should come
    to no harm,
    But he could do little for them; and now he is gone."

If, when hearing that I have been stilled at last, they stand at the
    door,
  Watching the full-starred heavens that winter sees,
Will this thought rise on those who will meet my face no more,
  "He was one who had an eye for such mysteries"?

And will any say when my bell of quittance is heard in the gloom,
  And a crossing breeze cuts a pause in its outrollings,
Till they rise again, as they were a new bell's boom,
  "He hears it not now, but used to notice such things"?

These twenty hexametric lines are the glory of English
poetry, and they owe all that they've got precisely to hexameter. The good question is to what does hexameter itself
owe its appearance here, and the answer is so that the old
man can breathe more easily. Hexameter is here not for its
epic or by the same classical token elegiac connotations but
for its trimeter-long, inhale-exhale properties. On the subconscious level, this comfort translates into the availability
of time, into a generous margin. Hexameter, if you will, is
a moment stretched, and with every next word Thomas
Hardy in "Afterwards" stretches it even further.

    The conceit in this poem is fairly simple: while consid-
ering his immanent passing, the poet produces cameo representations of each one of the four seasons as his departure's
probable backdrop. Remarkably well served by its title and
free of the emotional investment usually accompanying a
poet when such prospects are entertained, the poem proceeds at a pace of melancholy meditation—which is what
Mr. Hardy, one imagines, wanted it to be. It appears, however, that somewhere along the way the poem escaped his
control and things began to occur in it not according to the
initial plan. In other words, art has overtaken craft.

But first things first, and the first season here is spring, which is ushered in with an awkward, almost creaking septuagenarian elegance: no sooner does May get in than it is hit by a stress. This is all the more noticeable after the indeed highly arch and creaking "When the Present has latched its postern behind my tremulous stay," with its wonderfully hissing confluence of sibilants toward the end of the line. "Tremulous stay" is a splendid conjunction, evocative, one would imagine, of the poet's very voice at this stage, and thus setting the tone for the rest of the poem.

Of course, we have to bear in mind that we are viewing the whole thing through the prism of the modern, late-twentieth-century idiom in poetry. What seems arch and antiquated through this lens wouldn't necessarily have produced the same effect at the time. When it comes to generating circumlocutions, death has no equals, and at the Last Judgment it could cite them in its defense. And as such circumlocutions go, "When the Present has latched its postern behind my tremulous stay" is wonderful if only because it shows a poet more concerned with his diction than with the prospect he describes. There is a peace in this line, not least because the stressed words here are two and three syllables long; the unstressed syllables play the rest of these words down with the air of a postscript or an afterthought.

Actually, the stretching of the hexameter—i.e., time—and filling it up begins with "tremulous stay." But things really get busy once the stress hits "May" in the second line, which consists solely of monosyllables. Euphonically, the net result in the second line is an impression that Mr. Hardy's spring is more rich in leaf than any August. Psychologically, however, one has the sense of piling-up qualifiers spilling well into the third line, with its hyphenated, Homer-like epithets. The overall sensation (embodied in the future perfect tense) is that of time slowed down, stalled by its every second, for that's what monosyllabic words are: uttered—or printed—seconds.

"The best eye for natural detail," enthused Yvor Winters about Thomas Hardy. And we, of course, can admire this eye sharp enough to liken the reverse side of a leaf to newly spun silk—but only at the expense of praising the ear. As you read these lines out loud, you stumble through the second, and you've got to mumble fast through the first half of the third. And it occurs to you that the poet has stuffed these lines with so much natural detail not for its own sake but for reasons of metric vacancy.

The truth, of course, is that it's both: that's your real natural detail: the ratio of, say, a leaf to the amount of space in a line. It may fit, and then it may not. This is the way a poet learns the value of that leaf as well as of those available stresses. And it is to alleviate the syllabic density of the preceding line that Mr. Hardy produces the almost trochaic "Delicate-filmed as new-spun silk" qualifier, not out of attachment to this leaf and this particular sensation. Had he been attached to them, he'd have moved them to the rhyming position, or in any case out of the tonal limbo where you find them.

Still, technically speaking, this line and a half do show off what Mr. Winters appreciates so much about our poet. And our poet himself is cognizant of trotting out natural detail here, and polishing it up a bit on top of that. And this is what enables him to wrap it up with the colloquial " 'He was a man who used to notice such things.' " This understatement, nicely counterbalancing the opening line's ramshackle grandeur, is what he was perhaps after in the first place. It's highly quotable, so he attributes it to the neighbors, clearing the line of the charge of self-consciousness, let alone of being an autoepitaph.

There is no way for me to prove this—though there is also no way to refute it—but I think the first and last lines, "When the Present has latched its postern behind my tremulous stay" and " 'He was a man who used to notice such things,' " existed long before "Afterwards" was conceived, independently. Natural detail got in between them by chance, because it provided a rhyme (not a very spectacular one, so it needed a qualifier). Once there, it gave the poet a stanza, and with that came the pattern for the rest of the poem.

One indication of this is the uncertainty of the season in the next stanza. I'd suggest it's autumn, since the stanzas after deal respectively with summer and winter; and the leafless thorn seems fallow and chilled. This succession is slightly odd in Hardy, who is a superb plotter and who, you might think, would be one to handle the seasons in the traditional, orderly manner. That said, however, the second stanza is a work of unique beauty.

It all starts with yet another confluence of sibilants in "eyelid's soundless blink." Again, proving and refuting may be a problem, but I tend to think that "an eyelid's soundless blink" is a reference to Petrarch's "One life is shorter than an eyelid's blink"; "Afterwards," as we know, is a poem about one's demise.

But even if we abandon the first line with its splendid caesura followed by those two rustling *s*'s between "eyelid's" and "soundless," ending with two more *s*'s, we've got plenty here. First, we have this very cinematographic, slow-motion passage of "The dewfall-hawk" that "comes crossing the shades to alight . . ." And we have to pay attention to his choice of the word "shades," considering our subject. And if we do, we may further wonder about this "dewfall-hawk," about its "dewfall" bit especially. What, we may ask, does this "dewfall," following an eyelid's blink and preceding "shade," try to do here, and is it, perhaps, a well-buried tear? And don't we hear in "to alight/Upon the wind-warped upland thorn" a reined-in or overpowered emotion?

Perhaps we don't. Perhaps all we hear is a pileup of stresses, at best evoking through their "up/warp/up" sound the clapping of wind-pestered shrubs. Against such a backdrop, an impersonal, unreacting "gazer" would be an apt way to describe the onlooker, stripped of any human characteristics, reduced to eyesight. "Gazer" is fitting, since he observes our speaker's absence and thus can't be described in detail: probability can't be terribly particular. Similarly the hawk, batting its wings like eyelids through "the shades," is moving through the same absence. The refrainlike "To him this must have been a familiar sight" is all the more poignant because it cuts both ways: the hawk's flight here is as real as it is posthumous.

On the whole, the beauty of "Afterwards" is that everything in it is multiplied by two.

The next stanza considers, I believe, the summer, and the opening line overwhelms you with its tactility in "mothy and warm," all the more palpable because it is isolated by a very bravely shifted caesura. Yet speaking of bravery, it should be noted that only a very healthy person can ponder the nocturnal blackness of the moment of his demise with such equipoise as we find in "If I pass during some nocturnal blackness . . ." Not to mention more cavalier treatment of the caesura. The only mark of possible alarm here is the "some" before "nocturnal blackness." On the other hand, "some" is one of those readily available bricks a poet uses to save his meter.

Be that as it may, the real winner in this stanza is obviously "When the hedgehog travels furtively over the lawn"—and within the line itself it is, of course, "furtively." The rest is slightly less animated and certainly less interesting, since our poet is clearly bent on endearing himself to the public with his animal-kingdom sympathies. That's quite unnecessary, since, given the subject, the reader is on his side as it is. Also, if one wanted to be really hard-nosed here, one could query whether that hedgehog was indeed in harm's way. At this stage, however, nobody wants to quibble. But the poet himself seems to be aware of the insufficiency of the material here; so he saddles his hexameter with three additional syllables ("One may say")—partly because the awkwardness of speech, he believes, suggests geniality, partly to stretch the dying man's time—or the time he is remembered.

It is in the fourth, winter stanza that the poem confronts absence in earnest.

If, when hearing that I have been stilled at last, they stand at the door,
    Watching the full-starred heavens that winter sees,
Will this thought rise on those who will meet my face no more,
    "He was one who had an eye for such mysteries"?

To begin with, being "stilled at last" includes within its euphemistic reach the author taking leave of the poem, as well as the poem's previous stanza growing silent. This way the audience, more numerous than "the neighbors," "a gazer," or "one," is ushered here into the text and asked to play the role of "Watching the full-starred heavens that winter sees." This is an extraordinary line; the natural detail here is positively terrifying and practically prefigures Robert Frost. For winter indeed sees more "heavens," since in winter trees are naked and the air is clear. If these heavens are full-starred, it, winter, sees more stars. The line is an apotheosis of absence, yet Mr. Hardy seeks to aggravate it further with "Will this thought rise on those who will meet my face no more." "Rise" imparts to the presumably cold features of the "stilled at last" the temperature of the moon.

Behind all this there is, of course, an old trope about the souls of the dead residing on stars. Still, the optical literalness of this rendition is blinding. Apparently when you see a winter sky you see Thomas Hardy. That's the kind of mystery he had an eye for, in his lifetime.

He had an eye for something closer to the ground, too. As you read "Afterwards," you begin to notice the higher and higher position in the lines of each stanza of those who are to comment on him. From the bottom in the first, they climb to the top in the fifth. This could be a coincidence with anyone other than Hardy. We also have to watch their progression from "the neighbours" to "a gazer" to "one" to "they" to "any." None of these designations is particular, let alone endearing. Well, who are these people?

Before we get to that, let's learn something about "any" and what he expects from them.

And will any say when my bell of quittance is heard in the gloom,
   And a crossing breeze cuts a pause in its outrollings,
Till they rise again, as they were a new bell's boom,
   "He hears it not now, but used to notice such things"?

There is no particular season here, which means it's any time. It's any backdrop also, presumably a countryside, with a church in the fields, and its bell tolling. The observation described in the second and third lines is lovely but too common for our poet to claim any distinction for making it. It's his ability to describe it that "any" might refer to by saying in his absence, "He hears it not now, but used to notice such things." Also, "such things" is a sound: interrupted by wind yet returning anew. An interrupted but resuming sound could be regarded here, at the end of this autoelegy, as a self-referential metaphor, and not because the sound in question is that of a bell tolling for Thomas Hardy.

It is so because an interrupted yet resuming sound is, in fact, a metaphor for poetry: for a succession of poems emerging from under the same pen, for a succession of stanzas within one poem. It is a metaphor for "Afterwards" itself, with all its peregrination of stresses and suddenly halting caesuras. In this sense, the bell of quittance never stops—not Mr. Hardy's, anyway. And it doesn't stop as long as his "neighbors," "gazers," "one," "they," and "any" are us.

IX

Extraordinary claims for a dead poet are best made on the basis of his entire oeuvre; as we are perusing only some of Thomas Hardy's work, we may dodge the temptation. Suffice it to say that he is one of the very few poets who, under minimal scrutiny, easily escape the past. What helps his escape is obviously the content of his poems: they are simply extraordinarily interesting to read. And to reread, since their texture is very often pleasure-resistant. That was his whole gamble, and he won.

Out of the past there is only one route, and it takes you into the present. However, Hardy's poetry is not a very comfortable presence here. He is seldom taught, still less read. First, with respect to content at least, he simply overshadows the bulk of poetry's subsequent achievement: a comparison renders too many a modern giant a simpleton. As for the general readership, his thirst for the inanimate comes off as unappealing and disconcerting. Rather than the general public's mental health, this bespeaks its mental diet.

As he escapes the past, and sits awkwardly in the present, one trains one's eye on the future as perhaps his more appropriate niche. It is possible, although the technological and demographic watershed we are witnessing would seem to obliterate any foresight or fantasy based on our own relatively coherent experience. Still, it is possible, and not only because the triumphant Immanent Will might decide to acknowledge, at the peak of its glory, its early champion.

It is possible because Thomas Hardy's poetry makes considerable inroads into what is the target of all cognition: inanimate matter. Our species embarked on this quest long ago, rightly suspecting that we share our own cellular mix-up with the stuff, and that should the truth about the world exist, it's bound to be nonhuman. Hardy is not an exception. What is exceptional about him, however, is the relentlessness of his pursuit, in the course of which his poems began to acquire certain impersonal traits of his very subject, especially tonally. That could be regarded, of course, as camouflage, like wearing fatigues in the trenches.

Or like a new line of fashion that set a trend in English poetry in this century: the dispassionate posture became practically the norm, indifference a trope. Still, these were just side effects; I daresay he went after the inanimate—not for its jugular, since it has none, but for its diction.

Come to think of it, the expression "matter-of-fact" could well apply to his idiom, except that the emphasis would be on matter. His poems very often sound as if matter has acquired the power of speech as yet another aspect of its human disguise. Perhaps this was indeed the case with Thomas Hardy. But then it's only natural, because as somebody—most likely it was I—once said, language is the inanimate's first line of information about itself, released to the animate. Or, to put it more accurately, language is a diluted aspect of matter.

It is perhaps because his poems almost invariably (once they exceed sixteen lines) either display the inanimate's touch or else keep an eye on it that the future may carve for him a somewhat larger niche than he occupies in the present. To paraphrase "Afterwards" somewhat, he used to notice unhuman things; hence his "eye for natural detail," and numerous tombstone musings. Whether the future will be able to comprehend the laws governing matter better than it has done thus far remains to be seen. But it doesn't seem to have much choice in acknowledging a greater degree of human affinity with the inanimate than literature and philosophical thought have been insisting on.

This is what enables one to see in a crystal ball unfamiliar multitudes in odd attire making a run on the Scribner's edition of Hardy's Collected Works or the Penguin Selected.

Ninety Years Later

~

I

Written in 1904, "Orpheus. Eurydice. Hermes," by Rainer Maria Rilke, makes one wonder whether the greatest work of the century wasn't done ninety years ago. At the moment of its composition, its German author was twenty-nine years old and leading a rather peripatetic life that brought him first to Rome, where the poem was started, and, later the same year, to Sweden, where it was finished. We should say no more about the circumstances of its emergence, for the simple reason that what this poem adds up to can't be squared with any experience.

To be sure, "Orpheus. Eurydice. Hermes" is as much a flight from biography as it is from geography. Of Sweden there is at best the diffused, gray, somber light enveloping the entire scene. Of Italy there is still less, save the frequently made claim that it was a bas relief in the Museo Nazionale in Naples depicting the poem's three characters that set Rilke's pen in motion.

The relief does exist, and that claim could be valid, but, one would think, of self-defeating consequence. For the copies of this particular marble are innumerable, as are this

myth's vastly various other renditions. The only way for us
to hook said relief with the poem and the poet's personal
circumstances would be to come up with proof that our poet
recognized, for instance, a physiognomic resemblance between the relief's female figure and either his sculptress
wife, at the time estranged, or better yet his great love, Lou
Andreas-Salomé, estranged from him at that time as well.
Yet we possess practically no evidence on that score. And
even had that evidence been in abundance, it would be of
no use. For a particular union, or its dissolution, is of interest
only so far as it avoids metaphor. Once metaphor is introduced, it steals the show. Besides, the features of all the
relief's characters appear too general—as befits a mythological subject treated for the past three millennia in every
art form with relentless frequency—for any particular allusion.

Estrangement, on the other hand, is everyone's forte,
and estrangement is what this poem, in part, is about. It is
to this part in particular that the poem owes its perennial
appeal; all the more so because it deals with the essence of
that sentiment rather than with the personalized version
specific to our poet's predicament. On the whole, what lies
at the core of "Orpheus. Eurydice. Hermes" is a common
enough locution which formulates that essence and goes approximately like this: "If you leave, I'll die." What our poet,
technically speaking, has done in this poem is simply cross
all the way over to the far end of this formula. That's why
we find ourselves at the outset of "Orpheus. Eurydice.
Hermes" squarely in the netherworld.

II

As conceits go, a journey to the netherworld is about as ur
as is the first traveler to undertake it: Orpheus, the ur-poet.

Which is to say that this conceit rivals in age literature as such, or perhaps even predates it.

For all the obvious attractions of a round-trip story, the origins of this conceit are not literary at all. They have to do, I believe, with the fear of being buried alive, sufficiently common even in our own time but, one imagines, quite rampant in days of yore, with their sweeping epidemics— particularly those of cholera.

As fears go, this one undoubtedly is a product of mass society—of a society in any case where the ratio between the mass and its individual members results in the former's relative disregard for the latter's actual end. In the days of yore such a ratio would be provided chiefly by an urban setting or perhaps by a military camp—fertile ground for epidemics and literature (oral or not) alike, since, in order to spread, both require human amassment.

It is suitable, then, that the subject of the earliest works of literature known to us is the military campaign. Several of them incorporate various versions of the myth of descent into the netherworld, with the subsequent return of the hero. That has to do as much with the underlying moribundity of any human endeavor, warfare in particular, as with the congeniality of such a myth—with its equivalent of a happy end—to a narrative suggesting the loss of life on a mass scale.

III

The notion of the netherworld as a ramified, subway-like underground structure derives in all likelihood from the (practically identical) limestone landscapes of Asia Minor and the northern Peloponnesus, rich in what used to serve as both a prehistoric and a historic human habitat: in caves.

The kingdom of Hades is essentially an echo of the pre-urban past, as the intricacy of the netherworld's topography suggests, and the most probable place of this notion's origin is ancient Cappadocia. (In our own civilization, the most audible echo of a cave, with all its otherworldly implications, is obviously a cathedral.) Any given cluster of Cappadocian caves might indeed have housed a population similar in size to that of a small modern township or big village, with the most privileged occupying presumably the spaces closer to fresh air and the rest more and more remote. Often, the caves meander for hundreds of meters into the rock.

It seems that the least accessible among them were used by the inhabitants for storage and as burial grounds. When a dweller in such a community died, he would be taken to the most remote end of the cave network, laid there, and the entrance to his resting place would be barred with a stone. With such a start, the imagination wouldn't have to work too hard to conceive of the caves' patterns' continuation farther into the porous limestone. On the whole, finality ushers in the idea of infinity more readily than the other way around.

IV

Some three thousand years of that imagination's steady work later, it's natural to liken the netherworld's domain to an abandoned mine. The opening lines of "Orpheus. Eurydice. Hermes" bespeak the degree of our fluency with the notion of the kingdom of the dead, whose familiarity somewhat wore off or fell into disuse because of more pressing matters:

> That was the strange unfathomed mine of souls.
> And they, like silent veins of silver ore,
> were winding through its darkness . . .

"Strange" serves here as an invitation to suspend the rational approach to the story, and the translator's amplification of *wunderlich*, as "unfathomed" suggests both the mental and the physical depth of the place we find ourselves in. These epithets qualify the only tangible noun the poem's opening line contains, which is "mine." However, whatever tangibility there is to speak of is blown away with another qualifier: "of souls."

As the netherworld's depictions and definitions go, a "mine of souls" is extremely effective, because "souls" here, meaning in the first place simply "the dead," carries with it also both its pagan and its Christian connotations. The netherworld thus is both a storage and a source of supplies. This warehouse aspect of the kingdom of the dead fuses the two metaphysics available to us, resulting, whether from pressure, shortage of oxygen, or high temperature, in the next line's "silver ore."

Such oxidation is a product of neither chemistry nor alchemy but of cultural metabolism, most immediately detectable in language; and nothing shows this better than "silver."

V

Museo Nazionale or no Museo Nazionale, this "silver" comes, as it were, from Naples, from another cave heading into the netherworld, about ten miles west of the city. This cave, which had about a hundred openings, was the dwelling place of the Sibyl of Cumae, whom Virgil's Aeneas consults about his descent into the kingdom of the dead, which he undertakes in Book VI of the *Aeneid*, to see his father. The Sibyl warns Aeneas about various difficulties attendant on this enterprise, chief among them breaking the Golden

Bough off a golden tree he will encounter along the way. Presenting this bough to Persephone, the Queen of Hades, is his only way to secure admission to her dark realm.

Now the Golden Bough, as well as its tree, obviously stands in for underground deposits of golden ore. Hence the difficulty of breaking it off, which is the difficulty of extracting a whole vein of ore from the rock. Unwittingly, or consciously trying to avoid imitating Virgil, Rilke changes the metal and, with it, the color of the scene, aspiring evidently to a somewhat more monochromatic rendition of Persephone's domain. With this change, of course, comes also a change in the trade value of his "ore," which is souls, suggesting both their plenitude and the narrator's own unemphatic posture. "Silver," in short, comes from the Sibyl via Virgil. This is what that metabolism is all about; but we've just scratched the surface.

VI

We'll do better than that, I hope, though we are dealing with this German poem in an English translation. Well, actually, precisely because of that. Translation is the father of civilization, and as translations go, this is a particularly good one. It's taken from *Rainer Maria Rilke: Selected Works, Volume II: Poetry*, published in 1976 by the Hogarth Press in London.

It was done by J. B. Leishman. What makes it particularly good is, in the first place, of course, Rilke himself. Rilke was a poet of simple words and by and large of regular meters. As for the latter, it was so much the case with him that only twice in the course of his roughly thirty-year career as a poet did he seek to break away from meter-and-rhyme constraints in a decisive manner. The first time he did it is in the 1907 collection called *Neue Gedichte* (*New Poems*), in the cycle of five poems treating—to put it superficially—themes related to Greek antiquity. The second attempt, spanning with intervals the years 1915 to 1923, comprises what came to be known as his *Duino Elegies*. Breathtaking though these elegies are, one has the feeling that our poet got more freedom there than he bargained for. The five pieces from *Neue Gedichte* are a different matter, and "Orpheus. Eurydice. Hermes" is one of them.

It is an iambic pentameter job done in blank verse: something that the English language feels quite comfortable with. Second, it is a straight-out narrative poem, with its exposition, development, and denouement fairly clearly defined. From the translator's point of view, this is not a language-driven but rather a story-driven proposition, and that sort of thing makes translators happy, for with a poem like this, accuracy becomes synonymous with felicity.

Leishman's performance is all the more admirable because he seems to regularize his pentameter to a greater degree than the German original offers. This brings the poem into a metric mold familiar to English readers, enabling them to observe the author's line-by-line achievements in greater confidence. Many a subsequent effort—and in the past three decades translating Rilke has become practically a fad—is marred either by attempts to produce stress for stress a metrical equivalency of the original or to subordinate this poem to the vagaries of *vers libre*. Whether this shows the translators' appetite for authenticity or for being *comme il faut* in the current poetic idiom, the distinct feature of their aspirations (often sharply argued in prefaces) is that they were not the author's. In Leishman's case, though, we clearly deal with the translator's surrender of his ego to the reader's comfort; that's how a poem ceases to be foreign. And here it is, in its entirety.

VII

ORPHEUS. EURYDICE. HERMES

That was the strange unfathomed mine of souls.
And they, like silent veins of silver ore,
were winding through its darkness. Between roots
welled up the blood that flows on to mankind,
like blocks of heavy porphyry in the darkness.
Else there was nothing red.

But there were rocks
and ghostly forests. Bridges over voidness
and that immense, gray, unreflecting pool
that hung above its so far distant bed
like a gray rainy sky above the landscape.
And between meadows, soft and full of patience,
appeared the pale strip of the single pathway,
like a long line of linen laid to bleach.

And on this single pathway they approached.

In front the slender man in the blue mantle,
gazing in dumb impatience straight before him.
His steps devoured the way in mighty chunks
they did not pause to chew; his hands were hanging,
heavy and clenched, out of the falling folds,
no longer conscious of the lightsome lyre,
the lyre which had grown into his left
like twines of rose into a branch of olive.
It seemed as though his senses were divided:
for, while his sight ran like a dog before him,
turned round, came back, and stood, time and again,
distant and waiting, at the path's next turn,

his hearing lagged behind him like a smell.
It seemed to him at times as though it stretched
back to the progress of those other two
who should be following up this whole ascent.
Then once more there was nothing else behind him
but his climb's echo and his mantle's wind.
He, though, assured himself they still were coming;
said it aloud and heard it die away.
They still were coming, only they were two
that trod with fearful lightness. If he durst
but once look back (if only looking back
were not undoing of this whole enterprise
still to be done), he could not fail to see them,
the two light-footers, following him in silence:

The god of faring and of distant message,
the traveling-hood over his shining eyes,
the slender wand held out before his body,
the wings around his ankles lightly beating,
and in his left hand, as entrusted, *her.*

She, so belov'd, that from a single lyre
more mourning rose than from all women-mourners—
that a whole world of mourning rose, wherein
all things were once more present: wood and vale
and road and hamlet, field and stream and beast—
and that around this world of mourning turned,
even as around the other earth, a sun
and a whole silent heaven full of stars,
a heaven of mourning with disfigured stars—
she, so beloved.

But hand in hand now with that god she walked,
her paces circumscribed by lengthy shroudings,

uncertain, gentle, and without impatience.
Wrapt in herself, like one whose time is near,
she thought not of the man who went before them,
nor of the road ascending into life.
Wrapt in herself she wandered. And her deadness
was filling her like fullness.
Full as a fruit with sweetness and with darkness
was she with her great death, which was so new
that for the time she could take nothing in.

She had attained a new virginity
and was intangible; her sex had closed
like a young flower at the approach of evening,
and her pale hands had grown so disaccustomed
to being a wife that even the slim god's
endlessly gentle contact as he led her
disturbed her like a too great intimacy.

Even now she was no longer that blond woman
who'd sometimes echoed in the poet's poems,
no longer the broad couch's scent and island,
nor yonder man's possession any longer.

She was already loosened like long hair,
and given far and wide like fallen rain,
and dealt out like a manifold supply.

She was already root.

And when, abruptly,
the god had halted her and, with an anguished
outcry, outspoke the words: He has turned round!—
she took in nothing, and said softly: Who?

But in the distance, dark in the bright exit,
someone or other stood, whose countenance
was indistinguishable. Stood and saw
how, on a strip of pathway between meadows,
with sorrow in his look, the god of message
turned silently to go behind the figure
already going back by that same pathway,
its paces circumscribed by lengthy shroudings,
uncertain, gentle, and without impatience.

VIII

The poem has the quality of an uneasy dream, in which you gain something extremely valuable, only to lose it the very next moment. Within the limitation of one's sleeping time, and perhaps precisely because of that, such dreams are excruciatingly convincing in their details; a poem is also limited, by definition. Both imply compression, except that a poem, being a conscious act, is not a paraphrase or a metaphor for reality but a reality itself.

For all the recent popularity of the subconscious, our dependence on the conscious is still greater. If responsibilities begin in dreams, as Delmore Schwartz once put it, poems are where they are ultimately articulated and fulfilled. For while it's silly to suggest a hierarchy among various realities, it can be argued that all reality aspires to the condition of a poem: if only for reasons of economy.

This economy is art's ultimate *raison d'être*, and all its history is the history of its means of compression and condensation. In poetry, it is language, itself a highly condensed version of reality. In short, a poem generates rather than reflects. So if a poem addresses a mythological subject, this amounts to a reality scrutinizing its own history, or, if you will, to an effect putting a magnifying glass to its cause and getting blinded by it.

"Orpheus. Eurydice. Hermes" is exactly that, as much as it is the author's self-portrait with that glass in hand, and one learns from this poem a lot more about him than any life of him will offer. What he is looking at is what made him; but he who does the looking is far more palpable, for you can look at something only from the outside. That's the difference between a dream and a poem for you. Say, the reality was language's, the economy was his.

IX

And the first example of that economy is the title. Titles are a quite difficult affair: they run so many risks. Of being didactic, overly emphatic, banal, ornate, or coy. This one eludes any definition and has the air of a caption underneath a photograph or a painting—or, for that matter, a bas relief.

And presumably it was intended as such. This would suit the purpose of a poem treating a Greek myth very well, proclaiming the subject matter and nothing else. Which is what this title does. It states the theme and is free of any emotional investment.

Except that we do not know whether the title preceded the composition of the poem or was thought up afterward. One is tempted, naturally, to assume the former, given the largely dispassionate tone throughout the poem. In other words, the title offers the reader a cue.

Well, so far, so good, and one may only marvel at the remarkable shrewdness of a twenty-nine-year-old putting full stops after each name here to avoid any semblance of melodrama. As on Greek vases, one thinks, and marvels at his intelligence again. But then one looks at the title and notices that something is missing. Did I say "after each name"?

There is no full stop after Hermes, and he is the last. Why?

Because he is a god, and punctuation is the province of mortals. To say the least, a period after a god's name won't do, because gods are eternal and can't be curbed. Hermes, "the god of faring and of distant message," least of all.

The use of divinity in poetry has its own etiquette, which goes at least as far back as the medieval period, and Dante, for instance, advised against rhyming anything in the Christian pantheon with low-level nouns. Rilke, as it were, takes this etiquette a dot further, pairing Orpheus and Eurydice in their finality but leaving the god literally open-ended. As far as giving cues is concerned, this is a superbly emblematic job; one almost wishes it were a typo. But then it would be divine intervention.

X

This blend of matter-of-factness and open-endedness is what constitutes the diction of the poem. Nothing could be more suitable for retelling a myth, which is to say that the choice of diction was as much Rilke's own achievement as it was the product of this myth's previous renditions—say, from the *Georgics* onward. It's those innumerable previous versions that push our poet into the flight from any flourish, into adopting this dispassionate timbre tinged now and then with a note of somber wistfulness, equally befitting the age and the tenor of his story.

What is more Rilke's own is, in the opening lines of the poem, the use of color. Its bleached pastel tones of gray, of opaque porphyry, all the way down to Orpheus' own blue mantle are straight out of the Worpswede-soft bed of Northern expressionism, with its subdued, washed-out sheets wrinkled by the pre-Raphaelite-cum-Art-Nouveau aesthetic idiom of the turn of the century.

That was the strange unfathomed mine of souls.
And they, like silent veins of silver ore,
were winding through its darkness. Between roots
welled up the blood that flows on to mankind,
like blocks of heavy porphyry in the darkness.
Else there was nothing red.

But there were rocks
and ghostly forests. Bridges over voidness
and that immense, gray, unreflecting pool
that hung above its so far distant bed
like a gray rainy sky above the landscape.
And between meadows, soft and full of patience,
appeared the pale strip of the single pathway,
like a long line of linen laid to bleach.

Now this is the exposition; so, naturally, the emphasis
on color is substantial. You may count up to two "grays,"
a couple of "darknesses," three "reds." Add to that the
"ghostly" of the forests and the "pale" of the pathway—as
belonging to the same monochrome-gravitating family of epithets, since the source of light is withdrawn.

This is a scene devoid of any sharp color. If anything
stands out, it is the souls' "veins of silver ore," whose glitter also amounts to an animated version of gray at best.
"Rocks" project a further absence of color, another degree
of gray perhaps, especially being preceded by the spectrum-
thwarting "Else there was nothing red."

It is an anticlimactic palette, fashionable at the time,
that Rilke uses here, obviously running the risk of turning
the poem into a period piece. Having read thus far, we learn
at least what kind of art was inspiring for him, and we may
wriggle our modern noses at this dated aesthetic idiom: at

best, it's somewhere between Odilon Redon and Edvard Munch.

XI

Yet for all his slaving as a secretary for Rodin, for all his tremendous sentiment for Cézanne, for all his immersion in the artistic milieu, he was a stranger to the visual arts, and his taste for them was incidental. A poet is always a conceptualist rather than a colorist, and having read thus far, we realize that his eye in the quoted passage is subordinate to his imagination, or, to put it more accurately, to his mind. For while we can trace the application of color in these lines to a certain period in European painting, the spatial construction of

> Bridges over voidness
> and that immense, gray, unreflecting pool
> that hung above its so far distant bed
> like a gray rainy sky above the landscape

has no detectable origin. Save, perhaps, a standard textbook figure of a river (or lake) in profile in a high-school geometry lesson. Or both.

For "Bridges over voidness" echoes an arc chalked upon a blackboard. Similarly, "and that immense, gray, unreflecting pool/that hung above its so far distant bed" evokes a horizontal line drawn on the same blackboard and supplemented with a semicircle underneath joining that line's two ends. Add to this "like a gray rainy sky above the landscape," which is yet another semicircle arching over that horizontal line, and what you get is the figure of a sphere with its diameter within it.

XII

Rilke's poems are brimming and bristling with such depictions of things-in-themselves, in *Neue Gedichte* particularly. Take, for instance, his famous "Panther," with its "dance of forces around their center." He does this sort of thing with relish, sometimes gratuitously, just at a rhyme's suggestion. Yet arbitrariness in poetry is a better architect, because it supplies a poem's structure with its climate.

Here, of course, this sketch of a sphere fits rather well into the notion of his subterranean landscape's utter autonomy. It performs nearly the same function as his use of "porphyry," with its strictly geological connotations. What's more interesting, however, is the psychological mechanism behind this drawing full circle, and I believe that in this iambic pentameter blank-verse job, the equivalence of the two semicircles is the echo of the rhyme principle—of, to put it rudely, the inertia of pairing and/or equating one thing with another—whose application this particular poem was meant to eschew.

It does; but the rhyme principle makes itself felt through this poem like a muscle through a shirt. A poet is a conceptualist if only because his mind is conditioned by the properties of his means, and nothing makes you connect heretofore disparate things and notions like rhyme. These connections are often unique or singular enough to create a sense of their result's autonomy. Furthermore, the longer our poet is at it, at generating or dealing with autonomous entities, the more the notion of autonomy rubs off on his own psychological makeup, his sense of himself.

This line of thinking may take us, of course, straight into Rilke's biography, but that's hardly necessary, since biography will avail us much less than the verse itself. For the shuttling and oscillating of verse, fueled by that rhyme principle while questioning conceptual consonance, offers a far greater mental and emotional reach than any romantic endeavor. That's why one settles for a literary career in the first place.

XIII

Underneath the exposition's alternative landscape, with all it contains, including the perfect sphere, runs, like a painter's signature, the wonderfully meandering "pale strip of the single pathway/like a long line of linen laid to bleach," whose alliterative beauty should be credited, no doubt, to its English translator, J. B. Leishman.

This is a remarkably good circumlocution for an untraveled road, which, we learn a line before, is the only one in this alternative, wholly autonomous world just created by the poet. This is not the only such creation in this poem; more are to come, and they, retroactively, will explain to us the poet's appetite for self-contained scenes. But this is indeed an exposition, and Rilke proceeds here as a good stage designer setting the scene for the movement of his characters.

So last comes the pathway, a meandering horizontal line "between meadows, soft and full of patience," i.e., accustomed to the absence of movement but implicitly waiting for it: like us.

Landscapes, after all, are to be inhabited; the ones sporting a road, in any case, are. In other words, now the poem ceases to be a painting and becomes a story: now he can start moving his figures.

XIV

And on this single pathway they approached.

In front the slender man in the blue mantle, gazing in dumb impatience straight before him.

His steps devoured the way in mighty chunks
they did not pause to chew; his hands were hanging,
heavy and clenched, out of the falling folds,
no longer conscious of the lightsome lyre,
the lyre which had grown into his left
like twines of rose into a branch of olive.
It seemed as though his senses were divided:
for, while his sight ran like a dog before him,
turned round, came back, and stood, time and again,
distant and waiting, at the path's next turn,
his hearing lagged behind him like a smell.
It seemed to him at times as though it stretched
back to the progress of those other two
who should be following up this whole ascent.
Then once more there was nothing else behind him
but his climb's echo and his mantle's wind.
He, though, assured himself they still were coming;
said it aloud and heard it die away.
They still were coming, only they were two
that trod with fearful lightness. If he durst
but once look back (if only looking back
were not undoing of this whole enterprise
still to be done), he could not fail to see them,
the two light-footers, following him in silence . . .

"The slender man in the blue mantle" is obviously Orpheus himself. We should be interested in this depiction for a variety of reasons, above all because if there is anyone in this poem to tell us about its author, it is Orpheus. First, because he is a poet. Second, because in the context of this myth, he is a suffering party. Third, because he also has to imagine what is going on. Among the three, the emergence of some semblance of the author's self-portrait is inevitable.

All the same, we shouldn't lose sight of the narrator,

for it is he who gave us this exposition. It's the narrator who provided the poem with its deadpan title, thus gaining our confidence as regards the rest. It's his version of the myth we are dealing with, not Orpheus'. In other words, Rilke and the poet shouldn't overlap in our minds completely, if only because no two poets are alike.

Still, if our Orpheus is only an aspect of our author, that's already of sufficient interest to us, because through his portrayal of our ur-poet we can espy the great German's own vantage point and what—as he stands at that point— he envies or disdains in the figure of Orpheus. Who knows, perhaps the whole purpose of this poem for its author was in sorting these things out.

So as tempting as this might be, we should avoid fusing in our minds the author and his character. It's more difficult, of course, for us to resist this temptation than it was for Rilke himself, for whom total identification with Orpheus would be just plain unseemly. Hence his rather hard look at the legendary bard from Thrace. We should attempt to follow suit as we look at them both.

XV

". . . the slender man in the blue mantle" gives you very little, save the complexion and perhaps the height. "Blue" doesn't seem to denote anything in particular; it simply makes the figure more visible against the colorless background.

"Gazing in dumb impatience straight before him" is a bit more loaded and appears unflattering. Although Orpheus is understandably anxious to get it over with, the author's choice of psychological detail is quite telling. Theoretically, there must have been some other options: Orpheus' joy at regaining his beloved wife, for instance. However, by selecting ostensibly negative characterization, the author achieves two goals. First, he distances himself from Orpheus. Second, "impatience" underscores the fact that we are dealing with a figure in motion: with human movements in the domain of gods. This couldn't be otherwise, since in our visual habits we are to the ancients what their gods are to us. And equally inevitable is the failure of Orpheus' mission, as human movements in divine precincts are doomed from the threshold: they are subject to a different clock. *Sub specie aeternitatis*, any human movement would appear a bit too choleric and impatient. Come to think of it, Rilke's rendition of the myth, removed as he is in time from antiquity, is in itself the product of that eternity's small part.

But like a germ that each spring shoots up a new leaf, a myth engenders its mouthpiece century after century in every culture. So Rilke's poem is not so much a rendition of the myth as its growth. For all the differences between the human and divine time patterns—a difference which is at the core of this myth—the poem is still the story of a mortal told by a mortal. A god perhaps would present Orpheus in a harsher light than Rilke—since, to the gods, Orpheus is just a trespasser. If he is to be clocked at all, it's just to time his expulsion, and the gods' epithets for Orpheus' movements would be, no doubt, tinged with *Schadenfreude*.

"Dumb impatience" is an utterly human characterization; it has an air of personal reminiscence, of hindsight, if you will, of belated regret. Airs of that kind abound in this poem, imparting to Rilke's retelling of this myth an aspect of recollection. But myths have no other seat in men save memory; and a myth whose subject is loss only more so. What makes this sort of myth memorable is one's own experience of a similar nature. When you talk of loss you are on home ground, antiquity or no antiquity. Let's jump the hurdle, then, and let's equate myth with memory; this way we'll spare ourselves likening the life of our psyche to the

vegetable kingdom; this way we might get some explanation
for myth's haunting powers over ourselves and of the detectable regularity of their recurrence in every culture.

For the source of memory's potency (often overshadowing our very reality) is a sense of unfinished business, of
interruption. The same, it must be noted, lies behind the
concept of history. Memory is essentially a continuation of
that business—be that the life of your mistress or affairs of
some nation—by different means. Partly because we learn
about myths in our childhood, partly because they belong
to antiquity, they are an integral part of our private past.
And toward our past we are normally either judgmental or
nostalgic, for we are not bossed around any longer by those
beloveds or by those gods. Hence, the sway of myths over
us; hence their blurring effect upon our own private record;
hence, to say the least, the invasion of self-referential diction
and imagery into the poem at hand. "Dumb impatience" is
a good example, since self-referential diction, by definition,
is bound to be unflattering.

Now, this is the beginning of a poem dealing with a
mythological subject, and Rilke elects to play here by the
rules of antiquity, stressing the one-dimensionality of mythological characters. On the whole, the representational pattern in myths boils down to the man-is-his-purpose principle
(athlete runs, god strikes, warrior fights, and so forth),
whereupon everyone is defined by his action. This is so not
because the ancients were unwitting Sartreans but because
everyone was then depicted in profile. A vase, or for that
matter a bas relief, accommodates ambiguity rather poorly.

So if Orpheus is presented here by the author as being
single-minded, it is pretty much in tune with the treatment
of the human figure in the art of Greek antiquity: because
on this "single pathway" we see him in profile. Whether
deliberately or not (which is in the final analysis of no con-

sequence, although one is tempted to credit the poet with more rather than with less), Rilke rules out any nuance. That's why we, accustomed as we are to multifarious, indeed stereoscopic representations of the human figure, find the first characterization of Orpheus unflattering.

XVI

Because things are not getting any better with "His steps devoured the way in mighty chunks/they did not pause to chew . . ." let's say here something really corny. Let's say that our poet operates in these lines like an archaeologist removing the sediment of centuries from his find, layer by layer. So the first thing he sees about the figure is that it's in motion, and that's what he registers. The cleaner the find gets, the more psychological detail emerges. Having debased ourselves with this corny simile, let's address those devouring steps.

XVII

"To devour" denotes a ravenous manner of eating and generally pertains to animals. The author resorts to this simile not only to describe the speed of Orpheus' movements but also to imply the source of that speed. The reference here is clearly to Cerberus, the three-headed dog guarding the entrance to Hades—as well as the exit from it, we must add, since it's one and the same gate. Orpheus, as we have him here, is on his way back to life from Hades, which is to say that he has seen that monstrous animal just recently and must feel terrified. So the speed of his movements owes as much to his desire to bring his beloved wife back to life as quickly as possible as to the desire to put as much distance as possible between himself and that dog.

By employing this verb in describing Orpheus' manner

of movement, the author suggests that the terror of Cerberus turns the ur-poet himself into a sort of animal, i.e., makes him unthinking. "His steps devoured the way in mighty chunks/they did not pause to chew . . ." is a remarkable job, if only because it implies the true reason behind our hero's failing in his mission, as well as the meaning of the divine taboo forbidding one to look back: don't fall prey to terror. Which is to say, don't accelerate.

Again, there is no reason for us to believe that the author set out to decipher the myth's main provision as he embarked on the poem. Most likely this came out intuitively, in the process of composition, after his pen drew out "devoured" —a common-enough intensification of diction. And then it suddenly jelled: speed and terror, Orpheus and Cerberus. Most likely the connection just flashed into his mind and determined the subsequent treatment of our ur-poet.

XVIII

For Orpheus appears to be literally dogged by fear. Four lines and a half later—lines that theoretically put a bit of distance between Orpheus and that fear's source—the dog overtakes him to the point of becoming practically his own physical aspect:

> It seemed as though his senses were divided:
> for, while his sight ran like a dog before him,
> turned round, came back, and stood, time and again,
> distant and waiting, at the path's next turn,
> his hearing lagged behind him like a smell.

What we are given in this simile is essentially the domestication of fear. Now our archaeologist has removed the last layer of soil from his find, and we see Orpheus' state of mind, which appears to be quite frantic. His sight's shuttling back and forth, however faithfully it serves him, compromises both his progress and his destination. Yet the little doggy seems to be doing far more running here than we initially realize, for Orpheus' hearing lagging behind him like a smell is yet another deployment of the same dog simile.

XIX

Now, quite apart from what these lines accomplish in portraying Orpheus' mental state, the mechanics behind their coupling of his senses (of sight and hearing) is of great significance itself. And attributing this to the poet's rhyming muscle showing won't tell us the whole story.

For the rest of the story has to do with the nature of verse as such, and for that we have to go somewhat back in time. At the moment let me point out to you the remarkably mimetic fluency of the lines we are dealing with. This fluency, you would agree, is directly proportionate to our doggy's ability to shuttle back and forth. To use I. A. Richards's terms, this little quadruped is indeed a vehicle here.

However, the danger with a successful metaphor lies precisely in the vehicle's ability to absorb the tenor entirely (or the other way around, which happens less often) and confuse the author—not to mention the reader—as to what is being qualified by what. And if the vehicle is a quadruped, it swallows the tenor real fast.

But now let's go somewhat back in time.

XX

Well, not too far: to approximately the first millennium B.C., and if you insist on a precise location, to that millennium's seventh century.

The standard mode of *écriture* (written language) in that particular century in Greek was called "boustrophedon." *Boustrophedon* literally means "ox way" and denotes the kind of writing which is similar to plowing a field, when a furrow reaching the end of that field turns and goes in the opposite direction. In writing, this amounts to a line running from left to right and, upon reaching the margin, turning and running from right to left, and so on. Most of writing in Greek at the time was done in this, I daresay, oxonian fashion, and one only wonders whether the term "boustrophedon" was contemporaneous with the phenomenon, or coined post-factum, or even in anticipation? For definitions normally bespeak the presence of an alternative.

Boustrophedon had a minimum of two: the Hebrew and the Sumerian ways of writing. The Hebrew went, as it still does, from right to left. As for the Sumerian cuneiform, it went pretty much the way we are doing things now: from left to right. It's not that a civilization is exactly shopping around for a way to deploy its written language; but the existence of the term reveals a recognized distinction, and a very loaded one.

Hebrew's right-to-left procedure (available to the Greeks via the Phoenicians) could be traced, I suppose, to stone carving, i.e., to the process in which the carver holds the stylus in his left hand and the mallet in the right. In other words, the origins of this written language were not exactly in writing: moving this way, an ancient scribe would inevitably smudge his work with his sleeve or his elbow. A Sumerian (available to the Greeks, alas, directly), on the other hand, relying on clay rather than stone for his narrative or documentation, could press his wedge into the soft surface as easily as he could use a pen (or whatever he would have instead) on the papyri or parchment. The other hand in this case would be the right one.

The Greek boustrophedon, with its shuttle-like movement, suggests the absence of sufficient physical obstacles to the scribe's progress. In other words, its procedure doesn't seem to be motivated by the nature of available writing material. It is so nonchalant in its treading back and forth that it looks almost decorative and brings to mind the lettering on Greek ceramics, with its pictorial and ornamental freedom. It's quite possible that precisely ceramics gave rise to Greek written language, since pictographs normally precede ideograms. We must also bear in mind that, unlike the Hebrew or Sumerian, Greek was the language of an archipelago civilization, and heaving boulders was not the best way to communicate between islands.

Ultimately, because ceramics employ paint, it's safe to assume that written language—lettering, actually—did likewise. Hence its fluency and the knack for continuing regardless of limits. All right, says a sentence hitting the edge of its ceramic tablet, I'll just turn and proceed with what I've got to say to the available surface—for it's most likely that both lettering and images, not to mention ornament, were executed by the same hand.

In other words, the very material used in Greek writing at the time, as well as its relative fragility, suggests the fairly immediate and frequent character of the procedure. In this sense alone, the Greek written language, boustrophedon or no boustrophedon, was much more an *écriture* than similar processes in Hebrew or Sumerian, and presumably evolved faster than the other two. To say the least, the relatively short history of boustrophedon and its status as an archaeological curiosity testifies to that evolution's pace. And as a part of that evolution, the emergence of poetry in Greek owes quite a lot to this archaeological curiosity, for it is difficult not to recognize in boustrophedon—at least visually—a precursor of verse.

XXI

For "verse," which comes from the Latin *versus*, means "turn." Of direction, of one thing into another: left, right, U-; of thesis into antithesis, metamorphosis, juxtaposition, paradox, metaphor, if you will, especially successful metaphor; ultimately, rhyme, when two things sound the same but their meanings diverge.

It all comes from the Latin *versus*. And in a sense this whole poem, as well as the very myth of Orpheus, is one large verse, because it is about *turning*. Or should we say it's about a U-turn within a U-turn, for it's about Orpheus turning his back on his trip back from Hades? And that divine taboo was as sound as your traffic regulations?

Perhaps. One thing we can be confident about, though, is that the division of Orpheus' senses and its simile owes first to the medium itself, which is verse, and the poet's imagination, which is conditioned by that medium. And that this simile's movement itself conveys extremely well the medium's own progress, being perhaps the best imitation by a dog of ox-ways on record.

XXII

It seemed to him at times as though it stretched
back to the progress of those other two
who should be following up this whole ascent.
Then once more there was nothing else behind him
but his climb's echo and his mantle's wind.
He, though, assured himself they still were coming;
said it aloud and heard it die away.
They still were coming, only they were two
that trod with fearful lightness. If he durst
but once look back (if only looking back

> were not undoing of this whole enterprise
> still to be done), he could not fail to see them,
> the two light-footers, following him in silence . . .

If one could speak of Rilke's emotional investment in his depiction of Orpheus—and our poet has done everything within his power from the title on to avoid any semblance of sentiment for his hero—it is in these lines that one may detect it. That's not surprising, since these lines deal with the extremes of self-awareness: something every poet is familiar with because of the nature of his enterprise, and something he can't detach himself from, as hard as he may try.

This passage, wonderful as it is in its psychological accuracy, warrants no particular comment save the small matter dealt with by the author in parentheses. Taken as a whole, though, these lines indeed represent a slight shift in the narrator's attitude toward the figure of the ur-poet: there is an air of reluctant sympathy here, although Rilke is doing everything to keep his sentiments in check, including the aforesaid matter in parentheses.

Or should we say, perhaps, matter *of* parentheses? Because this parenthetical matter is the most audacious job pulled off by any poet dealing with this sort of material in the history of our civilization.

What Mr. Rilke puts here in the parentheses, as a matter of some secondary or tertiary importance, is the main provision of the myth—nay, the very premise of the myth—nay again, the myth itself. For the entire story of Orpheus' descent into the netherworld to bring back his wife and of his unsuccessful return revolves precisely around the Olympians' taboo and his violating it. A good half of world poetry is about this taboo! Well, even if it's one-tenth, say from Virgil to Goethe, making a huge meal precisely of this taboo! And Rilke gives it such short shrift. Why?

Because he is a modern poet who sees everything as psychological conflict? Or is it because of all those exalted ornate jobs done before him, and his wanting to sound different—say, deadpan? Does he really perceive Orpheus as a severely fatigued, perplexed creature, saddled with one more problem to solve, working his way out of Hades, with the main condition of the deal stashed away at the back of his mind? Or is this something to do with that rhyming inertia and boustrophedon again?

XXIII

Well, what's modern here is not the poet but the reader, consideration for whose attention span prompts the poet to issue this reminder. Also, since the relevance of the whole story for this reader is not exactly a given, this business-like parenthetical reminder may do some good. For parenthesis is the typographical equivalent of the back of one's mind: the true seat of civilization in modern man.

So the smaller the shrift, the easier the reader's—not the poet's—identification with the poet's hero lubricated further by having been thrown into the midst of the situation, as though it were happening this week, with a minimum of alienating archaic features. The irony—and "if only looking back/were not undoing of this whole enterprise/still to be done" is highly ironical in its stumbling, prose-like cadence and cumbersome enjambments—also helps. Moreover, these lines are just the last brushstrokes completing the depiction of the ur-poet's appearance—not of his substance, which comes six lines later— so the more mortal he looks, the better for what lies ahead.

XXIV

But does our poet know what lies ahead? He certainly knows the ropes of the story—and so, especially after the reminder, does the reader. So he knows that there are two more figures to be introduced and moved through the poem. He also knows that the means of their transportation is blank verse, and that he has to keep the iambic pentameter under tight control, for it has a tendency to march to its own music, occasionally bursting into song. He knows that thus far he has managed to hold the poem to the key given by the title and rein the meter in pretty well, but after forty lines any meter acquires a certain critical mass that presses for vocal release, for a lyrical resolution. So the question is, where is he to let his meter sing, especially since his story, being a tragic one, presents him with constant opportunities? For instance, here, in the first line of the passage introducing Hermes, the pentameter is about to get out from under the poet's dispassionate control:

> The god of faring and of distant message,
> the traveling-hood over his shining eyes,
> the slender wand held out before his body,
> the wings around his ankles lightly beating,
> and in his left hand, as entrusted, *her*.

The pitch rises here as much because of the subject's elevated nature as because of the open-endedness of "faring," propped up by the caesura and followed with the spacious "distant message." Both designations are far more suggestive than they are precise; one registers their vowels rather than their meaning. Connected by a preposition which is supposed to link them, they end up qualifying their respective vagueness and limitlessness as notions. In other words, one hears here the meter itself rather than the mental properties of what it deploys, which are eroded, washed out by the meter's own flow. There is quite a lot of "airing" in "faring," and the "distant message" expands to "distant passage." But then poetry has always been a melic art, especially in Orpheus' time, and it is, after all, Orpheus' vision of Hermes that we get here, so we may let our meter go. Anyhow, the English here is as inviting as *"Den Gott des Ganges und der weiten Botschaft."*

Well, not yet. There may well be other opportunities warranting song more than this one. And the poet knows this not only because he knows the plot and that Eurydice's turn in the poem, for instance, is coming up. He knows this because of the accumulation we mentioned a while ago of the meter's critical mass: the longer he keeps it in check, the greater will be its vocal explosion.

So for the moment it's back to the business-like, matter-of-fact tonality of "the traveling-hood over his shining eyes," although with this poet the matter-of-fact approach is extraordinarily rich.

Hermes' eyes are described as "shining" not simply because we are in the netherworld with its absence of light and color and the hood's shadow makes his eyes more prominent. No, it's because Hermes is a god, and his eyes shine with—as Rilke's contemporary, the great Greek poet Constantine Cavafy, put it about one of those Greek gods—"the joy of being immortal in his eyes."

"Shining" is, of course, a standard epithet for "eyes"; however, neither Orpheus' nor, as we shall see shortly, Eurydice's —which would be most appropriate—eyes are referred to in this manner. Moreover, this is the first epithet with positive connotations to appear in the thus far opaque body of the poem. So it's not stylistic inertia that lies behind this adjective, although the remainder of Hermes' description proceeds indeed along very traditional lines for that god's representation:

> the slender wand held out before his body,
> the wings around his ankles lightly beating . . .

The only interesting things about these lines is the second appearance in the poem of "slender," perhaps not the most evocative choice in this case and making you think that, at the moment of the poem's composition, it was one of our poet's pet words. But then, he was twenty-nine years old, so his attachment to this epithet is perhaps understandable.

The wings around Hermes' ankles are, of course, as standard a detail of his attire as the lyre is of Orpheus'. That they are "lightly beating" denotes the slow pace at which the god moves, as Orpheus' hands hanging "heavy and clenched, out of the falling folds,/no longer conscious of the lightsome lyre,/the lyre which had grown into his left/like twines of rose into a branch of olive" denote the opposite: the speed with which he moves as well as where he moves, both excluding the use of his instrument to the point of turning it into a decorative detail, a motif, worthy of adorning some classical cornice.

Yet two lines later, it is all going to change.

XXV

Given human utterance's vocal properties, the most puzzling aspect of our *écriture* is its horizontality. Whether it runs from right to left or vice versa, all that it is armed with to convey numerous tonal modulations is the exclamation point and question mark. Comma, semicolon, colon, dash, parentheses, period—all these things punctuate the linear, which is to say horizontal, version of our verbal existence. In the end, we buy this form of representation of our speech to the point of imparting to our utterances a certain mental, to say the least, tonal equivalent of horizontality, billing it now as equipoise, now as logic. Come to think of it, virtue is horizontal.

This stands to reason, for so is the ground underfoot. Yet when it comes to our speech, one may find oneself feeling envious of Chinese characters, with their vertical arrangement: our voice darts in all directions; or else one may long for a pictogram over an ideogram. For late as we are in our happy process of evolution, we are short of means of conveying on paper tonal changes, shifts in emphasis, and the like. The graphics of our phonetic alphabets are far from being sufficient; typographic tricks such as line breaks or blank intervals between words fail as a system of notation and are plain wasteful.

It took *écriture* so long to emerge not necessarily because the ancients were slow-witted but due to the anticipated inadequacy of *écriture* to human speech. The potency of myths has to do perhaps precisely with their oral and vocal precedence over the written. Every record is reductive by definition. *Ecriture* is essentially a footprint—which I believe is the beginning of *écriture*—left by a dangerous or benevolent but elsewhere-bound body in the sand.

So two thousand years later (two thousand six hundred, to be precise, since the first mention of Orpheus took place in the sixth century B.C.) our poet, by using structured verse—structured precisely to highlight the euphonic (i.e., vocal) properties of written words and the caesuras that separate them—returns, as it were, this myth to its pre-*écriture* vocal origins. Vocally speaking, Rilke's poem and the ancient myth are one. More exactly, their euphonic difference equals nil. Which is what he is to show two lines later.

XXVI

Two lines below, Eurydice is introduced, and the vocal explosion goes off:

and in his left hand, as entrusted, *her*.

She, so belov'd, that from a single lyre
more mourning rose than from all women-mourners—

that a whole world of mourning rose, wherein
all things were once more present: wood and vale
and road and hamlet, field and stream and beast—
and that around this world of mourning turned,
even as around the other earth, a sun
and a whole silent heaven full of stars,
a heaven of mourning with disfigured stars—
she, so beloved.

The lyre motif erupts here into full-blown singing. What triggers this is not even Eurydice herself but the epithet "belov'd." And what we get here is not her portrait but the ultimate characterization of Orpheus, which comes extremely close to being the author's self-portrait, or, at any rate, the description of his métier.

This passage is very similar to the autonomous sphere we encountered at the poem's beginning, except in this case we have, as it were, a universe—also, if you will, a sphere, though not static but in the process of expansion. At the center of this universe we find a lyre, initially engaged in a mimetic reproduction of reality but subsequently increasing its reach, sort of like the traditional depiction of sound waves emitted by an antenna.

This, I daresay, is very much a formula for Rilke's own art, not to mention his vision of himself. The quoted passage echoes very closely the 1898 entry in his diary in which he, twenty-three years old and reasonably low on self-esteem, ponders restructuring himself into a semblance of a demiurge omnipresent at every layer of his creations and traceable to the center: "There will be nothing outside this solitary figure [i.e., himself], for trees and hills, clouds and waves will only be symbols of those realities which he finds within himself."

A rather exalted vision, perhaps, to go by, but surely

transferrable, and, when applied to Orpheus, a fitting one. What matters is not so much the ownership or authorship of the emerging universe but its constantly widening radius; for its provenance (the lyre) is less important than its truly astronomical destination.

And the astronomy here, it must be noted, is very appropriately far from being heliocentric. It's deliberately epicyclic or, better yet, egocentric, since it's an Orphic, vocal astronomy, an astronomy of imagination and mourning. Hence its disfigured—refracted by tears—stars. Which, apparently, constitute the outer end of his cosmos.

But what I think is crucial for our understanding of Rilke is that these ever-widening concentric circles of sound bespeak a unique metaphysical appetite, to satisfy which he is capable of detaching his imagination from any reality, including that of himself, and proceeding autonomously within a mental equivalent of the galaxy or, with luck, beyond it. Herein lies the greatness of this poet; herein, too, lies the recipe for losing anything humanly attained—which is what presumably attracted him to the myth of Orpheus and Eurydice in the first place. After all, Orpheus was known specifically for his ability to move the inhabitants of the Celestial Mansions with his singing.

Which is to say that our author's notion of the world was free of any definable creed, since for him mimesis precedes genesis. Which is also to say that the origin of this centrifugal force enabling him to overcome gravitational pull to any center was that of verse itself. In a rhymed poem with a sustained stanzaic design this happens earlier. In an iambic pentameter blank-verse poem, it takes roughly forty or fifty lines. That is, if it occurs at all. It's simply that after covering such a distance, verse gets tired of its rhymelessness and wants to avenge it. Especially upon hearing the word *Geliebte*.

XXVII

This effectively completes the portrait of Orpheus, son of Apollo and the Muse Calliope, husband of Eurydice. Here and there a few touches will be added, but on the whole, here he is, the bard from Thrace whose singing was so enrapturing that rivers would slow down and mountains would shift their places to hear his song more clearly. A man who loved his wife so much that when she suddenly died he went, lyre in hand, all the way to Hades to bring her back, and who even after failing in this mission kept mourning her and proved unsusceptible to the wiles of the Maenads with their understandable designs on him. Angry, they killed him and dismembered his body and threw it into the sea. His head drifted away and ended up at the island of Lesbos, where it was buried. His lyre drifted much farther away and became a constellation.

We see him at a point in his mythic career which promises to be high but ends up very low. And we see him depicted with, for all we can tell, unflattering sobriety: a terrified, self-absorbed man of genius, alone on a single, not much traveled pathway, concerned no doubt about making it to the exit. Were it not for the set piece about his mourning, we wouldn't believe him much capable of loving; perhaps we would not wish him success either.

For why should we empathize with him? Less highborn and less gifted than he is, we never will be exempt from the law of nature. With us, the journey to Hades is a one-way trip. What can we possibly learn from his story? That a lyre takes one farther than a plow or a hammer and anvil? That we should emulate geniuses and heroes? That perhaps audacity is what does it? For what if not sheer audacity was it that made him undertake this pilgrimage? And where does that audacity come from? Apollo's genes, or Calliope's? From his lyre, whose sound, not to mention its echo, travels farther than the man himself? Or is this belief that he may return from no matter where he goes simply a spin-off from too much boustrophedon reading? Or does that audacity come perhaps from the Greeks' instinctive realization that loving is essentially a one-way street, and that mourning is its continuation? In the pre-*écriture* culture, one could arrive at this realization rather easily.

XXVIII

And now it's time to move the third figure:

> But hand in hand now with that god she walked,
> her paces circumscribed by lengthy shroudings,
> uncertain, gentle, and without impatience.
> Wrapt in herself, like one whose time is near,
> she thought not of the man who went before them,
> nor of the road ascending into life.
> Wrapt in herself she wandered. And her deadness
> was filling her like fullness.
> Full as a fruit with sweetness and with darkness
> was she with her great death, which was so new
> that for the time she could take nothing in.

Here she goes, Eurydice, Orpheus' wife, who died of snake-bite, fleeing from the pursuit of Aristaeus (also sired by Apollo and thus her husband's half brother). Now she moves very slowly: like somebody just woken up, or else like a statue, whose marble "lengthy shroudings" interfere with her small steps.

Her appearance in the poem presents the author with a number of problems. The first among them is the necessity of changing the pitch, especially after the vocal outburst of the preceding passage about Orpheus' mourning, to a more lyrical one, as she is a woman. This is partly accomplished by the repetition of "she, so beloved," which comes off as a choked wail.

More important, her arrival calls for the author's altering his entire posture in the poem, that of manly restraint fit for dealing with the figure of Orpheus—whose place the narrator may occasionally occupy—being unseemly (at least in Rilke's time) vis-à-vis a female heroine, and one who is dead at that. The narrative, in other words, will be infused with a substantial portion of eulogizing and elegiac tonality, if not wholly subverted by them.

This is so much so that "uncertain, gentle, and without impatience" sounds more like the author's inner monologue, like a set of commands he issues to himself on embarking on the description of Eurydice, than like an account of this statue's progress. Clearly a certitude—or a definitive attitude, at any rate—displayed by the poet in the Orpheus part of the poem is lacking: our poet is groping here. But, then, she is dead.

And to describe the state of death is the tallest order in this line of work. This is so in no small part because of the number and quality of the jobs already done in this, shall we say, vein. Also, because of the general affinity of poetry with this subject, if only because every poem, in its own right, gravitates toward a finale.

Rilke chooses, assuming that the process is at least in part conscious, a tactic we may expect from him: he presents Eurydice as an utterly autonomous entity. The only distinction is that instead of the centrifugal procedure employed in the portrayal of Orpheus—who was, for the poem's intents and purposes, after all alive—he goes here for the centripetal one.

XXIX

And the centripetal treatment starts, naturally, at the outer limits of an autonomous entity. For Eurydice, it's the shroud. Hence the first word of her description, "wrapt"; Rilke, to his great credit, proceeds not by unwrapping his heroine but by following the shroud itself to the entity's center.

"Thought not of the man who went before them" approaches the mental, subjective layers of herself, going, as it were, from the more outer ones to the more inner and, in a manner of speaking, more warm, since time is more abstract a notion than man. She is defined by these notions, but she is not them: she fills them up.

And what fills *her* up is her death. The underlying metaphor of the next four lines is that of a vessel defined by its contents rather than by its own shape and design. The cumbersomeness, or, more accurately, bulkiness of that shape ushers in the oblique but nonetheless extremely palpable imagery of pregnancy highlighting the richness and mysteriousness of Eurydice's new state, as well as its alienating aspect of total withdrawal. Naturally, "one whose time is near" comes off loaded with grief translated into the guilt of surviving, or, to put it more accurately, of responsibility for perceiving death from the outside, for filling up, as it were, the beloved with that perception.

This is Rilke at his best. He is a poet of isolation, and isolating the subject is his forte. Give him a subject and he will turn it immediately into an object, take it out of its context, and go for its core, inhabiting it with his extraordinary erudition, intuitions, and instinct for allusion. The net result is that the subject becomes his, colonized by the intensity of his attention and imagination. Death, somebody else's especially, certainly warrants this approach.

X X X

Notice, for instance, that there is not a word about the heroine's physical beauty—which is something to expect when a dead woman, and the wife of Orpheus at that, is being eulogized. Yet there is this line, "She had attained a new virginity," which accomplishes a lot more than reams of the most imaginative praise. Apart from being, like the above allusion to pregnancy, one more take on the notion of Eurydice's total alienation from her poet, this is obviously a reference to Venus, the goddess of love, endowed like many a goddess with the enviable (by some) capacity for self-renewing virginity—a capacity that had much less to do with the value the ancients placed on virginity as such than with their notion of divine exemption from the standard principles of causality binding mortals.

Be that as it might have been, the underlying meaning of this line is that our heroine even in death resembles Venus. This is, of course, the highest compliment one can possibly be paid, because what comes to your mind first is beauty synonymous with the goddess, thanks to her numerous depictions; her miraculous properties, including her regaining virginity after each sexual encounter with a god or a mortal, you recall later if at all.

Still, our poet here seems to be after something larger than imaginative compliments per se, since that could have been accomplished by the just quoted line. The line, however, ends not with a period but with a line break, after which we read "and was intangible." Naturally, one shouldn't read too much into lines, especially translated ones; but beyond this wonderfully evocative, very much fin-de-siècle qualifier lies a kind of equation between a mortal and a goddess which the latter could regard only as a backhanded compliment.

Of course, being a product of a later civilization, and a German on top of that, our poet can't avoid making a bit of heavy weather of Eros and Thanatos once he sees an opening. So the suggestion that, to the goddess, the outcome of a sexual encounter is never anything other than *le petit mort* can be put down to that. Yet what appears dramatic to a mortal, to the immortals, whose métier is infinity, may be less so, if not downright attractive. And the equation of love and death is presumably one of those things.

So in the end Venus perhaps wouldn't be much disturbed to be used as a vehicle to Eurydice's tenor. What's more, the goddess might be the first to appreciate the poet's resolution to drive the whole notion of existence, of being, inside: for that's what divinity in the final analysis is all about. So his stressing the heroine's corporeality, indeed her carnality, seals the vessel further off, practically promoting Eurydice to divine status, and infinity to sensual pleasure.

XXXI

That the narrator's and Orpheus' perspective on Eurydice diverge here is beside the point. To Orpheus, Eurydice's death is a pure loss that he wants to reverse. To the narrator, it is his and her gain, which he wants to extend.

A seeker of autonomy for his objects, Rilke certainly couldn't fail to detect this property in either his notion of death or that of love. What makes him equate them is their common rejection of the previous state. To wit, of life or of indifference. The clearest manifestation of that rejection is, of course, oblivion, and this is what our poet zeroes in on here with understandable gusto:

> her sex had closed
> like a young flower at the approach of evening,
> and her pale hands had grown so disaccustomed
> to being a wife that even the slim god's
> endlessly gentle contact as he led her
> disturbed her like a too great intimacy.

For oblivion is obviously the first cry of infinity. One gets here the sense that Rilke is stealing Eurydice from Orpheus to a far greater degree than the myth itself calls for. In particular, he rules out even Hermes as a possible object of Orpheus' envy or jealousy, which is to say that her infinity might exclude the entire Greek pantheon. One thing is certain: our poet is far more interested in the forces pulling the heroine away from life than in those that might bring her back to it. In this, however, he doesn't contradict the myth but extends its vector.

XXXII

The question is, who uses whom—Rilke the myth, or the myth Rilke? Myths are essentially a revelatory genre. They deal in the interplay of gods and mortals or, to put it a bit more bluntly, of infinities with finalities. Normally the confines of the story are such that they leave a poet very little room for maneuvering the plot line, reducing him to the role of a mouthpiece. Faced with that and with his public's assumed prior knowledge of the story, a poet tries to excel in his lines. The better the myth is known, the tougher the poet's job.

As we said before, the myth of Orpheus and Eurydice

is a very popular one, tried by an extraordinary number of hands. To embark on rendering it anew, one should have a compelling reason indeed. Yet the compelling reason (whatever it might be), in order to be felt as such, itself must have something to do with both finalities and infinities. In other words, the compelling reason is itself myth's relative.

Whatever it was that possessed Rilke in 1904 to undertake a rendering of this myth, it is not reducible to personal anguish or sexual anxiety, as some of his modern critics would have it, since those things are manifestly finite. What plays to a big audience in, say, Berkeley wouldn't ruffle the ink pot of the twenty-nine-year-old German poet in 1904, however much such things might happen to trigger a particular insight or—more likely—might themselves be the by-product of that insight's effects. Whatever it was that possessed him to write this poem must have had an aspect of myth, a sense of infinity.

XXXIII

Now, a poet arrives at this sense fastest by employing metrical verse, since meters are a means of restructuring time. This is so because every syllable has a temporal value. A line of iambic pentameter, for instance, is an equivalent of five seconds, though it could be read faster, especially if not out loud. A poet, however, always reads what he has written out loud. The meanings of words and their acoustics are saddled in his mind, therefore, with duration. Or, if you will, the other way around. In any case, a line of pentameter means five seconds spent differently from any other five seconds, including those of the next pentameter line.

This goes for any other meter, and a poet's sense of infinity is temporal rather than spatial practically by default. But few other meters are capable of generating the dispassionate monotone of blank verse, all the more perceptible, in Rilke's case, after a decade of practically nonstop rhyming. Quite apart from alluding to the poetry of Greco-Roman antiquity, habitually rendered in blank verse, this meter must have smelled to Rilke in 1904 of pure time, simply because it promised him neutrality of tone and freedom from the emphasis inevitable in rhymed verse. So up to a certain point in Eurydice's detachment from her previous state one discerns an echo of the poet's attitude to his previous diction, for she is neutral and free of emphasis. This is about as autobiographical as it gets.

XXXIV

> Even now she was no longer that blond woman
> who'd sometimes echoed in the poet's poems,
> no longer the broad couch's scent and island,
> nor yonder man's possession any longer.

Or as self-referential as it gets. Because the above four lines certainly suggest a personal perspective. It is marked not so much by the physical distance from which Eurydice is observed as by the mental one from which she is, and used to be, perceived. In other words, now, as then, she is being objectified, and the sensuality of this object owes all to its surface. And though it would be best to attribute this perspective to Orpheus' shielding thus Rilke from feminist critics, the vantage point here is unmistakably the narrator's. Its clearest indication is "the broad couch's scent and island," objectifying and literally isolating the heroine. But even "that blond woman" would suffice, since the ur-poet's wife was bound to be dark-haired.

On the other hand, verisimilitude and fear of anachronism are the least relevant concerns in rendering a myth:

its time frame overshoots both archaeology and utopia. Besides, here, toward the end of the poem, all the author aims at is a heightening of the pitch and a softening of the focus. The latter is certainly in keeping with Orpheus' own: Eurydice, if seen at all, is to be seen from afar.

XXXV

And here we are given by Rilke the greatest sequence of three similes in the entire history of poetry, and these deal precisely with going out of focus. More exactly, they deal with retreating into infinity. But first of all they deal with each other:

> She was already loosened like long hair,
> and given far and wide like fallen rain,
> and dealt out like a manifold supply.

The hair, presumably still blond, gets loosened, presumably for the night, connoting presumably the eternal one; and its strands, presumably turning grayish, become a rain, obscuring with its hairlike lines the horizon, to the point of replacing it with a distant plenitude.

In principle, this is the same type of job that gave you the sphere at the beginning of the poem and the concentric layers of Orpheus' universe-spinning lyre in the middle, except that this time a geometric pattern is replaced by plain penciling. This vision of one's ultimate dissipation has no equal. To say the least, the line "and given far and wide like fallen rain" doesn't. Now, this is, of course, a spatial rendition of infinity; but that's how infinity, temporal by definition, tends to introduce itself to mortals: it practically has no other choice.

Therefore it can be depicted only at our end, which is

to say, the netherworld's. Rilke, to his immense credit, manages to elongate the perspective: the above lines suggest Hades' open-endedness, its fanning out, if you will, and into a utopian rather than an archaeological dimension at that.

Well, an organic one, to say the least. Seizing on the notion of "supply," our poet finishes his description of the heroine in the next line—"She was already root"—by firmly planting her in his "mine of souls," between those roots where "welled up the blood that flows on to mankind." This signals the poem's return to its plot line.

XXXVI

For now the explication of the characters is finished. Now they can interact. We know, however, what's going to happen, and if we are continuing to read this poem, it is for two reasons. First, because the poet has told us *to whom* it is going to happen; second, because we want to know why.

Myth, as we've said before, is a revelatory genre, because myths illuminate the forces that, to put it crassly, control human destiny. The gods and heroes inhabiting them are essentially those forces' sometimes more, sometimes less tangible stand-ins or figureheads. No matter how stereoscopic or palpable a poet renders them, the job may remain in the end decorative, especially if he is obsessed with perfecting the details or if he identifies himself with one or several characters in the story, in which case it turns into a *poème à clef*. In this case the poet imparts to the forces his characters represent an imbalance alien to their own logic or volatility. To put it bluntly, his becomes an inside story. Whereas the forces' is an outside one. As we've seen, Rilke shields himself from too close an affinity with Orpheus right from the outset. Thus, the risk he runs is that of concentrating on the detail, particularly in Eurydice's case. Luckily, the details here are of a metaphysical nature and, if only because of that, resist elaboration. In short, his lack of partiality vis-à-vis his material resembles that of the forces themselves. Combined with the built-in unpredictability of verse's every next word, this amounts nearly to his affinity, not to say parity, with those forces. In any case, it makes him available to their self-expression, alias revelation, and he is not one to miss it.

XXXVII

The first opportunity emerges right now, offered by the plot. And yet it is precisely the plot, with its need for conclusion and denouement, that sidetracks him.

> And when, abruptly,
> the god had halted her and, with an anguished
> outcry, outspoke the words: He has turned round!—
> she took in nothing, and said softly: Who?

This is a stunning scene. The monosyllabic "who" is oblivion's own voice, an ultimate exhaling. Because forces, divine powers, abstract energies, etc., tend to operate in monosyllables; that's one way of recognizing them in everyday reality.

Our poet could have easily arrested the revelatory moment had the poem been a rhymed one. Since he had blank verse on his hands, however, he was denied the euphonic finality provided by rhyme and had to let this vastness compressed into the one vowel of "who" go.

Remember that Orpheus' turning is the pivotal moment of the myth. Remember that verse means "turn." Remember, above all, that "Do not turn" was the divine taboo. Applied to Orpheus it means, "In the netherworld, don't behave like a poet." Or, for that matter, like verse. He does, however, since he can't help it, since verse is his second nature—perhaps his first. Therefore he turns and, boustrophedon or no boustrophedon, his mind and his eyesight go back, violating the taboo. The price of that is Eurydice's "Who?"

In English, in any case, this could be rhymed.

XXXVIII

And had it been rhymed, the poem might well have stopped here. With the effect of euphonic finality and the vocal equivalent of distant menace contained in the *oo*.

It continues, however, not only because it is in blank verse, in German, and for compositional reasons requiring a denouement—though these could be enough. It continues because Rilke has two more things up his sleeve. One of them is highly personal, the other is the myth's own.

First, the personal; and here we are entering the murky domain of surmise. To begin with, "she took in nothing, and said softly: Who?" is modeled, I believe, on the poet's personal experience of, shall we say, romantic alienation. In fact, the entire poem could be construed as a metaphor for romantic estrangement between two participants in an affair, with the initiative belonging to the woman and the desire to restore things to normal to the man, who would naturally be the author's alter ego.

The arguments against such an interpretation are numerous; some of them have been mentioned here, including the dread of self-aggrandizement manifested in our author. Nonetheless, such an interpretation shouldn't be ruled out entirely, precisely because of his awareness of such a possibility, or else because the possibility of an affair gone bad on his part shouldn't be ruled out.

So having imagined that the level of personal reference is present here, we should take the next logical step and imagine a particular context and psychological significance informing the heroine's utterance in the poem.

That's not too difficult. Put yourself into any rejected lover's shoes and imagine yourself, say, on a rainy night passing after a protracted hiatus the all-too-familiar entrance of your beloved's house, stopping, and pressing the bell. And imagine the voice coming over, say, an intercom, inquiring who is there, and imagine yourself replying something like, "It's me, John." And imagine the voice, familiar to you in its slightest modulation, returning to you with a soft, colorless "Who?"

You would assume then not so much that you'd been entirely forgotten as that you'd been replaced. This is the worst possible interpretation of "Who?" in your current situation, and you may go for it. Whether you're right is a different matter. But if eventually you find yourself writing a poem about alienation or the worst possible thing a human being can encounter, for instance, death, you might draw on this experience of being replaced to add, so to speak, local color. All the more so because, being replaced, you seldom know by whom.

XXXIX

This is what might or might not have been behind this line, which cost Rilke an insight into the nature of the forces running the Orpheus-Eurydice hiatus. It took him seven more lines to get to the myth's own story, but it was worth waiting for.

The myth's own story is like this:

Orpheus and Eurydice seem to be pulled in opposite directions by conflicting forces: he, to life; she, to death.

Which is to say, he is claimed by finality while she is by infinity.

Ostensibly, there is a semblance of parity between the two, with life showing perhaps some edge over death, for the latter allows the former to make an inroad into death's domain. Or it may be the other way around and Pluto and Persephone allow Orpheus to enter Hades to collect his wife and bring her back to life precisely because they are confident that he is going to fail. Perhaps even the taboo they issue, forbidding him to turn and look back, reflects their apprehension that Orpheus may find their realm too seductive to return to life, and they don't want to offend their fellow god Apollo by claiming his son before his time.

Ultimately, of course, it appears that the force that controls Eurydice is stronger than the one that controls Orpheus. This stands to reason, for one remains dead longer than one may be alive. And it follows that infinity yields nothing to finality—save perhaps in verse—for, being categories of time, neither can change. And it also follows that these categories use mortals not so much to manifest their forces' presence or power as to mark the boundaries of their respective domains.

XL

All this is pretty absorbing, no doubt, but in the final analysis it doesn't explain how or, for that matter, why the divine taboo works. For that, it turns out, the myth needs a poet, and it's this myth's great fortune that it finds Rainer Maria Rilke.

Here is the poem's final part, which tells you about the mechanism of that taboo as well as who is using whom: a poet a myth, or a myth a poet:

> But in the distance, dark in the bright exit,
> someone or other stood, whose countenance
> was indistinguishable. Stood and saw
> how, on a strip of pathway between meadows,
> with sorrow in his look, the god of message
> turned silently to go behind the figure
> already going back by that same pathway,
> its paces circumscribed by lengthy shroudings,
> uncertain, gentle, and without impatience.

Now, the "bright exit" is obviously the exit from Hades into life, and the "someone or other" who is standing there, and whose "countenance" is "indistinguishable," is Orpheus. He is "someone or other" for two reasons: because he is of no relevance to Eurydice and because he is just a silhouette for Hermes, the god, who looks at Orpheus standing on the threshold of life from the dark depth of the netherworld.

In other words, Hermes at this point is still facing in the same direction as he did before, throughout the poem. Whereas Orpheus, as we've been told, *has turned.* As to Eurydice . . . and here comes the greatest job of the entire poem.

"Stood and saw," says the narrator, emphasizing by the change of tense in the verb "to stand" Orpheus' regret and acknowledgment of failure. But what he sees is truly remarkable. For he sees the god *turning,* but only *now,* to follow "behind the figure/already going back . . ." Which is to say that Eurydice has turned also. Which is to say, the god is the last to turn.

And the question is, *when* did Eurydice turn? And the answer is "already," and what it boils down to is that Orpheus and Eurydice turned simultaneously.

Our poet, in other words, has synchronized their movements, telling us thereby that the forces controlling finality and infinity themselves are controlled from a certain—let's call it panel, and that this control panel is, on top of that, automatic.

Our next question is, presumably, a soft "Who?"

XLI

The Greeks certainly would know the answer and say, Chronos, since he is the one to whom all myths point anyway. At the moment, though, he is beyond our concern or, for that matter, reach. We should stop here, where roughly six hundred seconds, or ten minutes, of this poem written ninety years ago leave us.

It is not a bad place, though it is only a finality. Except that we don't see it as such—perhaps because we don't wish to identify with Orpheus, rejected and failed. We see it rather as an infinity, and we even would prefer to identify with Eurydice, because it's easier to identify with beauty, especially dissipating and "given far and wide like fallen rain."

These, however, are the extremes. What makes the place where we are left by this poem indeed attractive is that while we are here, we have the chance to identify with its author, Rainer Maria Rilke, wherever he is.

Torö, Sweden

1994

Letter to Horace

My dear Horace,

If what Suetonius tells us about your lining your bedroom walls with mirrors to enjoy coitus from every angle is true, you may find this letter a bit dull. On the other hand, you may be entertained by its coming to you from a part of the world whose existence you never suspected, and some two thousand years after your death, at that. Not bad for a reflection, is it?

You were almost fifty-seven, I believe, when you died in 8 B.C., though you weren't aware of either C. Himself or a new millennium coming. As for myself, I am fifty-four now; my own millennium, too, has only a few years to run. Whatever new order of things the future has in store, I anticipate none of it either. So we may talk, I suppose, man to man, Horace. And I may as well begin with a locker-room kind of story.

Last night I was in bed rereading your *Odes*, and I bumped into that one to your fellow poet Rufus Valgius in which you are trying to convince him not to grieve so much over the loss of his son (according to some) or his lover (according to others). You proceed for a couple of stanzas with your exempla, telling him that So-and-so lost this person and Such-and-such another, and then you suggest to Rufus that he, as a kind of self-therapy, get engaged in praising Augustus' new triumphs. You mention several recent conquests, among them grabbing some space from the Scythians.

Actually, that must have been the Geloni; but it doesn't matter. Funny, I hadn't noticed this ode before. My people—well, in a manner of speaking—aren't mentioned that often by great poets of Roman antiquity. The Greeks are a different matter, since they rubbed shoulders with us quite a bit. But even with them we don't fare that well. A few bits in Homer (of which Strabo makes such a meal afterward!), a dozen lines in Aeschylus, not much more in Euripides. Passing references, basically; but nomads don't deserve any better. Of the Romans, I used to think, it was only poor Ovid who paid us any heed; but then he had no choice. There is practically nothing about us in Virgil, not to mention Catullus or Propertius, not to mention Lucretius. And now, lo and behold, a crumb from your table.

Perhaps, I said to myself, if I scratch him hard enough, I may find a reference to the part of the world I find myself in now. Who knows, he might have had a fantasy, a vision. In this line of work that happens.

But you never were a visionary. Quirky, unpredictable, yes—but not a visionary. To advise a grief-stricken fellow to change his tune and sing Caesar's victories—this you could do; but to imagine another land and another heaven—well, for that one should turn, I guess, to Ovid. Or wait for another millennium. On the whole, you Latin poets were bigger on reflection and rumination than on conjecture. I suppose because the empire was large enough as it was to strain one's own imagination.

———

So there I was, lying across my unkempt bed, in this un-imaginable (for you) place, on a cold February night, some two thousand years later. The only thing I had in common with you, I thought, was the latitude and, of course, the little volume of your Collected, in Russian translations. At the time you wrote all this, you see, we didn't have a language. We weren't even we; we were Geloni, Getae, Budini, etc.: just bubbles in our own future gene pool. So two thousand years were not for nothing, after all. Now we can read you in our own highly inflected language, with its famous gutta-percha syntax suiting the translation of the likes of you marvelously.

Still, I am writing this to you in a language with whose alphabet you are more familiar. A lot more, I should add, than I am. Cyrillic, I am afraid, would only bewilder you even further, though you no doubt would recognize the Greek characters. Of course the distance between us is too large to worry about increasing it—or, for that matter, about trying to shrink it. But the sight of Latin letters may be of some comfort to you, no matter how bewildering their use may look.

So I was lying atop my bed with the little volume of your *Carmina*. The heat was on, but the cold night outside was winning. It is a small, two-storied wooden affair I live in here, and my bedroom is upstairs. As I looked at the ceiling, I could almost see cold seeping through my gambrel roof: a sort of anti-haze. No mirrors here. At a certain age one doesn't care for one's own reflection, company or no company; especially if no. That's why I wonder whether Suetonius tells the truth. Although I imagine you would be pretty sanguine about that as well. Your famous equipoise! Besides, for all this latitudinal identity, in Rome it never gets that cold. A couple of thousand years ago the climate perhaps was different; your lines, though, bear no witness to that. Anyhow, I was getting sleepy.

And I remembered a beauty I once knew in your town. She lived in the Suburra, in a small apartment bristling with flowerpots but redolent with the smell of the crumbling paperbacks the place was stuffed with. They were everywhere, but mostly on shelves reaching the ceiling (the ceiling, admittedly, was low). Most of them were not hers but belonged to her neighbor across the hall, about whom I heard a lot but whom I never met. The neighbor was an old woman, a widow, who was born and spent her entire life in Libya, in Leptis Magna. She was Italian but of Jewish extraction—or maybe it was her husband who was Jewish. At any rate, when he died and when things began to heat up in Libya, the old lady sold her house, packed up her stuff, and came to Rome. Her apartment was apparently even smaller than my tender companion's, and jammed with a lifetime's accretions. So the two women, the old and the young, struck a deal whereupon the latter's bedroom began to resemble a regular second-hand-book store. What jarred with this impression wasn't so much the bed as the large, heavily framed mirror leaning somewhat precariously against a rickety bookshelf right across from the bed, and at such an angle that whenever I or my tender companion wanted to imitate you, we had to strain and crane our necks rather desperately. Otherwise the mirror would frame only more paperbacks. In the early hours it could give one an eerie feeling of being transparent.

All that happened ages ago, though something nudges me to mutter, centuries ago. In an emotional sense, that would be valid. In fact, the distance between that place in Subura and my present precincts psychologically is larger than the one between you and me. Which is to say that in neither case are "millennia" inapplicable. Or to say that, to me, your reality is practically greater than that of my private memory. Besides, the name of Leptis Magna interferes with both. I've always wanted to visit there; in fact, it became a sort of obsession with me once I began to frequent your town and Mediterranean shores in general. Well, partly because one of the floor mosaics in some bath there contains the only surviving likeness of Virgil, and a likeness done in his lifetime, at that! Or so I was told; but maybe it's in Tunisia. In Africa, anyway. When one is cold, one remembers Africa. And when it's hot, also.

Ah, what I wouldn't give to know what the four of you looked like! To put a face to the lyric, not to mention the epic. I would settle for a mosaic, though I'd prefer a fresco. Worse comes to worse, I would resign myself to the marbles, except that the marbles are too generic—everybody gets blond in marble—and too questionable. Somehow, you are the least of my concerns, i.e., you are the easiest to picture. If what Suetonius tells us about your appearance is indeed true— at least something in his account must be true!—and you were short and portly, then you most likely looked like Eugenio Montale or Charlie Chaplin in the *King in New York* period. The one I can't picture for the life of me is Ovid. Even Propertius is easier: skinny, sickly, obsessed with his equally skinny and sickly redhead, he is imaginable. Say, a cross between William Powell and Zbigniew Cybulski. But not Ovid, though he lasted longer than all of you. Alas, not in those parts where they carved likenesses. Or laid mosaics. Or bothered with frescoes. And if anything of the sort was done before your beloved Augustus kicked him out of Rome, then it was no doubt destroyed. So as not to offend high sensibilities. And afterward—well, afterward any slab of marble would do. As we used to say in northern Scythia— Hyperborea to you—paper can endure anything, and in your day marble was a kind of paper.

You think I am rambling, but I am just trying to reproduce the train of thought that took me late last night to an unusually graphic destination. It meandered a bit, for sure; but not that much. For, one way or another, I've always been thinking about you four, especially about Ovid. About Publius Ovidius Naso. And not for reasons of some particular affinity. No matter how similar my circumstances may now and then appear to his in the eyes of some beholder, I won't produce any *Metamorphoses*. Besides, twenty-two years in these parts won't rival ten in Sarmatia. Not to mention that I saw my Terza Roma crumble. I have my vanity, but it has its limits. Now that they are drawn by age, they are more palpable than before. But even as a young pup, kicked out of my home to the Polar Circle, I never fancied myself playing his double. Though then my empire looked indeed eternal, and one could roam on the ice of our many deltas all winter long.

No, I never could conjure Naso's face. Sometimes I see him played by James Mason—a hazel eye soggy with grief and mischief; at other times, though, it's Paul Newman's winter-gray stare. But, then, Naso was a very protean fellow, with Janus no doubt presiding over his lares. Did you two get along, or was the age difference too big to bother? Twenty-two years, after all. You must have known him, at least through Maecenas. Or did you just think him too frivolous, saw it coming? Was there bad blood between you? He must have thought you ridiculously loyal, true blue in a sort of quaint, self-made man's kind of way. And to you he was just a punk, an aristo, privileged from the cradle, etc. Not like you and Anthony Perkins's Virgil, practically working-class boys, only five years' difference. Or is this too much Karl Marx reading and moviegoing, Horace? Perhaps. But wait, there is more. There is Dr. Freud coming into this, too, for what sort of interpretation of dreams is it, if it's not filtered through good old Ziggy? For it was my good old subconscious the train of thought I just mentioned was taking me to, late last night, and at some speed.

Anyhow, Naso was greater than both of you—well, at least as far as I'm concerned. Metrically, of course, more monotonous; but so is Virgil. And so is Propertius, for all his emotional intensity. In any case, my Latin stinks; that's why I read you all in Russian. It copes with your asclepiadic verse in a far more convincing way than the language I am writing this in, for all the familiarity of the latter's alphabet. The latter just can't handle dactyls. Which were your forte. More exactly, Latin's forte. And your *Carmina* is, of course, their showcase. So I am reduced to judging the stuff by the quality of imagination. (Here's your defense, if you need one.) And on that score Naso beats you all.

All the same, I can't conjure up your faces, his especially; not even in a dream. Funny, isn't it, not to have any idea how those whom you think you know most intimately looked? For nothing is more revealing than one's use of iambs and trochees. And, by the same token, those who don't use meters are always a closed book, even if you know them physically, inside out. How did John Clare put it? "Even those whom I knew best / Are strange, nay! stranger than the rest." At any rate, metrically, Flaccus, you were the most diverse among them. Small wonder that this huffing and puffing train took you for its engineer as it was leaving its own millennium and heading for yours, unaccustomed as it may have been to electricity. Hence I was traveling in the dark.

Few things are more boring than other people's dreams, unless they are nightmares or highly carnal. This one, Flaccus, was of the latter denomination. I was in some very sparsely furnished bedroom, in a bed sitting next to the sea-serpent-like, though extremely dusty, radiator. The walls were absolutely naked, but I was convinced I was in Rome. In fact, I was sure I was in the Suburra, in the apartment of that pretty friend of mine from days of yore. Except that she wasn't there. Neither were the paperbacks, nor the mirror. But the brown flowerpots stood absolutely intact, emitting not so much the aroma of their plants as the tint of their own clay: the whole scene was done in terra-cotta-cum-sepia tones. That's how I knew I was in Rome.

Everything was terra-cotta-cum-sepia-shaded. Even the crumpled bedsheets. Even the bodice of my affections' target. Even those looming parts of her anatomy that wouldn't have benefited from a suntan, I imagine, in your day either. The whole thing was positively monochrome; I felt that, had I been able to see myself, I would be in sepia, too. Still, there was no mirror. Imagine those Greek vases with their multifigured design running around, and you'll get the texture.

This was the most vigorous session of its kind I've ever taken part in, whether in real life or in my imagination. Such distinctions, however, should have been dispensed with already, given the character of this letter. Which is to say, I was as much impressed by my stamina as by my concupiscence. Given my age, not to mention my cardiovascular predicament, this distinction is worth sustaining, dream or no dream. Admittedly, the target of my affections—a target long since reached—was markedly younger than I, but not by a huge margin. The body in question seemed in its late thirties, bony, yet supple and of great elasticity. Still, its most exacting aspect was its tremendous agility, wholly devoted to the single purpose of escaping the banality of bed. To condense the entire endeavor into one cameo, my target's upper torso would be plunged into the narrow, one-foot-wide trough between the bed and the radiator, with the

tanless rump and me atop it floating at the mattress's brink.
The bodice's laced hem would do as foam.

Throughout all this I didn't see her face. For the above-
implied reasons. All I knew about her was that she was from
Leptis Magna, although I have no idea how I learned this.
There was no sound track to this session, nor do I believe
we exchanged two words. If we did, that was before I became
cognizant of the process, and the words must have been in
Latin: I have a faint sense of some obstacle regarding our
communication. Still, all along I seem to have known, or
else managed to surmise in advance, that there was something of Ingrid Thulin in the bone structure of her face.
Perhaps I espied this when, submerged as she was under
the bed, her right hand now and then, in an awkward backward motion, groped for the warm coils of that dusty radiator.

When I woke up the next—i.e., this—morning, my bedroom was dreadfully cold. A mealy, revolting daylight was ar-
riving through both windows like some kind of dust. Perhaps
dust is indeed daylight's leftover; well, this shouldn't be
ruled out. Momentarily, I shut my eyes; but the room in the
Suburra was gone. Its only evidence lingered in the dark under
my blanket where daylight couldn't reach, but clearly not for
long. Next to me, opened in the middle, was your book.

No doubt it's you whom I should thank for this dream, Flaccus. Now, the hand jerkily trying to clutch the radiator could
of course stand for the straining and craning in days of yore,
as that pretty friend of mine or I tried to catch a glimpse of
ourselves in that gilded mirror. But I rather doubt it—two
torsos can't shrink into one limb; no subconscious is that
economical. No, I believe that hand somehow echoed the
general motion of your verse, its utter unpredictability and,
with this, the inevitable stretching—nay, straining—of your

syntax in translation. As a result, practically every line of yours is surprising. This is not a compliment, though; just an observation. In our line of work, tricks, naturally, are *de rigueur*. And the standard ratio is something like one little miracle per stanza. If a poet is exceptionally good, he may come up with a couple. With you, practically each line is an adventure; sometimes there are several in one line. Of course, some of this has to do with having you in translation. But I suspect that in your native Latin, too, your readers seldom knew what the next word was going to be. It's like constantly walking on broken glass or something: on the mental—oral?—version of broken glass, limping and leaping. Or like that hand clutching the radiator: there was something distinctly logaoedic about its bursts and withdrawals. But, then, next to me I had your *Carmina*.

Had it been your *Epodes* or *Epistles*, not to mention *Satires* or, for that matter, *Ars Poetica*, the dream I am sure would have been different. That is, it would perhaps have been as carnal, but a good deal less memorable. For it's only in the *Carmina* that you are metrically enterprising, Flaccus. The rest is practically all done in couplets; the rest is bye-bye to asclepiads and Sapphics and hello to downright hexameters. The rest is not that twitching hand but the radiator itself, with its rhythmic coils like nothing more than elegiac couplets. Make this radiator stand on end and it will look like anything by Virgil. Or by Propertius. Or by Ovid. Or by you, save your *Carmina*.

It will look like any page of Latin poetry. It will look like—should I use the hateful word—text.

Well, I thought, what if it *was* Latin poetry? And what if that hand was simply trying to turn the page? And my efforts vis-à-vis that sepia-shaded body simply stood for my reading of a body of Latin poetry? If only because I still—even in a

dream!—couldn't make out her face. As for that glimpse of
her Ingrid Thulin features that I caught as she was straining
to turn the page, it had most likely to do with the Virgil
played in my mind by Tony Perkins. Because he and Ingrid
Thulin have sort of similar cheekbones; also since Virgil is
the one I've read most of all. Since he has penned more
lines than anybody. Well, I've never counted, but it sure
feels that way, thanks to the *Aeneid*. Though I, for one, by
far prefer his *Bucolics* or *Georgics* to his epic.

I'll tell you why later. The truth of the matter, however,
is that I honestly don't know whether I espied those cheekbones first and learned that my sepia-shaded target was from
Leptis Magna second, or vice versa. For I'd seen a reproduction of that floor-mosaic likeness some time before. And
I believed it was from Leptis Magna. I can't recall why or
where. On the frontispiece of some Russian edition, perhaps? Or maybe it was a postcard. Main thing, it was from
Leptis Magna and done in Virgil's lifetime, or shortly there-
after. So what I beheld in my dream was a somewhat familiar
sight; the sensation itself wasn't so much that of beholding
as that of recognition. Never mind the armpit muscle and
the breast bustling in the bodice.

Or precisely because of that: because, in Latin, poetry
is feminine. That's good for allegory, and what's good for
allegory is good for the subconscious. And if the target of
my affections stood—lay down, rather—for a body of Latin
poetry, its high cheekbones could just as well resemble Virgil's, regardless of his own sexual preferences, if only because
the body in my dream was from Leptis Magna. First, because
Leptis Magna is a ruin, and every bedroom endeavor resembles a ruin, what with sheets, pillows, and the prone and
jumbled limbs themselves. Second, because the very name
"Leptis Magna" always struck me as being feminine, like
Latin poetry, not to mention what I suppose it literally

means. Which is, a great offering. Although my Latin stinks. But be that as it may, what is Latin poetry after all if not a great offering? Except that my reading, as you no doubt would charge, only ruins it. Well, hence this dream.

Let's avoid murky waters, Flaccus; let's not saddle ourselves with exploring whether dream can be reciprocal. Let me hope at least you won't proceed in a similar fashion about my own scribblings should you ever get acquainted with them. You won't pun about pen and penis, will you? And why shouldn't you get acquainted with my stuff quite apart from this letter. Reciprocity or no reciprocity, I see no reason why you, so capable of messing up my dreams, won't take the next step and interfere with my reality.

You do, as it is; if anything, my writing you this letter is the proof. But beyond that, you know full well that I've written to you, in a manner of speaking, before. Since everything I've written is, technically, addressed to you: you personally, as well as the rest of you. Because when one writes verse, one's most immediate audience is not one's own contemporaries, let alone posterity, but one's predecessors. Those who gave one a language, those who gave one forms. Frankly, you know that far better than I. Who wrote those asclepiadics, Sapphics, hexameters, and Alcaics, and who were their addressees? Caesar? Maecenas? Rufus? Varus? Lydias and Glycerias? Fat lot they knew about or cared for trochees and dactyls! And you were not aiming at me, either. No, you were appealing to Asclepiades, to Alcaeus and Sappho, to Homer himself. You wanted to be appreciated by them, first of all. For where is Caesar? Obviously in his palace or smiting the Scythians. And Maecenas is in his villa. Ditto Rufus and Varus. And Lydia is with a client and Glyceria is out of town. Whereas your beloved Greeks are right here, in your head, or should I say in your heart, for you no doubt knew them by heart. They were your best audience, since you could summon them at any moment. It's they you were trying to impress most of all. Never mind the foreign language. In fact, it's easier to impress them in Latin: in Greek, you wouldn't have the mother tongue's latitude. And they were talking back to you. They were saying, Yeah, we're impressed. That's why your lines are so twisted with enjambments and qualifiers, that's why your argument is always so unpredictable. That's why you advise your grief-stricken pal to praise Augustus' triumphs.

So if you could do this to them, why can't I do that to you? The language difference at least is here; so one condition is being met. One way or the other, I've been responding to you, especially when I use iambic trimeters. And now I am following this up with a letter. Who knows, I may yet summon you here, you may yet materialize in the end even more than you've done already in my verses. For all I know, logaoedics with dactyls beat any old séance as a means of conjuring. In our line of work, this sort of thing is called pastiche. Once the beat of a classic enters one's system, its spirit moves in, too. And you are a classic, Flaccus, aren't you, in more ways than one, which alone would be complex enough.

And ultimately who else is there in this world one can talk to without revulsion, especially if one is of a misanthropic disposition by nurture. It is for this reason, not vanity, that I hope you get acquainted with my iambs and trochees in some netherworldly manner. Stranger things have happened, and my pen at least has done its bit to that end. I'd much rather, of course, talk to Naso or Propertius, but with you I have more in common metrically. They stuck to elegiac couplets and hexameters; I seldom use those. So it's between you and me here, presumptuous as this may sound to everybody. But not to you. "All the literati keep / An imaginary friend," says Auden. Why should I be an exception?

At the very least, I can sit myself down in front of my mirror and talk to it. That would be fairly close, although I don't believe that you looked like me. But when it comes to the human appearance, nature, in the final analysis, doesn't have that many options. What are they? A pair of eyes, a mouth, a nose, an oval. For all their diversity, in two thousand years nature is bound to repeat itself. Even a God will. So I could easily claim that that face in the mirror is ultimately yours, that you are me. Who is there to check, and in what way? As conjuring tricks go, this might do. But I am afraid I am going too far: I'll never write myself a letter. Even if I were truly your look-alike. So stay faceless, Flaccus, stay unconjured. This way, you may last for two millennia more. Otherwise, each time I mount a woman she might think that she is dealing with Horace. Well, in a sense she is, dream or no dream. Nowhere does time collapse as easily as in one's mind. That's why we so much like thinking about history, don't we? If I am right about nature's options, history is like surrounding oneself with mirrors, like living in a bordello.

Two thousand years—of what? By whose count, Flaccus? Certainly not in terms of metrics. Tetrameters are tetrameters, no matter when and no matter where. Be they in Greek, Latin, Russian, English. So are dactyls, and so are anapests. Et cetera. So two thousand years in what sense? When it comes to collapsing time, our trade, I am afraid, beats history, and smells, rather sharply, of geography. What Euterpe and Urania have in common is that both are Clio's seniors. You start talking your Rufus Valgius out of his protracted grieving by evoking the waves of Mare Caspium; even they, you write, do not remain rough forever. This means that you knew about that *mare* two thousand years ago—from some Greek author, no doubt, as your own people didn't cast their quills that wide. Herein, I suppose, lay this *mare*'s first attraction for you as a Roman poet. An exotic name and, on top of that, one connoting the farthest point of your Pax Romana, if not of the known world itself. Also, a Greek one (actually, perhaps even Persian, but you could bump into it only in Greek). The main thing, though, about "Caspium" is that this word is dactylic. That's why it sits at the second line's end, where every poem's meter gets established. And you are consoling Rufus in an asclepiad.

Whereas I—I crossed that Caspium once or twice. When I was either eighteen or nineteen, or maybe twenty. When—I am tempted to say—you were in Athens, learning your Greek. In those days, the distance between Caspium and Hellas, not to mention Rome, was in a sense even greater than it was two thousand years ago; it was, frankly, insurmountable. So we didn't meet. The *mare* itself was smooth and shiny, near its western shores especially. Thanks not so much to the propitious proximity to civilization as to vast oil spills, perennial in those parts. (I could say this was the real case of pouring oil upon troubled waters, but I am afraid you wouldn't catch the reference.) I was lying flat on the hot upper deck of a dirty steamer, hungry and penniless, but happy all the same, because I was participating in geography. When you are going by boat you always do. Had I read by that time your piece to Rufus, I would have realized that I was also participating in poetry. In a dactyl rather than in a sharpening horizon.

But in those days I wasn't that much of a reader. In those days I was working in Asia: mountain climbing and desert trekking. Prospecting for uranium, basically. You don't know what that stuff is, and I won't bore you with an explanation, Flaccus. Although "uranium" is another dactylic word. What does it feel like to learn a word you cannot use? Especially

—for you—a Greek one? Awful, I suppose; like, for me, your Latin. Perhaps if I were able to operate in it confidently, I could indeed conjure you up. On the other hand, perhaps not: I'd become for you just another Latin author, and that is a recipe for hiatus.

In any case, in those days I'd read none of you, except—if my memory doesn't play tricks on me—Virgil, i.e., his epic. I remember that I didn't care for it much, partly because against that backdrop of mountains and deserts few things managed to make sense; mainly because of the epic's rather sharp smell of commission. In those days, one's nostrils were very keen for that sort of thing. Besides, I simply couldn't make out 99 percent of his exempla, which were getting in the way rather frequently. What do you expect from an eighteen-year-old from Hyperborea? I am better with this sort of thing now, but it's taken a lifetime. On the whole, it seems to me that you all were overdoing it a bit with the references; they often strike one as filler. Although euphonically of course they—the Greek ones especially— do marvels for the texture.

What rattled me perhaps most in the *Aeneid* was that retroactive prophecy of Anchises, when the old man predicts what has already taken place. Here, I thought, your friend went a bit too far. I don't mind the conceit, but the dead should be allowed to be more imaginative. They ought to know more than just Augustus' pedigree; after all, they are not oracles. What a waste of that stunning, mind-boggling idea about souls being entitled to a second corporeality and lapping from the river Lethe to cleanse themselves of their previous memories! To reduce them to paving the road for the reign of the current master! Why, they could become Christians, Charlemagnes, Diderots, Communists, Hegels, us! Those who will come after, mongrels and mutants, and in more ways than one! That would be a real prophecy, a real flight of fancy. Instead, he rehashes the official record and serves it as hot news. The dead are free of causality, to begin with. The knowledge available to them is that about time—all time. That much he could have learned from Lucretius; your friend was a learned man. More than that, he had a terrific metaphysical instinct, a real nose for things' spiritual lining: his souls are far less physical than Dante's. True *manes*: gaseous and unpalpable. One is tempted to say his scholasticism here is practically medieval. But that would be a put-down. Because metaphysically your future turned out to be far less imaginative than your Greek past. For what is life eternal to a soul compared with a second corporeality? What is Paradise to it after the Pythagorean promise of another body? Just unemployment. Still, whatever his sources were—Pythagoras, Plato's *Phaedrus*, his own fancy—he blows it all for the sake of Caesar's lineage.

Well, the epic was his; he had the right to do with it what he liked. But I find it, frankly, unforgivable. It's failures of imagination like these that paved the road to the triumph of monotheism. The one, I guess, is always more graspable than the many; and after that gigantic Greek-and-homemade stew of gods and heroes, this sort of longing for something more graspable, more coherent, was practically inevitable. In other words, for all his expansive gestures, your friend, my dear Flaccus, was just craving metaphysical security. And that, I am afraid, is a contradiction in terms; perhaps the chief attraction of polytheism is that it would have none of that. But I suppose the place was getting too populous to indulge in insecurity of any kind. That's why your friend pins this whole thing, metaphysics and all, on his beloved Caesar in the first place. Civil wars, I should say, do wonders for one's spiritual orientation.

But it's no use talking to you like that. You all loved Augustus, didn't you? Even Naso, although he apparently was more curious about Caesar's sentimental property, beyond suspicion as it habitually was, than about his territorial conquests. But then, unlike your friend, Naso was a womanizer. Among other things, that's what makes it so difficult to picture his appearance, that's why I oscillate between Paul Newman and James Mason. A womanizer is an everyman: not that it means he should be trusted any more than a pedophile. And yet his account of what transpired between Dido and Aeneas sounds a bit more convincing than that of your friend. Naso's Dido claims that Aeneas is abandoning her and Carthage in such a hurry—remember, there was a storm looming and Aeneas must have had it with storms by then, what with being tossed on the high seas for seven years—not because he heeded the call of his divine mother but because Dido was pregnant with his child. And that's why she commits suicide: because her reputation is ruined. She is a queen, after all. Naso makes his Dido even question whether Venus was indeed the mother of Aeneas, for she was the goddess of love, and departure is an odd (though not unprecedented) way to manifest this sentiment. No doubt Naso spoofs your friend here. No doubt this depiction of Aeneas is unflattering and, given the fact that the legend of Rome's Trojan origins was the official historical orthodoxy from the third century B.C. onward, downright unpatriotic. Equally doubtless is that Virgil never read Naso's *Heroides*; otherwise, the former's treatment of Dido in the netherworld would be less reprehensible. For he simply stashes her away, together with Sychaeus, her former husband, in some remote nook of Elysium, where the two forgive and console each other. A retired couple in an old people's home. Out of our hero's way. To spare him agony, to provide him with a prophecy. Because the latter makes better copy. Anyhow, no second corporeality for Dido's soul.

You will argue that I am applying to him the standards that took two millennia to emerge. You are a good friend, Flaccus, but it's nonsense. I am judging him by his own standards, more evident actually in the *Bucolics* and the *Georgics* than in his epic. Don't play the innocent: you all had a minimum of seven centuries of poetry behind you. Five in Greek and two in your own Latin. Remember Euripides, remember his *Alcestis*: the wedding scene's scandal of King Admetus with his parents beats anything in Dostoevsky hands down —though you may not catch the reference. Which means it beats any psychological novel. Which is something we excelled at in Hyperborea a hundred years ago. Out there, you see, we are big on agony. Prophecy is a different matter. Which is to say, two thousand years were not in vain.

No, the standards are his, by way of the *Georgics*. Based on Lucretius and on Hesiod. In this line of work, Flaccus, there are no big secrets. Only small and guilty ones. Herein, I must add, lies their beauty. And the small and guilty secret of the *Georgics* is that their author, unlike Lucretius—and, for that matter, Hesiod—had no overriding philosophy. To say the least, he was no atomist, no epicurean. At best, I imagine, he hoped that the sum total of his lines would add up to a worldview, if he cared about such a thing in the first place. For he was a sponge, and a melancholic one at that. For him, the best—if not the only—way to understand the world was to list its contents, and if he missed anything in his *Bucolics* or in the *Georgics*, he caught up with that in his epic. He was an epic poet, indeed; an epic realist, if you will, since, speaking numerically, reality itself is quite epic. The cumulative effect of his output upon my reflective faculty has always been the sensation that this man has itemized the world, and in a rather meticulous fashion. Whether he talks of plants or planets, soils or souls, the deeds and/or destinies of the men of Rome, his close-ups are both blinding and binding; but so are things themselves, dear Flaccus, aren't they? No, your friend was no atomist, no epicurean; nor was he a stoic. If he believed in any principle, it was life's regeneration, and his *Georgics*' bees are no better than those souls chalked up for second corporeality in the *Aeneid*.

But perhaps they are better, and not so much because they don't end up buzzing "Caesar, Caesar" as because of the *Georgics*' tonality of utter detachment. Perhaps it's those days of yore I spent roaming the mountains and deserts of Central Asia that make this tonality most appealing. Back then, I suppose, it was the impersonality of the landscape I'd find myself in that impressed itself on the cortex. Now, a lifetime later, I might blame this taste for monotony on the human vista. Underneath either one lies, of course, an inkling that detachment is the final product of many intense attachments. Or else the modern predilection for a neutral voice, so characteristic of didactic genres in your times. Or both, which is more likely still. And even if the *Georgics*' impersonal drone is nothing but a Lucretian pastiche—as I strongly suspect it is—it is still appealing. Because of its implicit objectivity and explicit similarity to the monotonous clamor of days and years; to the sound time makes as it passes. The very absence of story, the absence of characters in the *Georgics* echo, as it were, time's own perspective on any existential predicament. I even remember myself thinking back then that should time have a pen of its own and decide to compose a poem, its lines would include leaves, grass, earth, wind, sheep, horses, trees, cows, bees. But not us. Maximum, our souls.

So the standards are indeed his. And the epic, for all

its splendors, as well as because of them, is a letdown as regards those standards. Plain and simple, he had a story to tell. And a story is bound to have us in it. Which is to say, those whom time dismisses. On top of that, the story wasn't his own. No, give me the *Georgics* any day. Or, should I say, any night, considering my present reading habits. Although I must confess that even in those days of yore, when the sperm count was much higher, hexameter would have left my dreams dry and uneventful. Logaoedics apparently are much more potent.

Two thousand years this, two thousand years that! Just imagine, Flaccus, if I'd had company last night. And imagine an—er—translation of this dream into reality. Well, half of humanity must be conceived that way, no? Wouldn't you be responsible, at least in part? Where would those two thousand years be; and wouldn't I have to call the offspring Horace? So, consider this letter a soiled sheet, if not your own by-blow.

And, by the same token, consider the part of the world I am writing to you from, the outskirts of the Pax Romana, ocean or no ocean, distance or no distance. We've got all sorts of flying contraptions here to handle that, not to mention a republic with the first among equals built in, to boot. And tetrameters, as I said, are still tetrameters. They alone can take care of any millennia, to say nothing of space or of the subconscious. I've been dwelling here for twenty-two years now, and I've noticed no difference. In all likelihood, here is where I'll die. So you can take my word for it: tetrameters are still tetrameters, and so are trimeters. And so forth.

It was a flying contraption, of course, that brought me here from Hyperborea twenty-two years ago, though I can as easily put down that flight to my rhymes and meters.

Except that the latter might add up to an even greater distance between me and the good old Hyperborea, as your dactylic Caspium does to the actual size of your Pax Romana. Contraptions—flying ones especially—only delay the inevitable: you gain time, but time can fool space only so far; in the end, space catches up. What are years, after all? What can they measure save the decay of one's epidermis, of one's wits? Yet the other day I was sitting in a café here with a fellow Hyperborean, and as we were chatting about our old town in the delta, it suddenly crossed my mind that should I, twenty-two years ago, have tossed a splinter of wood into that delta, it could, given the prevailing winds and currents, have crossed the ocean and reached by now the shores I am dwelling on, to witness my decay. That's how space catches up with time, my dear Flaccus; that's how one truly departs from Hyperborea.

Or: how one expands Pax Romana. By dreams, if necessary. Which, come to think of it, are yet another—perhaps the last—form of life's regeneration, especially if you've got no company. Also, it doesn't lead up to Caesar, beating in this sense even the bees. Although, I repeat, it's no use talking to you like this, since your sentiments toward him were in no way different from Virgil's. Nor were your methods of conveying them. You, too, preach Augustus' glory over man's grief, saddling with this task not—to your considerable credit—idling souls but geography and mythology. Commendable as this is, it implies, I'm afraid, that Augustus either owns or is sponsored by both. Ah, Flaccus, you might just as well have used hexameter. Asclepiads are just too good for this stuff, too lyrical. Yes, you're right: nothing breeds snobbery better than tyranny.

Well, I suppose I am just allergic to this sort of thing. If I am not reproaching you more venomously, it is because

I am not your contemporary: I am not he, because I am almost you. I've written in your meters, and in this one particularly. That, as I've said, is what makes me appreciate "Caspium," "Niphaten," and "Gelonos" sitting there at the end of your lines, expanding the empire. And so do "Aquilonibus" and "Vespero," but upward. My subject matter, of course, was more humble; besides, I used rhyme. The only way to overlap with you completely would be by setting myself the task of repeating all your stanzaic patterns in this tongue or in my native Hyperborean. Or else by translating you into either. Come to think of it, such an exercise is plausible—far more so than redoing, say, Ovid's hexameters and elegiac couplets. After all, your Collected is not such a large book, and the *Carmina* itself is just ninety-five pieces of varying length. But I am afraid the dog's too old for new and old tricks alike; I should have thought of that earlier. We are destined to stay separated, to remain pen pals at best. Not for long, I'm afraid, but long enough, I hope, to get close to you now and then. Even if not close enough to make out your face. In other words, I am doomed to my dreams; but this doom is welcome.

Because the body in question is so rum. Its greatest charm, Flaccus, is the total lack of the egocentricity that so often plagues its successors, and I daresay the Greeks also. It seldom pushes the first person singular—though that's partly the grammar. In a language so highly inflected, it's hard to zero in on one's own plight. Although Catullus managed; that's why he is loved so universally. But among you four, even with Propertius, the most ardent of all of you, that was out. And certainly with your friend, treating as he did both man and nature *sui generis*. Most of all with Naso, which, given some of his subject matter, must be what turned the Romantics against him so sharply. Still, in my proprietary (after last night) capacity, this pleases me considerably. Come to think of it, the absence of egocentricity may be a body's best defense.

It is—in my day and age, in any case. Actually, of all of you, Flaccus, it is you who are perhaps the most egocentric. Which is to say, the most palpable. But that isn't so much a matter of pronouns, either: it is, again, the distinctness of your metrics. Standing out against the other guys' sprawling hexameters, they suggest some unique sensibility, a character that can be judged—while the others are largely opaque. Sort of like a solo versus the chorus. Perhaps they went for this hexametric drone precisely for reasons of humility, for purposes of camouflage. Or else they just wanted to play by the rules. And hexameter was that game's standard net; to put it differently, its terra-cotta. Of course, your logaoedics don't make you a cheat; still, they flash rather than obscure individuality. That's why for the next two thousand years practically everybody, including the Romantics, would embrace you so readily. Which rattles me, naturally —in my proprietary capacity, that is. In a manner of speaking, you were that body's tanless part, its private marble.

And with the passage of time you got whiter and whiter: more private and more desirable. Suggesting that you can be an egocentric and still handle a Caesar; that it's only a matter of equipoise. Music to so many ears! But what if your famous equipoise was just a matter of the phlegmatic temperament, easily passing for personal wisdom? Like Virgil's melancholy, say. But unlike the choleric upsurges of Propertius. And certainly unlike Naso's sanguine endeavors. Now, here's one who paved not an inch of that highway leading to monotheism. Here's one who was short on equipoise and had no system, let alone a wisdom or a philosophy. His imagination couldn't get curbed, neither by its own insights nor by doctrine. Only by hexameter; better yet, by elegiac couplets.

Well, one way or another, he taught me practically everything, the explication of dreams included. Which begins with that of reality. Next to him, somebody like the Viennese doctor—never mind not catching the reference! —is kindergarten, child's play. And frankly, you, too. And so is Virgil. To put it bluntly, Naso insists that in this world *one thing is another*. That, in the final analysis, reality is one large rhetorical figure and you are lucky if it is just a polyptoton or a chiasmus. With him a man evolves into an object, and vice versa, with the immanent logic of grammar, like a statement sprouting a subordinate clause. With Naso the tenor is the vehicle, Flaccus, and/or the other way around, and the source of it all is the ink pot. So long as there was a drop of that dark liquid in it, he would go on— which is to say, the world would go on. Sounds like "In the beginning was the word"? Well, not to you. To him, though, this adage would not be news, and he would add that there will be a word in the end as well. Give him anything and he will extend it—or turn it inside out—which is still an extension. To him, language was a godsend; more exactly, its grammar was. More exactly still, to him the world was the language: one thing was another, and as to which was more real, it was a toss-up. In any case, if one thing was palpable, the other was bound to be also. Often in the same line, especially if it was hexameter: there is a big caesura. Failing that, in the next line; especially if it is an elegiac couplet. For measures to him were a godsend also.

He would be the first to confirm this, Flaccus, and so would you. Remember his recalling in *Tristia* how amid the storm that hit the ship taking him into exile (to my parts, roughly; to the outskirts of Hyperborea) he caught himself again composing verses? Naturally you don't. That was some sixteen years after you died. On the other hand, where is one better informed than in the netherworld? So I shouldn't worry that much about my references: you are catching them all. And meters are always meters, in the netherworld especially. Iambs and dactyls are forever, like stars and stripes. More exactly: whenever. Not to mention, wherever. Small wonder that he eventually came to compose in the local dialect. As long as vowels and consonants were there, he could go on, Pax Romana or no Pax Romana. In the end, what is a foreign tongue if not just another set of synonyms. Besides, my good old Geloni had no *écriture*. And even if they had, it would be only natural for him, the genius of metamorphosis, to mutate into an alien alphabet.

That, too, if you will, is how one expands the Pax Romana. Although that never happened. He never stepped into our genetic pool. The linguistic one was enough, though: it took practically these two thousand years for him to enter Cyrillic. Ah, but life without an alphabet has its merits! Existence can be very poignant when it's just oral. Actually, as regards *écriture*, my nomads were in no hurry. To scribble, it takes a settler: someone who's got nowhere to go. That's why civilizations blossom more readily on islands, Flaccus: take, for instance, your dear Greeks. Or in cities. What is a city if not an island surrounded by space? Anyway, if he indeed barged into the local dialect, as he tells us, it was not so much out of necessity, not in order to endear himself to the natives, but because of verse's omnivorous nature: it claims everything. Hexameter does: it is not so sprawling for nothing. And an elegiac couplet is even more so.

Lengthy letters are anathema everywhere, Flaccus, including in the afterlife. By now, I guess, you've quit reading, you've had enough. What with these aspersions cast on your pal and praise of Ovid practically at your expense. I continue because, as I said, who is there to talk to, anyway? Even assuming that Pythagorean fantasy about virtuous souls' second corporeality every thousand years is true, and that you've had a minimum of two opportunities so far, and now with Auden dead and the millennium having only four years to go, that quota seems to be busted. So it's back to the original you, even if by now, as I suspect, you've quit reading. In our line of work, addressing the vacuum comes with the territory. So you can't surprise me with your absence, nor can I you with my perseverance.

Besides, I have a vested interest—and you, too. There is that dream that once was your reality. By interpreting it, one gets two for the price of one. And that's what Naso is all about. For him, one thing was another; for him, I'd say, A was B. To him, a body—a girl's especially—could become—nay, *was*—a stone, a river, a bird, a tree, a sound, a star. And guess why? Because, say, a running girl with her mane undone looks in profile like a river? Or asleep on a couch, like a stone? Or, with her arms up, like a tree or a bird? Or, vanishing from sight, being theoretically everywhere, like a sound? And, triumphant or remote, like a star? Hardly. That would suffice for a good simile, while what Naso was after wasn't even a metaphor. His game was morphology, and his take was metamorphosis. When the same substance attains a different form. The main thing is the sameness of substance. And, unlike the rest of you, he managed to grasp the simple truth of us all being composed of the stuff the world is made of. Since we are of this world. So we all contain water, quartz, hydrogen, fiber, et cetera, albeit in different proportions. Which can be reshuffled. Which already have been reshuffled into that girl. Small wonder she becomes a tree. Just a shift in her cellular makeup. Anyhow, with our species, shifting from the animate to the inanimate is the trend. You know what I mean, being where you are.

Smaller wonder, then, that a body of Latin poetry—of its Golden Age—became the target of my relentless affection last night. Well, regard it perhaps as a last gasp of your joint Pythagorean quota. And yours was the last part to submerge: because it was less burdened with hexameters. And attribute the agility with which that body strove to escape the banality of bed to its flight from my reading you in translation. For I am accustomed to rhyme, and hexameters won't have it. And you, who came closest to it in your logaoedics, you too gravitated to hexameters: you groped for that radiator, you wanted to submerge. And for all the relentlessness of my pursuit, which stood—no pun intended—for a lifetime of reading you, the dream never turned wet, not because I am fifty-four, but precisely because all of you were rhymeless. Hence the terra-cotta sheen of that Golden Age body; hence, too, the absence of your beloved mirror, not to mention its gilded frame.

And do you know why it wasn't there? Because, as I said, I am accustomed to rhyme. And rhyme, my dear Flaccus, is itself a metamorphosis, and metamorphosis is not a mirror. Rhyme is when one thing turns into another without changing its substance, which is sound. As far as language is concerned, to say the least. It is a condensation of Naso's approach, if you will—a distillation, perhaps. Naturally he comes frightfully close to it himself in that scene with Narcissus and Echo. Frankly, closer even than you, to whom he is metrically inferior. I say "frightfully" because, had he done so, for the next two thousand years we all would have been out of business. Thank God, then, for the hexametric inertia that kept him off, in that scene in particular; thank

God for that myth's own insistence on keeping eyesight and hearing apart. For that's what we've been at for the past two thousand years: grafting one onto another, fusing his vision with your meters. It is a gold mine, Flaccus, a full-time occupation, and no mirror can reflect a lifetime of reading.

At any rate, this should account for at least half of the body in question and its efforts to escape me. Perhaps, had my Latin stunk less, this dream would never have occurred in the first place. Well, at a certain age, it appears, one has reasons to be grateful for one's ignorance. For meters are still meters, Flaccus, and anatomy is still anatomy. One may claim to possess the whole body, even though its upper part is submerged somewhere between the mattress and the radiator: as long as this part belongs to Virgil or Propertius. It is still tanned, it is still terra-cotta, because it is still hexametric and pentametric. One may even conclude it is not a dream, since a brain can't dream about itself: most likely, it is reality—because it is a tautology.

Just because there is a word, "dream," it doesn't follow that reality has an alternative. A dream, Flaccus, is at best a momentary metamorphosis: far less lasting than that of rhyme. That's why I haven't been rhyming here—not because you wouldn't appreciate the effort. The netherworld, I presume, is a polyglot kingdom. And if I've resorted to writing at all, it is because the interpretation of a dream—of an erotic one especially—is, strictly speaking, a reading. As such, it is profoundly anti-metamorphic, for it is the undoing of a fabric: thread by thread, line by line. And its repetitive nature is its ultimate giveaway: it asks for an equation mark between the reading and the erotic endeavor itself. Which is erotic because it is repetitive. Turning pages: that's what it is; and that's what you are or should be doing now,

Flaccus. Well, this is one way of conjuring you up, isn't it? Because repetition, you see, is the primary trait of reality.

Someday, when I end up in your part of the netherworld, my gaseous entity will ask your gaseous entity whether you've read this letter. And if your gaseous entity should reply, No, mine won't feel offended. On the contrary, it will rejoice at this proof of reality's extension into the domain of shadows. For you've never read me to begin with. In this sense, you'll be like many people above who never read either one of us. To say the least, that's one thing that constitutes reality.

But should your gaseous entity reply, Yes, my gaseous entity will not be much worried either about having offended you with my letter, especially its smutty bits. Being a Latin author, you would be the first to appreciate an approach triggered in one by a language in which "poetry" is feminine. And as for "body," what else can one expect from a man in general, and a Hyperborean at that, not to mention the cold February night. I wouldn't even have to remind you that it was just a dream. To say the least, next to death, dream is reality.

So we may get along famously. As for the language, the realm, as I said, is most likely poli- or supra-glot. Besides, being just back from filling up your Pythagorean quota as Auden, you may still retain some English. That's perhaps how I would recognize you. Though he was a far greater poet than you, of course. But that's why you sought to assume his shape last time you were around, in reality.

Worse comes to worse, we can communicate through meters. I can tap the First Asclepiadic stanza easily, for all its dactyls. The second one also, not to mention the Sapphics. That might work; you know, like inmates in an institution.

After all, meters are meters even in the netherworld, since they are time units. For this reason, they are perhaps better known now in Elysium than in the asinine world above. That's why using them feels more like communicating with the likes of you than with reality.

And naturally I would like you to introduce me to Naso. For I wouldn't know him by sight, since he never assumed anyone else's shape. I guess it's his elegiacs and hexameters that conspired against this. For the past two thousand years, fewer and fewer people have tried them. Auden again? But even he rendered hexameter as two trimeters. So I wouldn't aspire to a chat with Naso. All I would ask is to take a look at him. Even among souls he should be a rarity.

I shall not bother you with the rest of the crowd. Not even with Virgil: he's been back to reality, I should say, in so many guises. Nor with Tibullus, Gallus, Varus, and the others: your Golden Age was quite populous, but Elysium is no place for affinities, and I won't be there as a tourist. As for Propertius, I think I'll look him up myself. I believe it should be relatively easy to spot him: he must feel comfortable among the *manes* in whose existence he believed so much in reality.

No, the two of you will be enough for me. One's taste sustained in the netherworld amounts to an extension of reality into the domain of shadows. I should hope I'll be able to do this, at least initially. Ah, Flaccus! Reality, like the Pax Romana, wants to expand. That's why it dreams; that's why it sticks to its guns as it dies.

1995

In Memory of
Stephen Spender

I

Twenty-three years later, the exchange with the Immigration
Officer at Heathrow is brisk. "Business or pleasure?"
  "What do you call a funeral?"
  He waves me through.

II

Twenty-three years ago, it took me nearly two hours to pass
his predecessors. The fault, as it were, was mine. I had just
left Russia and was heading for the States via London, where
I had been invited to take part in the Poetry International
festival. I had no proper passport, just a U.S. transit visa in
a huge manila envelope issued to me at the American Con-
sulate in Vienna.

  Apart from the natural anxiety, the wait was extremely
uncomfortable for me because of Wystan Auden, with whom
I had come on the same plane from Vienna. As the customs
officials grappled with that manila envelope, I saw him pacing
frantically behind the barrier, in a state of growing irritation.
Now and then he'd try to talk to one or another of them,

only to be told off. He knew that I knew nobody in London and he couldn't leave me there alone. I felt terrible, if only because he was twice my age.

When in the end we emerged from customs, we were greeted by a strikingly beautiful woman, tall and almost regal in her deportment. She kissed Wystan on the cheek and introduced herself. "I am Natasha," she said. "I hope you don't mind staying with us. Wystan is staying with us also." And as I began to mumble something not entirely grammatical, Auden intervened, "She is Stephen Spender's wife. Best if you say yes. They've prepared a room for you."

The next thing, we were in a car, with Natasha Spender at the wheel. Evidently they'd thought of everything; perhaps they'd discussed it over the phone—although I was a total stranger. Wystan hardly knew me, the Spenders even less. And yet . . . The London suburbs were flashing by in the car window and I tried to read signs. The most frequent was BED AND BREAKFAST; I understood the words, but luckily couldn't grasp—due to the absence of a verb—their meaning.

III

Later that evening, as the three of us sat down for supper, I tried to explain to Natasha (all the while marveling at the discrepancy between that wonderfully chiseled face and the homey-sounding Russian name) that I was not exactly a total stranger. That in fact back in Russia I'd had in my possession some items from this household, brought to me by Anna Akhmatova upon her return from England, where she had received an honorary doctorate from Oxford in 1965. The items were two records (*Dido and Aeneas* by Purcell and Richard Burton reading a selection from the English poets) and a veritable tricolor of some college scarf. They were given to her, she told me, by an extraordinarily handsome English poet whose name was Stephen Spender and who asked her to pass these things on to me.

"Yes," said Natasha. "She told us a lot about you. You were in prison, and we were all terribly worried that you would be cold. Hence the scarf."

Presently the doorbell rang and she went off to open the door. I was in the middle of a conversation with Wystan, or more exactly, I was listening to him, as my grammar would allow for very little initiative. Although I'd translated quite a bit from English (mostly the Elizabethans, as well as some modern American poetry and a couple of plays), my conversational skills at that time were minimal. I'd say "trepidation of the ground" instead of "earthquake." Besides, Wystan's speech, because of its extraordinary speed and truly transatlantic texture, required considerable concentration on my part.

But momentarily I lost it completely. In walked a very tall, slightly stooped, white-haired man with a gentle, almost apologetic smile on his face. He moved about what I assumed was his own dining room with the tentativeness of a newcomer rather than the master of the house's certitude. "Hello, Wystan," he said, and then he greeted me.

I don't remember the exact words, but I remember being stunned by the beauty of their utterance. It felt as if all the nobility, civility, grace, and detachment of the English language suddenly filled the room. Like an instrument's chords being played all at once. To me, with my then untrained ear, the effect was spellbinding. It owed, no doubt, in part to the instrument's stooping frame: one felt not so much this music's audience as its accomplice. I looked about the room: nobody betrayed the slightest emotion. But then accomplices never do.

IV

Still later that same night, Stephen Spender—for that was he—and I went to the BBC television station, for the late-news program's on-camera interview. Twenty-three years ago the arrival in London of somebody like me still counted as news. The whole thing took two hours, including the round trip by taxi. During those two hours—and during the taxi ride especially—the spell I was under began to let up somewhat, since we were talking logistics. Of the TV interview, of the Poetry International that began the next day, of my stay in England. Suddenly conversation was easy: we were just two men discussing relatively tangible matters. I felt oddly comfortable in the presence of this six-foot-tall, blue-eyed, white-haired old man I had never met before, and I marveled, Why? Most likely, I simply felt protected by his superior height and age, not to mention his Oxonian. But quite apart from that, in the gentle tentativeness of his deportment, bordering on the awkward and accompanied by a guilty smile, I sensed his awareness of the provisional, faintly absurd nature of any reality at hand. To this attitude I wasn't a stranger myself, as it comes not from one's physique or temperament but from one's métier. Some people are less ready to display this, some more. Then there are those incapable of concealing it. I sensed that he and I belonged in the latter category.

V

I'd pick this as the main reason for the subsequent twenty-three years of our unlikely friendship. There were several others, and I'll mention some. Yet before I go any further, I must say that if what follows sounds a bit too much like a personal memoir, with too much of my own presence in it, this is because I find it impossible—at least for now—to speak about Stephen Spender in the past tense. I don't intend to play the solipsistic game of denying the obvious: that he is no more. It would perhaps be an easy thing for me to do, since for all these twenty-three years that I've mentioned, we saw each other rather infrequently, and never for more than five days in a row. But what I think and do is so intertwined in my mind with his and Wystan Auden's lives and lines that to reminisce seems more appropriate at present than trying to comprehend my emotions. Living is like quoting, and once you've learned something by heart, it's yours as much as the author's.

VI

For the next few days that I stayed under their roof, I was mothered by the Spenders and by Wystan in the most minute way, from breakfast to supper and into the nightcap. At one point, Wystan tried to teach me how to use the English public phone and was alarmed at my slow-wittedness. Stephen attempted to explain the Underground system, but in the end Natasha drove me everywhere. We lunched at the Café Royal, the scene of their courtship during the Blitz, where they'd sit for a hot meal between air raids as the waiters swept away shards of the café's broken windows. ("As the Germans were pounding us, we were actually wondering how soon the Russian planes would join them. In those days we were expecting the Russian bombers anytime.") Or else we'd go for lunch to Sonia Orwell. ("*1984* is not a novel," Wystan declared. "It is a study.") Then there was dinner at the Garrick Club with Cyril Connolly, whose *Enemies of Promise* I'd read just a couple of years before, and Angus Wilson, of whom I knew nothing. The former looked gray, bloated, and oddly Russian; the latter, in his pink shirt, resembled a tropical bird. The conversation escaped me, and I was reduced to observation.

This was often the case with me at that time, and I felt rather awkward on a number of occasions. I explained that to Stephen, but he evidently believed in osmosis more than analysis. One evening he and Natasha took me to a dinner party somewhere in South London, at the local bishop's rectory. His Eminence turned out to be a bit too lively, not to say gregarious; too purple, not to say lavender, for my untrained eye. Still, the food was superb, so was the wine, and his stable of pretty young clerics waiting on the guests was lovely to look at. When the meal was over, the ladies departed to an adjacent chamber; the gentlemen stayed for their port and Havanas. I found myself sitting across from C. P. Snow, who began to extol to me the virtues and verities of Mikhail Sholokhov's prose. It took me about ten minutes to summon the appropriate entries from Partridge's dictionary of English slang (back in Russia, I had only Volume I) for an adequate reply. Mr. Snow's face went indeed white; Stephen laughed uproariously. In fact, I was aiming not so much at the pink novelist as at the lavender host, whose lacquered loafer was footsieing my honest Hush Puppy under the table.

I was trying to explain that to Stephen on the way back in the car, but he kept giggling. It was around midnight. As we crossed Westminster Bridge, he looked out the window and said, "They are still sitting." And to me: "Are you tired?" I said no. "Then let's go in." Natasha stopped the car; we got out and walked to the Houses of Parliament. We climbed several flights of stairs, entered a large hall, and landed in the gallery chairs. It was, I believe, the House of Commons, and some tax debate was in full swing. Men of more or less similar height and complexion would rise, deliver vehement-sounding tirades, and sit down, to rise again in a short while. Stephen tried to whisper in my ear what this was all about;

still, it remained, to me, largely impenetrable, practically a
pantomime. For a while I sat scrutinizing the rafters and
stained-glass windows. Here I was, face-to-face with the most
sacred notion of my youth, and I found the proximity blinding. I began to shake with silent laughter. The disparity
between my mental and physical realities suddenly gaped
vast: while the latter was occupying a green leather seat in
the heart of Westminster, the former dragged its feet, as it
were, somewhere behind the Urals. So much, I thought,
for air travel, and looked at Stephen. Apparently osmosis
worked.

VII

The Poetry International was a large, somewhat messy affair
held on the Thames's South Bank, in the Royal Festival Hall.
Few things could be worse than the mixture of poverty and
concrete, but the mixture of concrete and frivolity is one of
them. On the other hand, it matched what was transpiring
inside. The West Germans in particular got into the spirit
of the place, taking *vers libre* one step further by resorting
to plain body language, and I remember Wystan saying mo-
rosely into the backstage TV monitor, "This is not what you
were paid for." The pay was measly, but for me these were
the first pound notes I ever held in my hands, and I felt
thrilled at putting into my pocket practically the same tender
that was used by Dickens's and Joseph Conrad's characters.

The opening party was on the top floor of some high-
rise on Pall Mall; New Zealand House, I think, was the
name. As I write this, I look at a photograph taken there
that day: Stephen is saying something funny to Wystan, who
laughs heartily back, while John Ashbery and I look on.
Stephen is much taller than any of us, and there is an almost
detectable tenderness in his profile as he faces Wystan, who,

hands in his pockets, is immensely cheered. Their eyes meet; at this juncture, they have known each other for forty years, and they are happy in each other's company. Ah, this unbearable snapshot laughter! That's what one is left with—with these arrested instants stolen from life without any anticipation of the far greater theft ahead that will render your hoard the source of utter despair. A hundred years ago one would be spared at least that.

VIII

Stephen read on a different night than Wystan and I, and I wasn't present at the reading. But I know what he read because I have the *Selected* he gave me when he got back that night. There are seven pieces he had marked in the table of contents—the way we all do before a reading. The edition was a twin of what I'd had back home, courtesy of an English exchange student, and I knew it well enough to notice that my favorites—"Air Raid Across the Bay at Plymouth" and "Polar Exploration"—were not checked. I believe I asked him why, although I could partly foresee the answer, since both poems were fairly old. Perhaps it's for this reason that I don't remember his reply. What I remember, however, is that the conversation very quickly ran to Henry Moore's *Shelter Sketchbook* of the London Underground, and Natasha produced their dog-eared paperback edition, which I took with me to bed.

He mentioned Moore's *Sketchbook*, I suppose, because I mentioned the "Air Raid" poem. It had astounded me in my previous, Russian incarnation (in spite of my dim English) with its searchlight imagery's progression from the visual to the visionary. I thought the poem owed a lot to the contemporary, post-Cubist (what we called in Russia Constructivist) paintings, to somebody like Wyndham Lewis. Needless to say, searchlights were an integral part of my childhood: my earliest memory, in fact. So much so that till this day when I see Roman numerals I immediately recall the wartime night sky over my hometown. So I suppose I'd said something to that effect to Stephen, and the next thing was Henry Moore's little book of drawings.

IX

I'll never know now whether that was just a shift in conversation or a part of Stephen's osmosis game plan vis-à-vis my innocent self. Either way, the impact of the sketches was extraordinary. I'd seen a fair number of reproductions of Moore's work: all those reclining microcephalics, single or in groups. Mostly on postcards, though a couple of catalogues passed through my hands as well. I'd heard enough about pre-Columbian influences, organic forms, the hollow-versus-solid-mass concept, etc., and wasn't very much taken by any of it. The usual modern-art palaver, the song of insecurity.

Shelter Sketchbook had very little to do with modern art, and everything to do with security. If the sequence had any root, it must have been Mantegna's (or Bellini's) *Agony in the Garden*. Moore, evidently, was similarly obsessed with ellipsoids, and the Blitz provided him with a veritable safari. The whole thing takes place in the Underground, which is an apt word in more ways than one. Thus, no airborne angel carrying the cup is in sight here, though "Let it pass from me" is presumably on all lips. To paraphrase Wystan, *Shelter Sketchbook* is not a graphic work but a study. Above all, in ellipsoids, from the swaddled bodies covering platforms to the stations' vaults. But it is also a study in submission, since a body reduced to its generic form for reasons of safety won't forget this reduction, won't straighten up fully. Once you've crouched in submission to fear, the future of your vertebrae is set: you'll crouch again. Anthropologically speaking, war results in a backslide—unless of course you are a witless babe.

And that's what I was when Moore was busy with his study of ellipsoids and Stephen with his exploration of searchlights. As I looked at the *Sketchbook* I practically remembered the crypt-turned-bomb-shelter of our nearby cathedral, with its vaults and shrouded or swaddled bodies, my mother's and mine among them. While outside "Triangles, parallels, parallelograms,/experiment with hypotheses/on the blackboard sky . . ." At this rate, I said to myself as I was turning the obsessively penciled pages, I may remember even my own birth, perhaps even the time before; in fact, I may—perish the thought—go English.

X

Something of the sort had been well under way since I'd laid my hands on the Penguin anthology *Poetry of the Thirties*. If you are born in Russia, nostalgia for an alternative genesis is inevitable. The thirties were close enough, as I was born in 1940. What made the decade even more congenial was its grimy, monochrome denomination, owing chiefly to the printed word and black-and-white cinema: my native realm was of the same shade and stayed that way long after the Kodak invasion. MacNeice, Auden, and Spender —I mention them in the order I found them—made me feel at home at once. It wasn't their moral vision, since my enemy, I believe, was more formidable and ubiquitous than theirs; it was their poetics. It unshackled me: above all, metrically and stanzaically. After "Bagpipe Music," the good old tetrametric, quatrain-bound job seemed—initially at least—less tempting. The other thing I found terribly attractive was their common knack for taking a bewildered look at the familiar.

Call this influence; I'll call it affinity. Roughly from the age of twenty-eight on, I regarded them as my relatives rather than as masters or "imaginary friends." They were my mental family—far more so than anybody among my own contemporaries, inside or outside of Russia. Chalk this up to my immaturity or to disguised stylistic conservatism. Or else simply to vanity: to some puerile desire to be judged under a foreign code of conscience. On the other hand, consider the possibility that what they did could be loved from afar. Or that reading poets writing in a foreign tongue bespeaks one's appetite for worship. Stranger things have happened: you've seen the churches.

XI

I lived happily in that mental family. The wall-thick English-Russian dictionary was in fact a door, or should I say a window, since it was often foggy and staring through it required some concentration. This paid off particularly well because it was poetry, for in a poem every line is a choice. You can tell a lot about a man by his choice of an epithet. I thought MacNeice chaotic, musical, self-indulgent, and imagined him moody and reticent. I thought Auden brilliant, resolute, profoundly tragic, and witty; I imagined him quirky and gruff. I thought Spender more lyrical and ambitious with his imagery than either, though rather conspicuously modernist, but I couldn't picture him at all.

Reading, like loving, is a one-way street, and all that was going on unbeknownst to any of them. So when I ended up that summer in the West, I was a total stranger indeed. (I didn't know, for instance, that MacNeice had already been dead for nine years.) Less so perhaps to Wystan, since he wrote the introduction to my *Selected* and must have realized that my "Verses on the Death of T. S. Eliot" is based on his "In Memory of W. B. Yeats." But certainly to Stephen and Natasha, no matter what Akhmatova could possibly have told them. Neither then nor in the course of the subsequent twenty-three years did I talk to him about his poems, or vice versa. The same goes for his *World Within World, The Thirties and After, Love-Hate Relations, Journals.* Initially, I suppose, the culprit was my timidity, saddled with my Elizabethan vocabulary and shaky grammar. Eventually, it would be his or my transatlantic fatigue, public places, people around, or matters more absorbing to us than our own writings. Such as politics or press scandals, or Wystan. Somehow from the threshold it was assumed that we had more in common than not, the way it is in a family.

XII

Aside from our respective mother tongues, what would keep us apart were more than thirty years of life in this world, Wystan's and Stephen's superior intelligence, and their—with Wystan more and less with Stephen—private lives. That might seem like a lot; actually it wasn't much. I wasn't aware of their varying affections when I met them; besides, they were in their sixties. What I was aware of then, am now, and will be to my dying day is their extraordinary intelligence, to which thus far I've seen no approximation. Which of course puts my intellectual insecurity somewhat to rest, though it doesn't necessarily close the gap. As for their private lives, they came into focus, I believe, precisely for the reasons of their perceived intellectual superiority. In plain words, because in the thirties they were on the left, with Spender joining the Communist Party for a few days. What's done in a totalitarian state by the secret police in an open society presumably is the province of one's opponents or critics. Still, the reverse of this—attributing one's achievement to one's sexual identity—is perhaps even more silly. On the whole, the insistence on man's definition as a sexual being is breathtakingly reductive. If only because the ratio of one's sexual activity to other pursuits—say, earning a living, driving a car—is dismal even in one's prime. Theoretically, a poet has more time on his hands, but considering the way poetry is paid, his private life warrants less scrutiny than it gets. Especially if he writes in a language as cool about gender as English. And if the language is not concerned, why should its speakers be? Well, perhaps they are precisely because it isn't. At any rate, I indeed felt we had far more in common than not. The only gap I wouldn't be able to close was that of age. As for the difference in intelligence, at my best moments, I may convince myself I am getting near to their plane of regard. What remained was the language gap, and now and then I've tried to close it as best I could, though that required prose.

XIII

The only time I spoke to Stephen directly about his work, I am afraid, was when his *Temple* was published. By that time, I must admit, novels had ceased to be my preferred reading, and I wouldn't have talked to him about it at all, were it not for the book's being dedicated to Herbert List, a great German photographer with whose niece I was once in love. Spotting the dedication, I ran to him with the book in my teeth—I think this was in London—declaring triumphantly, "See, we are related!" He smiled wanly and said that the world is a small place, Europe in particular. Yes, I said, the world is a small place, and no next person makes it bigger. And no next time, he added, or something to that effect, and then asked whether I actually liked the book. I told him I'd always thought an autobiographical novel is a contradiction in terms; that it disguises more than it reveals even if the reader is partial. That to me, in any case, there was more of the author in the book's secondary characters than in its hero. He replied that this had a lot to do with the period's mental climate in general and with censorship in particular, and that he perhaps should have rewritten the whole thing. To that I protested, saying that disguise is the mother of literature and that censorship might even claim its fatherhood, and that there is nothing worse than when Proust's biographers scribble away to prove that Albertine was in fact Albert. Yes, he said, their pens move in a direction diametrically opposed to the author's: they are undoing the fabric.

XIV

I see the past tense creeping in, and I wonder whether I should really fight it. He died on July 16; today is August 5. Still, I can't think of him summarily. Whatever I may say about him will be provisional or one-sided. Definitions are always reductive, and his ability to escape them at the age of eighty-six is not surprising, even though I caught up with only a quarter of it. Somehow it's easier to question one's own presence than to believe he's gone.

This is so because gentleness and civility are most lasting. And his are of the most durable kind, borne as they were by the grimy, cruel, either/or era. To say the least, his manner of deportment—in verse as in life—appears to have been a matter of choice as much as temperament. In sissy times—like these—one, a writer especially, can afford to be brutal, lean, mean, etc. In fact, in sissy times one practically has to peddle gore and garbage, for otherwise one won't sell. With Hitler and Stalin around, one goes the other way . . . Ah, all this paperback brutal talent! So numerous and so unnecessary, and so awash in money. That alone can make you feel nostalgic for the thirties and play havoc with your affinities. In the final analysis, though, what matters in life as well as on paper—with deeds as well as with epithets—is what helps you to retain your dignity, and gentleness and civility do. For that reason alone he is, and will remain, palpable. More and more so, as days go by.

XV

My fanciful notions (affinity, mental family, etc.) aside, we got along very well. This partly had to do with the total unpredictability of his mind and its turns. With people around, he was terribly amusing—not so much for their sake as because he was organically incapable of banality. A received idea would appear on his lips only to get entirely subverted by the end of the sentence. However, he wasn't trying to amuse himself, either: it's simply that his speech was trying to catch up with the perpetually running train of his thought and therefore was rather unpredictable to the speaker himself. Given his age, the past was remarkably infrequently his subject; much less so than the present or the future, on which he was especially big.

In part, I think, this was the result of his métier. Poetry is a tremendous school of insecurity and uncertainty. You never know whether what you've done is any good, still less whether you'll be able to do anything good tomorrow. If this doesn't destroy you, insecurity and uncertainty in the end become your intimate friends and you almost attribute to them an intelligence all their own. That's why, I think, he showed such interest in the future, of countries, individuals, cultural trends: as though he tried to run the entire gamut of all possible mistakes in advance—not in order eventually to avoid them, but just to know those intimate friends of his better. For the same reason, he'd never make a meal of his past achievements or, for that matter, misfortunes.

XVI

This would give one the impression that he was free of ambition, devoid of vanity. And that impression, I think, would be by and large correct. I remember one day, many years ago, giving a poetry reading with Stephen in Atlanta, Georgia. Actually, we were raising funds for *Index on Censorship*—a magazine which, I believe, was essentially his brainchild and about whose fortunes, not to mention the issue of censorship itself, he cared deeply.

We had to spend about an hour and a half onstage and were sitting in the anteroom shuffling our papers. Normally when two poets share a reading, one reads for forty-five minutes solid, then the other. To present the public with a convincing notion of oneself. "Reckon with me" is the idea. So Stephen turns to me and says, "Joseph, why don't we do fifteen minutes each, and then have an interval with questions and answers, and then read for fifteen minutes each again. This way they won't be bored. How does that sound to you?" Marvelous, I say. For it was; it gave the whole undertaking the air of an entertainment. Which is what a poetry reading is in the first place, rather than an ego trip. It's a show, a piece of theater—especially if it's a fund-raiser.

That was Atlanta, Georgia, U.S.A. Where the public, even a well-meaning one, knows precious little about its own, American poetry, let alone about the Brits'. The procedure he suggested wouldn't advance his reputation, nor would it sell his books. Which is to say, he was not in it for himself, and he didn't read anything topical, either. I can't imagine anyone from among his American brethren (of his age, especially) deliberately short-changing himself—either for the sake of an issue or for the public's sake. There were about eight hundred people in that room, if not more.

"I suppose American poets all fall to pieces," he used to say (referring to the famous suicides in the profession), "because the stakes over there are so high. In Great Britain one is never paid so much and a national reputation is out of the question, although the place is much smaller." Then he would giggle and add, "Actually, precisely because of that."

XVII

It's not that he held himself in low esteem; he was simply genuinely humble. That virtue, too, I should think, was métier-inspired. If you are not born with some organic disorder, poetry—writing it as well as reading it—will teach you humility, and rather quickly at that. Especially if you are both writing and reading it. The dead alone will set you straight fast, not to mention your peers. Second-guessing yourself will become your second nature. You may be enamored with your own endeavors for some time, of course, provided your peers are worthless; but if in your undergraduate days you meet Wystan Auden, your self-infatuation is bound to be short.

After this encounter, nothing was easy: neither writing nor living. I may be wrong, but my impression is that he discarded far more than he printed. In living, however, where you can discard nothing, this unease resulted in extraordinary subtlety as well as in terrifying sobriety (with Auden becoming now and then its target but never a casualty). This mixture—of subtlety and sobriety—is what makes a gentleman, provided their ratio favors subtlety.

XVIII

And that is what he was, in a largely uncouth literary crowd on both sides of the Atlantic. He stood out, both literally and figuratively speaking. And the crowd's response, left and right, was predictable. X would chide him for being a pacifist in World War II (though he was nothing of the sort, having been turned down on medical grounds, after which he served as a fireman—and being a fireman during the Blitz in London is a far cry from being a conscientious objector at the time elsewhere). Y would accuse him of editing the CIA-financed *Encounter* in the fifties (although Stephen resigned this job once he learned the nature of the magazine's purse, and anyway, why didn't these people who were so squeamish about CIA money throw in any of their own to keep the publication afloat?). A righteous Z would jump on him for declaring his readiness to go immediately to Hanoi while it was being bombed but inquire who was to pay the fare. A man living by his pen—over thirty books, not to mention innumerable reviews by Stephen, tells one how he made his living—seldom has money to enact his convictions; on the other hand, he presumably didn't want to manifest his scruples at the expense of the Hanoi government. Well, that's only the end of the alphabet. Curiously—or predictably—enough, those reproaches and remonstrations were most often American in origin; i.e., they were coming from a place where ethics enjoys a greater proximity to cash than elsewhere. On the whole, the postwar world was a pretty crude show, and he would take part in it now and then, not for its applause and flowers, but—the way it appears in retrospect—as its saving grace.

XIX

I notice I am editorializing; the genre begins to dictate the content. This is sometimes acceptable, but not under the circumstances. Under the circumstances, the content should determine the genre—even if the net result is fragments. For that's what one's life becomes once it is entrusted to its beholder. So let me shut my eyes, and behold: an evening in some theater in Milan, ten or twelve years ago; lots of people, glitter, candelabra, TV, etc.; onstage—a bunch of Italian professors and literary critics as well as Stephen and myself; we are all members of a jury for some big award in poetry. Which goes this year to Carlo Bettocchi, a creaky, crusty octogenarian of rustic appearance, bearing some resemblance to Frost. The old man shuffles awkwardly along the aisle and with great difficulty starts to climb the stage, mumbling something inaudible to himself. Nobody moves; the Italian professors and literary critics in their chairs watch an old man struggling up the steps. At this point Stephen gets up and starts to applaud; I join him. Then comes an ovation.

XX

Or else it's an empty, windswept square in downtown Chicago, well past midnight, some twenty years ago. We crawl out of somebody's car into the winter rain and march toward some gigantic arrangement of cast iron and steel cables sitting there, dimly lit on a pedestal in the middle of the square. It's a Picasso sculpture; a woman's head, as it turns out, and Stephen wants to see it now because he leaves town in the morning. "Very Spanish," he says. "And very warlike." And suddenly, for me, it's 1937, the Spanish Civil War—to which he went, paying, I believe, out of his own pocket, because it was the last quest for the Just City on human record, not the superpowers' chess game, and we lost, and then the whole thing was dwarfed by World War II's carnage. The night is grainy with rain and wind, cold and thoroughly black-and-white. And the tall man with absolutely white hair, looking like a schoolboy with his hands stretching out from the sleeves of his old black jacket, is slowly circling these random pieces of metal twisted by the Spanish genius into a work of art that resembles a ruin.

XXI

Or it is the Café Royal, London, where I insist on taking him and Natasha for lunch each time I am there. For their memories' sake as well as for mine. So it's hard to tell what year it is—but not that long ago. Isaiah Berlin is with us, and also my wife, who cannot take her young eyes away from Stephen's face. For indeed, with that snowy-white hair of his, shining gray-blue eyes, and apologetic grin presiding over the six-foot-tall, stooping frame, he looks in his eighties like an allegory of some benevolent winter visiting the other seasons. Even when he is among his peers or his family, to say nothing of total strangers. Besides, it's summer. ("What's good about summer here," I hear him saying while uncorking a bottle in his garden, "is that you don't have to chill the wine.") We are making "the century's great writers" list: Proust, Joyce, Kafka, Musil, Faulkner, Beckett. "But that's only up to the fifties," says Stephen, and turns to me. "Anyone that good now?" "Perhaps John Coetzee," I say. "A South African. He is the only one who has a right to write prose after Beckett." "Never heard of him," says Stephen. "How do you spell his name?" So I get a piece of paper, spell the name, and add *Life and Times of Michael K* and pass it on to Stephen. Then the conversation reverts to gossip, a recent production of *Così fan tutte*, with the singers doing the arias prostrate on the floor, current knighthoods—after all, this is a lunch with two knights. Suddenly Stephen grins widely and says, "The nineties is a good time to die."

XXII

And, lunch over, we are giving him a lift home, but on the Strand he asks the cabbie to stop, bids us farewell, and disappears into a large bookstore waving that piece of paper with Coetzee's name on it. I worry how he'll get home; then I remember that London is his town more than mine.

XXIII

And speaking of fragments, I remember how, in 1986, when the *Challenger* blew up in the air over Cape Canaveral, I heard either the ABC or the CNN voice reading Stephen's "I think continually of those who were truly great," written fifty years ago.

Near the snow, near the sun, in the highest fields,
See how these names are fêted by the waving grass
And by the streamers of white cloud
And whispers of wind in the listening sky.
The names of those who in their lives fought for life,
Who wore at their hearts the fire's centre.
Born of the sun, they travelled a short while toward the sun,
And left the vivid air signed with their honour.

XXIV

I think I told him of this episode a few years later, and I believe he smiled, with that famous smile of his that conveyed at once pleasure, a sense of general absurdity, his partial culpability for that absurdity, pure warmth. If I am tentative here, it's because I can't quite picture the surroundings. (For some reason a hospital room keeps popping up.) As for his reaction, it couldn't have been otherwise: "I think continually" is his most tired, most anthologized piece. Of all his lines—written, discarded, unwritten, half or fully forgotten, yet glowing inside him nevertheless. For the métier claims its own one way or another. Hence his radiance, which stays on my retina whether I shut my eyes or not. Hence, in any case, that smile.

XXV

People are what we remember about them. What we call life is in the end a patchwork of someone else's recollections. With death, it gets unstitched, and one ends up with random, disjointed fragments. With shards or, if you will, with snapshots. Filled with their unbearable laughter or equally unbearable smiles. Which are unbearable because they are one-dimensional. I should know; after all, I am a photographer's son. And I may even go as far as suggesting a link between picture taking and verse writing—well, insofar as the fragments are black-and-white. Or insofar as writing means retention. Yet one can't pretend that what one beholds goes beyond its blank reverse side. Also, once one realizes how much somebody's life is a hostage of one's own memory, one balks at the jaws of the past tense. Apart from anything, it's too much like talking behind somebody's back, or like belonging to some virtuous, triumphant majority. One's heart should try to be more honest—if it can't be smarter—than one's grammar. Or else one should keep a journal whose entries, simply by definition, would keep that tense at bay.

XXVI

So now the last fragment. A journal entry, as it were: for July 20 to 21, 1995. Although I never kept a journal. Stephen, however, did.

Awfully hot night, worse than NY. D. [family friend] picks me up, and 45 minutes later we are at Loudoun Rd. Ah, how well I know this place's floors and basement! Natasha's first words: "Of all people, he was unlikeliest to die." I can't think of what the last four days were like for her, of what this night is going to be like. It's all in her eyes. The same goes for the children: for Matthew and Lizzie. Barry [Lizzie's husband] produces whiskey and treats my glass generously. No one is in good shape. Of all things, we are talking about Yugoslavia. I couldn't eat on the plane and still can't. More whiskey, then, and more Yugoslavia, and by now it's midnight for them. Matthew and Lizzie suggest that I stay either in Stephen's study or in Lizzie and Barry's attic. But M. booked a hotel for me, and they drive me there: it's a few blocks away.

In the morning D. drives us all to St. Mary's on Paddington Green. On account of my Russianness, Natasha arranges for me to see Stephen in an open coffin. He looks severe and settled for whatever it is ahead. I kiss him on his brow, saying, "Thank you for everything. Say hello to Wystan and my parents. Farewell." I remember his legs, in the hospital, protruding from the gown: bruised with burst blood vessels—exactly like my father's, who was older than Stephen by six years. No, it's not because I wasn't present at his death that I flew to London. Though that could be as good a reason as any. No, not because of that. Actually, after seeing Stephen in the open coffin, I feel much calmer. Presumably this custom has something to do with its therapeutic effect. This strikes me as a Wystan-like thought. He would be here if he could. So it might just as well be me. Even if I can't provide Natasha and the children with any comfort, I can be a distraction. Now Matthew screws the bolts into the coffin lid. He fights tears, but they are winning. One can't help him; nor do I think one should. This is a son's job.

XXVII

People begin to arrive for the service and stand outside in little groups. I recognize Valerie Eliot, and after some initial awkwardness we talk. She tells me this story: The day her husband died, the BBC broadcast a tribute to him over the wireless, read by Auden. "He was absolutely the right man," she says. "Still, I was somewhat surprised by his promptness." A little later, she says, he comes to London, calls on her, and tells her that when the BBC learned that Eliot was gravely ill, they telephoned and asked him to record an obituary. Wystan said that he refused to speak about T. S. Eliot in the past tense while he was alive. In that case, said the BBC, we'll go to somebody else. "So I had to grit my teeth and do it," said Auden. "I cannot be at peace until you absolve me."

Then the service begins. It is as beautiful as an affair of this kind can be. The window behind the altar gives onto a wonderfully sunlit churchyard. Haydn and Schubert. Except that, as the quartet goes into a crescendo, I see in the side window a lift with construction workers climbing to the umpteenth floor of the adjacent high-rise. This strikes me as the kind of thing Stephen himself would notice and later remark about. And throughout the service, totally inappropriate lines from Wystan's poem about Mozart keep running through my mind:

> How seemly, then, to celebrate the birth
> Of one who did no harm to our poor earth,
> Created masterpieces by the dozen,
> Indulged in toilet-humor with his cousin,
> And had a pauper's funeral in the rain,
> The like of whom we shall not see again.

So, after all, he is here: not as a comfort but as a distraction. And out of habit: I suppose his lines used to visit Stephen's mind quite frequently, and Stephen's his. Now in either case they will be homesick forever.

XXVIII

The service over, all adjourn to Loudoun Road for drinks in the garden. The sun is hard-hitting, the sky is a solid blue slate. General chatter; the most frequent openings are "The end of an era" and "What a perfect day." The whole thing looks more like a garden party than anything. Perhaps this is the way the English keep their real sentiments in check, though some faces betray confusion. Lady R. says hello and makes some remark to the effect that at all funerals one thinks inevitably of one's own, didn't I think? I say no and, when she professes disbelief, explain to her that in our line of work one learns to narrow the focus by writing elegies. That, I add, rubs off on one's attitudes in reality. "I meant that one implicitly wishes to last as long as the person who's just died," maneuvers Lady R. I buy the implication and move toward the exit. As I step outside, I run into a just-arriving couple. The man is about my age and looks vaguely familiar (somebody in publishing). We greet each other hesitantly and he says, "The end of an era." No, I want to say to him, not the end of an era. Of a life. Which was longer and better than either yours or mine. Instead I just muster a broad, cheerful, Stephen-like grin and say, "I don't think so," and walk away.

August 10, 1995

Made in the USA
Middletown, DE
01 December 2019